Local Clusters in Global Value Chains

The international fragmentation of economic activities – from research and design to production and marketing – described through the lens of the global value chain (GVC) approach impacts the structure and performance of small and medium-sized enterprises (SMEs) agglomerated in economic clusters. The consolidation of GVCs ruled by global lead firms and the recession of 2008–09 exacerbated the pressures on cluster actors that based their competitive advantage on local systems, spurring an increasing heterogeneity, both across and within clusters, that is still overlooked in the literature.

Drawing on detailed studies of different industries and countries, *Local Clusters in Global Value Chains* shows the co-evolutionary trajectories of clusters and GVCs, and the role of firms and their strategies in organizing manufacturing and innovation activities in the context of ongoing technological shifts. The book explores the tension between place-based variables and global drivers of change, and the possibility for territories containing such clusters to prosper in the new global scenario. By adopting insights from the GVC framework and management studies, the book discusses how the internationalization strategies of firms create opportunities as well as constraints for adaptive upgrading in clusters.

This book is relevant to both researchers and policy-makers who are interested in the dynamic sources of competitive advantage in the global economy.

Valentina De Marchi is Assistant Professor at the Department of Economics and Management at the University of Padova, Italy. Her research focuses on the managerial implications of environmental innovations and on the evolution of industrial districts within global value chains.

Eleonora Di Maria is Associate Professor at the Department of Economics and Management at the University of Padova, Italy. Her research focuses on internationalization, innovation and sustainability strategies of firms and local economic systems, as well as on evolutionary trends of knowledge-intensive business services.

Gary Gereffi is Professor of Sociology and Founding Director of the Center on Globalization, Governance & Competitiveness at Duke University. He published numerous books and articles on globalization and social and economic development; he is one of the originators of the global value chain framework.

Routledge Studies in Global Competition
Edited by John Cantwell,
Rutgers, the State University of New Jersey, USA
and
David Mowery,
University of California, Berkeley, USA

For a full list of titles in this series, please visit www.routledge.com/Routledge-Studies-in-Global-Competition/book-series/RSGC

60 The Economics of Creativity
Ideas, Firms and Markets
Edited by Thierry Burger-Helmchen

61 Epistemic Economics and Organization
Forms of Rationality and Governance for a Discovery Oriented Economy
Anna Grandori

62 Universities, Cities and Regions
Loci for Knowledge and Innovation Creation
Edited by Roberta Capello, Agnieszka Olechnicka and Grzegorz Gorzelak

63 Strategies for Shaping Territorial Competitiveness
Edited by Jesús M. Valdaliso and James R. Wilson

64 The Economics of Knowledge, Innovation and Systemic Technology Policy
Edited by Francesco Crespi and Francesco Quatraro

65 University Technology Transfer
The Globalization of Academic Innovation
Edited by Shiri Breznitz and Henry Etzkowitz

66 Innovation, Alliances, and Networks in High-Tech Environments
Edited by Fiorenza Belussi and Luigi Orsi

67 The Global Management of Creativity
Edited by Marcus Wagner, Jaume Valls-Pasola and Thierry Burger-Helmchen

68 Catching Up and Leapfrogging
The New Latecomers in the Integrated Circuits Industry
Xiao-Shan Yap and Rajah Rasiah

69 Local Clusters in Global Value Chains
Linking Actors and Territories Through Manufacturing and Innovation
Edited by Valentina De Marchi, Eleonora Di Maria and Gary Gereffi

Local Clusters in Global Value Chains

Linking Actors and Territories Through Manufacturing and Innovation

**Edited by Valentina De Marchi,
Eleonora Di Maria and Gary Gereffi**

LONDON AND NEW YORK

First published 2018 by Routledge

2 Park Square, Milton Park, Abingdon, Oxfordshire OX14 4RN
52 Vanderbilt Avenue, New York, NY 10017

Routledge is an imprint of the Taylor & Francis Group, an informa business

First issued in paperback 2019

British Library Cataloguing-in-Publication Data
A catalogue record for this book is available from the British Library

Library of Congress Cataloging-in-Publication Data
A catalog record for this book has been requested

ISBN: 978-1-138-74286-4 (hbk)
ISBN: 978-0-367-88706-3 (pbk)

Typeset in Times New Roman
by Apex CoVantage, LLC

Contents

List of figures — vii
List of tables — viii
Contributors — x
Foreword and acknowledgements — xii
Abbreviations — xiii

1 Industrial districts, clusters and global value chains: toward an integrated framework — 1
VALENTINA DE MARCHI, ELEONORA DI MARIA AND GARY GEREFFI

PART I
Co-evolution of clusters and global value chains — 19

2 Italian industrial districts today: between decline and openness to global value chains — 21
ELISA GIULIANI AND ROBERTA RABELLOTTI

3 Evolutionary trajectories of industrial districts in global value chains — 33
VALENTINA DE MARCHI, GARY GEREFFI AND ROBERTO GRANDINETTI

4 Clusters, industrial districts and the impact of their growing intersection with global value chains — 51
MARIO DAVIDE PARRILLI AND JIŘÍ BLAŽEK

PART II
The role of lead firms in global value chains and clusters — 69

5 MNEs and clusters: the creation of place-anchored value chains — 71
FIORENZA BELUSSI, ANNALISA CALOFFI AND SILVIA RITA SEDITA

6 **Global value chains and the role of MNEs in local production systems**   94
MARIACHIARA BARZOTTO, GIANCARLO CORÒ AND MARIO VOLPE

7 **Knowledge, systemic contribution and brokerage in industrial clusters**   114
FRANCESC XAVIER MOLINA-MORALES, LUIS MARTÍNEZ-CHÁFER AND
JOSÉ ANTONIO BELSO-MARTÍNEZ

8 **Local liabilities between immigrant and native entrepreneurship in clusters and global value chains**   133
SIMONE GUERCINI

PART III
Value chain activities: rethinking the role of manufacturing and innovation   153

9 **Manufacturing, where art thou? Value chain organization and cluster-firm strategies between local and global**   155
MARCO BETTIOL, MARIA CHIARVESIO, ELEONORA DI MARIA AND
STEFANO MICELLI

10 **Networks of clusters within global value chains: the case of the European ceramic tile districts in Spain and Italy**   175
JOSE LUIS HERVAS-OLIVER AND MARIO DAVIDE PARRILLI

11 **The role of manufacturing within industrial districts: proposing and testing an innovative methodology**   193
RUGGERO GOLINI AND ALBACHIARA BOFFELLI

12 **New frontiers for competitiveness and innovation in clusters and value-chains research**   213
VALENTINA DE MARCHI, ELEONORA DI MARIA AND GARY GEREFFI

Index   227

Figures

2.1	Stylized models of ID-GVC involvement in Italy	25
4.1	Typical intersections between types of clusters and types of GVCs	53
4.2	Streamlining the supply base within GVC and the resulting "cascade effect"	56
4.3	The development of global R&D centres – the case of Intel	61
6.1	Offshoring index for Italy and the Veneto region 1999–2011	100
7.1	Types of brokerage	124
9.1	Governance of value chain in the case studies analysed: the Montebelluna cluster	168
9.2	Governance of value chain in the case studies analysed: the furniture cluster	168
9.3	Governance of value chain in the case studies analysed: the Belluno eyewear cluster	169
10.1	Historic transformation of value chains	177
10.2	Production evolution in Castellon and Sassuolo IDs	185
10.3	Employment evolution in Castellon and Sassuolo IDs	186
11.1	Phases, stages and activities in textile and clothing value chain	197
11.2	Detail of percentage of sales and purchases by location for each manufacturing stage	201
11.3	Coverage of value chain stages by the manufacturing companies in the sample	202
11.4	Companies distribution in terms of variety and uniqueness	204

Tables

1.1   Comparing the cluster and GVC literatures on key analytical dimensions   8

3.1   Trajectories of ID evolution in GVCs   35

3.2   Identifying the IDs analysed   37

3.3   Overview of the Vicenza, Belluno, Montebelluna and Riviera del Brenta clusters and their position in the GVC   43

3.4   Key local/global determinants of ID trajectories in GVCs   44

3.5   Key local/global determinants of ID trajectories in GVCs in the cases analysed   45

4.1   Types of upgrading in GVCs and clusters and their frequency   58

5.1   Scientific literature about timing of entry of MNEs in clusters   74

5.2   Basic characteristics of the four clusters analysed   79

5.3   Overview of the Montebelluna, Dongguan, Riviera del Brenta and Timişoara clusters in the GVC   80

6.1   Case study main characteristics   103

7.1   Overview of the ceramic tile and toy valley clusters in the GVC   120

7.2   Sample firms' profile   123

7.3   Dependent, independent and control variables   124

7.4   Results for the toy sector   125

7.5   Results for the ceramic tile sector   125

8.1   Native and immigrant firms in textile and clothing in the local Prato area (2002–14)   138

8.2   Evolution of the positions covered by native and immigrant local firms of Prato in their global value chain   141

8.3   Overview of Prato Italian-native and Chinese-immigrant clusters in the GVC   143

8.4   Liability of foreignness, liability of outsidership and local liabilities   145

8.5   Overcoming "local liabilities": an adaptation from the Uppsala Model   146

9.1   Overview of the Italian clusters analysed   160

9.2   Overview of the Italian sportsystem, furniture, eyewear clusters in the GVC   161

9.3   Case studies overview   163

9.4   Internationalization strategies of the cluster firms analysed   167

10.1   Overview of the Castellon and Sassuolo clusters in the GVC   181

10.1   Overview (cont.d)   182

11.1   Overview of the Bergamo cluster in the GVC   195

11.2   Turnover and number of employees of the manufacturing companies   200

11.3   Integration models of the sample   203

11.4 An example on how to calculate variety and uniqueness in a two-stages value chain   204

11.5 Correlations among the indicators and the company size   205

11.6 Kruskal-Wallis test results and mean of the sub-samples of finished products producers and not   205

Contributors

Mariachiara Barzotto is Post-Doctoral Marie Skłodowska-Curie Research Fellow at the Birmingham Business School, Birmingham University, UK.

José Antonio Belso-Martínez is Associate Professor of Applied Economics at the Department of Economics and Financial Studies, Universidad Miguel Hernández de Elche, Spain.

Fiorenza Belussi is Full Professor of Management at the Department of Economics and Management "Marco Fanno", University of Padova, Italy.

Marco Bettiol is Assistant Professor of Management at the Department of Economics and Management "Marco Fanno", University of Padova, Italy.

Jiří Blažek is Associate Professor of Social Geography and Regional Development at the Department of Social Geography and Regional Development, Charles University in Prague, Czechia.

Albachiara Boffelli is Ph.D. Student at the Department of Management, Information and Production Engineering, University of Bergamo, Italy.

Annalisa Caloffi is Assistant Professor of Economics at the Department of Economics and Management "Marco Fanno", University of Padova, Italy.

Maria Chiarvesio is Associate Professor of Management at the Department of Economics and Statistics, University of Udine, Italy.

Giancarlo Corò is Associate Professor of Applied Economics at the Department of Economics, Ca' Foscari University of Venice, Italy.

Valentina De Marchi is Assistant Professor of Management at the Department of Economics and Management "Marco Fanno", University of Padova, Italy.

Eleonora Di Maria is Associate Professor of Management at the Department of Economics and Management "Marco Fanno", University of Padova, Italy.

Gary Gereffi is Full Professor of Sociology at the Department of Sociology and Founding Director of the Center on Globalization, Governance, & Competitiveness, Duke University, USA.

Elisa Giuliani is Full Professor of Management at the Department of Economics & Management of the University of Pisa, Italy.

Ruggero Golini is Associate Professor of General Management and Supply Chain Management at the Department of Management, Information and Production Engineering, University of Bergamo, Italy.

Roberto Grandinetti is Full Professor of Management at the Department of Economics and Management "Marco Fanno", University of Padova, Italy.

Simone Guercini is Full Professor of Management at the Department of Economics and Management, University of Florence, Italy.

Jose Luis Hervas-Oliver is Full Professor of Strategy and Innovation at the Department of Management, Universitat Politecnica Valencia, Spain.

Luis Martínez-Cháfer is Assistant Professor of Organization and Management at the Department of Business Administration and Marketing, Universidad Jaume I de Castelló, Spain.

Stefano Micelli is Associate Professor of Management at the Department of Management, Ca' Foscari University of Venice, Italy.

Francesc Xavier Molina-Morales is Full Professor of Organization and Management at the Department of Business Administration and Marketing, Universidad Jaume I de Castelló, Spain.

Mario Davide Parrilli is Associate Professor of Regional Economic Development at the Department of Accounting, Finance and Economics, Bournemouth University, UK.

Roberta Rabellotti is Full Professor of Economics at Department of Political and Social Sciences, University of Pavia, Italy and Assigned Professor at the University of Aalborg in Denmark.

Silvia Rita Sedita is Associate Professor of Management at the Department of Economics and Management "Marco Fanno", University of Padova, Italy.

Mario Volpe is Associate Professor of Political Economy at the Department of Economics, Ca' Foscari University of Venice, Italy.

Foreword and acknowledgements

This book is the outcome of a joint effort aimed at understanding how local and global forces interact to support the competitiveness of territories, leveraging on two perspectives that so far have grown mostly independently from one another: the industrial districts and clusters literature (ID), which focuses on local development issues; and the global value chain (GVC) literature, which developed to capture the global forces shaping industries. On the one hand, the more we observed industrial districts in the Old World, and in Italy in particular, which is the cradle of the ID literature and the location of some of the best-known districts, the more we realized that a global perspective was also needed to fully understand the dynamics at stake. On the other hand, the heterogeneity of development outcomes of different geographic areas participating in GVCs gave us a deeper appreciation of the need to include regional and firm-level analysis to understand which factors contribute to local development in GVCs. Since these research questions are increasingly addressed by a large set of interdisciplinary researchers in journals as well as academic conferences, we decided to collect a set of fresh empirical studies that could tackle these issues from different perspectives.

We would like to thank the participants at the International Workshop "Evolving industrial districts within global and regional value chains and the role of manufacturing and innovation capabilities" held on April 7, 2016 at the Department of Economics and Management "Marco Fanno", Padova (Italy) and at the workshop "Italy in the GVC. Country, region and firms analyses", held on April 28, 2016 at the Centro Rossi-Doria of Roma Tre, Rome (Italy) for useful feedbacks on earlier versions of the book chapters. The editors gained useful hints on the ideas developed in the book through discussion with participants at the SASE (Society for the Advancement of Socio-Economics) conference at the panels "Resilience in Local Systems and Emerging Issues in Industrial District, Cluster and Global Value Chain Analysis" (organized by Valentina De Marchi, Joonkoo Lee and Khalid Nadvi) and "Management studies and the Global Value Chain framework: future perspectives" (organized by Maria Chiarvesio, Eleonora Di Maria, and Stefano Micelli) (London, 2015), and "Industrial Districts and Global Value Chains: Emerging Issues" (organized by Valentina De Marchi and Joonkoo Lee) (Chicago, 2014).

Acknowledgements specific to each chapter are reported at the end of the chapters.

Abbreviations

ATC	Agreement on Textile and Clothing
ATECO	Classificazione ATtività ECOnomiche (Statistical Classification of Economic Activities in Italy)
B2B	Business-To-Business
CEO	Chief Executive Offices
DIY	Do-It-Yourself
EU	European Union
FDI	Foreign Direct Investment
GDP	Gross Domestic Product
GIN	Global Innovation Network
GLF	Global Lead Firms
GVA	Gross Value Added
GVC	Global Value Chain
H&S	Hub & Spoke Clusters
HH	Herfindal-Hirschman
HR	Human Resource
ICT	Information and Communication Technology
ID	Industrial District
ILO	International Labour Organization
IT	Information Technology
LDA	Local Dynamic Actors
LLs	Local Liabilities
LOF	Liability of Foreignness
LOO	Liability of Outsidership
LVMH	Louis Vuitton Moët Hennessy
MFA	Multi-Fiber Arrangement
MIDs	Marshallian Industrial Districts
MNCs	Multinational Companies
MNEs	Multinational Enterprises
NACE	Nomenclature Statistique Des Activités Économiques Dans La Communauté Européenne (Statistical classification of economic activities in the European community)
OBM	Original Brand Manufacturer
ODM	Original Design Manufacturer
OECD	Organization for Economic Cooperation and Development

OEM	Original Equipment Manufacturer
R&D	Research and Development
RIS	Regional Innovation System
SMEs	Small and Medium-sized Enterprises
SNA	Social Network Analysis
Sq.M	Square Meters
UK	United Kingdom
UNCTAD	United Nations Conference on Trade and Development
USA	United States of America

1 Industrial districts, clusters and global value chains

Toward an integrated framework

Valentina De Marchi, Eleonora Di Maria and Gary Gereffi

Introduction

The location of economic activities in specific territories and the reorganization of industries into global value chains have reshaped analysis on the competitiveness of regions and countries in recent decades. Starting in the 1970s in several developed countries, especially in Europe, industrial districts or clusters[1] represented the backbone of manufacturing, primarily in low-technology sectors, which drove exceptional export growth in international markets. Beginning with the seminal contributions by Becattini (1986), Piore and Sabel (1984), and Porter (1998), a broad literature developed supporting and explaining the specific advantages related to local production systems and their role in the development of regions and nations. Indeed, the cluster concept has enjoyed enormous success over the years (Schmitz and Nadvi, 1999; Lazzeretti et al., 2014), and this perspective became central in the action programs of many international institutions to support the competitiveness of SMEs and to foster the growth of less-developed countries and regions (e.g. Eastern Europe and Latin America).

International trade and cross-border production networks, however, shape the ability of clusters to deliver competitive advantages in the global arena. After the 1980s, manufacturing activities swiftly shifted from advanced to developing countries, due to the global outsourcing strategies of firms from the European Union (EU) and the United States (USA). Due to the transfers of knowledge and technologies related to the offshoring of manufacturing activities (Pietrobelli and Rabellotti, 2011), developing countries became central players in global supply chains, thus challenging the role of clusters in developed countries.

The global value chain (GVC) framework, whose origins date back to the mid-1990s, is particularly useful to analyse these global transformations and how industries are organized at the global level (Gereffi and Korzeniewick, 1994; Gereffi et al., 2005; Gereffi and Fernandez-Stark, 2016). This approach has been increasingly adopted by international organizations such as the World Bank, the Organization for Economic Cooperation and Development (OECD), the International Labour Organization (ILO), and the United Nations Conference on Trade and Development (UNCTAD) to guide development programs in poorer countries (Cattaneo et al., 2010; Gereffi, 2014; Werner et al., 2014). With specific industries or countries as the empirical focus of analysis, the GVC framework has been widely adopted to understand how industries and places (including clusters) evolve and how value is captured and distributed across diverse economic actors. Main players in this process are large multinational enterprises (MNEs) – including global buyers and brands, as well as producers – governing the activities of the chain, which is fragmented at the international level, and affecting the opportunities for firms, regions and countries to compete in global markets (Gereffi et al., 2005; Gereffi and Fernandez-Stark, 2016).

Over the years, the industrial district and GVC literatures have evolved considerably, impacting the international development agenda as well as policy intervention programs, but in a fragmented way. There are varied perspectives and goals: one emphasizing "local factors for competing in global markets" (Schmitz and Nadvi, 1999, p. 1503), and the other the role of large global firms in shaping local development, especially in developing economies (Gereffi, 1994, 1999; Morrison et al., 2008). This book aims at advancing concepts and theories that merge these perspectives to meet the challenges firms, regions and countries must cope with, and question the way the global-local nexus is rendered (Bair, 2008; Pietrobelli and Rabellotti, 2011). On the one hand, emerging economies are no longer just the factories for Western companies but are increasingly performing more value-added activities; "emerging giants" are playing a critical role in an increasing number of sectors (Khanna and Palepu, 2006; Sinkovics et al., 2014; Azmeh and Nadvi, 2014). On the other hand, recent discussions about backshoring and re-shoring scrutinize the consolidated position of advanced and emerging countries in the "smile" curve – depicting value-added at each stage of the chain (Mudambi, 2008; Gray et al., 2013; Bailey and De Propris, 2014; Fratocchi et al., 2014).

Researchers need new theoretical syntheses to integrate the global and local perspectives for a more comprehensive picture of how economic activities and economic systems are structured in the contemporary era. Indeed, complex interdependencies between the local and the global contexts – such as the access and use of technologies, knowledge creation and capture, product and process upgrading, stricter international regulations and standards, and management of social and environmental sustainability – call for an enrichment and synthesis of current theoretical frameworks. In this chapter, we outline a framework to enhance our understanding of the global/local nexus incorporating key elements from the GVC and industrial district/cluster perspectives.

Industrial districts and clusters: a brief overview

Research on clusters reflects multiple literatures and disciplines, including mainstream economics, business economics, regional science, and innovation studies (Lazzeretti et al., 2014). The goal is to understand how the local organization of economic activities based on SMEs in a specific socio-cultural context – compared to the production activities of large firms (Pyke et al., 1990) – could provide the same or better outcomes in terms of employment, value creation and innovation. In Europe, and in Italy in particular, the "industrial districts" literature highlights the role of social structure (the so-called "communitarian factor") in supporting local externalities. In other settings, the cluster concept is more commonly used, including business economics starting with Porter (1998), who considered larger geographic areas and different combinations of firms and institutions beyond SMEs (Porter and Ketels, 2009), as well as economic geography (e.g. Bathelt et al., 2004) and development studies (e.g. Humphrey and Schmitz, 2002).[2]

Based on the inspiring studies of Alfred Marshall, Giacomo Becattini and other Italian scholars, Piore and Sabel (1984) were among the first to popularize the ability of small-scale districts to successfully enter international markets (Schmitz and Nadvi, 1999). Flexible specialization emerged as a new paradigm, in contrast to the Fordist mass production model dominated by large corporations. Italy became an interesting case since it offered an extraordinary research setting to explore the characteristics of industry-specialized networks of SMEs embedded in particular locales (Brusco, 1982; Pyke et al., 1990). Because of the concentration of small and export-oriented firms in traditional manufacturing industries, the Italian experience was a useful reference point for the developing country agenda as well (Schmitz, 1989; Rabellotti, 1997; Saxenian, 2006; Long and Zhang, 2011; Bellandi and Lombardi, 2012).

A key element of the ID is the division of labour across a number of co-localized SMEs involved in the different manufacturing steps needed to make a final product. Several agglomeration effects benefit firms participating in such networks (Belussi, 2006). The concentration of a critical mass of firms in a given industry increases firm-level efficiency and productivity due to the availability at the local level of specialized suppliers within an intense division of labour among local actors, with positive impacts on economic performance and competitiveness (Porter, 1990; Molina-Morales, 2002). Moreover, the local labour market ensures easy access to skilled labour and market mobility of workers among local firms. Industrial districts also facilitate entrepreneurship and new firm start-ups (Garofoli, 1992; Delgado et al., 2010); existing firms often support spin-off processes or sustain new ventures through collaborative supply-chain management practices.

Due to physical and cognitive proximity, firms within clusters benefit from explicit and tacit processes of knowledge sharing, where specialized knowledge flows between the firm and its suppliers, and among the many other actors of the clusters (e.g. training and research centres, local institutions) (Pyke et al., 1990; Corno et al., 1999). The knowledge dimension (Camuffo and Grandinetti, 2011) has been utilized as an explanation of the competitiveness and innovation of firms located in clusters. Thanks to knowledge spillovers, rooted in agglomeration, firms gain key knowledge to nurture their activities and support positive economic outcomes, based on specializations within the cluster. Scholars have devoted particular attention to exploring innovation paths and the dynamics of learning in clusters. Innovation in clusters can be rooted in informal processes related to learning-by-doing and social interaction, as well as more structured activities of knowledge exchange where research and development (R&D) is important (see Camuffo and Grandinetti, 2011 for a review).

Industrial districts are viewed as systems made up of a number of small and medium-sized companies (SMEs). Whereas in the traditional Marshallian model the homogeneity across local companies was considered a constitutive element (Becattini, 1990) – even if some larger trees are admitted within the forest, to quote a famous metaphor of Marshall's (1919) – different typologies of firms within clusters have been studied as well. Along with the canonical Marshallian district, Markusen (1996) proposed a classification including two additional configurations: the hub-and-spoke and the satellite-platform districts. The former is characterized by the presence of a large firm dominating the relationships locally (where small firms depend on it) and linking the local systems internationally, while the latter refers to an agglomeration generated by the branch facilities of external players (firms but also government) in a specific location.

Studies on clusters have emphasized the role of local institutions[3] – training centres, local research and certification centres, industry associations, municipalities or other local associations – in sustaining their competitive advantage (see Brusco, 1982; Porter, 1990; Corno et al., 1999, Molina-Morales and Martínez-Cháfer, 2016). Through dedicated intervention policies, shared projects or other initiatives, such institutions have facilitated knowledge sharing and collaboration among cluster firms and nurtured local "industrial commons" (Pisano and Shih, 2012) useful for the competitiveness of clusters and their firms.

Indeed, a key focus of the cluster literature has been the relationships across local actors. Within clusters, *collaboration and competition* among firms usually coexist, creating a fascinating mix that pushes forward innovation and even different forms of imitation, considered in positive terms (see Shenkar, 2010). Collaboration between the firm and its suppliers enables knowledge transfer, but also knowledge co-creation to achieve shared goals. Collaboration activities are particularly frequent in clusters formed by a large number of SMEs, where social and cultural proximity favours these dynamics and gives birth to communitarian structures among local economic actors (Lazerson, 1995; Dei Ottati, 1996).

Recent research directions in the ID literature

Considering the deep changes occurring at the local and global levels during the last 15 years, the research on IDs has developed along several trajectories, including: 1) the evolutionary processes of clusters; and 2) the opening up of the geographical boundaries of clusters.

An important stream of work focuses on the evolutionary processes of particular types of clusters (Whitford, 2001; De Marchi and Grandinetti, 2014; Tomas-Miquel et al., 2012; Hervas-Oliver et al., 2015). One topic is the evolving relationships among cluster firms due to different internal and external factors (Belso-Martinez, 2008). Clusters are classified in terms of their variety (Paniccia, 1998), suggesting it is no longer possible to talk about a single model for IDs (see also De Marchi and Grandinetti, 2014). Despite homogeneity in the size of firms as SMEs, many scholars note an increasing within-ID heterogeneity in terms of firm strategies, especially as far as internationalization is concerned (Chiarvesio et al., 2010; Rabellotti et al., 2009), and they highlight the rise of leading firms within clusters (Lorenzoni and Lipparini, 1999; Lazerson and Lorenzoni, 1999; Camuffo, 2003). Leading firms are generally larger, more vertically integrated, and able to develop advanced strategies in terms of innovation, marketing and internationalization.

A second topic related to the cluster model is the opening up of cluster boundaries. Scholars described the cluster by emphasizing internal dynamics that facilitated local agglomeration. However, globalization and stiff international competition, shifting geographic markets and the rise of new technologies have heavily impacted local systems (Belussi et al., 2003; Chiarvesio et al., 2004; Iammarino and McCann, 2006). On the one hand, many scholars focused their attention on the entrance of MNEs in the cluster, which acquired specialized knowledge through local direct investments and relationships with cluster firms. The presence of MNEs at the cluster level also activates knowledge transfers related to markets or technology towards cluster firms (Belussi et al., 2003; Hervas-Oliver and Albors-Garrigos, 2008).

On the other hand, the emergence of leading firms has changed the cluster landscape due to the internationalization strategies of those firms. MNE lead firms may play the role of gatekeepers (Morrison, 2008), acquiring knowledge from outside the cluster that is transferred to local suppliers (and local actors in general) (Nachum and Keeble, 2003). At the same time, those firms also transfer knowledge outside the cluster through global sourcing, foreign direct investment or commercial internationalization (Belussi et al., 2008; Chiarvesio et al., 2010). In this perspective, the cluster becomes an open learning system, where internationalization and innovation processes are intertwined. Through inward and outward internationalization processes, the cluster becomes more connected with activities in the GVCs of which it is a part. Internationalization of specialized suppliers and subcontractors (Bocconcelli and Tunisini, 2001; Furlan et al., 2009) further enhances this trend, where production activities are no longer self-contained within the cluster boundaries, but are linked to the productive and knowledge networks in GVCs.

Global value chains: a brief overview

Globalization has given rise to a new era of international competition that is reshaping global production and trade, and altering the organization of industries (Gereffi and Lee, 2012). In the 1970s and 1980s, US retailers and brand-name companies joined manufacturers in the search for low-cost and capable offshore suppliers of consumer goods, which led to a fundamental shift from "producer-driven" to "buyer-driven" commodity chains (Gereffi, 1994).

The geography of these chains expanded from regional production-sharing arrangements to full-fledged global production networks, with a main emphasis on East Asia (Gereffi, 1999). In the 1990s and 2000s, the activities and industries encompassed by global supply chains grew exponentially, covering not only finished goods but also components and subassemblies. While perhaps most visible in manufacturing industries, they also encompass energy, food production and all kinds of services, from call centres and accounting, to medical procedures and core R&D activities of the world's leading MNEs (Dicken, 2011; Staritz et al., 2011; Cattaneo et al., 2013).

Today the organization of the global economy is entering a new phase – what some have referred to as a "major inflection point" (Fung, 2011). By the mid-2000s, the Washington Consensus development model was already beginning to unravel (Gereffi, 2014). US hegemony was eroding, and the large emerging economies, led by China and India, were transforming the organization of production; consolidation was growing at both the country and supply chain levels in a number of global industries. When the global economic recession hit in 2008–09, this ended all prospects of a return to the old order. As the consumption of advanced industrial economies was cut back, developing countries around the world looked for alternatives to declining or stagnant Northern markets. Large emerging economies turned inward and redirected production to their domestic markets and regional neighbours, and the role of GVC-oriented industrial policies in these economies grew rapidly (Gereffi and Sturgeon, 2013).

The GVC framework focuses on globally expanding supply chains and how value is created and captured therein. By analyzing the sequences of activities that firms and workers perform to bring a specific product from its conception to its end use and beyond (Gereffi and Fernandez-Stark, 2016), the GVC approach provides a holistic view of global industries from two contrasting vantage points: top-down and bottom-up. The key concept for the top-down view is the "governance" of global value chains, which focuses mainly on lead firms and the organization of global industries; the main concept for the bottom-up perspective is "upgrading", which focuses on the strategies used by countries, regions and other economic stakeholders to maintain or improve their positions in the global economy.

The concept of governance is the centrepiece of GVC analysis. It examines the ways in which corporate power can actively shape the distribution of profits and risk in an industry. Power in GVCs is exerted by lead firms. The distinction between producer-driven and buyer-driven chains was an early contribution to the governance literature (Gereffi, 1994). Later, a more elaborate typology was introduced that highlighted multiple ways in which the relationship between firms in global supply chains could be coordinated (Gereffi et al., 2005).[4] At the market and hierarchy poles of the GVC governance continuum, inter-firm relations are driven by price and ownership within vertically integrated firms, respectively. The remaining three categories are stable forms of network governance (modular, relational and captive), in which different kinds of GVC lead firms control to a large degree how global supply chains operate and the main winners and losers within these chains.[5]

While governance issues have attracted a good deal of attention among GVC scholars, the research on economic upgrading has been at least as important because many of the people who use the GVC framework have a very strong development focus. "Economic upgrading" is defined as the process by which economic actors – firms and workers – move from low-value to relatively high-value activities in GVCs (Gereffi, 2005, p. 171). The challenge of economic upgrading in GVCs is to identify the conditions under which developing and developed countries and firms can "climb the value chain" from basic assembly activities using low-cost and unskilled labour to more advanced forms of "full package" supply and integrated manufacturing.

In the past two decades, profound changes in the structure of the global economy have reshaped cross-border production and trade and have altered the organization of industries and national economies (Gereffi, 2014). As supply chains became global in scope, more intermediate goods were traded across borders, and more imported parts and components were integrated into exports (Krugman, 1995; Feenstra, 1998). In 2009, world exports of intermediate goods exceeded the combined export values of final and capital goods for the first time, representing 51% of non-fuel merchandise exports (WTO and IDE-JETRO, 2011, p. 81). Because of the unique ability of the GVC framework to show how international supply chains link economic activities at global, regional, national, and local levels within particular industries, international organizations such as UNCTAD, OECD, the World Bank, and the World Economic Forum are utilizing the GVC approach to structure new donor initiatives and data collection programs on global trade and development.

Recent research directions in the GVC literature

Several new trends in GVC research are relevant to understanding the connections between global chains, national development and local clusters: 1) the growing prominence of emerging economies as key actors in GVCs; 2) shifting end markets and the regionalization of value chains; and 3) efforts to examine the conditions under which social and economic upgrading can be combined.

Emerging economies are playing significant and diverse roles in GVCs (Gereffi and Sturgeon, 2013). During the 2000s, they became major exporters of intermediate and final manufactured goods (China, South Korea and Mexico) and primary products (Brazil, Russia and South Africa). However, growth in emerging economies has also led to shifting end markets in GVCs, as more trade has occurred between developing economies (often referred to as South-South trade in the literature), especially since the 2008–09 economic recession (Staritz et al., 2011, pp. 1–12). China has been the focal point of both trends: it is the world's leading exporter of manufactured goods and the world's largest importer of many raw materials, thereby contributing to the primary product export boom.

As world trade bounced back from the 2008–09 economic crisis, developing economies became a main engine of world economic recovery. Stagnant growth in demand in the global North since the mid-1980s was exacerbated by the crisis, whereas demand grew in the global South, particularly in large emerging economies like China, India and Brazil (Staritz et al., 2011). Over the period of 2005–10, the merchandise imports of the European Union and the United States increased by 27% and 14%, respectively, while emerging economies expanded their merchandise imports much faster: Brazil (147%), India (129%), China (111%) and South Africa (51%). In 2010, 52% of Asia's manufactured exports were destined to developing countries (WTO, 2011), signalling shifting end markets in the global economy.

The GVC literature shows that value chains oriented to different end markets often entail distinct upgrading opportunities (Palpacuer et al., 2005; Gibbon, 2008). For example, the demand in lower-income countries for less sophisticated products with regard to quality and variety can have major upgrading implications (Kaplinsky et al., 2011). On the one hand, lower entry barriers and less stringent product and process standards in emerging markets can facilitate the participation of developing country firms in global supply chains. They can engage in higher value-added activities, such as product development and design, which they would have little chance to do in chains oriented to advanced economies. On the other hand, solely focusing on low-income markets could lock suppliers into slimmer margins and cutthroat competition. Their knowledge advantage in local markets often quickly evaporates when MNEs catch up in learning the markets, as found in the Chinese mobile phone industry (Brandt and Thun, 2011).

A final GVC research trend stems from the growing concern in both developed and developing countries that the economic gains of participating in global supply chains do not necessarily translate into good jobs or stable employment, and in the worst case, economic upgrading may be linked to a significant deterioration of labour conditions, or social and environmental downgrading (Barrientos et al., 2011).[6] Studies are being carried out to determine under what conditions participation in global value chains can contribute to both economic and social upgrading in developing countries (Lee et al., 2011). This kind of research requires us to develop precise indicators of "upgrading" (economic, social or environmental) (see Bernhardt and Pollak, 2016; De Marchi et al., 2013), and it also raises the question of the extent to which GVCs are "inclusive" or "exclusive" in terms of facilitating the upgrading of lower-level firms or less-skilled workers, as well as supporting local communities connected to the industry.

A joint framework for the analysis of GVCs and clusters

As discussed in the previous paragraphs, the cluster and GVC frameworks reflect opposite premises – the first stemming from the need to understand local dynamics spurring competitiveness in export markets, and the second from the interest in explaining the organization of industries at the global level considering the role of lead firms and their impact on the development of countries and regions. Driven by the integration of activities at the global level and by the evidence of the enduring role of some regions and clusters in global supply chains, the two literatures are converging in certain aspects.

Indeed, even if the GVC framework developed mostly to describe the growth of international subcontracting by large multinationals, whether global buyers or producers (Gereffi, 2005), it has not denied the role of local areas (clusters) as key production nodes within global industries. Indeed, a large part of the literature on GVCs has focused on clusters, especially in developing countries (e.g. Bair and Gereffi, 2001; Nadvi and Halder, 2005; Giuliani et al., 2005). As discussed in Sturgeon et al. (2008) in the context of the automotive industry, GVCs are conceived as nested structures, and their production activities tend to be organized within clusters contained within national production systems, which collectively constitute the global industry. At the macro level, however, the nested structure of GVCs also includes globe-spanning business relationships between MNE lead firms and their global suppliers, which simultaneously operate in multiple countries and regions. Thus, Italy, China and Mexico compete with each other in real time in the GVC world, which is why the strategies and activities of lead firms in global chains must be integrated to the study of national economies and local clusters.

Conversely, while Marshallian industrial districts – the most studied cluster variant in the context of developed countries – highlighted the relationships between the actors located within the district (Dei Ottati, 2003), other typologies of clusters (such as those proposed by Markusen, 1996) base their competitive advantage on linkages with external firms. Furthermore "downstream" internationalization (mostly exports) has generally been considered a key channel for growth in all clusters.

On this basis, we propose a joint framework to advance our understanding of clusters and GVCs by leveraging the existing literature to build a common vocabulary using analytical dimensions present in both literatures, as summarized in Table 1.1.

Table 1.1 Comparing the cluster and GVC literatures on key analytical dimensions

	Cluster literature	*GVC literature*
Economic activities	Local division of labor (focus on local "complete" chain)	Value-chain mapping (smile curve and geography of related international activities)
Key actors	Key local firms Local institutions	Global lead firms (buyer/producer) Global institutions (standards)
Relationships	(Local) buyer-supplier relationships, "industrial atmosphere" or collective efficiency (horizontal governance)	Governance (vertical inter-firm ties)

Source: Authors.

The cluster and GVC literatures are based on three key analytical dimensions: economic activities, key actors and relationships. With respect to *economic activities*, the cluster literature focuses on the local division of labour. For example, all the activities needed to produce a shoe or a ski boot are realized by different actors within the same restricted area as enabling factors for the cluster's productivity and agglomeration effects (Belussi, 2006). A similar dimension is found in the GVC framework, which is based on the division of activities at the global level. In this context, value chain mapping and the smile curve[7] are two key tools used for understanding how industries are organized globally and the dynamics of GVC upgrading, respectively.

The focus on *key actors* is another common element of both frameworks, even if applied in a very different way. The cluster literature examines the role played by key actors in supporting the birth and evolution of clusters,[8] thanks to their strategic approach and distinctive capabilities. Often smaller companies are relevant for the local system but not necessarily for the industry as a whole (see De Marchi et al., 2013), since the homogeneity of cluster firms helps external economies to take place. Local institutions are another actor supporting cluster development. As highlighted in Table 1.1, a central element of the GVC framework is global lead firms, either buyers or producers, that shape the governance structure of GVCs (Gereffi, 1994; Gereffi et al., 2005). In more recent contributions, the role of global standards is also acknowledged, which might be set by actors such as international agencies or non-governmental organizations (Gibbon et al., 2008; Ponte and Sturgeon, 2014; Gereffi and Lee, 2016).

Third, *relationships* are a major dimension in explaining developmental outcomes in both literatures, again with a different accent. Cluster studies have looked at the structure of supplier-buyer and horizontal relationships among SMEs, especially in terms of innovation (Molina-Morales and Martínez-Fernández, 2010), as well as the role of local mechanisms to support collective efficiency (Schmitz, 1995). In the GVC context, both vertical and horizontal relationships give rise to private, public and social forms of governance that can facilitate social and economic upgrading (Gereffi and Lee, 2016), in addition to knowledge transfers and upgrading opportunities derived from purposeful connections with lead firms (Pietrobelli and Rabellotti, 2011).

Emerging research questions

By adopting the joint GVC/ID framework, we seek to enrich the debate on the evolution of the cluster model and the linkages between SMEs and GVCs. Starting in the 2000s, scholars noted that profound changes are taking place within clusters in the countries where such systems have spurred the local economy, namely Italy and Spain, and these shifts were connected to globalization and the consolidation of GVCs (e.g. Rabellotti et al., 2009; De Marchi and Grandinetti, 2014). Considerable heterogeneity is reported but still largely unexplored, both across clusters – in terms of resilience and ability to reproduce the local roots of their competitive advantage – and within them – with highly diversified competitiveness and innovation outcomes across firms, especially large companies vs. SMEs (e.g. Belso-Martinez, 2008; De Marchi et al., 2014). We are interested in how the GVC framework can help us better understanding these trends and, at the same time, how it can be extended to include them. Leveraging the joint framework outlined in Table 1.1, we propose three emerging questions that are going to be addressed in this book.

Co-evolution of clusters and GVCs

A first research question deals with the *evolutionary trends* that are reflected in both clusters and GVCs, and the extent to which their potential intersections can be seen as a co-evolutionary process. By adopting a temporal perspective, cluster studies have identified tipping points that have modified the internal structure of clusters based on a variety of factors (e.g. Belussi and Sedita, 2009). Studies on GVCs have also explored changes in the governance of value chains in specific industries and territories, showing how local and global systems co-evolve (Sturgeon et al., 2008; Ponte and Sturgeon, 2014) and how the co-evolution of geographic and organizational concentration within GVCs impacts the development of industries (Lee et al., 2012).

The GVC framework devotes particular attention to evolutionary trends in industries by emphasizing upgrading (or downgrading) trajectories of firms, regions and countries, a topic of particular importance for clusters. Longitudinal analysis is crucial to describe how actors and places are able to create additional value or modify their position in value chains by stressing the drivers of these changes (such as regulations, technological trends, market changes etc.). In this respect, the book offers new insights on how globalization trends depicted by GVC studies – such as the rise of large retailers, the internationalization strategies of brand vendors, new industry standards or regulations, and concentration in the production and distribution segments of chains – are modifying the opportunity of clusters to compete globally and their ability to capture value locally. At the same time, the empirical evidence provided will show how the trajectories of change at the cluster level – in particular in advanced countries – can contribute to the transformation of GVCs, thanks to their innovation efforts or the rise of new global actors with roots at the cluster level.

The first section of the book includes three contributions that address several research questions: *What are the key drivers of change within traditional, manufacturing clusters? What are the major transformations that are taking place? What determines the different evolutionary trajectories of clusters? What enabling elements are supporting the reproduction of local industrial commons?*

In Chapter 2, Giuliani and Rabellotti discuss how Italian IDs are linked to globalization dynamics, with an overview of the major transformations that have taken place in traditional IDs as well as a reflection from the policymaker perspective. The authors provide evidence for the increasing heterogeneity across IDs, based on their export strategies and their involvement in GVCs. A new typology of Italian ID organizational models is proposed (low-road IDs, locally rooted GVC-led IDs, and outward-oriented GVC-led IDs) to highlight the intersection between the ID and GVC models with an emphasis on the value-chain activities that are performed locally.

Leveraging the debate on the transformations of clusters, Chapter 3 by De Marchi, Gereffi, and Grandinetti offers a framework to categorize the heterogeneous evolutionary trajectories of IDs embedded in GVCs, based on their diversified resilience in global markets and the distribution of resources within the cluster. Focusing on four Italian districts in the Veneto region, they identify the presence of Global Lead Firms (GLFs) and Local Dynamic Actors (LDAs) (including both capable firms and institutions) as key determinants for a resilient development trajectory.

In Chapter 4, Parrilli and Blažek explore how upgrading processes affect the evolutionary trends of clusters within GVCs by considering supply chain management strategies of lead firms and their suppliers (with special attention on the transformation in the number and role of local suppliers). Using typologies of clusters and examples from different industries and countries, they provide a framework for how to contextualize upgrading in GVCs within the broader perspective of innovation. In particular, they explore how Global Innovation Networks (GIN) and Regional Innovation Systems (RIS) can affect and sustain cluster upgrading trajectories.

The role of lead firms in GVCs and clusters

A second major research issue concerns the role of lead firms in the increasingly diverse industrial structures of both local clusters and GVCs. As shown in Table 1.1, the focus on key actors is a component of the governance structures identified by the GVC framework (where they are called global "lead firms"), since it highlights who exercises the power to orchestrate and shape outcomes among firms and territories that participate in GVCs. In producer-driven chains, lead firms are typically large, vertically integrated manufacturers, while in buyer-driven chains, the lead firms could either be large retailers or global brands (Gereffi, 1994). The power of these lead firms is based on various assets: large manufacturers rely on their scale of production and technological prowess in global factory networks (e.g. Toyota or General Electric); giant retailers leverage direct access to consumers through their commercial outlets (e.g. Walmart, Tesco or Carrefour); and global brands use extensive marketing campaigns to generate awareness and sales of their products (e.g. Nike, Armani or Disney).

The significance of local actors in determining the development of clusters or IDs in global markets has been relatively overlooked. Studies of IDs contain diversified sets of actors – 1) final product firms, 2) stage-firms, and 3) firms belonging to vertically integrated sectors, to use Brusco's labels – that are quite homogeneous in size, which prevents them from having "a centre for strategic decision-making" (Brusco, 1990, p. 14). More recent studies, however, point to the rise of leading firms at the cluster level. Such firms have power within the cluster due to their technological competencies, commercial capabilities, innovation propensity or ability to internationalize, and might act as important "knowledge gatekeepers" to support ID evolution (see Camuffo and Grandinetti, 2011). Thanks to their strategies, they push the cluster system through the reconfiguration of value chain activities that are situated between the local and the global.

Thus, the second section of the book deals with the evolutionary trajectories of clusters looking at intra-district heterogeneity, giving special attention to the key actors in such changes, considering both local lead firms and global lead firms, whose specificities and characteristics will be described in Chapter 3. *How is the interplay of those local and global lead firms working for cluster evolution? Which features of these actors are necessary for the cluster to retain competitiveness in global markets? Are local lead firms needed for the emergence and survival of dynamic clusters in the globalization era?*

In Chapter 5, Belussi, Caloffi and Sedita explore the role of foreign MNEs in the evolution of clusters, emphasizing the timing of entry of MNEs in relation to the cluster life cycle. By comparing the process and impact of foreign MNE (often global lead firm) investments in Italian, Chinese, and Romanian clusters, the authors show the implications for the acquisition and transfer of knowledge between local and global players according to the phase of the cluster life cycle (initial versus maturity). The chapter highlights the heterogeneity of evolutionary paths related to governance issues and innovation opportunities.

Chapter 6 by Barzotto, Corò and Volpe offers the complementary perspective of ID companies that have internationalized their value chains, focusing on the rationale behind their decision to keep value-added activities at the local level. Based on a qualitative analysis of 10 MNEs operating in different clusters in the Veneto Region (Italy) with different positions in the value chain, the authors discuss how such firms contribute to sustaining the industrial commons at the cluster level, and they question whether IDs still represent an anchor within the internationalization strategies of these firms.

Chapter 7 also emphasizes the diverse roles that local actors can play in clusters, which introduces a major condition for ID resilience: its ability to remain a locus for innovation. Based on a quantitative analysis of two Spanish districts specializing in ceramic tiles and toys, Molina-Morales, Martínez-Cháfer and Belso-Martínez explore intra-district heterogeneity by measuring the impact on innovation of different knowledge brokerage roles that local firms adopt, taking into account their technical and business networks, the type of knowledge shared and the ability to connect with global flows of knowledge.

In Chapter 8, Guercini offers an original perspective on the inter-firm dynamics of local (cluster) and global linkages by exploring immigrant entrepreneurship. This allows for a deeper understanding of intra-district heterogeneity by discussing how the presence, within the same cluster, of firms that belong to two different value chains (and social communities) might affect the cluster's development. Through the analysis of the upgrading processes of Chinese firms in the Prato textile cluster (Italy), the author discusses local liability and shows how those firms were able to modify the organization of value chain activities and their relationship with indigenous cluster firms through their linkages with GVCs based in their home country, China.

Value-chain activities: rethinking the balance between manufacturing, services and innovation

A third issue that needs to be better understood is the description and analysis of the full array of value-chain activities (including pre-production, production and post-production phases) and their mapping within the industry being studied. In cluster/GVC analysis, this focus will improve our comprehension of: 1) how single activities contribute to the process of local value generation (links with the "smile" framework); and 2) the geographical distribution of activities (with particular attention to production tasks) and the role of different locations across global, country, regional and district levels of analysis.

Most GVC studies have emphasized a division of labour between global lead firms located in advanced countries (specializing in the upper branches or extremities of the "smile" curve, i.e. the pre and post-production phases) and suppliers in emerging countries (which focus on the lower-value-added stages, i.e. production processes). By contrast, studies of industrial districts have emphasized the relevance of production activities to enable ID competitiveness, especially in terms of innovation outcomes.

The third section of the book thus offers fresh insights into manufacturing as a value-adding activity and its impact on the geographical organization of production in light of technological transformations, the increasing costs of managing supply chains in developing countries and the growing attention toward country-of-origin products. *How will such trends impact the organization of GVCs as well as the role of clusters in the global division of labour from the perspective of manufacturing? What new configurations of activities exist for value creation and innovation development? Will the cluster as a system remain a competitive milieu for local companies and still be supportive of their innovative efforts?*

In Chapter 9, Bettiol, Chiarvesio, Di Maria and Micelli discuss why companies choose to locate manufacturing activities in the cluster or abroad based on their analysis of local lead firms operating in Italian furniture, sports system and eyewear clusters. The authors suggest that controlling manufacturing activities at the cluster level is crucial for innovation purposes, but also that the global scale of production (in emerging countries) is a crucial factor to enable global competitiveness and efficiency gains enabled by mass production.

In Chapter 10, Hervas-Oliver and Parrilli offer insights on how innovation can be developed and diffused across two co-evolving IDs by analyzing a recent break-through innovation that modified ceramic tile production in the Castellon (Spain) and Sassuolo (Italy) tile clusters: inkjet printing. The authors argue that the presence of home-grown global lead firms (often having facilities in both IDs) and of strong manufacturing capabilities at the local level have enabled the new technology to be developed, starting from an innovation initially created in the United Kingdom and subsequently diffused within the two clusters (Castellon first and Sassuolo later).

In Chapter 11, Golini and Boffelli propose an original methodology to map manufacturing activities at the cluster level based on the GVC framework. Through a survey-based analysis of the Bergamo textile cluster (Italy), the authors explore how firms at the cluster level control value-chain activities (within and across segments of the textile value chain) and operationalize their upgrading strategies into several distinctive patterns to exploit competitive niches within both the local and global economies.

Finally, Chapter 12, by the editors (De Marchi, Di Maria and Gereffi), reflects on the volume's key contributions with respect to the central research questions addressed. In addition, it discusses the policy implications and avenues for further research opened up by the chapters in this book.

In summary, the book's chapters explore the intersection between clusters and GVCs through a variety of methodological approaches, facilitating a broader understanding of the complex issues at stake. Chapters 7 and 11, for example, adopt quantitative approaches based on samples of cluster firms. Chapter 6 and 9, by contrast, utilize the comparative case-study approach, offering a richer picture of strategies of key firms within the cluster. Chapter 5 reports a meta-analysis of previous studies on the MNEs' investments at the cluster level. The various chapters in this book provide complementary narratives also with respect to the different units of analysis adopted, including: 1) the cluster as a whole, approached through a systemic perspective ((Chapters 2, 3, 8 and 10)); 2) the firm-level (Chapters 5 and 9); and 3) the GVC level (Chapters 6 and 11).

Due to this diversity of empirical approaches, which are rooted in similar theoretical frameworks, this book is uniquely positioned to offer an integrated view of the evolution of clusters within GVCs. It reveals not only how cluster (and firm) activities are connected with global markets, but also the heterogeneous internal structure of local clusters refracted through a GVC lens. The diversity of industries considered (jewellery, toys, textiles, ceramics, eyewear, furniture, footwear, ICT and metal-mechanics) as well as the countries explored (Italy, Spain, China and Romania) further enrich the picture and provide better grounding for the generalizations across clusters as well as their intersection with GVCs.

Notes

1 These can be defined as a population of firms, mostly small and medium-sized enterprises (SMEs), carrying out different activities in the same industry and located in a geographically bounded area.
2 While acknowledging the differences across these diverse literatures (see e.g. De Marchi and Grandinetti, 2014; Ortega-Colomer et al., 2016), in this chapter and the book, unless otherwise specified, we will use the terms cluster and industrial district as synonymous.
3 This is especially true in the configuration that Brusco (1990) named *Mark II*, as opposed to *Mark I*, which has no external local government intervention.
4 These typologies are based on detailed GVC case studies. The research required to map governance structures typically involves two steps: first, the input-output structure of the value chain needs to be identified in considerable detail (GVC case studies almost always contain diagrams of these input-output structures composed of boxes and arrows that map interconnected goods and services); and second, the research needs to overlay the main companies involved in different stages of the supply chain, and figure out where the "lead firms" are located. This gives us the governance structure of an industry.
5 Current studies show that most global industries are made up of a mix of these governance structures in different parts of the global supply chain, and these structures change over time and across different regional and country settings (Gereffi and Fernandez-Stark, 2016).
6 For example, the offshore production of high-tech electronics, such as Apple products, has led to the disappearance of middle-income jobs in the United States while generating a large group of Chinese workers suffering excessive working hours, violation of labour laws and hazardous factory conditions (see Duhigg and Bradsher, 2012; Duhigg and Barboza, 2012).
7 In this model, which depicts value-added activities at each stage of the chain, production itself is usually represented as relatively low-value-added activities, compared with higher value pre- and post-production services (see Gereffi and Fernandez-Stark, 2016, p. 14).
8 See, for example, the role of anchor or seed firms (Belussi, 2015).

References

Azmeh, S., and Nadvi, K. (2014). Asian firms and the restructuring of global value chains. *International Business Review*, 23(4): 708–717.
Bailey, D., and De Propris, L. (2014). Manufacturing reshoring and its limits: The UK automotive case. *Cambridge Journal of Regions, Economy and Society*, 7: 379–395.
Bair, J. (2008). Analysing economic organization: Embedded networks and global chains compared. *Economy and Society*, 37(3): 339–364.
Bair, J., and Gereffi, G. (2001). Local clusters in global chains: The causes and consequences of export dynamism in Torreon's blue jeans industry. *World Development*, 29(11): 1885–1903.
Barrientos, S., Gereffi, G., and Rossi, A. (2011). Economic and social upgrading in global production networks: A new paradigm for a changing world. *International Labour Review*, 150(3–4): 319–340.
Bathelt, H., Malmberg, A., and Maskell, P. (2004). Clusters and knowledge: Local buzz, global pipelines and the process of knowledge creation. *Progress in Human Geography*, 28(1): 31–56.
Becattini, G. (1986). Small firms and industrial districts: The experience of Italy. *Economia Internazionale*, 39(2–3–4): 98–103.
Becattini, G. (1990). The Marshallian industrial district as a socioeconomic notion. In F. Pyke, G. Becattini and W. Sengerberger (eds.), *Industrial Districts and Inter-firm Cooperation in Italy*. Geneva: International Institute of Labour Studies.

Bellandi, M., and Lombardi, S. (2012). Specialized markets and Chinese industrial clusters: The experience of Zhejiang Province. *China Economic Review*, 23: 623–638.

Belso-Martinez, J.A. (2008). Differences in survival strategies among footwear industrial districts: The role of international outsourcing. *European Planning Studies*, 16(9): 1229–1248.

Belussi, F. (2006). In search of a useful theory of spatial clustering. In B. Asheim, P. Cook and R. Martin (eds.), *Clusters and Regional Development*. Abingdon: Routledge.

Belussi, F. (2015). The international resilience of Italian industrial districts/clusters (ID/C) between knowledge re-shoring and manufacturing off (near)-shoring. *Investigaciones Regionales*, 32: 89–113.

Belussi, F., Gottardi, G., and Rullani, E. (eds.). (2003). *The Technological Evolution of Industrial Districts*. Boston: Kluwer.

Belussi, F., and Sedita, S.R. (2009). Life cycle vs. multiple path dependency in industrial districts. *European Planning Studies*, 17(4): 505–528.

Belussi, F., Sedita, S.R., and Pilotti, L. (2008). Learning at the boundaries for industrial districts between exploitation of local resources and exploration of global knowledge flows. In R. Leoncini and S. Montresor (eds.), *Dynamic Capabilities Between Firm Organization and Local Systems of Production*. London: Routledge, pp. 181–215.

Bernhardt, T., and Pollak, R. (2016). Economic and social upgrading dynamics in global manufacturing value chains: A comparative analysis. *Environment and Planning A*, 48(7): 1220–1243.

Bocconcelli, R., and Tunisini, A. (2001). La costellazione del mobile nel Pesarese. Un'analisi interpretativa. *Piccola Impresa*, 2: 83–112.

Brandt, L., and Thun, E. (2011). Going mobile in China: Shifting value chains and upgrading in the mobile telecom sector. *International Journal of Technological Learning, Innovation and Development*, 4(1–3): 148–180.

Brusco, S. (1982). The Emilian model: Productive decentralisation and social integration. *Cambridge Journal of Economics*, 6: 167–184.

Brusco, S. (1990). The idea of the industrial district: Its genesis. In F. Pyke, G. Becattini and W. Sengenberger (eds.), *Industrial Districts and Local Economic Regeneration*. Geneva: International Institute for Labour Studies, pp. 10–19.

Camuffo, A. (2003). Transforming industrial districts: Large firms and small business networks in the Italian eyewear industry. *Industry and Innovation*, 10: 377–401.

Camuffo, A., and Grandinetti, R. (2011). Italian industrial districts as cognitive systems: Are they still reproducible? *Entrepreneurship & Regional Development*, 23(9–10): 37–41.

Cattaneo, O., Gereffi, G., Miroudot, S., and Taglioni, D. (2013). *Joining, Upgrading and Being Competitive in Global Value Chains: A Strategic Framework*. World Bank Policy Research Working Paper 6406. Available at: www-wds.worldbank.org/external/default/WDSContentServer/IW3P/IB/2013/04/09/000158349_20130409182129/Rendered/PDF/wps6406.pdf.

Cattaneo, O., Gereffi, G., and Staritz, C. (eds.). (2010). *Global Value Chains in a Postcrisis World: A Development Perspective*. Washington, DC: The World Bank.

Chiarvesio, M., Di Maria, E., and Micelli, S. (2004). From local networks of SMEs to virtual districts? Evidence from recent trends in Italy. *Research Policy*, 33(10): 1509–1528.

Chiarvesio, M., Di Maria, E., and Micelli, S. (2010). Global value chains and open networks: The case of Italian industrial districts. *European Planning Studies*, 18(3): 333–350.

Corno, F., Reinmoeller, P., and Nonaka, I. (1999). Knowledge creation within industrial systems. *Journal of Management and Governance*, 3: 379–394.

Dei Ottati, G. (1996). Trust, interlinking transactions and credit in industrial districts. *Cambridge Journal of Economics*, 18: 529–546.

Dei Ottati, G. (2003). The governance of transactions in the industrial district: The 'community market'. In G. Becattini, M. Bellandi, G. Dei Ottati and F. Sforzi (eds.), *From Industrial Districts to Local Development: An Itinerary of Research*. Cheltenham: Edward Elgar.

Delgado, M., Porter, M.E., and Stern, S. (2010). Clusters and entrepreneurship. *Journal of Economic Geography*, 10(4): 495–518.

De Marchi, V., Di Maria, E., and Ponte, S. (2013). The greening of global value chains: Insights from the furniture industry. *Competition and Change*, 17(4): 299–318.

De Marchi, V., and Grandinetti, R. (2014). Industrial districts and the collapse of the Marshallian model: Looking at the Italian experience. *Competition & Change*, 18(1): 70–87.

Dicken, P. (2011). Global Shift: Mapping the Changing Contours of the World Economy, 6th ed. New York: Guilford.

Duhigg, C., and Barboza, D. (2012). In China, human costs are built into an iPad. *The New York Times*, January 26.

Duhigg, C., and Bradsher, K. (2012). How the U.S. lost out on iPhone work. *The New York Times*, January 22.

Feenstra, R. (1998). Integration of trade and disintegration of production in the global economy. *Journal of Economic Perspectives*, 12(4): 31–50.

Fratocchi, L., Di Mauro, C., Barbieri, P., Nassimbeni, G., and Zanoni, A. (2014). When manufacturing moves back: Concepts and questions. *Journal of Purchasing and Supply Management*, 20(1): 54–59.

Fung, V.K. (2011). *Global Supply Chains – Past Developments, Emerging Trends*. Speech to the Executive Committee of the Federation of Indian Chambers of Commerce and Industry, Oct. 11. Available at: www.fungglobalinstitute.org/en/global-supply-chains-%E2%80%93-past-developments-emerging-trends.

Furlan, A., Grandinetti, R., and Campagnolo, D. (2009). Local networks in global networks: Is it possible? *The IMP Journal*, 3(3): 3–20.

Garofoli, G. (1992). New firm formation and local development: The Italian experience. *Entrepreneurship & Regional Development*, 4: 101–125.

Gereffi, G. (1994). The organization of buyer-driven global commodity chains: How U.S. retailers shape overseas production networks. In G. Gereffi and M. Korzeniewicz (eds.), *Commodity Chains and Global Capitalism*. Westport, CT: Praeger, pp. 95–122.

Gereffi, G. (1999). International trade and industrial upgrading in the apparel commodity chain. *Journal of International Economics*, 48(1): 37–70.

Gereffi, G. (2005). The global economy: Organization, governance, and development. In N.J. Smelser and R. Swedberg (eds.), *The Handbook of Economic Sociology*, 2nd ed. Princeton, NJ: Princeton University Press, pp. 160–182.

Gereffi, G. (2014). Global value chains in a post-Washington consensus world. *Review of International Political Economy*, 21(1): 9–37.

Gereffi, G. and Fernandez-Stark, K. (2016). *Global Value Chain Analysis: A Primer*, 2nd ed. Durham, NC: Duke CGGC. Available at: www.cggc.duke.edu/pdfs/Duke_CGGC_Global_Value_Chain_GVC_Analysis_Primer_2nd_Ed_2016.pdf.

Gereffi, G., Humphrey, J., and Sturgeon, T. (2005). The governance of global value chains. *Review of International Political Economy*, 121: 78–104.

Gereffi, G., and Lee, J. (2012). Why the world suddenly cares about global supply chains. *Journal of Supply Chain Management*, 48(3): 24–32.

Gereffi, G., and Lee, J. (2016). Economic and social upgrading in global value chains and industrial clusters: Why governance matters. *Journal of Business Ethics*, 133(1): 25–38.

Gereffi, G., and Sturgeon, T. (2013). Global value chain-oriented industrial policy: The role of emerging economies. In D.K. Elms and P. Low (eds.), *Global Value Chains in a Changing World*. Geneva: World Trade Organization, Fung Global Institute and Temasek Foundation Centre for Trade & Negotiations, pp. 329–360.

Gibbon, P. (2008). Governance, entry barriers, upgrading: A re-interpretation of some GVC concepts from the experience of African clothing exports. *Competition and Change*, 12(1): 29–48.

Gibbon, P., Bair, J., and Ponte, S. (2008). Governing global value chains: An introduction. *Economy and Society*, 37(3): 315–338.

Giuliani, E., Pietrobelli, C., and Rabellotti, R. (2005). Upgrading in global value chains: Lessons from Latin American clusters. *World Development*, 33(4): 549–573.

Gray, J.V., Skowronski, K., Esenduran, G., and Johnny Rungtusanatham, M. (2013). The reshoring phenomenon: What supply chain academics ought to know and should do. *Journal of Supply Chain Management*, 49(2): 27–33.

Hervas-Oliver, J.L., and Albors-Garrigos, J. (2008). Local knowledge domains and the role of MNE affiliates in bridging and complementing a cluster's knowledge. *Entrepreneurship and Regional Development*, 20(6): 581–598.

Hervas-Oliver, J.-L., Gonzalez, G., Caja, P., and Sempere-Ripoll, F. (2015). Clusters and industrial districts: Where is the literature going? Identifying emerging sub-fields of research. *European Planning Studies*, 4313(April): 1–46.

Humphrey, J., and Schmitz, H. (2002). How does insertion in global value chains affect upgrading in industrial clusters? *Regional Studies*, 36(9): 1017–1027.

Iammarino, S., and McCann, P. (2006). The structure and evolution of industrial clusters: Transactions, technology and knowledge spillovers. *Research Policy*, 35(7): 1018–1036.

Kaplinsky, R., Terheggen, A., and Tijaja, J. (2011). China as a final market: The Gabon timber and Thai cassava value chains. *World Development*, 39(7): 1177–1190.

Khanna, T., and Palepu, K. (2006). Emerging giants: Building world class companies from emerging markets. *Harvard Business Review*, 84(10): 60–69.

Krugman, P. (1995). Growing world trade. *Brookings Papers on Economic Activity*, 1: 327–377.

Lazerson, M.H. (1995). A new phoenix? Modern putting-out in the Modena knitwear industry. *Administrative Science Quarterly*, 40(1): 34–59.

Lazerson, M.H., and Lorenzoni, G. (1999). The firms that feed industrial districts: A return to the Italian source. *Industrial and Corporate Change*, 8: 235–266.

Lazzeretti, L., Sedita, S.R., and Caloffi, A. (2014). Founders and disseminators of cluster research. *Journal of Economic Geography*, 14(1): 21–43.

Lee, J., Gereffi, G., and Barrientos, S. (2011). *Global Value Chains, Upgrading and Poverty Reduction*. Capturing the Gains Briefing Note, No. 3. Available at: www.capturingthegains.org/pdf/ctg_briefing_note_3.pdf.

Lee, J., Gereffi, G., and Beauvais, J. (2012). Global value chains and agrifood standards: Challenges and possibilities for smallholders in developing countries. *Proceedings of the National Academy of Sciences*, 109(31): 12326–12331.

Long, C., and Zhang, X. (2011). Cluster-based industrialization in China: Financing and performance. *Journal of International Economics*, 84(1): 112–123.

Lorenzoni, G., and Lipparini, A. (1999). The leveraging of interfirm relationships as a distinctive organizational capability: A longitudinal study. *Strategic Management Journal*, 204: 317–338.

Markusen, A. (1996). Sticky places in slippery space: A typology of industrial districts. *Economic Geography*, 723: 293–313.

Marshall, A. (1919). *Industry and Trade*. London: MacMillan.

Molina-Morales, F.X. (2002). European industrial districts: Influence of geographic concentration on performance of the firm. *Journal of International Management*, 7(4): 277–294.

Molina-Morales, F.X., and Martínez-Cháfer, L. (2016). Cluster firms: You'll never walk alone. *Regional Studies*, 50(5): 877–893.

Molina-Morales, F.X., and Martínez-Fernández, M.T. (2010). Social networks: Effects of social capital on firm innovation. *Journal of Small Business Management*, 48(2): 258–279.

Morrison, A. (2008). Gatekeepers of knowledge within industrial districts: Who they are, how they interact. *Regional Studies*, 42(6): 817–835.

Morrison, A., Pietrobelli, C., and Rabellotti, R. (2008). Global value chains and technological capabilities: A framework to study learning and innovation in developing countries. *Oxford Development Studies*, 36(1): 39–58.

Mudambi, R. (2008). Location, control and innovation in knowledge-intensive industries. *Journal of Economic Geography*, 8(5): 699–725.

Nachum, L., and Keeble, D. (2003). Neo-Marshallian clusters and global networks: The linkages of media firms in Central London. *Long Range Planning*, 36(5): 459–480.

Nadvi, K., and Halder, G. (2005). Local clusters in global value chains: Exploring dynamic linkages between Germany and Pakistan. *Entrepreneurship and Regional Development*, 17(5): 339–363.

Ortega-Colomer, F.J., Molina-Morales, F.X., and Fernandez de Lucio, I. (2016). Discussing the concepts of cluster and industrial district. *Journal of Technology Management & Innovation*, 11(2): 139–147.

Palpacuer, F., Gibbon, P., and Thomsen, L. (2005). New challenges for developing country suppliers in global clothing chains: A comparative European perspective. *World Development*, 33(3): 409–430.

Paniccia, I. (1998). One, a hundred, thousands of industrial districts: Organizational variety in local networks of small and medium-sized enterprises. *Organization Studies*, 4(19): 1–24.

Pietrobelli, C., and Rabellotti, R. (2011). Global value chains meet innovation systems: Are there learning opportunities for developing countries? *World Development*, 39(7): 1261–1269.

Piore, M.J., and Sabel, C.F. (1984). *The Second Industrial Divide: Possibilities for Prosperity*. New York: Basic Books.

Pisano, G., and Shih, W. (2012). *Producing Prosperity: Why America Needs a Manufacturing Renaissance*. Boston: Harvard Business School Press.

Ponte, S., and Sturgeon, T. (2014). Explaining governance in global value chains: A modular theory-building effort. *Review of International Political Economy*, 21(1): 195–223.

Porter, M.E. (1990). *The Competitive Advantage of Nations*. New York: Free Press.

Porter, M.E. (1998). Clusters and the new economics of competition. *Harvard Business Review*, 76: 77–90.

Porter, M.E., and Ketels, D. (2009). Clusters and industrial districts: Common roots, different perspectives. In G. Becattini, M. Bellandi and L. De Propris (eds.), *A Handbook of Industrial Districts*. Cheltenham: Edward Elgar, pp. 172–183.

Pyke, F., Becattini, G., and Sengerberger, W. (eds.). (1990). *Industrial Districts and Inter-firm Cooperation in Italy*. Geneva: International Institute of Labour Studies.

Rabellotti, R. (1997). External Economies and Cooperation in Industrial Districts: A Comparison of Italy and Mexico. London: Macmillan.

Rabellotti, R., Carabelli, A., and Hirsch, G. (2009). Italian industrial districts on the move: Where are they going? *European Planning Studies*, 17(1): 19–41.

Saxenian, A. (2006). *The New Argonauts: Regional Advantage in a Global Economy*. Cambridge, MA: Harvard University Press.

Schmitz, H. (1989). *Flexible Specialization: A New Paradigm of Small-Scale Industrialization*. Discussion Paper, No. 261, Institute of Development Studies, University of Sussex, Brigthon.

Schmitz, H. (1995). Collective efficiency: growth path for small-scale industry. *Journal of Development Studies*, 31(4): 529–566.

Schmitz, H., and Nadvi, K. (1999). Clustering and industrialization: Introduction. *World Development*, 27(9): 1503–1514.

Shenkar, O. (2010). Copycats: How Smart Companies Use Imitation to Gain a Strategic Edge. Cambridge, MA: Harvard Business Press.

Sinkovics, R.R., Yamin, M., Nadvi, K., and Zhang Zhang, Y. (2014). Rising powers from emerging markets? The changing face of international business. *International Business Review*, 23(4): 675–679.

Staritz, C., Gereffi, G., and Cattaneo, O. (eds.). (2011). Special Issue on shifting end markets and upgrading prospects in global value chains. *International Journal of Technological Learning, Innovation and Development*, 4(1–3): 1–12.

Sturgeon, T., Van Biesebroeck, J., and Gereffi, G. (2008). Value chains, networks and clusters: Reframing the global automotive industry. *Journal of Economic Geography*, 8(3): 297–321.

Tomas-Miquel, J., Molina-Morales, F.X., and Exposito-Langa, M. (2012). 19. Evolution of Spanish industrial districts: How are they evolving and adapting in the face of globalization? In F. Belussi and U.H. Staber (eds.), *Managing Networks of Creativity*. Abingdon: Routledge.

Werner, M., Bair, J., and Fernández, V.R. (2014). Linking up to development? Global value chains and the making of a post-Washington consensus. *Development and Change*, 45(6): 1219–1247.

Whitford, J. (2001). The decline of a model? Challenge and response in the Italian industrial districts. *Economy and Society*, 30(1): 38–65.

WTO. (2011). *International Trade Statistics 2011*. Geneva: World Trade Organization.

WTO and IDE-JETRO. (2011). *Trade Patterns and Global Value Chains in East Asia: From Trade in Goods to Trade in Tasks*. World Trade Organization and Institute of Developing Economies, Geneva and Tokyo. Available at: www.ide.go.jp/English/Press/pdf/20110606_news.pdf.

Part I

Co-evolution of clusters and global value chains

2 Italian industrial districts today

Between decline and openness to global value chains

Elisa Giuliani and Roberta Rabellotti

Introduction

In 1979, Giacomo Becattini resuscitated the Marshallian industrial district (ID) concept[1] to explain the rapid process of industrialization during the 1970s in the central and north-eastern parts of Italy. In these areas, numerous spatial agglomerations of small and medium-sized enterprises (SMEs), specialized in different phases of the same production process, had achieved economies of scale comparable to those enjoyed by large firms. In particular, Becattini emphasized the social dimension of the ID, stressing the co-existence of populations of firms and the local community of people, and a shared homogenous system of values and norms, which was the ground for trustful interactions.

During the 1980s, the Italian industrial growth model based on IDs was widely celebrated in the international literature, and was often presented as an answer to the crisis in the capitalist system based on large companies (Piore and Sabel, 1984). IDs or as the international literature describes them, industrial clusters,[2] proliferated also outside of Italy, with many agglomerations of small, specialized firms being established around the world.[3] The concept rapidly became relevant for policy, and in the early 1990s several programs were initiated across Europe, mainly in Italy, Spain and Denmark, alongside some examples in the USA, to facilitate the emergence and sustain the development of clusters (OECD, 2007).

Up to the early 1990s, Italian IDs displayed remarkable economic dynamism in sales, exports, employees and profits, and certainly played a central role in the growth of the domestic manufacturing system (Signorini, 2000; Brusco and Paba, 1997). However, in the succeeding years, which coincided with a general downturn in the Italian economy, IDs have been at the centre of a lively economic and political debate in which the widespread enthusiasm of the past was replaced by increasing and diffused criticism (OECD, 2014). According to many scholars, districts are one of the main culprits of Italy's industrial decline, unfitted to face the challenges of globalization and the information and communication technology (ICT) revolution, due mainly to the *dwarfism* of their manufacturing firms, and their specialization in traditional industries (among others see Onida, 2004; Nardozzi, 2004; Ramazzotti, 2010).

The debate on the contribution of IDs to the most recent downward trends in the Italian economic system has been fuelled by a rich empirical literature, which explores the many structural changes occurring in the districts. In this context, Rabellotti et al. (2009) argue that currently, Italian IDs are undergoing radical transformations, and are evolving towards new industrial organization forms: some districts are experiencing deep crisis, while others are successfully facing globalization and increased international competition.

The aim of this chapter is to document these changes by surveying the numerous empirical studies in the literature, and by discussing the challenges that Italian IDs must overcome to survive and prosper in a highly competitive global market. Based on the available evidence, this chapter discusses how the emergence of aggressive international competitors in low-cost countries, the stagnation of "traditional" target markets (i.e. the domestic and EU markets), the growing demand from emerging countries, rising technological complexity, and the increasing organization of production along global value chains (GVC) are influencing Italian IDs' strategies and outcomes.

The fading of the district effect

Several empirical studies confirm the existence of a district effect tied to the presence of ID-level external economies and spillovers, and consisting of superior local availability of knowledge, technology, skilled labour, specialized suppliers and other resources (Fabiani et al., 2000; Cainelli and De Liso, 2005). Thus, most research on IDs conducted before and/or during the 1990s suggests that district firms outperform non-district firms in terms of returns on investment and equity, value added per worker and propensity for product and process innovation.

However, some recent studies find that this difference in the performance of district and non-district firms holds (Foresti et al., 2008) only in the case of urban clusters whose firms still appear to benefit from a *district effect* (Di Giacinto et al., 2014).[4] Di Giacinto and colleagues show that Italian districts generate local productivity advantages which are appropriated more effectively by less efficient firms, while the externalities arising in cities are exploited better by more efficient enterprises. In the same vein, Iuzzolino and Menon (2011) study clusters located in the Northeast of Italy, and test for the existence of two different types of *district effects*. For 1993 to 2006, they find a slightly positive agglomeration effect for quality of infrastructures, business services and human capital across all cluster firms, and over the whole period 1993–08, a negative specialization effect for knowledge spillovers, specialized labour pool and availability of high-quality inputs exploitable only by firms in the main sector of cluster specialization. After this, from 2006 the effect becomes zero or slightly negative. A consequence of this finding of decreasing importance of the district effect is increased diversity of performance (i.e. employment and firm profitability) both within and between clusters. This diversity is the focus of the next section.

Diversity within and between districts

Diversity among district firms

Firms in Italian districts have proven to be far more heterogeneous – in terms of both size and performance – than conventionally is envisaged (Bronzini et al., 2013). Compared to larger firms, small firms (with turnover of less than EUR 10 million) are more fragile and less capable of coping with globalization and innovation challenges (Intesa Sanpaolo, 2013; Bronzini et al., 2013). Many of these firms have been unable to survive in the new highly competitive global context, which is confirmed by their recent massive exit from the market. According to Confindustria (2013), in Italy 55,000 manufacturing companies closed between 2009 and 2012, with small enterprises in the Northeast where many districts are located being the most affected in the country. Among sectors, the worst affected were pharmaceuticals, textiles and clothing, and leather. Empirical analysis confirms that in the north-eastern districts medium-large firms (with turnover greater than EUR 50 million) are faring better than smaller firms (Iuzzolino and Menon, 2011). The increasing importance of medium-large firms is also made evident by the emergence of leading firms in some districts, such as Tod's in the footwear sector, Luxottica in the optical industry, Zegna in the luxury wool sector and Riello, which is specialized in heating equipment. Many of these firms are still family-run and find IDs to be a natural environment for their development (Colli, 2005).

Business groups, which are groups of firms with the same ownership but which are legally independent, often populate districts (Iacobucci and Rosa, 2005). Apart from minimizing transaction costs (Williamson, 1979), in Italian districts the creation of business groups often is motivated by the need to resolve conflicts within families arising from generational changes, and a desire to absorb new human resources without losing ownership control. This results in new linked enterprises, often owned by former employees of the group's leader (Cainelli et al., 2006). Groups can be created also to reduce transparency, often for fiscal reasons because complex groups are more likely to be involved in tax evasion. Cainelli et al. (2006) show empirically that groups are more widespread in district than in non-district areas, and can be considered an organizational strategy adopted by many enterprises to grow, expand and diversify their economic activities. The increasing number of business groups is forcing a reconsideration of the average dimension of Italian firms. According to Cainelli and Iacobucci (2005), if business group is the economic unit of analysis, this increases the average size of Italian firms from 43 to 156 employees. Thus, the available empirical evidence shows there is wide diversity among cluster firms depending on their size, performance and patterns of local and global involvement described in detail below, which has consequences for the distribution of capital, knowledge and market power in the district.

Diversity among districts

District-level performance varies widely across industries: mechanical IDs have been one of the best performers with steady positive trends in employment over the period 1993–2008; in contrast "Made in Italy" IDs specialized in the production of clothing and shoes, have registered more negative trends, especially in employment (Accetturo et al., 2013).

There has been a tendency also for IDs to change their specialization over time. There is increasing systematic evidence that countries and regions are more likely to diversify into sectors that are closely related to their traditional activities (Hidalgo et al., 2007). Diversification in related sectors is often a path-dependent process, arising from the re-use and adaptation of existing technological, knowledge, organizational and commercial capabilities and assets. This movement of firms and clusters into new but often related industries is described in the GVC literature as chain upgrading (Gereffi et al., 2005).

In response to the widening of market opportunities to include new countries, a number of Italian districts have experienced a spontaneous shift in specialization from final goods such as clothing and shoes, which often are characterized by cost-based competition, to capital goods such as clothing and footwear industry machinery. In this case, technological capabilities provide competitive advantage over competitors in emerging markets. Between 1991 and 2001, 21 Italian IDs changed their industry specialization with one-third moving into the mechanical industry (Rabellotti et al., 2009). Diversification in a related field is common. Some examples of specialization shifts include Schio and San Bonifacio (Veneto) previously specialized in textiles are now producers of textiles machinery, and Canelli which is located in the core wine region of Piedmont is now a centre for the production of machinery for the wine industry, while Mirandola (Emilia-Romagna) has shifted from textiles to the mechanical and biomedical industries.

The internationalization of IDs and their connections to global value chains

IDs and exports

Clusters traditionally have been important contributors to Italy's international trade performance. In industries such as jewellery, glass and musical instruments, IDs account for more than 90% of Italian exports, and in the textile, clothing and leather sector they account for more than 80% of exports (ISTAT, 2015). Overall, Italian ID firms' exports account for approximately 30% of total national manufacturing exports (ISTAT, 2015) with certain IDs accounting for very significant world market shares, for example Sassuolo with 27% of world exports in ceramic tiles, Prato with 4% of world textile exports and Arezzo which contributes 3.5% to world jewellery sales (Fortis and Carminati, 2009).

Since the 1990s, IDs exporting firms have progressively upgraded the quality of their products in an effort to avoid direct competition with emerging market production. Initially, this strategy was successful, and firms were able to apply mark ups to the marginal costs of many products and in many destination markets (Monti, 2005). The Biella cluster is an example here. Following a severe crisis characterized by the exit of a high number of small firms, a few local companies assumed leading roles in the GVCs coordinating local and external suppliers. They then reoriented their production towards very high-quality luxury fabrics such as cashmere, alpaca and vicuna, and increased their investments in marketing and branding.

However, a study by Giovannetti et al. (2013) shows that China is challenging Italy even in its prime market segments. The Italian IDs most at risk though, are those specialized in low-tech, traditional goods whose quality differs very little from the offers from low-cost competing countries such as China. Since patterns of national export specialization tend to change slowly over time, Italy's vulnerability to China appears unlikely to diminish in the near future. Bugamelli et al. (2010) show that the pressure of Chinese competition is stronger in low-skill sectors such as textile, apparel, leather goods and furniture, and is highly heterogeneous across firms depending on their productivity levels. The competition is more severe for less productive firms, which presumably, are less capable of responding to this pressure by applying product upgrading and specialization strategies. At the same time, China has been pursuing a strategy of upgrading in order to produce higher quality items for export, which makes it an even tougher competitor for Italy. Thus, the challenge is to do more than quality up-scaling.

IDs involvement in global value chains

For district firms, connection to GVCs can be a viable strategy to revamp districts, and avoid their slow down. As discussed in the Introduction to this book, production increasingly is organized along value chains, which cross countries. One or more lead firms, typically multinationals corporations with considerable market power, usually coordinate these GVCs. IDs' involvement in GVCs is a relatively new phenomenon; the economic success of Italian IDs originally was based on deep specialization along a value chain confined predominantly within a geographically bounded area. However, in the current global competition landscape, many firms have extended their supply chains beyond district borders (Belussi and Sammarra, 2010; Chiarvesio et al., 2010; De Marchi et al., 2014; Rabellotti, 2004).

The involvement in GVCs of Italian clusters differs depending on the characteristics of their firms, and their competitiveness strategies. Based on these differences, we propose

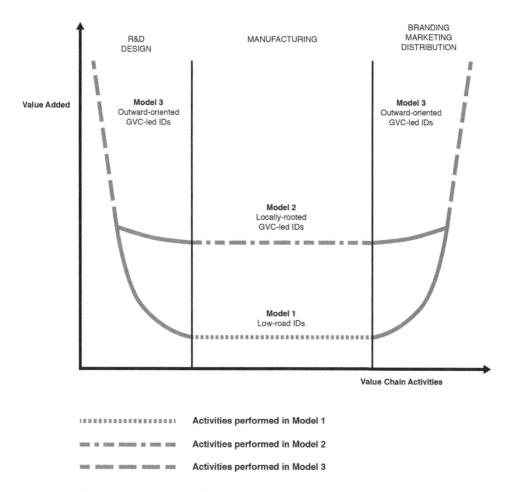

Figure 2.1 Stylized models of ID-GVC involvement in Italy
Source: Authors.

three stylized models of ID-GVC involvement which we consider to characterize Italian IDs: (1) *Low-road IDs*, (2) *Locally rooted GVC-led IDs*, and (3) *Outward-oriented GVC-led IDs* (see Figure 2.1). We discuss these models in the context of the value chain activities performed within the IDs, and in terms of the value-added generated at district level. We conjecture that the relationships between these factors take the form of the Stan Shi's smiling curve. In what follows, we describe the three models and their characteristics.

Model 1: low-road IDs

Low-road IDs models include districts characterized by a predominance of small and rather inefficient firms, mainly undertaking low-value added manufacturing that the literature suggests has been negatively affected by the fading of the *district effect*. Firms in low-road IDs have reacted to international pressures mainly by outsourcing large parts of their production to countries with comparative advantage in labour costs (Humphrey and Schmitz, 2002). For instance, Amighini and Rabellotti (2006) found that some footwear districts in the south of Italy, specialized in low-price market segments, had outsourced a large proportion of their intermediate production abroad. This left very few production activities within the district, and few possibilities for adding value due to the very low investments in branding and design by district firms. The pressure of cost-based international competition has caused these districts to suffer a general decline the numbers of both employees and firms. In some cases, this has resulted in a crisis that has threatened the survival of the district. For instance in Barletta (Apulia) domestic production has been dismantled and transferred to lower labour cost countries on the other side of the Adriatic Sea.

In a comparative analysis of three jewellery clusters, De Marchi et al. (2014) describe Vicenza as a district competing mainly on cost: "the majority of firms [in Vicenza] are still unbranded subcontractors, which are very hard hit by the crisis. These firms based their competitive advantage on economies of scale, rather than product differentiation" (p. 871). De Marchi et al. (pp. 879–80) say also that:

> there is evidence that during the recession, some firms reacted by "downgrading" their production – e.g. substituting silver for gold (not always successfully because this shift requires new and different competences than the use of gold) – while others engaged in partial upgrading, improving their products and processes but not performing higher value-added activities like design, marketing and retail.

In general, involvement in GVCs by low-road clusters has been less than successful, and resulted only in specialization in low value-added manufacturing (see Figure 2.1). Also, due to the strong cost competition from suppliers located in developing countries, in some cases this has resulted in reduced domestic production. Thus, in this type of district, GVCs have had a negative impact on the ability of district firms to capture value-added, and has favoured lower cost competitors.

Model 2: Locally rooted GVC-led IDs

This model is characterized by a concentration of medium to large-sized firms, which are highly embedded in their districts via backward and forward linkages with other local firms and organizations. These companies consider the local supply chain as key to their business success because it facilitates quality, lead times and easy monitoring and control, none of which can be guaranteed by distant suppliers (Buciuni and Pisano, 2015; Capasso et al., 2013). However, several local ID firms have ceased to undertake high value-added activities related to design/product development, or branding and marketing (or both), and have opted to become manufacturing suppliers to larger Italian and/or international luxury brands which retain most of these high value-added activities (Rabellotti, 2004).

An example here is Riviera del Brenta district where several local companies have become subcontractors of Italian and international luxury brands that offer a relatively safe high-end final market for these district firms (Rabellotti, 2004). However, Riviera del Brenta is not just a supplier to international firms; some have invested in the district by setting up new production facilities or acquiring incumbent firms. The first of these investments involved Louis Vuitton Moët Hennessy (LVMH) which acquired Rossimoda, a local flagship company. Next, Chanel, Yves Saint Laurent, and Dior established headquarters for shoe production in the area. Through their activity in high-end markets, many Riviera del Brenta firms have maintained most of their supply relations within the district which has allowed them to monitor quality and lead times – key competitive factors in the context of luxury goods and other high-end products. Riviera del Brenta is considered an interesting location for GVC lead firms because the local system has proven capable of improving its production capabilities, dealing with challenging requests from global designers and leveraging local ecosystem in order to compete.

The Livenza furniture district cluster, which is located in the Northeast of Italy, has adopted a similar model. The Livenza district includes the largest IKEA supplier in Europe (Buciuni and Pisano, 2015). This company is supported by a large network of local suppliers, and is responsible for connecting global design knowledge to local sources of manufacturing and technical production know-how. Another interesting case is the hosiery district of Castel Goffredo (Capasso and Morrison, 2013) where ID firms' involvement in GVCs has resulted in improved production capabilities, and higher product quality, which has allowed local firms to enter new and more demanding global markets.

Compared to *Low-road IDs*, this model currently generates more value added at district level (see Figure 2.1). However, whether this strategy of maintaining only manufacturing and giving up higher value-added activities will endanger the survival of these districts over the longer term, it remains to be seen since other countries are rapidly acquiring highly skilled production capacity at lower costs.

Model 3: outward-oriented GVC-led IDs

This model of ID-GVC connection is characterized mainly by the presence of medium to large-sized firms, which are strongly outward-oriented. These firms privilege international or otherwise extra-ID commercial, supply, and knowledge linkages, over local linkages with other district firms and/or organizations. Some of these firms have grown by establishing business groups; others have been acquired by foreign multinational enterprises and/or are strongly embedded in GVCs.

In these types of districts, firms compete in high-end, specialized, or niche markets, they globally outsource most of their manufacturing activities but they keep the high value-added activities such as R&D, product development, design, branding and marketing within the district boundary. Their outward connections are oriented towards efficiency-seeking on the production side (see Figure 2.1). Given that not all the firms in IDs are capable of becoming prominent actors, this model risks generating a disconnection between the largest ID firms and the local ecosystem (De Marchi and Grandinetti, 2014).

A case that nicely describes this model is Montebelluna (Veneto), a district focusing on production of sportswear including ski boots. The largest firms offshore production to lower cost countries, and focus their district activities on R&D, marketing and distribution. Sammarra and Belussi (2006, pp. 556–557) emphasize the relevance of external knowledge transfer through the multinational enterprises in Montebelluna:

> a fundamental mechanism that fostered the process of acquisition of external knowledge is related to the entry of foreign multinationals in the Montebelluna district through the acquisition of district companies . . . [because multinationals] are generally prone to facilitate knowledge transfer within their own network of foreign subsidiaries, fostering their functional upgrading through the transfer of product, process and management skills and innovations between the units of their transnational network.

Similarly, the Belluno eyewear district includes Luxottica which has become the world's largest eyewear group, and a few other business groups that are vertically integrated or connected to an international network of suppliers (De Marchi and Grandinetti, 2014). De Marchi et al. (2014) identify a similar pattern of GVC involvement in the jewellery industry in Arezzo (Tuscany). The cluster survived a major crisis following the decision of the district lead firm to delocalize a considerable part of its manufacturing activities and its supply chain to Jordan and other developing countries.

In these types of districts, the challenge clearly is maintaining and sustaining local engagement to avoid the risk of local firms and GVC lead companies progressively relocating their business activities, and separating from and negatively affecting the ID. Empirical evidence in McCaffrey (2013) on textile and clothing Italian IDs shows that in some cases, leading companies have reduced their local subcontracting arrangements and their engagement with local organizations, and increasingly are relying on external links to access knowledge.

To sum up, these three models of ID-GVC connection include *low-road IDs* mainly specialized in low value-added manufacturing activities; *locally rooted GVC-led IDs* focusing on higher value-added manufacturing and *outward-oriented GVC-led IDs* concentrating in R&D, design, marketing, branding and distribution phases. We note, first, that the global dispersion of activities is not always accompanied by higher value added at district level as shown by *low-road IDs*, which have outsourced manufacturing without being able to move up the value chain towards design or marketing. Second, to achieve higher value-added requires district firms to make the right strategic choices about markets and the potential for generating value-added. Escaping the low cost-low value-added trap seems to be one reason for exploiting GVC connections in order to achieve long-term development.

Conclusions and policy recommendations

The empirical evidence on recent developments in Italian IDs shows that they have reorganized their activities strategically and in different ways. They are very different from the 1970s and1980s IDs. Our analysis (see Figure 2.1) shows that not all ID models are equally successful. That is, the global dispersion of activities does not result in higher value-added production at the district level. Many districts have chosen the route of downgrading of their activities and searching for ways to reduce costs. However, these strategies are unlikely to be successful since the global competition scenario is becoming stronger.

The strategy of escaping the low cost-low value-added trap seems a more promising development strategy, and firms in outward-oriented GVC-led IDs are exploiting their GVC connections to favour their long-term development. These types of firms are more strategic and more forward-looking, and have invested rather than divested, even during crises. They have responded to the uncertainty of a rapidly changing global production and innovation landscape, by devoting resources to activities – such as R&D, or design – which rarely yield immediate results, and need constant, steady firm-level commitment. They have challenged the dwarfism characterizing ID firms, and have grown, in some cases – for example Luxottica; they have become the international leader in their industry. This is clearly the right direction; however, lack of or badly designed policies are not supporting these firms and these IDs. This might be the reason why many IDs chose the easy route and have become low-road IDs, or locally rooted GVC-led IDs.

There are several implications for policy that can be derived from this chapter. First, IDs are changing; they are complex adaptive systems made up of different components with evolving functions and interrelationships. The population of the firms in a district is likely to change further due to high entry and exit dynamics. Martin and Sunley (2011, p. 1300) point out that: "[districts] come and go; they emerge, grow, may change in complexion and orientation, may undergo reinvention and transformation, and may eventually decline and even disappear. In short, they evolve." Policy-makers need to be aware of and take account of these changes. They must abandon any romantic notions of Italian IDs, and avoid designing policies inspired by earlier Marshallian ID models. These former ID models and the macro-economic conditions that prevailed in the 1970s and 1980s no longer exist. Italian IDs can no longer compete on costs, this is not viable and will result only in a race to the bottom, which the experience of many developing countries shows is not conducive to a sustainable economic development process.

Policy-makers should design long-term industrial policies; these have been lacking in Italy for at least two decades (De Blasio and Lotti, 2008, Onida and Viesti, 2016). These policies should identify potential development paths for IDs that recognize and enable transformations to industry specializations, and facilitate internationalization and GVC involvement. These efforts must be coordinated by national government, which must participate directly in an overall, country-level industry strategy. Policy-makers need to be better informed about strategic industries, and districts that are in need of support or incentives. This would be in the spirit of mission-oriented policy making. However, it will require policy-makers to have adequate levels of knowledge and skills, and in Italy, this cannot be taken for granted. A recent Bank of Italy study states that:

> policy-makers have limited information about the development potential of industries and other economic activities, and moreover, they often follow the specific interests of corporative groups, thereby biasing the allocation of public funds. By so doing, they run the risk of taking decisions that might hamper rather than promote economic growth.
>
> (Accetturo et al., 2013, p. 30, our translation)

Finally, although this Chapter has focused on Italian IDs and their evolution towards connection to GVCs, we believe that this discussion and the proposed ID organizational models could apply to other European countries facing similar challenges, which includes most of continental and Southern European countries. Given the decline suffered by most of these economies, policies able to support and promote the co-evolution of districts and GVCs are strongly needed. The objective could be to design policies that would strengthen IDs' external connections (including across different clusters worldwide) and sustaining local firms' insertion in GVCs. This would increase SMEs' market shares in international markets, and foster their (often too weak) levels of internationalization. To achieve this will require the development of programs that would help local firms to meet quality standards, and certification requirements, which often are essential for connection to GVCs, and help to identify new market opportunities and new market segments. Support for domestic medium and large firms to move to the head of GVCs in order to capture the highest value segments is crucial. Gereffi and Sturgeon (2013, p. 355) conclude that: "GVC-oriented industrialization and GVC-oriented industrial policies appear to be elements of the current industrial landscape that are here to stay."

Acknowledgements

We would like to thank the editors of the book for their comments on earlier versions of this chapter. Thanks go also to Flavio Calvino for his help in the collection of empirical evidence, and to Alessia Scatena and Fabio Pomini for their graphical support. The initial research work for this chapter was done on behalf of the OECD. All usual disclaimers apply.

Notes

1 Recall that in the late 19th century in England, Alfred Marshall (1920, p. 221) was the first to introduce the concept of industrial district defined as a "concentrations of small businesses of a similar character in particular localities", taking advantage of external economies and industrial atmosphere.
2 In this chapter, the terms cluster and district are used interchangeably.
3 Pyke and Sengenberger (1992) present a collection of empirical studies on clusters in Denmark, Germany, Spain and Canada, among others. For empirical cases in developing countries, see van Dijk and Rabellotti (1996). Becattini et al. (2009) provide a recent survey of empirical studies on clusters within and outside Europe.
4 A possible reason why district effects have faded recently might be related to Audretsch and Feldman's (1996) intuition that local knowledge spillovers matter most during the early stages of an industry development cycle, and less so for mature clusters when technology is consolidated and there is less scope for innovation.

References

Accetturo, A., Bassanetti, A., Bugamelli, M., Faiella, I., Finaldi Russo, P., Franco, D., Giacomelli, S., and Omiccioli, M. (2013). *Il sistema industriale italiano tra globalizzazione e crisi*. Bank of Italy Occasional Paper, 193, Rome.

Amighini, A., and Rabellotti, R. (2006). The effects of globalization on Italian industrial districts: Evidence from the footwear sector. *European Planning Studies*, 14(4): 485–502.

Audretsch, D.B., and Feldman, M.P. (1996). Innovative clusters and the industry life cycle. *Review of Industrial Organization*, 11(2): 253–273.

Becattini, G. (1979). Dal settore industriale al distretto industriale. Alcune considerazioni sull'unità di indagine dell'economia industriale. *Rivista di economia e politica industriale*, 1(1): 35–48 (reprinted as Sectors and/or districts: Some remarks on the conceptual foundations of industrial economics in E.J. Goodman, J. Bamford and P. Saynor (eds.). (1989). *Small Firms and Industrial Districts in Italy*. London: Taylor & Francis, pp. 123–135.

Becattini, G., Bellandi, M., and De Propris, L. (eds.). (2009). *A Handbook of Industrial Districts*. Cheltenham: Edward Elgar Publishing.

Belussi, F., and Sammarra, A. (eds.). (2010). Business Networks in Clusters and Industrial Districts: The Governance of the Global Value Chain. New York: Routledge.

Bronzini, R., Cannari, L., Staderini, A., Conti, L., D'Aurizio, L., Fabbrini, A., Filippone, A., Ilardi, G., Iuzzolino, G., Montanaro, P., and Paccagnella, M. (2013). *L'Industria Meridionale E La Crisi*. Bank of Italy Occasional Paper, 194, Rome.

Brusco, S., and Paba, S. (1997). Per una storia dei distretti industriali italiani dal secondo dopoguerra agli anni novanta. In F. Barca (ed.), *Storia del capitalismo italiano dal dopoguerra ad oggi*. Rome: Donzelli, pp. 265–334.

Buciuni, G., and Pisano, G.P. (2015). *Can Marshall's Clusters Survive Globalization?* Harvard Business School Working Paper, No. 15–088, May.

Bugamelli, M., Fabiani, S., and Sette, E. (2010). *The Age of the Dragon: Chinese Competition and the Pricing Behavior of the Italian Firms*. Department of the Treasury Working Paper, No 4, Ministry of Economy and Finance, Rome.

Cainelli, G., and De Liso, N. (2005). Innovation in industrial districts: Evidence from Italy. *Industry and Innovation*, 12(3): 383–398.

Cainelli, G., and Iacobucci, D. (2005). I gruppi d'impresa e le nuove forme organizzative del capitalismo locale italiano. *L'Industria*, 26(2): 237–256.

Cainelli, G., Iacobucci, D., and Morganti, E. (2006). Spatial agglomeration and business groups: New evidence from Italian industrial districts. *Regional Studies*, 40(5): 507–518.

Capasso, M., Cusmano, L., and Morrison, A. (2013). The determinants of outsourcing and offshoring strategies in industrial districts: Evidence from Italy. *Regional Studies*, 47(4): 465–479.

Capasso, M., and Morrison, A. (2013). Innovation in industrial districts: Evidence from Italy. *Management Decision*, 51(6): 1225–1249.

Chiarvesio, M., Di Maria, E., and Micelli, S. (2010). Global value chains and open networks: The case of Italian industrial districts. *European Planning Studies*, 18(3): 333–350.

Colli, A. (2005). Il quarto capitalismo. *L'Industria*, 26(2): 219–235.

Confindustria. (2013). L'alto prezzo della crisi per l'Italia. Crescono i paesi che costruiscono le condizioni per lo sviluppo manifatturiero. Scenari Industriali, 4, June, Centro Studi Confindustria, Rome.

De Blasio, G., and Lotti, F. (eds.). (2008). *La valutazione degli aiuti alle imprese*. Bologna: Il Mulino.

De Marchi, V., and Grandinetti, R. (2014). Industrial districts and the collapse of the Marshallian model: Looking at the Italian experience. *Competition & Change*, 18(1): 70–87.

De Marchi, V., Lee, J., and Gereffi, G. (2014). Globalization, recession and the internationalization of industrial districts: Experiences from the Italian gold jewellery industry. *European Planning Studies*, 22(4): 866–884.

Di Giacinto, V., Gomellini, M., Micucci, G., and Pagnini, M. (2014). Mapping local productivity advantages in Italy: Industrial districts, cities or both? *Journal of Economic Geography*, 14(2): 365–394.

Fabiani, S., Pellegrini, G., Romagnano, E., and Signorini, L.F. (2000). Efficiency and localisation: The case of Italian districts. In M. Bagella and L. Beccchetti (eds.), *The Competitive Advantage of Industrial Districts*. Heidelberger: Physica-Verlag, pp. 45–69.

Foresti, G., Guelpa, F., and Trenti, S. (2008). 'Effetto distretto': Esiste ancora? *Sviluppo locale*, 13(31): 3–38.

Fortis, M., and Carminati, M. (2009). Sectors of excellence in the Italian industrial districts. In Becattini et al. (eds.), *A Handbook of Industrial Districts*. Cheltenham: Edward Elgar Publishing, pp. 417–428.

Gereffi, G., Humphrey, J., and Sturgeon, T. (2005). The governance of global value chains. *Review of International Political Economy*, 12(1): 78–104.

Gereffi, G., and Sturgeon, T. (2013). Global value chain-oriented industrial policy: The role of emerging economies. In D. Elms and P. Low (eds.), *Global Value Chains in a Changing World*. Geneva: World Trade Organization, pp. 329–360.

Giovannetti, G., Sanfilippo, M., and Velucchi, M. (2013). The 'China effect' on EU exports to OECD markets: A focus on Italy. In G. Gomel, D. Manconi, I. Musu and B. Quintieri (eds.), *The Chinese Economy*. Heidelberg: Springer, pp. 163–180.

Hidalgo, C.A., Klinger, B., Barabási, A.L., and Hausmann, R. (2007). The product space conditions the development of nations. *Science*, 317(5837): 482–487.

Humphrey, J., and Schmitz, H. (2002). How does insertion in global value chains affect upgrading in industrial clusters? *Regional Studies*, 36(9): 1017–1027.

Iacobucci, D., and Rosa, P. (2005). Growth, diversification and business group formation in entrepreneurial firms. *Small Business Economics*, 25: 65–82.

Intesa Sanpaolo. (2013). *Economia e finanza dei distretti industriali*. Rapporto Annuale, No. 5, Servizio studi e ricerche, Intesa Sanpaolo, Turin.

ISTAT. (2015). *Rapporto Annuale Istat 2015*. Rome: ISTAT.

Iuzzolino, G., and Menon, C. (2011). Le agglomerazioni industriali del Nord Est: Segnali di discontinuità negli anni Duemila. *L'industria*, 32(4): 615–654.

Marshall, A. (1920). *Principles of Economics*, 8th ed. London: Macmillan.

Martin, R., and Sunley, P. (2011). Conceptualizing cluster evolution: Beyond the life cycle model? *Regional Studies*, 45(10): 1299–1318.

McCaffrey, S.J. (2013). Tacit-rich districts and globalization: Changes in the Italian textile and apparel production system. *Socio-Economic Review*, 11(4): 657–685.

Monti, P. (2005). Caratteristiche e Mutamenti della Specializzazione delle Esportazioni Italiane. Temi e Discussioni, 559, Banca d'Italia, Rome.

Nardozzi, G. (2004). Miracolo e declino. L'Italia tra concorrenza e protezione. Rome and Bari: Editori Laterza.

Onida, F. (2004). Se il piccolo non cresce. Piccole e medie imprese italiane in affanno. Bologna: Il Mulino.

Onida, F., and Viesti, G. (2016). Una Nuova Politica Industriale in Italia: Investimenti Innovazione, Trasferimento Tecnologico. Florence: Passigli Editori.

Organisation for Economic Cooperation and Development (OECD). (2007). *Competitive Regional Clusters: National Policy Approaches*. Paris: OECD.

Organisation for Economic Cooperation and Development (OECD). (2014). *Italy: Key Issues and Policies, OECD Studies on SMEs and Entrepreneurship*. Paris: OECD.

Piore, M., and Sabel, C. (1984). *The Second Industrial Divide*. New York: Basic Books.

Pyke, F., and Sengenberger, W. (eds.). (1992). *Industrial Districts and Local Economic Regeneration*. Geneva: International Labour Organization.

Rabellotti, R. (2004). How globalization affects Italian industrial districts: The case of Brenta. In H. Schmitz (ed.), *Local Enterprises in the Global Economy: Issues of Governance and Upgrading*. Cheltenham: Edward Elgar, pp. 140–173.

Rabellotti, R., Carabelli, A., and Hirsch, G. (2009). Italian industrial districts on the move: Where are they going? *European Planning Studies*, 17(1): 19–41.

Ramazzotti, P. (2010). Industrial districts, social cohesion and economic decline in Italy. *Cambridge Journal of Economics*, 34(6): 955–974.

Sammarra, A., and Belussi, F. (2006). Evolution and relocation in fashion-led Italian districts: Evidence from two case-studies. *Entrepreneurship and Regional Development*, 18(6): 543–562.

Signorini, F. (ed.). (2000). Lo sviluppo locale: Un'indagine della Banca d'Italia sui distretti italiani. Bari: Donzelli.

van Dijk, M.P., and Rabellotti, R. (eds.). (1996). Enterprise Clusters and Networks as Sources of Cooperation and Technology Diffusion for Small Firms in Developing Countries. London: Frank Cass.

Williamson, O.E. (1979). Transaction-cost economics: The governance of contractual relations. *Journal of Law & Economics*, 22(2): 233–261.

3 Evolutionary trajectories of industrial districts in global value chains

Valentina De Marchi, Gary Gereffi and Roberto Grandinetti

Introduction

Italian industrial districts (IDs) or clusters have been undergoing profound structural changes in the last 15 years, mostly driven by globalization (e.g. Rabellotti et al., 2009, De Marchi and Grandinetti, 2014b; Giuliani and Rabellotti, Chapter 2 in this book). But that does not necessarily mean that Italy's industrial districts have come to the end of their life cycle and can no longer be a source of global competitiveness for district firms. Rather, such changes call for a new framework to understand their actual configurations and opportunities for growth considering their capacity to respond to global changes and evolutionary trajectories, ranging from decline to resiliency (Grandinetti and De Marchi, 2012; De Marchi and Grandinetti, 2014b).

Interestingly, a resilient performance in today's global economy cannot be ascribed to particular industries per se, since comparative studies of clusters specialized in the same industry have revealed quite different performances across clusters (e.g. footwear, Belso-Martinez, 2008; or gold jewellery, De Marchi et al., 2014). Rather, studies suggest that a key determinant of the heterogeneous capacity of IDs to compete in global markets may be their position in global value chains (GVCs) (e.g. Rabellotti, 2004; Chiarvesio et al., 2010), which leverages the international interdependence of economic activities and its economic and social implications for countries and regions (Gereffi, 2014).

The value-added activities performed by suppliers of global lead firms (GLFs), which are the key actors shaping how value is created and captured along GVCs, define three distinct roles suppliers can play in GVCs: 1) focusing just on manufacturing activities to work under the lead firm's specifications (original equipment manufacturer, OEM); 2) carrying out pre-production activities such as R&D and design (original design manufacturer, ODM); or 3) adding branding and marketing functions (original brand manufacturer, OBM) (Gereffi, 1999). While the GVC framework has been applied mostly to understand the implication of the participation in GVCs for firms based in developing economies, we believe that this approach can be used to investigate the development of industrial districts in advanced countries as well (see also De Marchi et al., Chapter 1 in this book).

Although a rich literature exists to describe recent changes in IDs – mostly focusing on one or a few districts at a time (e.g. Alberti, 2006) or treating them as a homogenous category (e.g. Rabellotti et al., 2009; Chiarvesio et al., 2010) – a comprehensive understanding of the role of global-local linkages in shaping trajectories of local development is still missing. What factors drive the ability of some IDs to compete and capture value within GVCs, while other districts are stagnant or in decline?

Based on different configurations of ID evolution contained in the literature (see De Marchi and Grandinetti, 2014a), a key contribution of this chapter is to investigate the factors related to the emergence of IDs as well as implications for their future competitiveness.[1] We analyse four IDs based in the Veneto region of Italy, characterized by a very high number of IDs, and we provide an integrative framework including internal (ID-related) elements and global (GVC-related) ones to understand how clusters based in developed countries evolve and compete in the global context, addressing the challenge of adopting jointly the global and local levels of analysis proposed by Gereffi and Lee (2016). While the results provided are based on IDs located in a developed country – Italy, the archetype of an ID-based development model – we wish to set out a research agenda for understanding the developmental trajectories of advanced manufacturing clusters based in developing countries as well.

Factors affecting the evolution of IDs in the global economy

The traditional type of IDs was a dynamic component of the Italian economy and an essential factor in explaining the success of "Made in Italy" products in international markets during the 1970s and 1980s, but times have changed. Some new factors were already evident in the 1990s (e.g. Harrison, 1994; Crestanello, 1997; Corò and Grandinetti, 1999), but the transformation that occurred in the last 20 years was more dramatic and characterized by different drivers, mostly related to globalization but exacerbated by internal difficulties (Rabellotti et al., 2009; Grandinetti and De Marchi, 2012).

All the IDs in the "old" world had to come to terms with a formidable intensification of global competition since the arrival of newcomers on the world market, mainly from Asia, capable of offering a wide range of export products at lower costs. This external challenge was exacerbated in the last decade due to the effects of the 2008–09 world recession. The increasing geographic and organizational consolidations in most industries, both at country and firm levels (Cattaneo et al., 2010), is further hindering the ability of the small and -micro-sized enterprises within IDs to compete. This has prompted a sizable number of firms, specialized both in the production of final goods as well as intermediate inputs, to shut down. The former suffered from the aggressive pricing policies of their developing country competitors, especially for low-cost products. The latter are being displaced by the surviving firms, as many local final-goods companies have turned to foreign suppliers for their intermediate inputs in order to remain competitive, changing the geography of product and knowledge sourcing and eroding the fabric of local relationships (Dunford, 2006; Tattara et al., 2006; De Propris et al., 2008).

In addition to the decreasing numbers of ID firms, a second threat to the traditional district model is the heightened significance of larger firms in IDs (Rabellotti, 2009). Relatively large enterprises emerged in a number of IDs, both as end-product firms or specialized suppliers (Chiarvesio et al., 2010; Camuffo and Grandinetti, 2011), and occasionally attained global leadership status in their industry. In other cases, large foreign firms entered many IDs from the outside and played a major role in their development (Belussi, 2003). These include the global buyers, brands or producers described by the GVC literature as the key lead firms shaping how, where, when and by whom value is added within global industries (Gereffi, 1999; Bair and Gereffi, 2001; Cattaneo et al., 2010).

The impact of such transformations has been exacerbated by a deep change in the social structure of local entrepreneurship. Local entrepreneurs have become a scarce element because of cultural changes: fewer new companies are founded (high birth rates were a common feature of traditional IDs) and many existing enterprises are facing succession problems (De Marchi and Grandinetti, 2014b). The strong influx of immigrant employees and entrepreneurs further weakens the "communitarian factor" typical of the traditional ID configuration (Dei Ottati, 2014; Guercini, Chapter 8 in this book).

Identifying ID evolutionary trajectories

Taken together, these changes have modified the core features of the ID model, which was characterized by a large population of interconnected businesses (mainly SMEs) operating in the same industry with different specializations and displaying high competitiveness on foreign markets. First, they have impacted the population of ID firms, determined both by the exit of existing companies, net of the entries by foreign firms, and by a reduction in their birth rate. Second, they affect concentration within IDs, with a few companies becoming considerably larger and more capable on international markets, whereas in the traditional model resources and competencies (often measured in terms of firm size) were distributed among a plurality of interdependent and quite homogeneous firms. Third, they spurred a reduction in the overall ID capacity to generate value and diminished their role in GVCs, in contrast to traditional IDs that were known for employment growth, innovation and extraordinary performance on international markets.

Such changes, however, have not affected all IDs in the same way. Three distinct trajectories appear within the traditional configuration of Italian IDs: decline, hierarchization and resiliency (De Marchi and Grandinetti, 2014a). As summarized in Table 3.1, we suggest that such evolutionary trajectories are related to the intensity of change along the three dimensions identified above. We describe each trajectory below according to this model.

Decline identifies districts characterized by a strong reduction in the number of firms able to face global competition and in the overall ability of the ID to produce value, which is not associated with the emergence of few large players. Scholarly contributions support the emergence of this trajectory for the textile ID of Como (Alberti, 2006), the Vibrata-Tordino-Vomano clothing ID (Sammarra and Belussi, 2006), the Maniago cutlery ID (Corò and Grandinetti, 2001), and the Barletta footwear ID (Amighini and Rabellotti, 2006), among others.

Hierarchization involves a marked depletion of the population of district enterprises, to the advantage of a few large corporations that might (at least partially) compensate for employment losses and that generate and capture the largest part of the value produced in IDs. Districts along this trajectory have a concentration of employment and revenues in a few big corporations, which are not necessarily connected with the local context. The scholarly description of the Castel Goffredo hosiery and Santa Croce sull'Arno leather IDs (Carminucci and Casucci, 1997), and the Sassuolo ceramic tile (Bursi and Nardin, 2008) and Belluno eyewear (Camuffo, 2003) clusters resemble this trajectory.

The *resilience* trajectory characterizes IDs that have experienced a moderate contraction in their population of firms and employment, and a good capacity to generate value. While concentration does not increase strongly, a number of dynamic firms are emerging. The literature suggests that such a trajectory may describe the mechanics ID of Pordenone (Bortoluzzi et al., 2006; Furlan et al., 2009), the Arzignano leather district ID (Belussi and Sedita, 2008), and the Montebelluna sportsystem ID (Sammarra and Belussi, 2006; Gottardi and Scarso, 2009). While decline and hierarchization have fairly clear-cut boundaries, the

Table 3.1 Trajectories of ID evolution in GVCs

	Decline	*Hierarchization*	*Resilience*
Reduction of ID firm population	High	High	Moderate
Increase of resource concentration	Moderate	High	Moderate
Reduction of ID value production	High	Negligible	Negligible

Source: Authors.

trajectory describing the districts with a resilient capability is more heterogeneous, but these IDs manifest the capability to adapt to relevant changes and to compete in global markets.

Trajectories of IDs in GVCs: learning from the Veneto case

The methodology adopted

The identification of the decline, hierarchization and resilience trajectories allows us to recognize the variety of Italian traditional IDs that was spurred by drivers external and internal to the clusters. The question remains open, however, about what features allowed one trajectory or the other to emerge. Why have some districts gone into decline, while others have been resilient in global markets? Which characteristics, internal to the district and inherent to the GVC, have supported such diversified outcomes?

We have explored these questions via a case-study approach, using the district as the object of the analysis. Such a methodology is appropriate considering the guidelines by Yin (2003), due to the "why?" nature of the research questions under scrutiny. Our objective is to generate new hypotheses and expand our existing knowledge, since the case-study literature is still relatively limited. We decided to focus on districts based in the Veneto region, located in the Northeast of Italy, which is the second most active region in Italy for IDs according to the ISTAT 2001 and 2011 census, with a high prevalence of traditional IDs. The focus on a single region allows us to control for the potential impact of contextual factors not related specifically to the IDs or GVCs being analysed (e.g. infrastructure quality, policy and regulation, workforce development, institutions, cultural factors). Adopting a theoretical sampling strategy (Eisenhardt and Graebner, 2007), we selected four districts within this region: one each representative of the decline and the hierarchization trajectories (the Vicenza gold jewellery and Belluno eyewear districts, respectively); and two representative of the resilience trajectory (Riviera del Brenta footwear and Montebelluna sportsystems), given the greater heterogeneity characterizing this trajectory and our interest in learning more about the most "successful" cases.

Starting from the list (and definitions) of IDs acknowledged by the latest Regional Law on industrial districts (L.R. 13/2014),[2] we identified districts based on a preliminary review of the existing literature and on the actual values of the three key dimensions identified in Table 3.1.[3] We operationalized them as follows:

- Reduction of the population of ID firms has been calculated as the variation of active firms between 2004 and 2014, using Movimprese data.[4]
- Increase in the resource concentration has been calculated employing the Herfindal-Hirshman (HH) concentration index on turnover, measured as the sum of the squared turnover of each firm on the total turnover of the districts.[5] Data have been extracted by the AIDA Bureau Van Dijk dataset[6] – including balance sheet data on limited liability companies only, the subgroup of companies responsible for the largest share of the overall turnover. Instead of evaluating the variation of the index, which should be calculated on a longer time span than the one allowed by the data at hand, we use a static measure (2014 data) to examine the outcome of concentration over the years.
- The reduction of ID value production, consistent with the previous measures, has been calculated in terms of variation of turnover by ID firms, based on AIDA data during the period 2008–14.[7]

Table 3.2 Identifying the IDs analysed

	Vicenza Jewellery	Belluno Eyewear	Montebelluna Sport System	Riviera del Brenta Footwear
Reduction of ID firm population				
Active firms var. (2004–14) (*)	−41.2%	−49.8%	−12.6%	−2.4%
Number of active firms (2014) (*)	623	313	525	548
Increase of resource concentration				
HH index (2014) (§)	4.7	63.7	14.3	6.4
Turnover by top firm (2014) (§)	12.2%	78.7%	33.4%	21.2%
Reduction of ID value production				
ID Turnover var. (2008–14) (§)	−4.5%	39.3%	7.7%	17.6%

Source: Authors, based on Movimprese (*) and AIDA Bureau Van Dijk (§) data.

Note: Definition of size classes: small (less than 50 employees); medium (between 50 and 250 employees); and large (more than 250 employees).

Focused interviews are the most relevant qualitative data source for our analysis. Since our study deals with a complex system, we have interviewed several of its elements, including both ID institutions and firms representative of the universe of ID firms. Information collected has been triangulated with evidence emerging from documentary information (academic contributions, industry reports and newspaper articles). Table 3.2 reports for each ID the values of the three dimensions as we have operationalized them.

The Vicenza gold jewellery district

Jewellery production in the Vicenza province has a long tradition but boomed in the 1960s thanks to mechanization, which supported the development of a relatively large average firm size. Having the US mass market as the major destination, exports from the district grew fast, especially through the selling of machinery-produced affordable jewels (e.g. chains), even though artisan-like, higher-value-added firms were also present (De Marchi et al., 2014; Gaggio, 2007). During the 1980s and up to the early 2000s, the ID reached its peak in terms of exports and output, and a number of companies invested heavily in mechanization. Other companies gave up local manufacturing activities to import and sell jewellery produced in the Far East. Until this period, the majority of firms were small ODMs, specialized mostly in design and manufacturing activities. All the products were easily sold to foreign wholesalers and exporters, mostly through the local Vicenza fair. Additionally, there were specialized suppliers (chain producers being the strongest) and a few OBMs.

In the 2000s, the district experienced a severe crisis; the number of active firms dropped by 41.2% between 2004 and 2014; during 2008–14 turnover fell by 4.5%, despite the increasing price of gold and silver, making up a large part of the final value of the products. The crisis was driven by strong foreign competition in Vicenza's major export markets (mainly Thailand, Turkey and, to a lesser extent, China), and also by changes in global demand and the consolidation of the retail system, especially in the United States (De Marchi et al., 2014). Companies specialized in lower quality products, and those with no local manufacturing capabilities quickly exited the market with small ODMs suffering the most. Before the mid-2000s, several district firms responded by delocalizing production or importing components, and/or reducing the amount of gold employed or substituting it with the cheaper silver, but these strategies did not prove to be effective.

Starting in 2008–09, as the recession crisis magnified the effect of the earlier "globalization" crisis (see De Marchi et al., 2014), a diverse set of upgrading strategies were implemented by resilient and successful local companies. All entailed substantial quality improvement, moving from the mass market, where foreign competition was stiffer to higher value niche markets. Some firms invested in product and process upgrading for smaller batch sizes or higher quality products, in some case making the jewellery more affordable thanks to process upgrading (e.g. Facco), as well as jewellery in higher quality niches (e.g. F.lli Bovo). Functional upgrading took place as well: larger companies (specialized suppliers like Better Silver and Chrysos, or OBMs like F.lli Bovo) invested in branding (creating new brands or improving existing ones), and in marketing and distribution (selling directly to selected jewellery chains rather than wholesalers, and providing them with additional services, like Fope or Facco).[8]

Very few firms (mostly larger and more consolidated ones) are working for global brands (either jewellery brands, such as Tiffany and Swarovski, or non-jewellery brands like Bottega Veneta), which is viewed as an additional and minor business. No local firms have been acquired by global companies either. Up to now, the largest companies are gold or silver chain producers (such as Vieri, Asolo Gold, Filk and Better Silver), which often are vertically integrated to support efficiency. A handful of medium-sized OBMs that have solid reputations abroad in medium-high quality jewellery are present as well (e.g. Marco Bicego, Cielo Venezia, Roberto Coin, Chimento, Lorenzo Muraro). However, they do not seem to drive local development[9] and in some cases have been experiencing serious financial problems in recent years. Additionally, many companies are still working as ODMs, despite the market power of global buyers with which they interact. The two sets of firms suffering the most have been medium-sized companies with their own brand or design capabilities but with no strong marketing and distribution capabilities, and non-specialized small sub-suppliers serving local companies.

Overall, relationships within the Vicenza jewellery district have been weakening. A few larger companies are still competitive but no one is emerging as a key player, and they have little connection to local producers. Thus, they are not working to upgrade their suppliers; indeed, many of the most successful companies are vertically integrated. Data on turnover concentration support this view: the top company makes up 12.2% of overall sales (see Table 3.2). Despite the strong reduction in final-product firms, the district is still perceived to be an important knowledge repository.[10] The presence of numerous competitors, customers and suppliers (especially in supporting industries such as machinery and chemistry) is a key spur and a resource to develop innovative solutions and improve product and process quality for the most dynamic firms of the industry, which are located both within and outside the ID. Several district institutions are present and active in the ID (including the local Vicenza trade show, plus an institution representing the larger/most structured companies and one pooling SMEs mostly from Vicenza but also from other Italian gold jewellery IDs), but they do not seem to play as critical a role as they did in the past.[11]

The Belluno eyewear district

Eyewear production in Belluno started in the mid-19th century thanks to the presence of skilled and low-cost manpower and the abundance of energy, but developed in a district form in the 1970s and 1980s, when many spin-offs were founded that specialized in eyewear production. Local output and the district's leadership in foreign markets boomed in the 1990s, as branded sunglasses were introduced thanks to agreements with global-brand firms such as Armani, Bulgari, Yves Saint Laurent and Versace. Beginning in the mid-1990s, the number of local firms fell dramatically, whereas employment kept increasing, with capacity suppliers suffering the most. Recent data support this view: between 2004 and 2014, active firms dropped by 49.8% (see Table 3.2), but employment increased by 28% (ANFAO data).

In the same period, local concentration grew within the district, which became evident during the 2000s. In the early 1980s, large firms represented 17.6% of local employment (Bramanti and Gambarotto, 2008); in 2014, the largest company alone was responsible for 78.7% of ID turnover (see Table 3.2). Whereas in the 1980s and 1990s production was ensured by the coordination of numerous capacity and specialized suppliers located in the ID, the largest companies became vertically integrated and developed as leaders in international markets thanks to the opening of new factories abroad (mostly in China) and the development of an international network of suppliers to lower production costs and support innovation (Camuffo, 2003; Nassimbeni, 2003).

The unquestioned leading enterprise is Luxottica, a company born and nurtured in the district that became the eyewear industry's global leader with net sales of more than €8.8 billion in 2015 and roughly 79,000 employees. The business runs a fully integrated production cycle with six manufacturing plants in Italy,[12] three in China, and others in Brazil, India and the United States. In early 2017, it completed its vertical integration strategy by merging with the French multinational Essilor, specialized in the complementary specialization of the production of ophthalmic lenses and optical equipment. Luxottica's brand portfolio is very broad, including house brands like Ray-Ban, and licensed brands like Giorgio Armani, Versace and Prada. The firm's vertical integration policy also extends to distribution, with a growing level of direct control over the wholesale and retail stages, in part as a result of international acquisitions. Today, nearly three-quarters of the group's employees work in its wholesale or retail operations.

Safilo, the second largest enterprise in the district, has adopted the Luxottica model, albeit with lower levels of upstream and downstream vertical integration. Thus, the two firms show different GVC configurations. Safilo's downstream integration stops at the wholesale stage, while its production is concentrated in five plants owned by the group, one of which is within the district and two are abroad (in Slovenia and China). Unlike Luxottica, however, Safilo uses a global supplier network based on capacity subcontractors to cope with peaks in demand for products that are not part of the luxury segment (Bramanti and Gambarotto, 2008). In the most recent years (2014 on), re-shoring of the higher-end products of large firms is taking place (ANFAO, 2015). Both companies are opening new plants in the ID (2016 data).

Other than a handful of lead firms (including De Rigo, Marcolin, Marchon and Fedon, the last being a case producer), the firms surviving in the district are very small; in 2014, 85.9% of the firms had less than 50 employees (Table 3.2, see also Bettiol et al., Chapter 9 in this book). While capacity suppliers of local companies and firms in the low-end of the market were most affected by the crisis, there is a small group of dynamic firms: OBMs serving specific niches, especially abroad and in the luxury segment (e.g. Dolpi, producing wooden eyewear), or specialized component suppliers, engineering service providers, technology specialists and case producers (e.g. Visottica-Comotec) (Campagnolo and Camuffo, 2011).

The Montebelluna sportsystem district

As reported in Codara and Morato (2002), production of leather mountain boots in the Montebelluna area dates back to the early 19th century, a competence that during the following decades was adapted to make ski boots. Production boomed as plastic ski boots were introduced in the mid-1960s (a break-through innovation developed by a local company), thanks to spin-off processes that started to take shape in the ID with the development of sub-suppliers and supporting industries. The Montebelluna district enjoyed a world leadership in these products due to the innovation and flexibility enabled by the traditional ID configuration.

Since the 1970s, ID production became increasingly diversified as other mountain-related products were introduced (e.g. après-ski boots). In the 1980s, following a strong demand crisis and increasing foreign competition, trekking, soccer, motorcycle, bicycle and tennis shoes were all developed in the ID, and in the 1990s, skates production and sport-related performance outerwear grew in prominence. The 2000s was marked by the growth of everyday/casual shoes, driven by the success of Geox, now by far the largest company in the ID.

In sum, there was a concentric pattern of diversification driven by product diversity (e.g. ski and clothing for motorcycles), user diversity (athletes of racing, climbing, trekking and skiing) and technological diversity (e.g. the use of plastic for the production of ski boots vs. high-performance textiles to produce apparel for motorcycles). The process originated with lead users (e.g. Calzaturificio SCARPA to develop the new climbing line), which drove important and successful innovation in those markets (Ciappei and Simoni, 2005).

In addition to diversification, other factors, such as the delocalization of manufacturing activities and the increasing role of GLFs (home-grown and foreign), began to shape the district. Companies specialized in component manufacturing (especially producers of uppers) were most seriously affected in the 1990s, as local OBMs, especially the largest firms, developed global supply chains. Components production was increasingly moved offshore, either via foreign direct investment or, more often, via outsourcing to foreign suppliers, especially in East European countries (mostly Romania, in the Timisoara region), a strategy that became mainstream in the 2000s (see also Belussi and Asheim, 2010). Suppliers of specialized services (such as prototyping and new materials development) are still a dynamic component of the ID (e.g. Novation Tech, Claudio Franco Design&Develop), but they employ the knowledge developed in the district to serve international clients/firms specialized in different industries.

Today, most of the local companies are brand manufacturers, designing and branding the final products but having delocalized production. While some of these OBMs face shrinking sales (even large ones as in the case of Tecnica), a number of local OBMs grew and have garnered global recognition. These include very large companies working in mass markets (such as Diadora), or medium-sized companies that became leaders of specific sport niches because of their innovation and quality capabilities (e.g. Alpinestar for motorcycle boots and clothing; Aku and Asolo for performance trekking shoes) (Chapter 9).

Starting in the 1990s, GLFs began to play a key role in the Montebelluna district. The high manufacturing and innovation capabilities present in the area attracted global companies that acquired existing medium/large OBMs (see Belussi et al., Chapter 5 in this book) and worked with local ODMs (as in the case of Grisport for Decathlon). Interestingly they also opened R&D labs and some production facilities within the ID in order to learn specific manufacturing capabilities (e.g. regarding soccer shoe production), as in the cases of Nike and Adidas. Although they all left by the mid-2000s after they acquired the key competences they sought when entering the ID, these companies are still drawing on Montebelluna's knowledge base by acquiring high-skilled personnel, which are employed in the US R&D offices. This can be interpreted as evidence that relevant knowledge is still "sticky" in manufacturing locales that are attractive to GLFs.

As reported in Table 3.2, during 2004–14 the number of firms in the district dropped by 12.6%; since the start of the recession (2008), turnover increased by 7.7%.[13] Concentration in the district is moderate; the largest company, being a homegrown GLF – Geox – makes up 33.4% of the ID overall turnover; medium and large companies make up 84.2% of total employment. Due to the increasing importance of large companies (local and foreign), district institutions, once very effective, are no longer playing a significant role, and the sense of belonging to the district has faded quite substantially due to the extensive diversification.

The Riviera del Brenta footwear district

The district developed at the beginning of the 20th century after the first company was set up by an entrepreneur that merged technical and commercial knowledge acquired during his stay in the United States with craftsmanship skills available in the area (Fontana et al., 1998). During the 1950s and 1960s, the number of firms and production boomed, thanks to the growth in export markets. In the mid-1970s, Riviera del Brenta firms gradually improved the quality of their product; luxury shoes for women became the main product offered, while production was carried out by independent SMEs rather than centralized within companies. The major clients were Italian and increasingly German retailers.

From the mid-1990s, the district entered into a deep transformation in terms of the role of its final product companies. On the one hand, lower value-added activities were increasingly outsourced to Eastern Europe (see also Amighini and Rabellotti, 2006) or carried out by immigrant entrepreneurs, especially the most labour-intensive activities related to the manufacturing of components (e.g. upper shoes). In the 2000s, production of lower-end products (such as everyday shoes) moved to the same locations or closed (e.g. Donna Carolina, Calzaturificio Ca' D'Oro). Some district entrepreneurs subsequently moved to Romania, Serbia and China to teach shoe-making to local companies.

On the other hand, local companies that specialized in the production of high-end shoes gradually gave up their own brands to produce for global brands such as Kering Group, LVMH, Prada and Armani. While these GVC leaders are responsible for the design, marketing and distribution of the final products, local firms cooperate on the development of the products and are responsible for prototyping and carrying out the final steps required for manufacturing luxury footwear. Thus, they could be defined as OEM suppliers, who can also perform activities similar to ODMs. In order to accommodate these global brands, the local firms heavily invested in upgrading their processes in order to ensure they could produce at the requisite scale or to deal with certifications required by the brands. Although the largest and most successful OEMs tended to be vertically integrated, other district OEMs worked with a limited number of local and, to a lesser extent, foreign suppliers.

According to a survey by Rabellotti (2004), in the mid-2000s half of the firms investigated worked only as OEMs for global brands; recent interviews indicate that 90% of the district's production is now carried out for global brands. In addition to the "simple" OEMs, which often work for several brands at a time, there are other approaches: a few OEMs pursue a "hybrid strategy" with a small fraction of turnover from their own brand (such as Ballin shoes); super-luxury, established OBMs (such as Renè Caovilla); and a growing number of small OBMs specialized in different products (e.g. fashion, high-end sneakers for women, like Philippe Model).

In an initial phase, GLFs entered the district developing long-term relationships with local firms. In the mid-2000s, however, they shifted to broader investment strategies that included vertical integration, whereby they acquired their major local suppliers, as well as greenfield investments, which has been the most popular strategy in recent years (see also Chapter 5 by Belussi et al.).[14] Such global companies are now the largest enterprises in the ID in term of employment and turnover; concentration is modest but increasing.

The number of active firms in Riviera del Brenta has been relatively stable (a mild decline of 2.4% between 2004 and 2014), as lower-end production was gradually abandoned and many companies proved unable to work with GLFs (either because they were too small or not capable of keeping pace with their production requirements). All in all, however, interviews and turnover figures (+17.6% between 2008–14) support the finding that, despite the huge transformation that took place in the ID during the last 20 years, the Riviera de Brenta district is still performing well, and its integration with global brands, while challenging, is perceived more as a strong asset than a threat. Concentration remains quite limited (Table 3.2).

The local industry association (ACRIB, developed in the 1960s) is still playing an active role within the ID, both providing technical knowledge (via the "politecnico calzaturiero" school), supporting the internationalization of SMEs (via the "Consorzio Maestri Calzaturieri"), and ensuring that the high-value-added competences of the ID are maintained and preserved.[15] The role of local unions has proved to be supportive as well (see also Azzariti and Candoni, 2007; De Stefani, 2012).

A theory of ID evolution in GVCs

The detailed analyses of the four districts covered in this chapter, summarized in Table 3.3, highlight a major transformation that has taken place in the Veneto's IDs during recent years – a very different landscape from that described in the traditional Marshallian ID model (Becattini (1990). Our narratives of the four districts, which 20 years ago had very similar industrial structures, showcase their great heterogeneity today and their ability to respond to both internal and external challenges.

The decline, hierarchization, and resilience trajectories – as corroborated by the Vicenza, Belluno, Montebelluna and Riviera del Brenta cases – typify three distinct pathways from the traditional ID model, implying diverse journeys within GVCs. While the decline trajectory points to the inability of these IDs to reproduce the basis of their success in the changed global scenario – even if there is a number of successful firms locally, they do not appear to boost other local companies to develop in GVCs – both the hierarchization and the resilience trajectories represent two positive responses to globalization, denoting a capability to adapt to global challenges. However, they entail a different distribution of the value created and a distinct industrial organization model too, with non-trivial differences in terms of policy implications. Indeed, both have retained a large portion of value-added in the ID (being driven rather by pre- and post-production activities in Belluno and Montebelluna, and by production activities in Riviera del Brenta). In the hierarchization trajectory, however, such a capacity is concentrated in only a few companies, which might be disconnected from the rest of the ID, whereas in the resilience trajectory, growth is driven and value is spread among a larger amount of actors, which allows these IDs to better support the development and upgrading of SMEs.

The strategies that local firms put in place in response to recent global challenges to engage in GVCs have been quite diverse, representing different sets of capabilities. In some cases, local producers have integrated with GLFs by focusing only on the manufacturing activities (from OBM to OEM), which is by far the most common strategy in Riviera del Brenta. However, it also occurred in some of the largest companies within the Vicenza and Montebelluna districts, where it has mostly taken the form of a "hybrid" strategy (OEM *and* OBM). In other cases, local producers have tried to change their role in the GVC by performing more value-added activities (e.g. in Vicenza, specialized suppliers getting OBM, or OBM focusing just on branding activities). Finally, the growth of home-grown GLFs, which are focusing on pre- and post-production activities, has been observed in Belluno and Montebelluna (where the greater degree of diversification supported a lower level of concentration).

Table 3.3 Overview of the Vicenza, Belluno, Montebelluna and Riviera del Brenta clusters and their position in the GVC

	Vicenza Jewellery	Belluno Eyewear	Montebelluna SportSystem	Riviera del Brenta Footwear
Share of companies by size classes (2014) §				
Large	0.0%	5.1%	4.3%	0.7%
Medium	5.7%	9.1%	10.1%	12.3%
Small	94.3%	85.9%	85.5%	87.0%
Share of employment by size classes (2014) §				
Large	0.0%	97.9%	70.5%	9.6%
Medium	35.2%	0.9%	13.7%	40.8%
Small	64.8%	1.2%	15.8%	49.7%
Activities mostly performed locally	Pre-production, production, (some post-production)	Pre-production, production and post-production	Pre-production (some post-production)	Production
Upgrading trajectories	Process upgrading, branding and distribution	Vertical Integration, control of retailing activities	Product diversification, internationalization of sourcing, branding (OBM)	From OBM to OEM (producing for global brands)
Global lead firms (GLF)	None	Home-grown	Home-grown and foreign	Foreign
Key local companies	Specialized suppliers	Global leaders (Luxottica, Safilo)	Internationally recognized OBMs; global leaders (Geox); KIBS	Capable OEMs
Support by local institutions	Internationalization	Training, internationalization, product certifications	No support activity recently	Training, internationalization

Source: Authors, based on AIDA Bureau Van Dijk (§) data and interviews.

Table 3.4 Key local/global determinants of ID trajectories in GVCs

		Decline	Hierarchization	Resilience
Global lead firms (GLFs)	Home-grown (*inside-out*) Foreign (*outside-in*)	Absent	Present	Present
Local dynamic actors (LDAs)	OEMs or ODMs with advanced *production capabilities*	Absent	Absent	Present (variety)
	OBMs with advanced post-production capabilities			
	Highly specialized suppliers with distinct *manuf./service capabilities*			
	Capable local institutions			

Source: Authors.

What are the key factors explaining the ability of IDs to effectively compete in GVCs? In order to create a theory that is useful to policy-makers who wish to support local development, we simplify and abstract from the rich and heterogeneous evidence collected and identify the main factors that determine the different trajectories. While acknowledging the role that ID history, industry specificities, institutions, and the local social context might play in the evolution of the ID, we believe that the major factors characterizing the trajectories (see Table 3.4) are:

1) the presence of global lead firms (GLFs) – well described in the GVC literature; and
2) the presence of a variety of local dynamic actors (LDAs) – emerging in many recent scholarly contributions on IDs.

All the IDs that proved to be successful in GVCs are characterized by the presence of GLFs, which might have grown within the ID itself until becoming a global leader (home-grown GLF) or it might be an MNE that decided to directly invest in the ID (through acquisition, greenfield investments or orchestrating sourcing locally) (foreign GLF). Whatever the case, such a GLF represents a channel for the ID to participate in GVCs, especially to the extent it is actively engaging with a network of local ID firms.

What distinguishes the hierarchization and the resilience trajectories is the presence of a large base of local dynamic actors (LDAs), entailing peculiar and hard-to-replicate value-adding capabilities, and maintaining, albeit selectively, relationships with other ID firms. Such firms work as knowledge integrators or gatekeepers (Camuffo and Grandinetti, 2011) between the knowledge (mostly related to the market) embedded in GVCs and the knowledge embedded in the local context (mostly related to the technology). This is diffused via local relationships, similarly to what has been described earlier with GVC lead firms.

Different types of LDAs might be envisioned, depending on the specificity of the industry/ID:

• OEMs or ODMs with advanced production capabilities;
• OBMs with advanced post-production capabilities;
• Highly specialized suppliers with distinct manufacturing or service capabilities; and
• Capable local institutions.

The first category refers to *OEMs or ODMs* able to respond to the requests by global brands, with production capabilities that can combine the high manufacturing quality of artisanal production with the structured organization needed to meet GLF standards. This is particularly relevant where manufacturing represents a high value-adding activity (as in the case of luxury products). Relevant international relationships for such firms are *downstream* with the GLFs.

OBMs with advanced post-production capabilities are able to preside over their own final markets (e.g. having developed their own distributions channels, such as shops, franchising or shop-in-shop) and/or having developed a leadership in a market niche (see also Corò and Grandinetti, 1999; Guercini, 2004; Capasso et al., 2013). Relevant international relationships for such firms are both *downstream*, in terms of presence in international markets, and *upstream*, in terms of managing global supply networks.

The third category includes *highly specialized suppliers* with distinct manufacturing capabilities, providers of knowledge-intensive business services (e.g. design, prototyping, development of new materials, quality tests, customized software, marketing services, advanced logistics), or manufacturers of machine tools and other high-value components (see also Camuffo and Grandinetti, 2011; Di Maria et al., 2012; Tunisini and Bocconcelli, 2009). Relevant international relationships for such firms are mostly *downstream*, since they serve customers outside of the ID (and of the country); in some cases, they also are specialized in different industries.[16]

Finally, a fourth LDA is represented by *local institutions* that support the reproduction of the local knowledge and capabilities base (e.g. by providing training on high-value activities, implementing collective marketing to create and communicate the intangible value of the ID, or provide certifications and R&D activities) (see also Grandinetti, 2011; De Michele, 2015). Based on the narrative in the previous paragraphs, Table 3.5 provides some examples of the four types of LDAs and the two GLFs for each ID analysed.

Table 3.5 Key local/global determinants of ID trajectories in GVCs in the cases analysed

	Decline	Hierarchization	Resilience	
	Vicenza Jewellery	*Belluno eyewear*	*Montebelluna sportsystem*	*Riviera del Brenta footwear*
Global lead firms (GLFs)				
Home-grown	–	(Luxottica, Safilo)	(Geox)	–
Foreign	–	–	–	(LVMH, Kering Group, Prada, . . .)
Variety of local dynamic actors (LDAs)				
OEMs/ODMs w. advanced production capabilities	–	–	–	(Nillab, Rossimoda, . . .)
OBMs w. advanced post-production capabilities	–	–	(AKU, Asolo, Alpinestar, . . .)	(Renè Caovilla)
Highly specialized suppliers w. distinct manuf./ service capabilities	(Better Silver, . . .)	–	(Novation tech, Claudio Franco Design&Develop, . . .)	–
Capable local institutions	(Gold&Silver Italian group)	–	–	(ACRIB)

Source: Authors.

The larger the set of LDAs located in a district – either several companies of the same category or a mix of the possible categories listed – the greater the likelihood that it will hold a competitive position in GVCs, if a GLF is embedded in the ID. This variety is what makes the framework different from the role of the "local lead firms" identified in earlier studies on IDs (Lazerson and Lorenzoni, 1999), which are "solo" actors in the ID. An additional difference is that LDAs also involve relationships external to the ID (e.g. OEMs interacting with GLFs; OBMs having direct contact with the final markets and/or relying on international suppliers; and specialized suppliers working for global customers). Such a distributed knowledge interface can support the reproduction of the ID competence base and its adaptation to global needs. Finally, size is a third distinguishing element of LDAs, since managing international relationships, achieving the standards required by GLFs, and leadership in niche markets based on innovation or branding capabilities all require investments and resources. Small firm size is usually an impediment to this role. This characterization is corroborated by data in Table 3.3, reporting that resilient IDs contain a higher proportion of medium and large companies.

Conclusion

Italian IDs no longer fit the traditional model that characterized them up until 20–30 years ago. At least three evolutionary trajectories can be found in the literature: decline, hierarchization and resiliency. In this chapter, we addressed the challenge of identifying the key determinants of the different trajectories utilizing the GVC framework. First, via a critical review of the existing literature, we operationalized the main changes taking place in Italian IDs with respect to the traditional ID model in three variables: 1) the reduction in the population of firms; 2) the concentration of resources within few firms; and 3) the reduction in value addition within the IDs. Such variables are subsequently used to identify empirically the three trajectories of ID transformation defined by the literature.

Second, based on the detailed histories of change in the Vicenza gold jewellery ID (exemplifying the decline trajectory), the Belluno eyewear ID (the hierarchization trajectory), and the Montebelluna sportsystem and the Riviera del Brenta footwear IDs (resilience trajectories), we suggested that the direct engagement of Global Lead Firms (GLFs) and the presence of Local Dynamic Actors (i.e. OEMs/ODMs with advanced production capabilities, OBMs with advanced post-production capabilities, highly specialized suppliers, and/or capable local institutions) are the main determinants that shape which trajectory occurs. In particular, the presence of GLFs is a necessary condition for hierarchization and resilience to take place, enabling the IDs to effectively participate in GVCs; the presence of a large set of LDAs facilitates the resilience trajectory – acting as knowledge integrators between local and global knowledge flows, they support a diffused capability to retain value locally.

During the "golden age" of IDs, the focus was on IDs as a system. We suggest that two additional levels of analysis are needed to track resiliency: the GVC level and the local-firm level. A key implication of our analysis is that it is no longer possible to understand the evolution of IDs without including the GVCs in which they are embedded. GVC tools are fundamental to understand the role that local companies play in their industries, with an emphasis on the activities they are performing (pre-production, production, post-production) and the ability to create and capture local value-added (via the capabilities embedded in their OEM, ODM and OBM roles). Similarly, the interplay of GLFs and LDAs is of utmost importance for determining the future of IDs. To keep pace with global challenges, the activities performed and relationships implemented within IDs have evolved in significant ways. For example, "downgrading" design and branding functions to participate in GVCs led by GLFs may allow capable OEMs and ODMs to gain competitiveness in high-value market niches. An increase in size has been a prerequisite and a consequence for such diversified strategies, supporting the importance of medium-sized and relatively large firms for the resilience of local clusters.

In this chapter, we adopted a parsimonious approach to theory building that highlighted salient differences across clusters that are most relevant to our research focus. Indeed, this analysis is neither a recipe for future development nor a comprehensive schema of all the specificities that may support the evolution of IDs. Rather, trajectories are intended to serve as useful scenarios for the interpretation of a complex reality, offering potential insights for policy-makers interested to support the development of IDs through tailored and selective policies (rather than a one-size-fits-all approach). "Entrepreneurial" cluster institutions can play a key role in this respect.

Moreover, the three trajectories are neither prescriptive nor immutable; districts that were in decline might move toward a more resilient configuration, provided that a sufficient number of capable companies link up with GLFs (e.g. Valenza Po jewellery, in De Marchi et al., 2014). IDs in the hierarchization trajectory could decline if the supporting GLF presence fades away (e.g. the textile ID headed by Benetton – see Harrison, 1994). Similarly, while some trends might be clear cut in an ID (like the move from OBM to OEM in Riviera del Brenta), firms implementing different strategies could flourish in the same ID as well (e.g. firms developing their own brands via collaboration with foreign designers). This underlines the need to continuously assess the presence and nature of LDAs in the context of the broader GVC system.

Notes

1 We do not intend to study the entire evolutionary experience of clusters or IDs, but rather the analysis of recent trajectories (the last 15–20 years, when globalization has hit the hardest) for those IDs that: 1) had a traditional, Marshallian, configuration; 2) are specialized in a traditional, manufacturing industry; and 3) are participating in GVCs.

2 See: http://bur.regione.veneto.it/BurvServices/pubblica/DettaglioLegge.aspx?id=275529

3 We have not considered the mechanical IDs (Treviso Inox Valley, Vicenza mechanics, Padova refrigeration) and the Polesine fishing and Valdobbiadene prosecco IDs because of peculiarities of these industries with respect to the traditional Marshallian IDs. Veneto IDs have been identified based on the municipalities and the ATECO (Classificazione ATtività ECOnomiche or Statistical Classification of Economic Activities in Italy) industry code indicated by the regional law. We have included additional municipalities if they were reported in the existing literature and, in 2014, there were firms with a turnover higher than 2.5 million euros or employing more than 50 people (based on AIDA data), or if there were more than 10 active firms in the municipality (based on Movimprese data). In some cases, we have included additional industry codes if this was consistent with the existing literature or to support consistencies in the correspondence between ATECO 2002 codes (used for the years 2004–08) and ATECO 2007 codes (used from 2009 on). Industry codes and city considered are available upon request.

4 We do not consider the possibility of an increase in the ID population as the empirical evidence today indicates a reduction of companies across all industries in developed countries such as Italy.

5 Because we aim at comparing IDs specialized in different industries and because of data availability, we measured concentration and value production in terms of turnover. Future research, however, should think of this choice in a critical way, considering case by case, if other measures such as employees, value-added, or export levels might be better. A similar reflection is relevant to the time period analysed. We focused on transformations from 2004 on, this year being a tipping point for globalization dynamics (see De Marchi et al., 2014), but each industry might be characterized by different turning points.

6 Data for 2008 are calculated summing turnover by all firms present in that year, irrespective if they were present in 2014 as well; the opposite for 2014. Consolidated balance sheets have been considered when available (*Luxottica, Safilo, Marcolin, Fedon* for the Belluno eyewear ID; *Geox,*

Tecnica, Grisport, Calzaturificio SCARPA, Lotto sport, Bonis, Stonefly for the Montebelluna Sportsystem).

7 Unfortunately, it was not possible to use data on earlier years due to data constraints. Even though the phenomena may have a longer time span, we assume the results for the later years (starting with the recession) to be coherent and therefore indicative.

8 There were also cases of 'functional downgrading': OBMs/ODMs giving up their manufacturing capabilities; pooling production by small ODMs to increase market power; and selling products to the wholesalers and foreign importers.

9 Often they are vertically integrated, which tends to diminish local linkages.

10 This may reflect the fact that Vicenza is home to a variety of IDs in diverse industries, including textiles and apparel, handicrafts, furniture, and engineering/computer components.

11 This is true especially for the trade show, whose centrality as a 'distribution channel' faded away due to changes in the global retailing systems.

12 The most important factory is located within the district, together with the group's head office.

13 This figure would be much higher if we excluded from the analysis the largest company in the ID specializing in winter sport equipment, which has been in trouble for several years. The performance of medium-sized companies is particularly positive (see De Marchi and Grandinetti, 2016).

14 For instance, LVHM and YSL opened new large factories in 2016.

15 They have been fighting the recent increase of companies led by immigrants, mostly Chinese, which established in the district and specialized in low-value-added steps of the value chain, exploiting a competitive advantage based on illegal practices and the violation of social standards.

16 Claudio Franco Design&Develop is a case in point; it is an agency offering design services, engineering, product steering and prototyping. It began as a knowledge-intensive supplier for ID companies, and from the recession crisis of 2009, it started to serve more and more external clients (it exports 80% of its services). It is specialized in very different sectors, such as eyewear and medical.

References

Alberti, F.G. (2006). The decline of the industrial district of Como: Recession, relocation or reconversion. *Entrepreneurship & Regional Development*, 18(6): 473–501.

Amighini, A., and Rabellotti, R. (2006). How do Italian footwear industrial districts face globalization? *European Planning Studies*, 14(4): 485–502.

ANFAO, (2015). Per l'occhialeria italiana un 2015 da ricordare. ANFAO communnications. Available at: www.anfao.it/documents/comunicati/CS_dati_Anfao_MIDO_2016_DEF_1469619598106.pdf

Azzariti, F., and Candoni, I. (2007). Oltre il distretto: Interviste, modelli aziendali e teorie di un fenomeno italiano. Milano: FrancoAngeli.

Bair, J., and Gereffi, G. (2001). Local clusters in global chains: The causes and consequences of export dynamism in Torreon's blue jeans industry. *World Development*, 29(11): 1885–1903.

Becattini, G. (1990). The Marshallian industrial district as a socioeconomic notion. In F. Pyke, G. Becattini and W. Sengerberger (eds.), *Industrial Districts and Inter-firm Cooperation in Italy*. Geneva: International Institute of Labour Studies, pp. 37–51.

Belso-Martinez, J. (2008). Differences in survival strategies among footwear industrial districts: The role of international outsourcing. *European Planning Studies*, 16(9): 1229–1248.

Belussi, F. (2003). 11. The changing governance of IDs: The entry of multinationals in local nets. In B.T. Asheim and Å. Mariussen (eds.), Innovations, Regions and Projects: Studies in New Forms of Knowledge Governance. Stockholm: Nordregio, pp. 317–346.

Belussi, F., and Asheim, B. (2010). Industrial districts and globalisation: Learning and innovation in local and global production systems. In F. Belussi and A. Sammarra (eds.), *Business Networks in Clusters and Industrial Districts: The Governance of the Global Value Chain*. New York: Routledge, pp. 136–145.

Belussi, F., and Sedita, S.R. (2008). L'evoluzione del modello distrettuale: La 'delocalizzazione inversa' e il caso del distretto della concia di Arzignano. *Economia e Politica Industriale*, 2(35): 51–72.

Bortoluzzi, G., Furlan, A., and Grandinetti, R. (2006). Il distretto della componentistica e della meccanica in provincia di Pordenone. Relazioni locali e apertura internazionale. Milano: FrancoAngeli.

Bramanti, A., and Gambarotto, F. (eds.). (2008). *Il distretto bellunese dell'occhialeria: Leadership mondiale e fine del distretto?* Milano: Fondazione Fiera Milano.

Bursi, T., and Nardin, G. (eds.). (2008). Il distretto delle piastrelle di ceramica di Sassuolo tra identita` e cambiamento. Milano: Franco Angeli.

Campagnolo, D., and Camuffo, A. (2011). Globalization and low-technology industries: The case of Italian eyewear. In P.L. Robertson and D. Jacobson (eds.), *Knowledge Transfer and Technology Diffusion*. Cheltenham: Edward Elgar, pp. 138–161.

Camuffo, A. (2003). Transforming industrial districts: Large firms and small business networks in the Italian eyewear industry. *Industry and Innovation*, 10(4): 377–401.

Camuffo, A., and Grandinetti, R. (2011). Italian industrial districts as cognitive systems: Are they still reproducible? *Entrepreneurship & Regional Development*, 23(9–10): 815–852.

Capasso, M., Cusmano, L., and Morrison, A. (2013). The determinants of outsourcing and offshoring strategies in industrial districts: Evidence from Italy. *Regional Studies*, 47(4): 465–479.

Carminucci, C., and Casucci, S. (1997). Il ciclo di vita dei distretti industriali: Ipotesi teoriche ed evidenze empiriche. *L'industria*, 18(2): 293–315.

Cattaneo, O., Gereffi, G., and Staritz, C. (eds.). (2010). *Global Value Chains in a Postcrisis World: A Development Perspective*. Washington, DC: World Bank.

Chiarvesio, M., Di Maria, E., and Micelli, S. (2010). Global value chains and open networks: The case of Italian industrial districts. *European Planning Studies*, 18(3): 333–350.

Ciappei, C., and Simoni, C. (2005). Drivers of new product success in the Italian sport shoe cluster of Montebelluna. *Journal of Fashion Marketing and Management: An International Journal*, 9(1): 20–42.

Codara, L., and Morato, E. (2002). Il distretto di Montebelluna tra locale e globale. In G. Provasi (ed.), *Le istituzioni dello sviluppo. I distretti industriali tra storia, sociologia ed economia*. Roma: Donzelli, pp. 99–143.

Corò, G., and Grandinetti, R. (1999). Evolutionary patterns of Italian industrial districts. *Human Systems Management*, 18(2): 117–129.

Corò, G., and Grandinetti, R. (2001). Industrial district responses to the network economy: Vertical integration versus pluralist global exploration. *Human Systems Management*, 20(3): 189–199.

Crestanello, R. (1997). La trasformazione in 10 distretti industriali durante gli anni '80. In R. Varaldo and L. Ferrucci (eds.), *Il distretto industriale tra logiche di impresa e logiche di sistema*. Milano: Franco Angeli, pp. 243–273.

Dei Ottati, G. (2014). A transnational fast fashion industrial district: An analysis of the Chinese businesses in Prato. *Cambridge Journal of Economics*, 38(5): 1247–1274.

De Marchi, V., and Grandinetti, R. (2014a). Industrial districts and the collapse of the Marshallian model: Looking at the Italian experience. *Competition & Change*, 18(1): 70–87.

De Marchi, V., and Grandinetti, R. (2014b). I distretti industriali veneti tra crisi ed evoluzione. In M. Bellandi and A. Caloffi (eds.), *I nuovi distretti industriali: Rapporto di Artimino sullo sviluppo locale 2012–2013*. Bologna: Il Mulino, pp. 141–153.

De Marchi, V., and Grandinetti, R. (2016). Lo sportsystem di Montebelluna: Il distretto dalle sette vite. *Economia e Società Regionale*, 34(1): 142–148.

De Marchi, V., Lee, J., and Gereffi, G. (2014). Globalization, recession and the internationalization of industrial districts: Experiences from the Italian gold jewellery industry. *European Planning Studies*, 22(4): 866–884.

De Michele, C. (2015). Il ruolo delle istituzioni locali nelle realta` distrettuali. In Intesa San Paolo (ed.), *Economia e finanza dei distretti industriali*. Roma: Intesa San Paolo, pp. 117–130.

De Propris, L., Menghinello, S., and Sudgen, R. (2008). The internationalisation of production systems: Embeddedness, openness and governance. *Entrepreneurship & Regional Development*, 20(6): 493–515.

De Stefani, S. (2012). *Skills for Competitiveness: Country Report for Italy, 4*. OECD Local Economic and Employment Development (LEED) Working Papers, OECD Publishing.

Di Maria, E., Bettiol, M., De Marchi, V., and Grandinetti, R. (2012). Developing and managing distant markets: The case of KIBS. *Economia Politica: Journal of Analytical and Institutional Economics*, 29(3): 361–379.

Dunford, M. (2006). Industrial districts, magic circles, and the restructuring of the Italian textile and clothing chain. *Economic Geography*, 82(1): 27–59.

Eisenhardt, K.M., and Graebner, M.E. (2007). Theory building from cases: Opportunities and challenges. *Academy of Management Journal*, 50(1): 25–32.

Fontana, G.L., Franceschetti, G., and Roverato, G. (1998). *100 anni di industria calzaturiera nella Riviera del Brenta*. Fiesso d'Artico: Consorzio Maestri Calzaturieri del Brenta.

Furlan, A., Grandinetti, R., and Camuffo, A. (2009). Business relationship portfolios and subcontractors' capabilities. *Industrial Marketing Management*, 38(8): 937–945.

Gaggio, D. (2007). In Gold We Trust: Social Capital and Economic Change in the Italian Jewellery Towns. Princeton, NJ: Princeton University Press.

Gereffi, G. (1999). International trade and industrial upgrading in the apparel commodity chain. *Journal of International Economics*, 48(1): 37–70.

Gereffi, G. (2014). Global value chains in a post-Washington consensus world. *Review of International Political Economy*, 21(1): 9–37.

Gereffi, G., and Lee, J. (2016). Economic and social upgrading in global value chains and industrial clusters: Why governance matters. *Journal of Business Ethics*, 133: 25–38.

Gottardi, G., and Scarso, E. (2009). Reti internazionali nelle calzature sportive. In G. Gottardi (ed.), *Nuovi modelli di gestione dell'impresa. Governare le reti internazionali di conoscenza*. Roma: Carocci, pp. 200–265.

Grandinetti, R. (2011). Local/global cognitive interfaces within industrial districts: An Italian case study. *The Learning Organization*, 18(4): 301–312.

Grandinetti, R., and De Marchi, V. (2012). Dove stanno andando i distretti industriali? Un tentativo di risposta a partire da un'indagine in Veneto. *Studi Organizzativi*, 14(2): 142–175.

Guercini, S. (2004). International competitive change and strategic behaviour of Italian textile-apparel firms. *Journal of Fashion Marketing and Management*, 8(3): 320–339.

Harrison, B. (1994). The Italian industrial districts and the crisis of the cooperative form: Part I. *European Planning Studies*, 2(1): 3–22.

Lazerson, M.H., and Lorenzoni, G. (1999). The firms that feed industrial districts: A return to the Italian source. *Industrial and Corporate Change*, 8(2): 235–266.

Nassimbeni, G. (2003). Local manufacturing systems and global economy: Are they compatible? The case of the Italian eyewear district. *Journal of Operations Management*, 21(2): 151–171.

Rabellotti, R. (2004). How globalisation affects Italian industrial districts: The case of Brenta. In H. Schmitz (ed.), *Local Enterprises in the Global Economy: Issues of Governance and Upgrading*. Cheltenham: Edward Elgar, pp. 140–173.

Rabellotti, R., Carabelli, A., and Hirsch, G. (2009). Italian industrial districts on the move: Where are they going? *European Planning Studies*, 17(1): 19–41.

Sammarra, A., and Belussi, F. (2006). Evolution and relocation in fashion-led Italian districts: Evidence from two case-studies. *Entrepreneurship and Regional Development*, 18(6): 543–562.

Tattara, G., Corò, G., and Volpe, M. (eds.). (2006). Andarsene per continuare a crescere: La delocalizzazione internazionale come strategia competitiva. Roma: Carocci.

Tunisini, A., and Bocconcelli, R. (2009). Reconfiguring supplier relationships between local and global: History matters. *Industrial Marketing Management*, 38(6): 671–678.

Yin, R.K. (2003). *Case Study Research: Design and Methods*, 3rd ed. Thousand Oaks: Sage Publications.

4 Clusters, industrial districts and the impact of their growing intersection with global value chains

Mario Davide Parrilli and Jiří Blažek

Introduction

Globalization has strongly affected the prospects of local and regional development over the past three decades. Economic development across countries is changing dynamically, thus countries and regions that were at the top of the table 30 years ago have lost their leading role (e.g. Piedmont and Tuscany in Italy, the Midlands in England), whilst others that were lagging behind have made significant steps forward (e.g. metropolitan regions in Poland, Hungary and Czechia in Europe, Malaysia, Thailand, and Colombia overseas). In this piece of research, we take a systematic look at new trends, problems and drivers of the evolution and competitiveness of clusters in globalized markets in general and global value chains (GVCs) in particular. In this way, the prospects of local and regional development are discussed more thoroughly, giving attention to all the key constraints, potentials and opportunities.

In this endeavour, we combine the literature on clusters (Porter, 1998; Schmitz, 1995a) and industrial districts (Becattini, 1990; Becattini et al., 2009) with the literature on globalization, particularly through the concept of global value chains (Bair and Gereffi, 2003; Gereffi et al., 2005), along the lines drawn by De Marchi et al. Chapter 1 in this book. These two areas of research are finally combined with the development of innovation dynamics as a means to promote a more competitive, "high-road" type of integration to GVCs. This includes individual business R&D efforts, regional innovation system (RIS) dynamics (Asheim and Gertler, 2005) and the more recent formation of global innovation networks led by multinational companies that may or may not be embedded in clusters (Cooke, 2013).

This multifaceted approach should allow us to provide an answer to our main research questions, namely:

- What upgrade options stem from the growing intersection of firms in clusters with GVCs?
- What are the key innovation strategies and the policy implications for those local economies (i.e. clusters) whose economic fabric has been traditionally based upon dense networks of firms closely cooperating within clusters?

The combination of the above-mentioned theoretical frameworks is applied primarily through the lenses of local stakeholders interested in promoting the development of local and regional economies. Yet, a number of constraints exist for such efforts (e.g. limited insertion in global markets, streamlining of the supply base in GVCs, and inexistent or ineffective RISs) that need to be clarified and discussed together with possible solutions aimed at controlling such constraints and promoting local forces and synergies.

Clusters in GVCs: conceptual aspects

Over more than 40 years, the literature on clusters has been deeply and thoroughly developed through a wide range of works focused on the different determinants of their competitiveness. The contributions of Piore and Sabel (1984) and Becattini (1990) on the key configuration of industrial districts, as well as Porter's (1998) and Schmitz's (1995b) work on clusters, have been taken one step further through the cluster typology developed by Markusen (1996). Later on, in the late 1990s and early 2000s, the study of typologies of local production systems paved the way for the analysis of their development trajectories (Swann, 1998; Knorringa, 2002; Parrilli, 2007; Guerrieri and Pietrobelli, 2004; Menzel and Fornhal, 2010; Boschma and Fornhal, 2011; Martin and Sunley, 2011). The importance of absorptive capacity and related variety is currently under intense study by scholars who point out the best strategies to support the competitive evolution of these local production systems based on optimal knowledge distance (Asheim et al., 2008; Boschma and Fornahl, 2011). This academic discussion is particularly important for the current emphasis, especially within Europe, given to smart specialization strategies (Foray, 2009) in which entrepreneurial discovery, specialization and diversification drivers are combined to ensure that regions strengthen, refocus and even diversify their competitive advantage in line with the prospected demand of more open, globalized markets (Foray, 2009; McCann and Ortega-Argilés, 2011; Asheim et al., 2008; Parrilli and Zabala, 2014).

It is a debate with great significance, because clusters exist almost everywhere, although they have a higher impact in countries such as China (Bellandi and Di Tommaso, 2005), Brazil (Lastres and Cassiolato, 2005), South Asia (Nadvi and Schmitz, 1999; Guerrieri and Pietrobelli, 2004), Spain (Boix and Galletto, 2009) and Italy (Sforzi, 2000), as well as across the whole of Latin America (Pietrobelli and Rabellotti, 2007).

Clusters are increasingly positioned within GVCs as their firms contribute to specific productions together with other suppliers scattered across the globe. This happens in complex type of productions such as automotive, computers and energy (Sturgeon et al., 2008; Yang and Coe, 2009; Hansen et al., 2016), as well as in more traditional industries such as textiles and footwear (Bair and Gereffi, 2003), amongst others.

Connecting clusters with GVCs requires a particular effort to adapt a framework that is supposed to study the "relationship" between specific firms connected through buyer-supplier links to the context of clusters. However, the work developed in the 1990s on the supply chain and the different tiers of suppliers studied in the context of the Japanese automotive industry (Aoki, 1988; Cusumano and Takeishi, 1991) set the basis for the identification of firms – including those localized in clusters – participating in the production and commercialization of final products. This was subsequently applied to a number of cases in developing and developed countries (Pietrobelli and Rabellotti, 2007; Artola and Parrilli, 2007; Navas-Aleman, 2011; Elola et al., 2013; Hervas-Oliver and Boix, 2013; De Marchi et al., Chapter 3 in this book).

Based upon earlier work of Humphrey and Schmitz (2002, 2004) and our own work (Parrilli, 2007), Figure 4.1 shows the possible combinations between the most typical kinds of clusters (Marshallian IDs, survival clusters, hub-and-spoke clusters and satellite clusters) and the various types of GVC forms of governance (i.e. relational, modular, market, captive and hierarchical – see Gereffi et al., 2005). As Humphrey and Schmitz (2004) stressed, the combination of cluster typologies with the different GVC configurations has important implications for the governance and upgrading of clusters and their firms. For instance, the horizontal network of local firms, which characterizes Marshallian industrial districts,

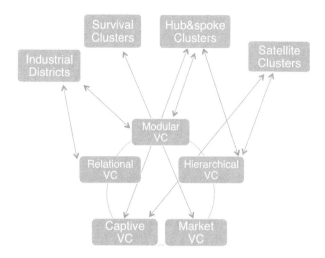

Figure 4.1 Typical intersections between types of clusters and types of GVCs
Source: Authors.

promotes balanced alliances among peers (typical of relational or modular GVCs) in favour of local development strategies (Amin and Thrift, 1994). By contrast, survival types of clusters, described as artisanal clusters with poor division and specialization of labour and patterns of capital accumulation (Altenburg and Meyer-Stamer, 1999), are another horizontal form of cluster. Yet, they do not develop intense networks of collaboration, but instead rely on market exchanges and market types of GVCs. Large embedded firms of typical hub-and-spoke clusters and satellite platforms (non-embedded in the case of satellite platforms) take the lead in designing long-range objectives and plans that they might discuss with their key first-tier suppliers (or impose upon second-tier suppliers), as well as with regional and national governments. This second case is mostly associated with hierarchical or captive types of GVCs, and in some cases (mostly first-tier suppliers) with modular GVCs (hub-and-spoke clusters). In the next section, we discuss current trends affecting GVCs and, as a consequence, firms and clusters that are integrated in such GVCs.

New GVC landscapes and changing vertical fragmentation of production

One of the key features of the changing organizational patterns of production on a global scale over the last few decades has been an extensive and ever-increasing vertical fragmentation of production. This vertical fragmentation, often orchestrated by large companies, has resulted in profound differentiation of functions performed by different firms and – to a large extent – also by regions and countries, even within the same industry (Gereffi, 2014). Typically, while high-end functions yielding high value-added are performed by companies in highly developed countries, low-end activities are largely decentralized to developing countries. This decentralization of production allows a much deeper integration of developing countries into the global economy via spurring large-volume production and rapidly expanding export of (semi)produced goods (in contrast to the export of mere raw materials)

(Dicken, 2015; Coe and Yeung, 2015). In addition, global buyers encourage their suppliers to upgrade production processes and often also their products. Thus, an extensive learning process even within the lowest tiers of GVCs has been initiated (Ernst and Kim, 2002; Ivarsson and Alvstam, 2011). Nevertheless, as a consequence of this vertical fragmentation of production, many suppliers and regions in developing countries are locked-in to the lowest tiers of GVCs and thus are trapped into performing only low-value-added activities (Kaplinsky et al., 2010). This position leaves only bleak perspectives for most of these lower-tier suppliers as well as for the socio-economic development of the regions concerned.

However, the trend of vertical fragmentation of production affects not only suppliers in developing countries, but also poses tremendous challenges as well as some opportunities for suppliers in developed countries, especially SMEs. In particular, joining GVCs is a possible alternative for SMEs with international ambitions that might be preferable (at least in some firms) to their own attempts to penetrate final markets in foreign countries. The latter is in fact bound to be extremely knowledge-demanding, time-consuming, costly and, evidently, a highly risky venture. Therefore, SMEs in developed countries can in principle choose from three basic strategies: 1) operate predominately in local markets, 2) penetrate foreign markets, or 3) become engaged in GVCs (and, obviously, through various combinations of these three basic options).

Recent research has shown that the third option, i.e. engagement with GVCs, represents a distinctive tendency in numerous SMEs in clusters (see De Marchi et al., Chapter 3 in this book). However, while both streams of literature (on clusters and on GVCs) maintain that process and product upgrading are being encouraged within clusters, as well as by lead firms or higher-tier suppliers in GVCs (Humphrey and Schmitz, 2002; Bettiol et al., Chapter 9 in this book), the case of functional upgrading – arguably the most desirable type of upgrading within a GVC – is largely different. Functional upgrading can be defined as a given supplier acquiring new functions that offer higher value-added or relinquishing functions with lower value-added (Humphrey and Schmitz, 2002). However, even within the GVC literature, there is disagreement about the scope to achieve such upgrading. The type of GVC governance, the capabilities of a given supplier to upgrade, and the quality of the regional innovation system within which the particular supplier is embedded are believed to be the key factors enabling this type of upgrading (Humphrey and Schmitz, 2002; Tokatli and Kizilgün, 2004).

Nevertheless, recently, it has been argued that functional upgrading represents a rather diverse category as in reality at least five different types of functional upgrading can be distinguished: 1) penetration among higher-tier suppliers or even among lead firms, 2) abandoning some activities with lower added value, 3) voluntary transfer of some high value-added functions by lead or higher-tier firms to their lower-tier suppliers, 4) developing new (intermediary) markets, and 5) upgrading via mergers or acquisitions (for discussion of these types, see Blažek, 2016). These types of functional upgrading differ in their strategic rationale and also in their cost-benefit ratios, which translate into sharply differing probabilities of whether particular firms would follow them.

Moreover, the dissonance in the literature over the possibilities of functional upgrading should also be re-assessed in the context of recent trends occurring in GVCs. In particular, the impact of recent changes in the organizational set-up of GVCs performed under the paradigm of "streamlining the supply base of production" – which is motivated by a quest for cutting the costs of coordination and by an effort to simplify the logistics – should be carefully considered. To start with, streamlining the supply base paradigm that is increasingly employed within GVCs provides vigorous stimuli for the voluntary transfer of some higher value-added functions by higher-tier suppliers to their most capable lower-tier suppliers

(Ivarsson and Alvstam, 2011). Namely, according to Özatağan (2011), in the automobile industry, first-tier suppliers are increasingly charged by lead firms (that are exposed to fierce competition on a global level) with responsibilities in the design and development of increasingly complex systems.

Consequently, first-tier suppliers are loaded with new functions, and, therefore, require their second-tier suppliers to undertake new functions, such as product development and design expertise. As a result, second-tier suppliers are also pushed vigorously by their buyers to innovate and to provide more complex (sub)systems. Thus, tendencies to relinquish functions with higher value-added are not limited to the highest level of the hierarchy, but are being replicated also at the lower levels (Özatağan, 2011) thus leading to a "cascade effect". The same cascade effect, consisting of spreading some higher-level functions across the whole chain, was identified in the Italian automotive industry (Follis and Enrietti, 2001). Importantly, these authors proved that the process of spreading higher-level functions down the GVC hierarchy has been driven predominately by a radical reduction in the number of first-tier suppliers induced by a paradigm of "streamlining the supply base" (see Figure 4.2).

The trend towards the drastic reduction in the number of suppliers is not limited to the automotive industry. Plank and Staritz (2015) provided the same evidence for the Romanian apparel industry, as large global buyers prefer suppliers that can take on new functions such as washing, labelling and packaging, as well as design/product development. Likewise, in her case study of the luxury retailer Burberry, Tokatli observed that the "number of Burberry suppliers has fallen from 240 to 100 during the last few years" (Tokatli, 2012, p. 71). In addition, a similar tendency has been reported in the case of a prime buyer-driven GVC, namely the case of IKEA (Ivarsson and Alvstam, 2011). According to these authors, the number of IKEA suppliers reduced over a period of 10 years from around 2,500 to 1,350 companies.

As a result, the remaining suppliers are being required to supply a wider spectrum of more complex (sub)systems or, in the case of buyer-driven GVCs such as IKEA, a wider spectrum of goods. This trend was intensified by the 2008–12 recession, as lead firms rationalized their supply chains even more to focus on fewer, larger and more capable suppliers (Gereffi, 2014). Therefore, taking up new higher-level functions that lead firms or higher-tier suppliers are willing to relinquish (cfr. the voluntary type of functional upgrading introduced above) seems to be a promising pathway for highly capable and efficient lower-tier suppliers. By contrast, suppliers that lack financial resources, human skills and, most importantly, the ambition to perform these new functions are relegated in importance or eliminated from the chain (Palpacuer et al., 2004).

Consequently, the intense global competition that gave rise to the paradigm of "streamlining the supply base" and the subsequent "cascade effect" that shifted some higher-level functions down the chain hierarchy represent a powerful process reshaping the organizational structure of GVCs. In fact, both these processes (i.e. streamlining the supply base as well as the cascade of additional requests) can be comprehended as vigorous selection mechanisms. In particular, while some firms might be able to functionally upgrade, those firms that are unable or unwilling to expand and to take up new functions tend to be gradually squeezed out of GVCs. As a result, lead firms and their key suppliers that were able to keep or even to enhance their position within the supply chain developed intensive mutual learning (Ivarsson and Alvstam, 2011), thus making the relationships among suppliers and their customers less unequal. This new form of inter-firm relationship was recently analysed in detail in the case of Chinese suppliers by Herrigel et al. (2013), who contended that global MNC production arrangements with suppliers are "strategic formally-governed systems focused not on making specific products, but on constructing collaborative continuous

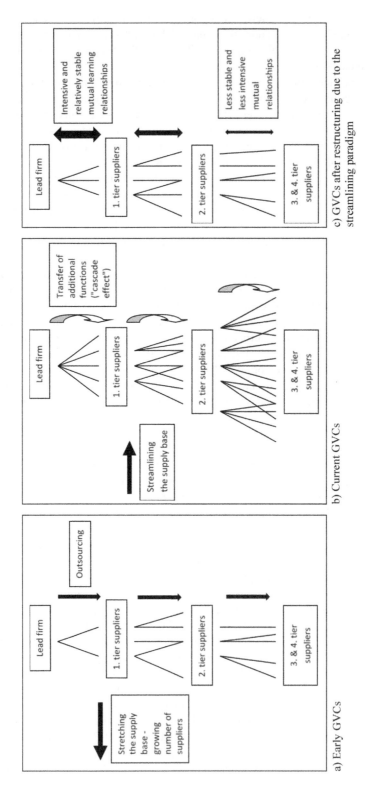

a) Early GVCs

b) Current GVCs

c) GVCs after restructuring due to the streamlining paradigm

Figure 4.2 Streamlining the supply base within GVC and the resulting "cascade effect"

Source: Authors.

learning processes that drive competence expansion, innovation, and self-transformation" (Herrigel et al., 2013, p. 122; see also Figure 4.2c).

Consequently, these new tendencies represent a fundamental challenge for firms that are ready to reposition themselves within GVCs by taking up new functions, for those suppliers that prefer to remain in their current seemingly "stable" and/or "safer" position, as well as for those firms that prefer (or are forced) to stay outside these vertical-learning and innovation systems.

In the following paragraphs, we investigate the intersection of clusters with GVCs to understand the possible match between the potential upgrading pathways identified in the literature on GVCs and the effective opportunities available to clusters in such a changing global scenario.

Development at the intersection between clusters and GVCs

The investigation of possible strategic options and evolutionary pathways for clusters is based upon various types of upgrading and repositioning shifts developed within the GVC framework. To start with, in the GVC literature there is a well-established four-fold typology of upgrading options – process upgrading, product upgrading, functional upgrading and inter-sectoral upgrading (Humphrey and Schmitz, 2002) (for a useful critique of this typology, see: Ponte and Ewert, 2009; Tokatli, 2013).

In reality, various combinations of these types of upgrading and repositioning shifts have been documented. For instance, a study by Rabellotti et al. (2009) on cluster evolution pathways identified a typology of patterns similar to those identified in GVC upgrading. These patterns included: attempts by some clusters to move to higher market segments or to higher value-added activities; the emergence of ethnic firms and the widespread offshoring to Balkan countries and beyond, both focused on cheap execution of the labour-intensive phases of production; the strategy of business-group formation consisting of several SMEs under single ownership; and, lastly, the strategy of cluster firms willing to engage with GVCs.

In the current work, we stress the importance of some types of GVC upgrading options that may have an important impact on cluster development. Functional upgrading, for example, represents a particularly important type of GVC upgrading, which corresponds to strategies that might seldom be available within predominately horizontal/networked clusters (cfr. the typology of clusters suggested by Markusen, 1996; see Table 4.1). Nevertheless, an example of far-reaching functional upgrading has been documented in the furniture cluster of Azpeitia and Azkoitia in the north of Spain, where former traditional furniture producers formed a wider cluster attracting producers of other components (e.g. electrical and acclimatization systems, domotic and security systems, design and engineering of complex buildings) that created new market options for the cluster as a whole, e.g. new hotel and restaurant chains (Parrilli and Zabala, 2014).

Another example of successful functional upgrading for clusters within GVCs is the case of the wind energy cluster in the Basque country, Spain. This represents an attempt by a cluster and its firms to move away from lower value-added operations to focus upon the most strategic, knowledge-based activities. For a decade, this cluster grew based on the national market demand sponsored by the Spanish government. In the mid-2000s, the lead companies started their globalization process to take on public bids in China, India, Brazil, and the United States, among others. In this way, the full value chain that was concentrated in the Basque country and Spain shrank, whilst the lower value-added operations were contracted out (e.g. China, India) to large companies in those host countries. Since then, the Basque

Table 4.1 Types of upgrading in GVCs and clusters and their frequency

Type of upgrading	GVCs	Examples	Clusters/IDs	Examples
Process upgrading	Common	Extensive use of Skype calls allowed setting up virtual teams (Tiits and Kalvet, 2012).	Common	Technological development, i.e. inkjet printing for tile production, Castellon cluster (Hervas-Oliver and Boix, 2013).
Product upgrading	Common	Developing new products with higher value for customers.	Common	All clusters present incremental and/or radical product innovations.
Functional upgrading				
1) Penetration among higher-tier suppliers	Infrequent	Former Turkish clothing supplier Erak Clothing successfully transformed itself even into an original brand-name manufacturer and retailer (Tokatli and Kizilgün, 2004).	Exceptional	Maniago knife district with a high percentage of 'developed subcontractors', capable of advanced market practices (direct exports) and technological operations (IT design, Furlan et al., 2007).
2) Abandoning lower value-added functions	Common	Outsourcing of low value-added production by apparel firms in Romania (Plank and Staritz, 2015).	Common	The Basque wind energy industry that focuses on more advanced stages of production and outsources the production of towers and nacelle (often abroad) (Elola et al., 2013).
3) Production of new type of good, thus forming a new market	Exceptional	Czech automotive producer Brano incorporated parking cameras into car locks, giving rise to a new type of product (Glogar, 2013).	Infrequent	The Basque furniture cluster of Azpeitia-Azkoitia that now assembles new turnkey solutions for hotel chains and government institutions (Parrilli and Zabala, 2014).
4) upgrading via mergers or acquisitions	Infrequent	A Chinese firm has upgraded to lead-firm position in the biomass power plant industry, mainly through acquisitions of Danish technological firms (Hansen et al., 2016).	Infrequent	Sassuolo tile cluster. The size of lead firms increased whilst they formed a consortium to develop intensive R&D and marketing (Brioschi et al., 2002)
5) voluntary taking up of new functions transferred by higher-tier supplier to lower-tier supplier	Frequent	The first-tier automotive suppliers require new functions such as design expertise from their second-tier suppliers (Özatağan, 2011).	Exceptional	n.a.

Type of upgrading	GVCs	Examples	Clusters/ IDs	Examples
Inter-sectoral upgrading	Infrequent	The South Moravian firm PBS (aircraft industry) has embarked upon developing special appliances for final customers with wider profit margins.	Infrequent	The Costa Rican software industry grew from the Intel-centred semiconductor industry (Parrilli and Sacchetti, 2008).
Chain or cluster upgrading	Infrequent	Under VW ownership, automobile manufacturer Škoda moved from low-end to mid-range market segment (Pavlínek and Ženka, 2011).	Common	Furniture cluster of Forli, Italy, targeting a higher income segment from the mid-1990s (Parrilli, 2009).
Decoupling and recoupling with GVC	Exceptional	Indian pharmaceutical firms Wockhardt, Cipla and Piramal Healthcare (Horner, 2014).	Exceptional	Footwear producers in Sinos Valley vis-à-vis global buyers (Schmitz, 1995).

Source: Author's elaboration based on the former work of Blažek (2016).

Notes: Frequency of particular types of upgrading is indicated at least tentatively on the basis of a literature review, as well as on the basis of own research of both authors on the following three-fold scale: common, infrequent, exceptional.

companies have narrowed down their operations to the most important and value-added phases of energy production and distribution (Elola et al., 2013). Similarly, the case of the knife-industry cluster in Veneto shows the increasing capacity of SME suppliers to develop higher value-added activities (e.g. direct exports, IT design), which represents another type of functional upgrading (Furlan et al., 2007).

These cases illustrate that at least some types of functional upgrading might represent a realistic strategic option for SME clusters. Recent research has shown that other types of upgrading can be identified, such as chain upgrading or "strategic decoupling" and subsequent "recoupling" with GVC in a much more favourable position (Horner, 2014). Chain upgrading represents a shift of a given chain to a more demanding market segment(s) within the same industry (e.g. from production of standard goods to a medium market segment or even to luxury goods) that often allow capturing a higher value (the Škoda auto-manufacturer under VW ownership is an example). This type of upgrading inter alia implies strong learning along the chain hierarchy orchestrated by lead firms and higher-tier suppliers, which contrasts with the efforts of individual firms in cases of functional upgrading. Such a shift can also be seen in the case of clusters, such as the furniture cluster of Forli, Italy, which moved from a lower and cheap market segment to a higher segment in the early 1990s after the national economic crisis and as a means to respond to the rising competition of Natuzzi and other industries based in transition and emerging countries (Parrilli, 2009).

Inter-sectoral upgrading is similar to the previous (chain), albeit more complex and demanding for the firms and clusters involved. An interesting example is the software cluster in San Jose, Costa Rica. In the mid-1990s, Intel created its own production plant and applied research centre. Based on Intel's investments and collaboration with the government (e.g. BA and MSc courses in electronic engineering and informatics in state universities, training in the National Training Institute, INA), a number of initiatives spurred the simultaneous growth of a software cluster that in a few years' time involved more than 100 companies producing advanced software and applications for a large variety of markets and countries (Parrilli and Sacchetti, 2008).

Strategic decoupling and subsequent recoupling represents a less obvious type of upgrading, as illustrated by Horner (2014) in the case of firms in the Indian pharmaceutical industry. In particular, Indian pharmaceutical firms, especially from Mumbai, Ahmedabad, Delhi, Hyderabad and Vadodara, have purposefully stopped supplying global pharmaceutical companies in order to break up the pre-existing highly unfavourable type of linkages. Subsequent development of local assets and capabilities enabled recoupling with the global pharmaceutical companies, but on a much more symmetrical and favourable basis (Horner, 2014). A similar case was identified a few years earlier by Schmitz (1995a) in the footwear cluster of Sinos Valley in Brazil, where large local producers started decoupling from large buyers (e.g. Bata) and selling their shoes autonomously whilst engaging with new buyers in national and international markets. Importantly, it should be emphasized that various combinations of upgrading types occur as an effect of the multiplicity and multidimensionality of strategies followed by particular (or particular groups of) firms at any given time.

Table 4.1 schematically shows examples of intersections between upgrading processes at work simultaneously in GVCs and in clusters. A few of these are quite common (i.e. product and process upgrading), whilst others are infrequent, especially in the context of clusters. Usually, lead firms in these local production systems are the guide for the whole cluster towards new upgrading forms; the rest of the clustered firms adjust to the trend.

The above examples of variegated firm strategies within GVCs, which open a myriad of new strategic options for the firms concerned, imply a trend towards even more complex internal restructuring of clusters and towards vastly divergent trajectories of particular companies within the same cluster. In addition, and very importantly, most of these strategies are the tools and mechanisms that firms and clusters currently adopt to face the new challenges represented by growing international competition and the aforementioned streamlining of GVCs.

In the next section, the discussion turns to the strategies adopted by firms and clusters to implement the upgrading options that promote the high-road development that local stakeholders target. Innovation is the keyword; yet the way firms and clusters go about innovation may differ significantly (i.e. own R&D, GINs and RISs), thus leading to specific effects and constraints upon local development.

Firm and cluster innovation strategies

The aforementioned upgrading efforts and strategies developed by firms and clusters are representative of a "high-road" type of development focused on creating new competitive edges vis-à-vis new and traditional competitors (Pyke and Sengenberger, 1992). The high road is undertaken with significant investments for enhancing innovation and the quality of goods and services. Where this has not happened, the decline of traditional clusters has taken place, e.g. some satellite textiles, footwear and furniture clusters in the South of Italy (on this process, see also: De Marchi and Grandinetti, 2014; De Marchi et al., Chapter 3 in this book).

"High-road development" can be pursued, provided that firms and clusters focus on effective upgrading processes. As mentioned in the previous section, these efforts include targeting product, process, organizational and commercial innovation, as well as the aforementioned functional, chain and inter-sectoral upgrading. The relevant question that we want to explore in this section focuses on the practical approach taken by firms and clusters to innovation. Three main strategies are currently adopted by individual and collective agents (i.e. firms and clusters): own R&D efforts, the formation of global innovation networks (GINs) and the creation of synergies with regional innovation systems (RISs).

Own R&D

Hub-and-spoke clusters and satellite platforms find it easier to progress through the first strategy as they rely on large firms, which are always in a condition to set up their own R&D departments with specialized personnel to focus directly on knowledge absorption, generation and related innovation output (Schumpeter, 1942). In the context of industrial clusters, this investment produces knowledge and innovation spillovers that benefit both local suppliers and other co-localized firms (Malmberg and Maskell, 2002), thus increasing the local capabilities that have an impact on productivity and performance.

Figure 4.3 shows the long-term R&D strategy of Intel in the semiconductor industry. Its efforts and investments have globalized not only its production operations, but also its R&D activities. At first, the company relied mostly on leading R&D locations such as other US or international leading centres (e.g. Boston and Cambridge). More recently, the expansion of this multinational has led to the development of (applied) R&D activities in developing and emerging economies, such as Costa Rica and China. Similarly, most multinational companies have developed wider production, innovation and market operations within and outside clusters. This is also the case in the wind energy industry, in which the lead companies Vestas and Gamesa opened new R&D operations in China and India (Elola et al., 2013; Lema et al., 2015).

In all these cases, lead firms have created new R&D centres as a means to benefit from the skills, competences and creativity of the local workforce (and from local financial and policy incentives) to respond to context-specific demands set by their specific regulations (e.g. norms of local contents) and by the preferences of local consumers.

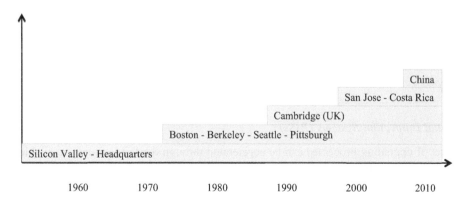

Figure 4.3 The development of global R&D centres – the case of Intel
Source: Author's elaboration based on Intel's web information (30/7/2016).

Global Innovation Networks (GINs)

Simultaneously, multinational companies (MNCs) and industries have developed a new, second type of strategy. In addition to setting up new R&D centres in emerging countries, they have created alliances with other MNCs in their industry and related sectors. Such partnerships have led to the creation of global innovation networks (GINs) that help these companies to connect to global knowledge pipelines and absorb the most advanced knowledge in the field, in addition to jointly developing new ideas, knowledge and innovation (Bathelt et al., 2004; Ernst, 2009; Cooke, 2013). This might lead to the formation of a monopoly power in industry innovation, which makes it more difficult for smaller firms to participate actively or to strengthen their competitive position in these industries.

Lead companies in the wind energy industry have formed an explicit global innovation network as a means of pulling together resources, capabilities and outputs to secure their market lead in future. Iberdrola is leading its own GINs, through in a rather collaborative approach with other MNCs specialized in different areas of expertise (e.g. Gamesa and Siemens in wind turbine production, Vicinay in anchoring offshore platforms, ABB in generators and energy distribution, Smulders in water-resistant materials). Similar networks can be found in any industry, such as the automotive industry with the Open Automotive Alliance that includes Ford, Audi, Citroen, Fiat, Honda, Hyundai, Panasonic, and Google, among others. These new systemic formations (GINs) are horizontal networks of multinational companies that collaborate usually through formal agreements with a view to drawing on each company's expertise and specialization, thus promoting innovation and strengthening their respective competitive position in the market. These networks usually unify large firms (MNCs) that collaborate on an "equal peer" basis due to their size and advanced knowledge in their area of expertise.

Second-, third- and fourth-tier suppliers (in general, SMEs) are usually excluded from such GINs. They tend to participate in other, more localized networks and usually hold a direct and binding relationship with the lead MNC. The fragmentation of innovation activities and networks between lead firms and their suppliers jeopardizes the participation of clusters in GVCs, as a good number of their firms that are marginalized from innovation activities also tend to be split from the rest of the GVC and have to re-direct their operations towards different industries and products. This is typical in energy industries, where third- and fourth-tier suppliers (e.g. local foundries producing towers, nacelles and other metallic components, or suppliers of materials and generic components) might be driven to close down their operations or to reorient their supplies towards other industries, e.g. automotive or shipbuilding (Elola et al., 2013). It is an important challenge that has to be addressed by clusters and their firms that want to maintain their competitive position in GVCs. The most appropriate strategy is discussed in the next subsection, where the role of regional innovation systems is considered.

Regional Innovation Systems (RISs)

This set of upgrading processes can be accelerated through the third strategy available for innovation. This implies a well-planned regional innovation approach that creates higher resources, skills and capabilities for the pool of local firms and clusters. The process raises the absorptive capacity of the regional actors, and thus their capacity to benefit from an active inflow of global knowledge that is used in upgrading production and commercialization practices.

For many years, local SMEs have coped with the demands of greater competition by lob-bying regional government to develop effective regional innovation policies (Cooke et al., 2004). These policies were based on significant public investment in R&D expenditure for the formation of purpose-specific infrastructure (e.g. universities, technology centres, science and technology parks) and highly qualified human capital (e.g. engineers and sci-entists). Several cases have been pointed out as successful examples of such public-led investment in innovation, such as regions in Germany (e.g. Baden-Wuerttemberg, Bayern), Italy (Emilia-Romagna, Piedmont, Lombardy), Spain (Valencia, Basque country), Norway (Agder), Denmark and Sweden (Medicon Valley), the UK (East and Southeast of England), as well as regions overseas, e.g. in Taiwan, Japan and Korea (see works of: Iammarino, 2005; Rodriguez-Pose and Crescenzi, 2008; Hollanders et al., 2009; Alberdi et al., 2016).

However, this reality is all but widespread, and many regions and clusters are not as effec-tive and efficient as portrayed in the literature based on those successful cases. In addition, policy-makers often try to replicate those successful cases, whilst practice shows that it is quite a difficult process as each country and region has its own specificities that need to be taken into account, with adequate adaptations and transformations (Tödtling and Trippl, 2005; Aranguren et al., 2014; Alberdi et al., 2016; Isaksen and Trippl, 2016).

This complex situation needs rethinking as a means to find the way to promote knowl-edge formation in the context of clusters. Namely, regional governments need to keep their pro-active role in innovation promotion and to work through appropriate round tables with local agents so as to identify issues, options and investments to target with a critical mass of agents, resources and programs. This has been carried out over the years, for example in the Basque country, Spain, where an agile cluster policy (identifying around 20 clusters in the region) has been successfully combined with a powerful innovation policy based on a set of programs focused on delivering meaningful resources to upgrade the knowledge and innovation capacity of the local agents, primarily the regional technology centres and the local SMEs (Olazaran et al., 2009).

Regional innovation strategies and policies need to be set up and evolve in a way that supports the capacity of the region and its clusters (Tödtling and Trippl, 2005; Parrilli et al., 2013; Isaksen and Trippl, 2016). One of the key mechanisms is certainly competence forma-tion. Human capital is in fact the critical asset to trigger higher productivity and efficiency in the use of physical assets (Pekkarinen and Harmaakorpi, 2006). In this respect, maps of competences can be formed for each specific industry/product so as to fully identify current knowledge and skills as well as those that will be needed in the near future. This prospect has been thoroughly discussed and is currently applied in the context of the new offshore wind energy cluster based in the Basque country, Spain, where the related clusters (energy, shipbuilding and logistics) involve numerous agents in a project that activates new resources, markets and development pathways (see Elola et al., 2013).

Conclusions and policy implications

This work has shown the upgrading options that are available to clusters positioned in GVCs. The current strategies implemented by firms are not necessarily pursuing better integration of their clusters within GVCs. Some of them (own R&D and the formation of GINs) might even lead to a fracture within clusters. For this reason, the RIS pathway is highlighted as the best means to achieve a "high-road of development" that benefits the cluster as a whole. Yet, as shown in the previous section, a set of reformulations and adjustments are needed in the RIS strategy to make it more effective.

The set of problems that we have indicated above require appropriate management and solution. In GVCs, the new paradigm of streamlining the supply chain results in a cascade of requests from lead companies to their first- and second-tier suppliers to take up new functions, whilst the less capable suppliers are gradually eliminated from the supply chain. This situation generates a progressive differentiation or even fragmentation and shrinking of the clusters that are integrated in GVCs.

The stronger (and private/bilateral) partnerships created by lead companies in GVCs (through their GINs) tend to make local SMEs and their regional innovation infrastructures inadequate and redundant. Unless they substantially upgrade their innovation capacities and output, they become irrelevant to the lead companies and their GVCs, which could shift their supply function to producers based elsewhere (e.g. in emerging economies). Therefore, concurrent with the effort of achieving various forms of upgrading, and particularly the above-mentioned functional and inter-sectoral upgrading, other efforts should target the innovation system so as to make it more efficient and effective in the delivery of relevant innovation outputs to small firms (Tödtling and Trippl, 2005; Iammarino, 2005; Rodríguez-Pose and Crescenzi, 2008; Hollanders et al., 2009; Alberdi et al., 2016: Isaksen and Trippl, 2016). For this task, five different operations seem to be essential:

- There is a need to overcome the gap in our knowledge about the existing types and extent of integration of local SMEs in GVCs. Without such knowledge, policies might be misdirected, whereas a thorough understanding of the extent and form of plugging local SMEs (and, as an extension, their clusters) into GVCs could become a cornerstone of a targeted and effective innovation policy. In fact, opportunities and challenges differ fundamentally between firms integrated into GVCs and firms that remain outside these chains. Subsequently, tailor-made support to particular types of upgrading and repositioning shifts of local companies and clusters should be considered (Tödtling and Trippl, 2005; Aranguren et al., 2014).
- Mapping competences across the different agents that form the clusters (Elola et al., 2013) tends to be crucial. In this way, policy-makers identify which resources and capacities are missing; they need to be built up so as to introduce more adequate knowledge and skills into the innovation system.
- Given the key role of RISs in the modern globalized economy, efforts targeting individual companies could be combined with cross-cutting/horizontal policies aimed at enhancing the overall quality of RISs. Accordingly, systemic measures in the sphere of education and labour-force training (Pekkarinen and Harmaakorpi, 2006), various forms of networking (both internal and external), high-quality mentoring programmes for SMEs, and access to modern financial instruments could be promoted.
- The results produced by innovation policies should be routinely assessed, in line with arguments by Georghiou (2001) and Nauwelaers and Wintjes (2003), amongst others, who understand that such operations offer both indications for improvement and peer pressure to raise the relevant delivery standards (Rodríguez-Pose and Crescenzi, 2008; Hollanders et al., 2009; Alberdi et al., 2016).
- In those regions and clusters where innovation policies are not yet in operation, the key task refers to setting them up in a gradual and reasonable form (without excess spending – see Blažek and Csank, 2016). Recently, this effort received a significant impetus in the form of EU requirements that regions set up and implement tailor-made smart specialization strategies. These strategies should be based upon efforts made by regional businesses and other stakeholders, as well as previous competences and new

competences that are likely to grow as a result of efficient education and training (Asheim et al., 2008; Foray, 2009).

Overall, the growing engagement of firms in clusters with GVCs opens a spectrum of new challenges and opportunities and, evidently, represents an important driver of change. The increasing diversification of innovation strategies and the resulting divergence in the performance of firms is likely to lead towards higher differentiation and fragmentation within clusters (Elola et al., 2013). Nevertheless, if these changes are countered by a specific and effective RIS strategy, most clusters could be expected to retain a relevant position in GVCs in the future.

References

Alberdi, X., Gibaja, J., and Parrilli, M. (2016). Innovation gaps: A typology for Spain. In M.D. Parrilli, R. Fitjar and A. Rodriguez-Pose (eds.), *Innovation Drivers and Regional Innovation Strategies*. New York: Routledge.

Altenburg, T., and Meyer-Stamer, J. (1999). How to promote clusters in Latin America. *World Development*, 27: 1693–1713.

Amin, A., and Thrift, N. (1994). Living in the global. In A. Amin and N. Thrift (eds.), *Globalization, Institutions and Regional Development in Europe*. Oxford: Oxford University Press.

Aoki, M. (1988). Information, Incentives and Bargaining in the Japanese Economy. New York: Cambridge University Press.

Aranguren, M., De la Maza, X., Parrilli, M., Vendrell, F., and Wilson, J. (2014). Nested methodological approach to cluster policy. *Regional Studies*, 48: 1547–1562.

Artola, N., and Parrilli, M.D. (2007). The dairy products cluster in Nicaragua: Issues for upgrading. In C. Pietrobelli and R. Rabellotti (eds.), *Upgrading to Compete: Global Value Chains, Clusters, and SMEs in Latin America*. Cambridge, MA: Harvard University Press.

Asheim, B., Boschma, R., and Cooke, P. (2008). Constructing Regional Advantage: Platform Policies Based on Related Variety and Differentiated Knowledge Bases. Papers in Evolutionary Economic Geography, Utrecht University.

Asheim, B.T., and Gertler, M.S. (2005). The geography of innovation: Regional innovation systems. In J. Fagerberg, D. Mowery and R. Nelson (eds.), *The Oxford Handbook of Innovation*. Oxford: Oxford University Press.

Bair, J., and Gereffi, G. (2003). Upgrading, uneven development and jobs in the North-American apparel industry. *Global Networks*, 3: 143–169.

Bathelt, H., Malmberg, A., and Maskell, P. (2004). Clusters and knowledge: Local buzz, global pipelines and the process of knowledge creation. *Progress in Human Geography*, 28(1): 31–56.

Becattini, G. (1990). The Marshallian industrial district as a socio-economic notion. In F. Pyke, G. Bacattini and W. Sengenberger (eds.), *Industrial Districts and Interfirm Cooperation in Italy*. Geneva: International Labour Organisation.

Becattini, G., Bellandi, M., and De Propris, L. (eds.). (2009). *Handbook of Industrial Districts*. Cheltenham: Edward Elgar.

Bellandi, M., and Di Tommaso, M. (2005). The case of specialized towns in Guangdong, China. *European Planning Studies*, 13: 707–729.

Blažek, J. (2016). Towards a typology of repositioning strategies of GVC/GPN suppliers: The case of functional upgrading and downgrading. *Journal of Economic Geography*, 16(4): 849–869.

Blažek, J., and Csank, P. (2016). Can emerging regional innovation strategies in less developed European regions bridge the main gaps in the innovation process? *Environment and Planning C: Government and Policy*, 34(4): 1095–1114.

Boix, R., and Galletto, V. (2009). Innovation and industrial districts. *Regional Studies*, 43(9): 1117–1133.

Boschma, R., and Fornahl, D. (2011). Cluster evolution and a roadmap for future research. *Regional Studies*, 45: 1295–1298.

Brioschi, F., Brioschi, M., and Cainelli, G. (2002). From the industrial district to the district group: Insight into the evolution of capitalism in Italy. *Regional Studies*, 36: 1037–1052.

Coe, N., and Yeung, H. (2015). Global Production Networks: Theoretizing Economic Development in an Interconnected World. Oxford: Oxford University Press.

Cooke, P. (2013). Asian dynamics: From global production networks to global innovation networks in ICTs. *European Planning Studies*, 21(7), 1081–1094.

Cooke, P., Braczick, M., and Heidenreich, M. (2004). *Regional Systems of Innovation*. London: Routledge.

Cusumano, M., and Takeishi, A. (1991). Supplier relations and management: A survey of Japanese, Japanese-Transplant and US autoplants. *Strategic Management Journal*, 12: 563–588.

De Marchi, V., and Grandinetti, R. (2014). Industrial district and the collapse of the marshallian model: Looking at the Italian experience. *Competition and Change*, 18: 70–87.

Dicken, P. (2015). Global Shift: Mapping the Changing Contours of the World Economy, 7th ed. London: Sage.

Elola, A., Parrilli, M.D., and Rabellotti, R. (2013). The resilience of clusters in the context of increasing globalization: The Basque wind energy value chain. *European Planning Studies*, 21(7), 989–1006.

Ernst, D. (2009). A New Geography of Knowledge in the Electronics Industry? Asia's Role in Global Innovation Networks. Policy Studies No. 54. Honolulu: East-West Center.

Ernst, D., and Kim, L. (2002). Global production network, knowledge diffusion and local capability formation. *Research Policy*, 31: 1417–1429.

Follis, M., and Enrietti, A. (2001). Improving performance at the second tier of the automotive supply chain: A draft case study of an innovative initiative in the Italian car industry. *Actes du GERPISA*, 33: 41–47.

Foray, D. (2009). *Understanding Smart Specialization*. The Questions of R&D Specialization: Perspectives and Policy Implications. JRC Scientific and Technical Reports, European Commission, pp. 19–25.

Furlan, A., Grandinetti, R., and Camuffo, A. (2007). How do subcontractors evolve? *International Journal of Operations & Production Management*, 27(1): 69–89.

Georghiou, L. (2001). Evolving framework for European collaboration in research and technology. *Research Policy*, 30: 891–903.

Gereffi, G. (2014). Global value chains in a post-Washington consensus world. *Review of International Political Economy*, 21: 9–37.

Gereffi, G., Humphrey, J., and Sturgeon, T. (2005). The governance of global value chains. *Review of International Political Economy*, 12(1): 78–104.

Glogar, L. (2013). *Position of Czech Automotive Firms in Global Value Chains*. Presentation at the workshop 'Global Production Networks: Theory and Practice', South Moravian Innovation Centre, Brno, June 2013.

Guerrieri, P., and Pietrobelli, C. (2004). Industrial districts' evolution and technological regimes: Italy and Taiwan. *Technovation*, 17(11): 899–914.

Hansen, U., Fold, N., and Hansen, T. (2016). Upgrading to lead firm position via international acquisition: Learning from the global biomass power plant industry. *Journal of Economic Geography*, 16(1): 131–153.

Herrigel, G., Wittke, V., and Voskamp, V. (2013). The process of Chinese manufacturing upgrading: Transitioning from unilateral to recursive mutual learning relations. *Global Sourcing Journal*, 3: 109–125.

Hervas-Oliver, J., and Boix, R. (2013). The economic geography of meso-global spaces: Integrating MNCs and clusters. *European Planning Studies*, 21(7): 1064–1080.

Hollanders, H., Tarantola, S., and Loschky, A. (2009). *Regional Innovation Scoreboard (RIS) 2009*. Maastricht: Economic and Social Research and Training Centre on Innovation and Technology, Joint Research Centre, Institute for the Protection and Security of the Citizen (IPSC). Available at: www.inovacijos.lt/inopagalba/cms/94lt.pdf

Horner, R. (2014). Strategic decoupling, recoupling and global production networks: India's pharmaceutical industry. *Journal of Economic Geography*, 14:1117–1140.

Humphrey, J., and Schmitz, H. (2002). How does insertion in global value chains affect upgrading in industrial clusters? *Regional Studies*, 36: 1017–1027.

Humphrey, J., and Schmitz, H. (2004). Chain governance and upgrading. In H. Schmitz (ed.), *Local Enterprises in the Global Economy: Governance and Upgrading*. Cheltenham: Elgar, pp. 349–381.

Iammarino, S. (2005). An evolutionary integrated view of regional innovation systems. *European Planning Studies*, 13: 497–519.

Isaksen, A., and Trippl, M. (2016). Path development in different regional innovation systems. In M. Parrilli, R. Fitjar and A. Rodriguez-Pose (eds.), *Innovation Drivers and Regional Innovation Strategies*. New York: Routledge.

Ivarsson, I., and Alvstam, C. (2011). Upgrading in global value-chains: A case study of technology-learning among IKEA-suppliers in China and Southeast Asia. *Journal of Economic Geography*, 11: 731–752.

Kaplinsky, R., Terheggen, A., and Tijaja, J. (2010). What happens when the market shifts to China? The Gabon timber and Thai cassava value chains. In O. Cataneo, G. Gereffi and C. Staritz (eds.), *Global Value Chains in a Post-Crisis World*. Washington: World Bank, pp. 125–153.

Knorringa, P. (2002). Cluster trajectories and the likelihood of endogenous upgrading. In M. van Dijk and H. Sandee (eds.), *Innovation and Small Firms in the Third World*. Cheltenham: Edward Elgar.

Lastres, A., and Cassiolato, J. (2005). Innovation systems and local productive arrangements. *Innovation, Management, Policy and Practice*, 7(2): 172–187.

Lema, R., Quadros, R., and Schmitz, H. (2015). Reorganizing global value chains and innovation capabilities in Brazil and India. *Research Policy*, 44: 1375–1386.

Malmberg, A., and Maskell, P. (2002). The elusive concept of localization economies: Towards a knowledge-based theory of spatial clustering. *Environment and Planning A*, 34: 429–449.

Markusen, A. (1996). Sticky places in slippery space: A typology of industrial districts. *Economic Geography*, 72(3): 293–313.

Martin, R., and Sunley, M. (2011). Conceptualizing cluster evolution: Beyond the lifecycle model. *Regional Studies*, 45(10): 1299–1318.

McCann, P., and Ortega-Argilés, R. (2011). *Smart Specialisation, Regional Growth and Applications to EU Cohesion Policy*. Economic Geography Working Papers, University of Groningen. Available at: http://ipts.jrc.ec.europa.eu/docs/s3_mccann_ortega.pdf.

Menzel, M., and Fornhal, D. (2010). Cluster lifecycle: Dimensions and rationales of cluster evolution. *Industrial and Corporate Change*, 19(1): 205–238.

Nadvi, K., and Schmitz, H. (1999). Clustering and industrialization: Introduction. *World Development*, 27(9): 1503–1514.

Nauwelaers, C., and Wintjes, R. (2003). Towards a new paradigm of innovation policy? In B. Asheim, A. Isaksen, C. Nauwelaers and F. Tödtling (eds.), *Regional Innovation Policy for Small Enterprises*. Cheltenham: Edward Elgar, pp. 193–218.

Navas-Aleman, L. (2011). The impact of operating in multiple value chains for upgrading: The case of the Brazilian furniture and footwear industries. *World Development*, 39(8): 1386–1397.

Olazaran, M., Albizu, E., and Otero, B. (2009). Technology transfer between technology centres and SMEs. *European Planning Studies*, 17: 345–363.

Özatağan, G. (2011). Dynamics of value chain governance: Increasing supplier competence and changing power relations in the periphery of automotive production – Evidence from Bursa, Turkey. *European Planning Studies*, 19: 77–95.

Palpacuer, F., Gibbon, P., and Thomsen, L. (2004). New challenges for developing country suppliers in global clothing chains: A comparative European perspective. *World Development*, 33: 409–430.

Parrilli, M.D. (2007). *SME Cluster Development*. Basingstoke: Palgrave-Macmillan.

Parrilli, M.D. (2009). Collective efficiency, policy-inducement and social embeddedness: Drivers of ID development. *Entrepreneurship and Regional Development*, 21: 1–24.

Parrilli, M.D., Nadvi, K., and Yeung, H. (2013). Local and regional development in global VCs, PNs and INs: A comparative review and challenges for future research. *European Planning Studies*, 21(7): 1–21.

Parrilli, M.D., and Sacchetti, S. (2008). Linking learning and governance in clusters and networks. *Entrepreneurship and Regional Development*, 20(4): 387–408.

Parrilli, M.D., and Zabala, J. (2014). Interrelated diversification and internationalization: New drives of global industries. *Revue d'Economie Industrielle*, 145: 71–101.

Pavlínek, P., and Ženka, J. (2011). Upgrading in the automotive industry: Firm-level evidence from Central Europe. *Journal of Economic Geography*, 11: 559–586.

Pekkarinen, S., and Harmaakorpi, V. (2006). Building regional innovation networks. *Regional Studies*, 40: 401–413.

Pietrobelli, C., and Rabellotti, R. (eds.). (2007). *Upgrading to Compete.* Cambridge, MA: Harvard University Press.

Piore, M., and Sabel, C. (1984). *The Second Industrial Divide.* New York: Basic Books.

Plank, L., and Staritz, C. (2015). Global competition, institutional context, and regional production networks: Up- and downgrading experiences in Romania's apparel industry. *Cambridge Journal of Regions, Economy and Society*, 8: 421–438.

Ponte, S., and Ewert, J. (2009). Which way is 'up' in upgrading? Trajectories of change in the value chain for South African wine. *World Development*, 37: 1637–1650.

Porter, M. (1998). Clusters and the new economics of competition. *Harvard Business Review*, November–December, 77–90.

Pyke, F., and Sengenberger, W. (1992). Introduction. In F. Pyke, P. Cossentino and W. Sengenberger (eds.), *Industrial Districts and Local Economic Regeneration.* Geneva: International Labour Office.

Rabellotti, R., Carabelli, A., and Hirsch, G. (2009). Italian industrial districts on the move. *European Planning Studies*, 17(1): 19–41.

Rodríguez-Pose, A., and Crescenzi, R. (2008). Research and development, spillovers, innovation systems, and the genesis of regional growth in Europe. *Regional Studies*, 42: 51–67.

Schmitz, H. (1995a). Collective efficiency: Growth path for small-scale industry. *Journal of Development Studies*, 31(4).

Schmitz, H. (1995b). Global competition and local cooperation: Success and failure in the Sinos Valley, Brazil. *World Development*, 27: 1627–1650.

Schumpeter, J. (1942). *Capitalism, Socialism and Democracy.* New York: Harper.

Sforzi, F. (2000). The industrial districts and the new Italian economic geography. *European Planning Studies*, 10: 439–447.

Sturgeon, T., van Biesebrock, J., and Gereffi, G. (2008). Value chains, networks and clusters: Reframing the global automotive industry. *Journal of Economic Geography*, 8: 297–321.

Swann, G. (1998). Introduction. In G. Swann, M. Prevezer and D. Stout (eds.), *The Dynamics of Industrial Clusters: International Comparisons in Computing and Biotechnology.* Oxford: Oxford University Press.

Tiits, M., Kalvet, T. (2012). Nordic Small Countries in the Global High-Tech Value Chains: The Case of Telecommunications Systems Production in Estonia. Working Papers in Technology Governance and Economic Dynamics, 38: 1–47.

Tödtling, F., and Trippl, M. (2005). One size fits all? Towards a differentiated regional innovation policy approach. *Research Policy*, 34: 1203–1219.

Tokatli, N. (2012). Old firms, new tricks and the quest for profits: Burberry's journey from success to failure and back to success again. *Journal of Economic Geography*, 12: 55–77.

Tokatli, N. (2013). Toward a better understanding of the apparel industry: A critique of the upgrading literature. *Journal of Economic Geography*, 13: 993–1011.

Tokatli, N., and Kizilgün, Ö. (2004). Upgrading in the global clothing industry: Mavie jeans and the transformation of a Turkish firm from full-package to brand-name manufacturing and retailing. *Economic Geography*, 80: 221–240.

Yang, D., and Coe, N. (2009). The governance of global production networks and regional development: A case study of Taiwanese PC production networks. *Growth and Change*, 40: 30–53.

Part II

The role of lead firms in global value chains and clusters

5 MNEs and clusters

The creation of place-anchored value chains

Fiorenza Belussi, Annalisa Caloffi and
Silvia Rita Sedita

Introduction

This chapter discusses the presence and the role played by multinationals (MNEs) in clusters. Recent empirical research has pointed out the increasing involvement of clusters in global value chains (GVCs) (Gereffi and Korzeniewicz, 1994; Gereffi, 1999; Gereffi and Kaplinsky, 2001; Gereffi and Bair, 2001; Gereffi et al., 2005). However, the role MNEs can play in clusters still requires further investigation.

Within the cluster literature, the phenomenon of MNEs-led clusters (Markusen, 1996) has often been considered as an incomplete local development model. The strong dependence of MNE subsidiaries on their headquarters make them incapable of embedding within the local *milieu*, and being active part in a network of knowledge flows within cluster organizations. In contrast, the international business literature has adopted a very optimistic view, suggesting that MNE subsidiaries may evolve within their corporation as well as within the cluster, building multiple knowledge flows that can sustain new development paths. Our chapter tries to integrate these two perspectives by analyzing the interplay and long-term evolution of clusters and MNEs under the lenses of the global supply chain approach (Sturgeon et al., 2008; Belussi and Sammarra, 2010). In particular, stemming from the cluster life cycle approach (Brenner, 2004; Feldman and Braunerhjelm, 2007; Belussi and Sedita, 2009; Menzel and Fornahl, 2010), we argue that the entry of MNEs in a local context is influenced by the specific stage of cluster evolution. MNEs may play a particular role during the initial stage of a cluster life cycle – the origin – giving rise to the cluster, and thus building place-anchored value chains. However, such anchoring may be more or less intense, and thus generate different effects on the subsequent life stages of the cluster. The extent to which those subsidiaries hire local labour force (not only to perform trivial tasks) and/or develop relationships with local organizations triggers local upgrading processes (Belussi and Sedita, 2009). A lack of embeddedness gives rise to the establishment of a satellite model – as suggested more than 20 years ago by Markusen (1996) – where subsidiaries do not integrate with local social/business/institutional actors and do not promote a local development trajectory. In fact, the entry of MNEs during cluster maturity represents a more intriguing case. The entry of MNEs through greenfield investments or the acquisition of firms having high-technical competences alters local governance mechanisms, and, particularly in the latter case, puts the local chain of subcontractors under heavy control. The more extensive or important the acquisitions of local firms, the more the place-anchored value chain will be managed by MNEs, within a top-down governance system.

We here illustrate the differences among alternative ways of MNEs' entry in different stages of the cluster life cycle through four case studies concerning clusters. Two of the observed clusters originated by foreign investments (the Dongguan electronics cluster and the Timisoara footwear cluster), while the other two clusters attracted MNEs in the maturity stage (the Montebelluna sportsystem cluster and the Riviera del Brenta footwear cluster). The latter cases differ for the intensity through which the phenomenon of MNEs' entry took place. In one case, MNEs were never able to dominate the local cluster, while in the other, MNEs acquired many local SMEs in just 10 years, exerting a deep control over the cluster. Drawing on these examples, we discuss the interwoven evolution of MNEs and clusters, also in relation to the changing position of clusters in global value chains. As we will show, MNEs do not necessarily play the role of cluster lead firms.[1] In the two first cases studied, clusters formed by MNEs lacked local dynamism in the long run: indigenous entrepreneurs never sprang up, and local companies did not activate learning processes for improving either the production process or the products. Firms remained blocked in their condition of low-cost subcontractors, without developing selling and marketing autonomous functions. They only slightly improved their relative position moving from a low-tech sector to a medium-tech sector, thus increasing the economic value of the individual activity performed. In the second two cases, we observed more variability. The Montebelluna sportsystem cluster was never widely penetrated by MNEs, and local firms grew, transforming into large transnationals or MNEs. By doing so, they were able to keep their position on international markets stable, competing with the largest global firms existing in the sportsystem sector (Nike, Adidas etc.). In the Montebelluna cluster, firms gave rise to a GVC either by creating a satellite district (in Timisoara, Romania) for the manufacturing of low-tech/low-costs activities, or by outsourcing some activities to firms located in China and other emergent/developing market economy countries.[2] In the Riviera del Brenta cluster, a wave of acquisitions from the two major worldwide fashion and luxury groups (LVMH and Kering) transformed the cluster, where the leading groups now coordinate some local supply chains. In this model the old industrial district has become a specialized area where MNEs have created "place-anchored" value chains. In the Riviera del Brenta cluster only 20–30% of the local activity is now in the hands of endogenous entrepreneurs, able to sell their products on international markets. This process has loosened the embeddedness of firms in the local context, also decreasing their relationships with local institutions, which, initially, were used to co-evolve with local cluster firms.[3]

MNEs, clusters and timing of entry: a literature review

Literature has shown that MNEs are often attracted into clusters (Dunning, 2000) in order to gain access to specific pools of resources and competences (Birkinshaw, 2000; McCann et al., 2002; Nachum and Keeble, 2003). Some research has focused on the role played by MNEs entering clusters for local development and for cluster upgrading (Humphrey and Schmitz, 2002; De Propris and Driffield, 2006; Sturgeon et al., 2008; De Marchi et al., 2014). However, little is known about the role MNEs can play in the different stages of cluster evolution.

In order to investigate this aspect, we refer to the concept of cluster life cycle (Brenner, 2004; Feldman and Braunerhjelm, 2007; Belussi and Sedita, 2009; Menzel and Fornahl, 2010). Literature has identified three main stages of cluster life cycle: origin, development and maturity. Along these stages we assist to variations in the local population of firms and workers, and in the structure of their social and business relationships. In addition, different phases of cluster development correspond to different stages of the evolution of cluster-specific conditions in terms of quantity and quality of the local pool of contextual knowledge and skills, social norms and business practices.

In the origin stage, the set of cluster-specific conditions are not present. Retrospectively, we can say that the local fabric of institutions, knowledge and competencies has not yet formed. However, the cluster can host some historical sediment of knowledge and competencies, as well as a local culture, not necessarily moulded on the features of a specific kind of industry – which at this stage does not yet exist (Brusco, 1986). The development stage is characterized by the emergence of a set of cluster-specific institutions, knowledge and competencies. The type of knowledge exchanged among the actors in the cluster is mainly tacit, and therefore difficult for external agents to grasp. In the maturity stage, the local population's growth rate slows down gradually, as does the virtuous cycle of the semi-automatic reproduction of cluster-specific conditions. Part of the tacit, cluster-specific knowledge, previously accumulated, progressively becomes codified, and the production of new pieces of tacit knowledge gradually slows down.

MNEs can enter in different stages of cluster evolution, possibly generating different effects on the inclusion or the positioning of cluster firms in GVCs. Drawing on a review of the literature on clusters and MNEs, the following Table 5.1 summarizes the determinants of MNEs' location choice in the different stages of cluster evolution.[4] In what follows, we gave special attention to cluster origin and maturity, because literature reports evidence of MNEs' entry in clusters mostly in these two stages (see Table 5.1 and Belussi et al., 2013).

MNEs can play an important role in giving rise to cluster emergence (Manning, 2008; Belussi and Sedita, 2009; Mudambi and Swift, 2012; Giblin and Ryan, 2015). Mudambi and Santangelo (2014) argue that the mode of entry, timing of entry and the corporate mandate of the subsidiary have an impact on the transformation of a region from a "shallow pool of resources" to an "emerging cluster". This process is activated in particular when subsidiaries are autonomous and "competence-creating" (Cantwell and Mudambi, 2005). Pioneering MNEs as first entrants in the region creates a legitimacy of the location that attracts other subsidiaries. The emergence of a cluster depends on linkages and knowledge transfer mechanisms created by these early pioneering entrants (Østergaard and Park, 2015). As a result, the cluster can be inserted in different global value chains. However, the outcomes of this insertion can be different. The entry of an MNE can bring an immediate benefit for the local area, in the form of new activities, new jobs, and new potential sources of knowledge spillovers. Nevertheless, the cluster does not exist independently of the MNE, but is instead a result of its presence (Bellandi, 2001; Rugman and Verbeke, 2003; Iammarino and McCann, 2010). If the MNE is inserted in a closed network, linking it to the parent company or to other subsidiaries, and does not develop any relationship with the local area, the knowledge, competencies and capabilities developed internally by the MNE will never spread to local firms. In the medium-term, this "closure" could produce relatively concentrated knowledge governance architectures (De Propris et al., 2008), being unable to stimulate local growth processes. Moreover, in case of crisis, the MNE might opt for disinvesting rapidly and move the affiliate in another more attractive location. The absence of embeddedness eases this process (Benito, 2005).

In the maturity phase, the entry of an MNE can produce an immediate benefit. In a phase when the local engines of innovation and growth are slowing down or even stopping, the entry of an MNE can help the cluster rejuvenate or substitute worn-out components of the engines. At this stage, local firms have accumulated some knowledge-specific capabilities, but the MNEs could be more effective than local firms in the process of recombination between local and external knowledge. To the extent that MNEs operate as bridges between local and global knowledge and competencies, and create relationships with local organizations – through which these external resources can enter the cluster – the entry of MNEs can positively influence the cluster (Raines et al., 2001; Bathelt and Li, 2014). Conversely, when MNEs operate within closed networks, disconnected from the local context, the effects on cluster development are uncertain.

Table 5.1 Scientific literature about timing of entry of MNEs in clusters

Reference	Short description	Determinants of MNEs' location choice
ORIGIN		
Giblin and Ryan (2015), IND_INNOV	Longitudinal study on the role of MNEs as conduits of knowledge flows, in the evolution of a technology cluster in medical technology in the West of Ireland.	No direct explanation of the motives
Mudambi and Santangelo (2016), REG_STUD	Investigation of the role of MNEs' subsidiaries in peripheral areas as conduits for global knowledge flows.	Knowledge, market and resource-seeking activities
Edgington and Hayter (2013), ECON_GEOGR	Japanese MNEs moved beyond simple assembly-based to embedded clustering in Malaysia. However, such MNEs did not promote a technology upgrading of the cluster because of the poor technological environment in Malaysia, as well as MNCs' strategies that depend on technology from headquarters.	Low production costs
Gibling and Ryan (2012), REG_STUD	Inward FDI can have a positive impact in instigating a clustering process. The unit of analysis is the medical technology sector in Galway (Ireland). Indigenous and foreign-owned MNEs are analyzed.	Policy-driven FDI
Manning, Ricart, Rique, and Lewin (2010), J_INT_MANAG	Many ICT clusters in Latin America are originated by FDI.	Access to an increasing large pool of science and engineering talent at relatively low cost.
Sajarattanochote and Poon (2009), REG_STUD	This paper examines the geography of technology flows among MNEs located in Bangkok. It finds evidence of limited regional spillovers to first- and second-order neighbours. Technology transfer to Thai firms varies by nationality, sector, size, and age of MNEs.	No direct explanation of the motives.
Zhou and Xin (2003), ECON_GEO; Chen and Karwan (2008), INNOV; Yang (2009), REG_STUD; Lo, Niu, Yang, and Wang (2010), J_CONTEMP_ASIA; Yang and Liao (2010), ANN_REGIONAL_SCI; Zhou, Sun, Wei, and Lin (2011), J_ECON_GEOGR	Fundamental role played by MNEs in the creation of ICT clusters in China (Guangdong in particular, but also Pudong area in Shanghai and Zhongguancun in Beijing). A particular role has been played by Taiwanese and Hong Kong FDI.	Large presence of research infrastructures attracts MNEs in Beijing, while relatively low production costs and market-driven factors attract firms in Guangdong and in Shanghai area. Pro-active IFDI policies play a fundamental role in all cases.

Manning (2008), ECON_DEV_Q	Pioneer MNCs promote the initial development of clusters by customizing local institutions and business practices in accordance with their sourcing needs. This can in turn lead to the attraction of further MNEs.	Access to an increasing large pool of science and engineering talent at relatively low cost, as well as to a number of specialized service providers.
Phelps (2008), REG_STUD	FDI in developing countries are at the first stage of cluster formation, while in the subsequent development phase regional policy is important to stimulate local development.	No explanation of the motives.
Depner and Bathelt (2005), ECON_GEOGR; Po (2006), GEOFORUM; Zhao and Zhang (2007), REG_STUD	Central role of foreign investors in the creation of several specialized clusters in China (non-ICT clusters such as: automotive, advertising, clothing).	Abundant presence of labour and other productive resources at relatively low cost. Presence of pro-active IFDI policies.
Finegold, Wong and Cheah (2004), EUR_PLAN_STUD	Industrial policy attracts FDI in the Singapore biotechnology cluster.	Availability of research infrastructures and public incentives. Presence of pro-active IFDI policies.
Fromhold-Eisebith (2002), ENVIRON_PLANN_A; Audirac (2003), J_AM_PLANN_ASSOC	MNEs triggered regional cycles of learning in the IT industry in Bangalore (India). Inferior cycles, characterized by the absence of MNEs are found instead in Bandung cluster.	Favourable geographical conditions, availability of an educated labour force, some R&D infrastructures. Availability of public subsidies & – in later stages of cluster development – availability of networks of suppliers that can meet the MNEs quality and delivery standards.
Sjöholm (2002), J_CONTEMP_ASIA	FDI in Indonesia often concentrate in clusters.	Availability of infrastructures and a rich pool of labour. Market-seeking motives.
Thompson (2002), WORLD_DEV	Hong Kong investments cluster around Hong Kong's neighbouring Guangdong province.	Geographical and cultural proximity; abundant presence of low-cost labour and other productive resources; market-seeking motives.
Kearns and Gorg (2002), INT_J_TECH_MANGE; Wickham and Vecchi (2008), EUR_PLAN_STUD	Irish software cluster originated by industrial policy, which included the attraction of FDI. Over time, foreign and indigenous firms link together.	Availability of various productive resources at relatively low cost; good institutional environment; availability of public incentives and presence of pro-active IFDI policies.

(Continued)

Table 5.1 Continued

Reference	Short description	Determinants of MNEs' location choice
Brown (2000), EUR_URBAN_REG_STUD; van Winden, van der Meer, and van den Berg (2004), INT_J_TECH_MANGE	The rise of ICT clusters in some European countries is centred on MNEs. Indigenous MNE quickly become key drivers of the Stockholm and Helsinki ICT clusters [H].	Strong role of IFDI policies in Ireland. MNEs locate in Amsterdam mostly because of the presence of a well-developed service industry and of a number of research infrastructures.
Harrison (1994), ENVIRON_PLANN_A	Silicon Valley was created by, and remains profoundly dependent on, major MNEs and on the fiscal and regulatory support of the national government.	Availability of research infrastructures and IFDI policies.
Young, Hood, and Peters (1994), REG_STUD	Review of the circumstances under which "developmental" MNE subsidiaries may emerge in host regions and give rise to clusters.	No direct explanation of the motives.
DEVELOPMENT		
Demirbag and Glaister (2010), J_MANAGE_STUD	MNEs offshore R&D projects to locations where science and engineering talents and infrastructures are strong.	Access to an increasing large pool of science and engineering talent at relatively low cost.
Bagchi-Sen and Lawton Smith (2008), REG_STUD	Bangalore's biotechnology cluster was funded by the state government of Karnataka. Later entrants were attracted by IFDI policies.	Presence of pro-active IFDI policies
Chen (2008), J_DEV_STUD; Zhou (2005), ENVIRON_PLANN_A	MNCs continue to enter in the Zhongguancun multimedia technologies district (Beijing) in the 1990s.	Presence of MNEs; access to an increasing large pool of science and engineering talent at relatively low cost; market-seeking behaviour
Ivarsson (2002), J_ECON_GEOGR	Swedish regions in their development phase attract FDI. Evidence of knowledge creation and transfer among cluster firms and MNEs.	Knowledge-seeking and competence-seeking motives.
MATURITY		
Østergaard and Park (2015) REG_STUD	Technological lock-in and exit of firms contribute to the decline of a wireless communication cluster in North Jutland (Denmark). MNEs have a contradicting effect, being quick to leave the cluster in case of crisis. Embeddedness is good to prevent rapid move of the MNE in case of troubles.	Knowledge-seeking and competence-seeking motives.

Reference	Description	Motives
Potter and Watts (2011) J_ECON_GEOGR	Global networks and MNCs appear in the mature stage of development, as demonstrated in the Sheffield metals industry cluster	Knowledge-seeking and competence-seeking motives.
Cantwell and Zhang (2011) INT_J_TECHNOL_MANAGE	The interaction between MNEs and local networks depends upon the type of cluster, whether a general centre of excellence or a specialized centre. These two principal kinds of cluster are associated with different structures of local knowledge spillovers between firms.	No direct explanation of the motives
Hervas-Oliver and Albors-Garrigos (2008), ENTREP_REGION_DEV; Hervas-Oliver, Albors-Garrigos, and Hidalgo (2011), INT_J_TECHNOL_MANAGE; Oliver, Garrigos, and Porta (2008), EUR_PLAN_STUD	In the Castellon (Spain) and Sassuolo (Italy) ceramics clusters, home-grown multinationals rose in the maturity phase and then create inter-cluster links along the GVC by locating foreign plants in the two clusters [H].	Knowledge sourcing, and in particular sourcing of cluster-specific knowledge. Presence of knowledge and productive complementarities; proximity to the clients.
Asmussen, Pedersen & Dhanaraj (2009), J_INT_BUS_STUD	The presence of a strong cluster is a sufficient condition for subsidiary competences to arise.	Market and knowledge-seeking purposes
Majocchi and Presutti (2009), INT_BUS_REV	MNEs invest in existing consolidated clusters, but not in the development phase, when local entrepreneurial activity is more consistent and the rate of creation of indigenous firms is high.	No direct explanation of the motives
Whitford (2001), ECON_SOC; De Propris, Menghinello, and Sugden (2008), ENTREP_REGION_DEV	Italian IDs internationalization has moved from exports to FDI. home-grown MNEs raised in the maturity phase of the home-cluster [H]	Abundant presence of labour and other productive resources at relatively low cost.
Amdam, Lunnan, and Ramanauskas (2007), ENG_ECON	Norwegian furniture cluster firms conducted FDI in Lithuania [H].	Abundant presence of labour and other productive resources at relatively low cost.
Biggiero (2006), ENTREP_REGION_DEV	Different patterns of IDs relocation, between selective and replicative strategies [H]	Mostly resource-access and cost-driven migration of firms from the West to the East of European clusters.
De Martino, Mc Hardy Reid, and Zygliodopoulos (2006), ENTREP_REGION_DEV	MNE invest in mature cluster in their home-country – the case of optics/photonics cluster in Rochester, New York.	Abundant presence of labour and other productive resources at relatively low cost and market seeking motives push location in Asia, while technology-seeking motives in Germany

(Continued)

Table 5.1 Continued

Reference	Short description	Determinants of MNEs' location choice
De Propris and Driffield (2006), CAMB_J_ECON	MNEs located in clusters are able to benefit from the spillovers generated by the cluster firms.	Technology-seeking motives.
Mason and Harrison (2006), REG_STUD	MNE enter the Scottish clusters in their maturity and trigger a process of positive entrepreneurial recycling.	No direct explanation of the motives
Perez-Aleman (2005), IND_CORP_CHANGE	Analysis of two successful clusters in Chile: the agro industry cluster for the conservation of tomatoes and the aquaculture cluster of salmon production. These cases reveal a positive interaction among the state, the MNEs and the local firms. The emergence of a dynamic cluster depends on building institutions that enable the coordination of learning, capabilities, and product/process improvements.	Resource-seeking motives (presence of a well-developed salmon aquaculture)
Tallman and Fladmoe-Lindquist (2002), CALIF_MANAGE_REV	The article shows how MNE can gain sustained competitive advantage in the global market place developing dynamic capabilities. In the area of capability building, firms can tap into foreign clusters acquiring knowledgeable firms	Knowledge-seeking and competence-seeking motives.
Teubal, Avnimelech, and Gayego (2002), EUR_PLAN_STUD	MNEs enter the Israel ICT cluster mostly at its maturity stage, acquiring some of its most successful firms.	Knowledge-seeking and competence-seeking motives. Availability of a large number of R&D infrastructures
Cornford and Robins (1992), REG_STUD	The development of the Northeast England cluster specialized in media tech has been eroded by the entry of MNEs.	No direct explanation of the motives

Source: Authors.

Notes: The scientific articles (ISI database) that explain the timing of entry of MNEs in cluster are listed in the table (origin and maturity stages). They are identified with authors' names, year of publication and ISI abbreviated journal title and are grouped by stage of entry/origin of the MNE in the cluster. On search criteria see note 2. [H] refers to the presence of home-grown MNEs, i.e. to local firms that become MNEs.

For sure, much also depends on the type of activities carried out by the multinational in the cluster. Following McCann and Mudambi (2004, 2005), MNEs' offshoring strategy starts to take advantage of low salaries, but over time they activate a process of local incremental learning and move rapidly toward a process of product improvement reengineering. In other cases, they start to benefit from their new location in terms of innovation and new knowledge absorption (Kenney et al., 2009). Literature has hypothesized that the entry of MNEs in clusters gives rise to a significant process of technology transfer between MNE subsidiaries and local firms (Dunning, 1998, 2000). Some empirical contributions have shown that this has occurred (Crone and Roper, 2001; Holm et al., 2003; Kim and Zhang, 2008; Menghinello et al., 2010; Gugler et al., 2015), while others have been more cautious or critical (Bair and Gereffi, 2001; Phelps et al., 2003; Görg and Greenaway, 2004; Lipsey, 2004; Østergaard and Park, 2015).

For those who claim a positive effect of MNEs, the latter can facilitate cluster upgrading thanks to the presence of spillover effects. However, literature has shown that in order to absorb and benefit from these knowledge spillovers, the cluster must have a certain degree of absorptive capacity (Dunning, 1994; Blomström et al., 2000; Görg and Greenaway, 2004; Humphrey and Schmitz, 2002; Giuliani et al., 2005; Nadvi and Halder, 2005; De Propris and Driffield, 2006). Thus, the improvement of cluster firms does not always come from functional upgrading, but by the extension and deepening of technological capabilities (Morrison et al., 2008).

Methodology and description of the four cases

The longitudinal, comparative case study research was based on a collection of surveys carried out by the authors, addressed to firms belonging to four important clusters: two in Italy, one in China, and one in Romania. Our selection was guided by the principle of covering different cases in terms of the cluster phase in which the MNE emerged or entered/originated in the cluster. More specifically, the units of analysis are firms located as follows: the Montebelluna sportsystem cluster, Italy; the Riviera del Brenta footwear cluster, Italy; the Dongguan information technology (IT) cluster, China; and the Timisoara footwear cluster, Romania. In each cluster, besides entrepreneurs, we also interviewed several members of local organizations such as business associations, local governments, universities or research centres. These original sources were complemented with secondary sources. Table 5.2 presents the case studies.

Table 5.2 Basic characteristics of the four clusters analysed

	Dongguan electronics cluster	*Timisoara footwear cluster*	*Montebelluna sportsystem cluster*	*Riviera del Brenta footwear cluster*
MNEs entry timing	Origin	Origin	Maturity	Maturity
Sample size	30 companies and 5 local organizations	30 companies and 9 local organizations	30 companies and 10 local organizations	50 companies and 2 main local organizations
Year of fieldwork	2004; 2005; 2010	2003; 2016	2003; 2004; 2006; 2011	2000; 2005; 2016
Related Publications	Bellandi and Caloffi (2008, 2010)	Belussi (2010b)	Belussi (2010a); Sammarra and Belussi (2006); Belussi et al. (2011)	Belussi and Scarpel (2002); Belussi and Caldari (2005)

Table 5.3 Overview of the Montebelluna, Dongguan, Riviera del Brenta and Timişoara clusters in the GVC

	Montebelluna	Dongguan	Riviera del Brenta	Timişoara
Product	Technical sport shoes, ski and trekking boots, motorcycle boots and bicycle shoes	Laptops and other IT products	High-quality fashion shoes, mostly for women	Former shoe cluster (mostly for women). Currently a wide array of products
Number of firms and employees	400 companies and 6000 employees	1500 companies in 2010	200 companies and 7000 employees	150 companies and about 5000 employees
Export propensity	Very high	Mainly indirect, through the MNEs located in the cluster	Very high	Low. Shoes producers supply the national demand
Local firms	Global lead firms and OBMs	OEMs, stage suppliers	Global lead firms, OBMs and OEMs	OMBs and OEMs
Supporting industries	Machinery, Chemical industry, mould producers; textile and clothing industry	Logistics	Pattern makers, Designers, Logistic	Logistics
Local institutions	Museo dello scarpone (Boot museum), Chamber of Commerce	Business associations of foreign producers	Politecnico Calzaturiero, specialized in innovation and training activities	None are relevant to the cluster activity
Major recent transformations	Concentration process that is favouring the most innovative firms and leads to a shrink of the total number of firms. Montebelluna is now a pole of excellence for technologies related to winter and summer sports items and leading firms are coordinating GVC	Emergence of diseconomies of agglomeration, rise in wages and low presence of skilled workers are diminishing the attractiveness of the cluster for low-cost activities. At the same time, the cluster is not yet enough attractive for high-value activities. MNEs are changing the structure of their GVC to locate some activities outside the cluster	With the entry of MNEs, Riviera del Brenta has transformed into a hub-and-spoke cluster	The footwear cluster imploded. Foreign companies have gradually left the cluster. Without those foreign firms, Timişoara exits the GVC in which it was inserted

Related publications made by the authors on the topic are also reported. Table 5.3 summarizes the information on the four clusters analysed.

The Montebelluna sportsystem cluster

The Montebelluna cluster, in the province of Treviso (Italy), includes about 400 companies and 6,000 employees located in the cluster, while about 11,200 workers are employed globally by Montebelluna firms (Aida 2013 and Museo dello Scarpone data) (Belussi, 2010a). Montebelluna is the world leader in technical sport shoes, ski and trekking boots, motorcycle boots and bicycle shoes. Its main competitors are specialized MNEs, while – to our knowledge – no other sportsystem clusters are competing with the district. The Montebelluna sportsystem cluster originated in the 1950s when the number of firms multiplied, forming a thick entrepreneurial area characterized by the diffused presence of SMEs. The cluster take-off was facilitated by the presence of several leading firms, such as Tecnica (established in 1890), Dolomite (1897) and Nordica (1926). The growth of the European markets during the 1950s, and the enthusiasm for mountain excursions, stimulated local firms to introduce innovative new products, such as plastic ski boots and various types of climbing and technical sport shoes, conceptualized by the most innovative local firms. The innovativeness of the cluster was strongly supported by the sedimentation of specific competencies of the local firms and their direct access to external sources of knowledge. The hub-and-spoke structure of the cluster became evident in the 1990s, when it embarked in a twofold model of international growth. Three important local firms (Tecnica, Geox and Stonefly) became MNEs, while huge external FDIs, made by GVC leading firms, entered the cluster (Rossignol, Roces, HTM, Lange etc.). Half of the founders of the district successfully remained active on the market even after the third generation. Some MNCs entered the cluster during the 1970s, such as Salomon that acquired S. Giorgio; Nike, which acquired Bauer; HTM (Head, Tyrolia and Mares), which acquired Brixia S. Marco and Munari. In the 1990s also Benetton – an Italian-owned company established in the Region of Veneto – started a process of local firms' acquisition by buying Nordica. After a while, Nordica was sold to another local firm (Tecnica). Nike, which acquired one local plant (Bauer) in order to gain access to local knowledge concerning several technical shoes' components, abandoned the cluster after a few years, selling the firm to a group of entrepreneurs (now Novation). Novation is a high-tech firm now producing new carbon components for various industries (auto, mechanics and frame glasses). In the last years, Tecnica acquired two important foreign companies, Blizzard and Lowa. Montebelluna firms (and in particular Garmont, Grisport, Lotto Sport, Tecnica, Scarpa, Alpinestars, and Geox) manage a larger number of productive and commercial units outside the cluster. They have now reached the status of MNEs, being large firms owing multiple firms and subsidiaries abroad.

For two decades, local leading firms activated an intense process of manufacturing relocation, and employment levels and the local number of firms decreased dramatically. The development of the Montebelluna cluster after the 1990s saw the leading firms and also some medium-size firms outsourcing abroad the low-value activities of manufacturing, giving rise to FDIs and GVCs located in emerging countries, in Asia and other Eastern countries (Romania and Hungary) (Chiarvesio et al., 2010). In recent years, MNEs have located their prototype development and design branches in Montebelluna. A concentration process is in place, favouring the most innovative firms and leading to a shrink in the total number of firms. In relation to the model of knowledge acquisition, the most important global innovative actors are located in Montebelluna, which is now a local pole of excellence for technologies related to winter and summer sports items, based on innovation in mechanical engineering and advanced plastic moulding. As regards employment, the interviewed firms confirmed the presence of a high percentage of qualified workers. When firms recur to off-shoring, they continue developing in-house the tertiary functions of design, management, logistics and research. The presence of designers within the firms is quite common. In addition, firms also use external (local and global) designers. The impact of multinationals in the cluster has been marginal, via a rapid entry and exit. One of the latest entries of famous MNEs is that of the Turkish group Zylan, which acquired Canguro in Verona and the brand Lamberjack, transferring in Montebelluna all of the group's design activity for high-fashion shoes. Zylan has also acquired the European distribution channels of Canguro, and now it is commercializing its "designed in Italy" Turkish sport shoes. Local large leading firms – which base most of their activity in the local context – possess high innovation and export capabilities, but they do not show an MNE-like growth path.

The Dongguan electronics cluster

The Dongguan IT cluster emerged during the 1980s, thanks to the localization of a group of MNEs in the area of Dongguan, in the Province of Guangdong (China). They were attracted by three main factors: the proximity to Hong Kong and the Shenzhen area (which hosted the first Special Economic Zone in China); the presence of a huge reservoir of low-cost labour; and the presence of FDI attraction policies. The Dongguan cluster exhibits the typical features of a satellite industrial platform, populated by a large number of MNEs.

The first foreign investors to settle in the town were a large group of Taiwan-based MNEs, which established the low-tech productive phases of personal computers and electronics production in the area. These MNEs were, and still are, first-tier suppliers in the GVC led by the most famous producers of personal computers. As the local environment could not offer qualified local suppliers, Taiwanese multinationals moved the whole subcontracting system and all suppliers from Taiwan to Dongguan. The number of MNEs has gradually increased (from around 100 in the beginning of the 1980s to around 1,500 in 2010), and the Taiwanese investors have been followed by a large number of European and Asian investors. Today, the area hosts Taiwanese MNEs such as Delta Electronics, GVC Corporation, BBK Electronics, Qisheng Electronics, Tecsun, Nintaus Digital and Gigabyte Electronics. "Foxconn city" or "iPod city" – named after the famous Taiwanese multinational Foxconn, which manufactures (also) for Apple – is located not far from Dongguan.

In the initial phase, Dongguan electronics factories were assembly plants of low-added value laptop components and similar IT products fuelled by the productive capacity of a large number of migrants coming from various areas of mainland China. Only in a later phase, companies started to carry out more complex manufacturing or logistical phases in the cluster.

The growing density and technological complexity of MNEs in the 2000s facilitated the development of the cluster. However, it never really became a high-tech and knowledge-oriented cluster. Indeed, to describe the behaviour of these multinationals, some authors have used the term "closed network" (Yang, 2006). In fact, the MNEs' subsidiaries have relationships with the parent company, other subsidiaries or with their Taiwanese subcontractors. Only a few authors report the existence of relationships between the Taiwanese subsidiaries located in China and Chinese companies (Tong and Wang, 2002). In most cases they have not established any backward or forward linkage with Chinese firms, and the cluster has remained relatively not much integrated in the local context. The fact that MNEs make an extensive use of migrant workers does not help the integration of the IT industry in the local context (Bellandi and Caloffi, 2010). Indeed, migrants are temporarily present in the city and after 2–3 years they return to their place of origin.

The inflow of FDIs slackened during the second half of the 2000s. Some MNEs reduced their activities in Dongguan, both by relocalizing some assembly plants in the cheapest areas of mainland China, or by moving some higher value-added activities in the area of Shanghai. The area was hit by two different forces. On the one hand, the local increase in the cost of labour and the competition from other areas that implemented FDI attraction policies (the Go-West policies constitute a striking example) diminished the attractiveness of Dongguan (and that of the whole Province of Guangdong) as a target area for the localization of assembly plants (Becker, 2014). In 2004, the monthly minimum wage was RMB 450 per month, while it amounted to 1,510 RMB in 2015 (Fang and Lin, 2015). On the other hand, the emergence of agglomeration diseconomies (pollution and overcrowding) and the low presence of well-educated human capital resulted in a business and social environment that was not attractive enough for high value-added investments.

The main impact of the presence of MNEs can be summarized as follows. In the first stage of cluster emergence, the presence of MNEs brought new jobs, infrastructure and knowledge on managerial practices that enriched the area. However, an indigenous industry has not emerged, at least not yet. In fact, only a very small group of Chinese-owned enterprises have started to work as subcontractors for the foreign enterprises localized within the cluster. Although some of these firms could survive the exit of the MNEs from the cluster, the overall medium-term impact is very uncertain (OECD, 2000; Whalley and Xian, 2010).

In order to change this trend, the local government has engaged in a continuous interaction with foreign investors, in order to try to embed them in loco. At the same time, huge investments in the creation of education and research infrastructure have been made in order to improve the absorptive capacity of local firms and workers, without being successful in creating a regional innovation system. Finally, the MNEs do not seem to have promoted social upgrading. A recent report by the National Labour Committee (2009) has denounced the very poor labour conditions of workers employed in the assembly lines of a Taiwanese MNE, and this is not the first case.

The Riviera del Brenta footwear cluster

The Riviera del Brenta footwear cluster originated in the 1960s (Italy) and rapidly grew as a typical Marshallian district. The area was already well-known for its artisanal specialization in shoe production, but the first industrial firm, Voltan, was created in 1898. Such firm was the first to introduce the automated machinery of the assembling line (manovia) in the production of women and men shoes. Voltan learned to use such machineries in the United States, where the entrepreneur had emigrated because of the poverty existing in Riviera del Brenta, as well as in the whole Region of Veneto. Voltan can be considered the anchor firm of the district. Throughout the years, many of its skilled technicians and qualified workers have created a number of spin-offs.

Initially, the district produced medium-quality shoes for the national market. The big development of the district occurred after WW II, and especially during the 1970s. Gradually, the district started to produce high-quality shoes for women (Belussi and Scarpel, 2002).

Nowadays, the Riviera del Brenta shoe production accounts for about 15% of the total amount of Italian sales of the sector. It produces about 20 million pairs yearly of which 90% are exported. At the end of the 1990s, after decades of development, the crisis arrived when the Chinese competition and the shrinking of the market for middle-quality shoes bitted the cluster. Considering only shoe producers, the number of firms decreased from 500 in 2000 to about 200 in 2015, and the local employment levels diminished from 8,000 to about 7,000 workers (clearly the average size of the firms grew over time). The craft abilities of the local firms were no longer sufficient to guarantee their survival. A process of hierarchal concentration initiated.

When MNEs started to enter the cluster, acquiring some of the local firms, they worked as gatekeepers of knowledge, bringing knowledge about fashion trends and design into the cluster, moving the cluster from a typical Marshallian district towards a hub-and-spoke model. Consequently, local firms began to produce fit-to-the-market luxury shoes, such as Rossimoda. At the same time, only in few cases very labour-intensive tasks were outsourced to low-cost foreign firms, mainly located in Eastern European countries. Many firms in the district have now been acquired by foreign MNEs, as in the case of: Rossimoda, acquired by Monique and Arcad (now Manufacture de Souliers Louis Vuitton – LVMH); Guardi by Armani; Lamos by Prada; and Iris by Gibò. Also, Dior is going to expand its investments in the area with a Greenfield investment, as well as François-Henri Pinault with Kering, and Yves Saint Laurent, Balenciaga, Stella McCartney, and Gucci entered the cluster with the brand Bottega Veneta. Two important local firms remained independent and built an aggressive brand policy: the Ballin group (a medium-sized firm) and the Calzaturificio Renè Caovilla (luxury brands, specialized in women shoes for haute-couture, well known among US actresses). Recently, the local association of entrepreneurs launched Restart, a project oriented to the "rejuvenation" of the local production, and Ci Divertiamo, a start-up company founded by Giuseppe Baiardo, which is oriented to scouting new talents and promoting the creation of new firms by local young stylists.

Even if the entry of global fashion multinationals (such as Armani, Kering-Gucci, Puma, Prada, LVMH-Louis Vuitton,) downgraded some firms, limiting their commercial capabilities (Amighini and Rabellotti, 2006), it did not penalize the overall innovative capability of the cluster, which still very much relies on the role played by the local Politecnico Calzaturiero (secondary school providing vocational training), specialized in innovation and training activities. Such entry has undoubtedly changed the structure of the local district, imposing a process of concentration led by foreign MNEs. Many small subcontractors, which did not start to work for the MNEs, have closed their activities. However, the cluster as a whole is still alive and has maintained a satisfactory level of activity. The interviewed entrepreneurs think that the entry of MNEs saved the Riviera del Brenta cluster, creating a fully place-anchored value chain. However, the "side effects" of loosing market autonomy must be still better evaluated. Contrary to Buciuni and Pisano (2015), we think that the effects of global knowledge integrators on the success of clusters will be fully understood only in the medium to long term. It is still too early to say that this district has overcome the crisis.

The Timişoara footwear cluster[5]

The origin of the Timişoara footwear cluster in Romania is rooted in the presence of a bulk of state-owned companies (such as Guban, Filty and Banatim in Timişoara; Libertatea in Arad; and Solidaritatea in Oradea) that produced shoes. Banatim was founded in 1900 by an Austrian entrepreneur. In 1948 the company was taken over by the State and its name changed to "Banatul". Filty, once the biggest local firm, was privatized after the revolution of 1989, and it still exists. The cluster took off after 1989, thanks to the entry of foreign investors who acquired many state companies on the brink of economic collapse, and created brand new plants. MNEs came to Romania mainly to explore the cost opportunity offered by local labour costs, and created a typical satellite cluster in Timişoara (Markusen, 1996). Since its beginning, the cluster was characterized by the presence of Italian entrepreneurs (from Veneto, Marche, and Emilia-Romagna) investing in Timişoara taking advantage of low salaries, good technical competences of local workers (thanks to the previous manufacturing tradition) and low cultural distance.

In the first years of the 1990s Filty was re-launched by a group of Romanian managers who founded a cooperative among former employers. The members of the cooperative started to work as subcontractors for several new Italian firms, but also continued to operate as subcontractors for Adidas and other foreign firms. Their large manufacturing capacity allowed them to reach the significant size – if we consider the typical footwear firm – of about 1,400 workers (data refer to 2003). The true problem is that they were not able to sell any part of their production abroad, because they had no contacts with international designers for the production of their collections, nor did they have any marketing and selling experience abroad. The lack of connections in the GVCs negatively affected the success of local firms, hampering the upgrading process. The Timişoara district lost its attractiveness over time, and its occupational levels continued to diminish; currently, the largest local firm, Filty, employs only 251 workers (2015). Considering the group of the most dated firms, only Filty and Guban are still active, covering only the national market demand with semi-luxury shoes.

Local firms are mainly subcontractors of Western companies and the main products are footwear items of medium-quality for men, women, teenagers and children. Outside of the MNEs' activities, the cluster has a very low share of endogenous entrepreneurs and of innovative capabilities. The firms' competences are limited to manufacturing, and they lack design and marketing capacities. Moreover, the cluster's collective organizations and institutions are weak.

MNEs were not interested in building these capabilities in Romania, because they were already developed in other well-established industrial districts, whose access was simpler for MNEs. MNEs located in the area do not have many knowledge links with other local firms, but they mainly work with their headquarters located in Italy or Germany. Thus, there are little knowledge spillovers at the local scale. The low degrees of technology transfer also depend on the low absorptive capabilities of local companies. The primary aim of the MNE is to use cheap labour and quickly re-export goods, without making any effort to upgrade the skills of the local labour force. Foreign firms operate just for one large client: that is, the company's headquarters or a leading foreign firm such as Cesare Paciotti or Calzaturificio Magli. The benefits of the MNE's entry in the cluster are ambiguous. On the one hand, they are the triggering factor behind the cluster development, but, on the other hand, they did not stimulate local entrepreneurship; the MNE subsidiaries appear to be footloose investments that could soon end up being relocated to lower salary countries. This was the case, for instance, of Geox, which dismissed the large plant Technic established in 2012, and moved the production to Chinese subcontractors with lower labour costs. During the years 2000–03, the cluster reached its maximum size of about 300 firms, employing about 30,000 workers. In the subsequent decade, no new important local start-ups (or MNE spin-offs) fed the cluster. Recently, also the old local firm Guban has been sold to foreign investors. Production moved to China and to other low-cost countries.

Local firms are currently small, with declining internal occupational levels, and the total employment has decreased to about 20,000 workers. A marginal fringe of Romanian entrepreneurs is now producing low-cost shoes for the internal market, but the cluster is no longer specialized in shoes; it is now formed by subcontractors working for electronics and components for the automotive industry. Timişoara does not exhibit any chain upgrading, but a horizontal transfer to new industries, which may pay higher wages and demand better skills.

All service activities – such as research, design and marketing – are developed in Italy and abroad in the MNEs' headquarters. Also for this reason, we did not find any evidence about knowledge transfer dynamics from the MNEs to the local context.

Discussion and conclusions

We explored the modality through which MNEs and clusters are intrinsically interlinked. Our paper analyses the heterogeneous evolutionary patterns of MNEs and clusters, and tries to detect some major implications in terms of prevailing knowledge acquisition, diffusion models and cluster performance. There are three ideal-type phases of cluster life cycle: origin (emergence), development (increased number of firms and employees) and maturity (stability or relative decline of firms and/or employees). Among said phases, we found the presence of an unavoidable heterogeneity, which characterizes not only the variety of triggering factors at the basis of the FDI choice of entry, but also the role played by MNEs in each phase, and the size distribution and roles played by local cluster firms. The cases presented above show that in some instances MNEs are the main actors that gave rise to the cluster. In other situations they entered (or emerged in) the cluster in the maturity phase. In both instances, MNEs are building place-anchored value chains, but in the latter case they operate also as competence seekers that are able to leverage their networks to effectively manage dispersed knowledge assets. They do this by tapping into a cluster to assimilate and integrate local knowledge (Mudambi, 2002).

The impact of MNEs on the knowledge governance of the cluster, and economic and innovative performance, does not indicate a unique direction. There is a relevant difference between types of clusters and timing of entry. In the case of clusters generated by MNEs, the MNEs that originated the cluster try to take advantage of resources that are abundant in the locality, which give them some short-term advantages. Being the cluster populated mostly by MNEs, each one keeping its knowledge linkages with headquarters and external-to-the-cluster partners, the knowledge acquisition model is the direct-peer (as illustrated by Belussi et al., 2011). Small indigenous firms (often subcontractors) are almost excluded by the process. This is the case of Dongguan and Timişoara, where the presence of external MNEs produces limited or no impact in terms of support for the growth of new endogenous entrepreneurship and innovation patterns.

In the maturity phase, the entry of foreign investors can result in increased levels of concentration in the governance of external knowledge flows. The process is exemplified by the Riviera del Brenta case: the pool of local knowledge – which is in a lock-in phase, with local entrepreneurs being less and less capable to find new uses for old knowledge bases – is captured and reused by the MNEs that enter the cluster through acquisitions or greenfield investments. The overall impact of the MNEs seems to be positive because they saved the productive capacity of the cluster. However, we are in the presence of a puzzling situation where processes of functional degrading combine with product upgrading.

In the Montebelluna cluster, the entry of MNEs generated a relative low increase in knowledge flows. Some types of knowledge spillovers arising from the presence of MNEs were produced, but mainly related to commercial strategies. Indeed, several local businesses have tried to imitate some marketing behaviours of MNEs. However, the role of foreign MNEs is still marginal, while home-grown MNEs are playing an important role in the district.

Nevertheless, it is worthy to notice that, in general, as the industry grows worldwide and the cluster reaches the maturity stage, the role of agglomeration and geographical proximity diminish in importance, leaving peripheral global firms, located outside the cluster, to grow faster. In addition to that, the maturity stage is often associated to a decline of the innovative activity of incumbent firms, due to 1) the exhaustion of the technological opportunities, 2) the decreasing variety across firms, and 3) the cognitive lock-in (Ter Wal and Boschma, 2011; Tödtling et al., 2017). Global producers gain increasing relevance, together with their global value chains. This happens, for instance, in the case of Nike and Adidas. Therefore, cluster evolution, as also suggested by Trippl et al. (2015), must be analysed from a multi-scalar perspective, which combines industry-driven explanations with cluster-specific ones, within an interpretative framework which accounts for the geographical scale of the growth driving factors. On the basis of these considerations, we argue that foreign firms localized in Northern countries show a better innovative and economic performance than firms in Montebelluna, because of their location within advanced regional or national innovation systems, which proved to be more dynamic than those of the Veneto region or Italy. Thus, a dynamic cluster such as Montebelluna suffers from being an "island" not supported by an advanced institutional and technological context.

In the Riviera del Brenta cluster, some localized pools of skills still play an important role: this happens where local craft skills are used for manufacturing luxury shoes. Nevertheless, the most crucial competitive capabilities are those of firms coming from outside the district, which are inserted in business networks stretching on a global scale and combine different types of resources, skills and market accesses. The presence of these MNEs in the cluster gives rise to a model of place-anchored value chains

Notes

1 A leading firm in a cluster can be defined in a kind of subjective way. It exhibits particular positive characteristics related to turn-over, size, number of employees, production capacity, market share, technological excellence, and centrality of relationships (Lomi and Lorenzoni, 1992; Lazerson and Lorenzoni. 1999; Belussi and Pilotti, 2002; Zanni, 2004; Klepper, 2010). This concept is similar to that developed by Boari (2001) on focal firms. While MNEs localized in clusters tend to be leading firms, the inverse is not true: not all leading firms are MNEs. The concept of anchor firms in clusters was developed, among others, by Feldman (2003) and Belussi and Sedita (2009) and it refers to the agglomerative process triggered by early founders.

2 The productive model of Nike and Adidas is still different, and more similar to the one discussed by the GVC literature, where the MNEs play the role of creative producers and large buyers of subcontracting activities spread around in low costs countries.

3 However, as we will discuss in what follows, the relationships with the local training school (Politecnico Calzaturiero) are still very important both for local and MNE firms.

4 Table 5.1 was constructed by collecting all publications present in the ISI-Thomson Reuters Web of Science database (ISI) in September 2016, covering all the literature published until the end of December 2015. We delimited the topic by searching for articles on: 'industrial district*' and 'multinational*'; or 'industrial district*' and FDI; or 'cluster*' and 'multinational*'; or 'cluster*' and FDI. The table shows the articles retrieved in the most relevant journals in the fields of economic geography, management and innovation, and international business.

5 We thank Ruscanu Loredana for her help with the 30 interviews conducted in June 2016.

References

Amighini, A., and Rabellotti, R. (2006). The effects of globalization on Italian industrial districts: Evidence from the footwear sector. *European Planning Studies*, 14(4): 485–502.

Asmussen, C.G., Pedersen, T., and Dhanaraj, C. (2009). Host-country environment and subsidiary competence: Extending the diamond network model. *Journal of International Business Studies*, 40(1): 42–57.

Audirac, I. (2003). Information-age landscapes outside the developed world Bangalore, India, and Guadalajara, Mexico. *Journal of the American Planning Association*, 69(1): 16–32.

Bagchi-Sen, S., and Lawton Smith, H. (2008). Science, institutions, and markets: Developments in the Indian biotechnology sector. *Regional Studies*, 42(7): 961–975.

Bair, J., and Gereffi, G. (2001). Local clusters in global chains: The causes and consequences of export dynamism in Torreon's blue jeans industry. *World Development*, 29: 1885–1903.

Bathelt, H., and Li, P.F. (2014). Global cluster networks – Foreign direct investment flows from Canada to China. *Journal of Economic Geography*, 14(1): 45–71.

Becker, J. (2014). Social Ties, Resources, and Migrant Labour Contention in Contemporary China: From Peasants to Protesters. Lanham: Lexington Books.

Bellandi, M. (2001). Local development and embedded large firms. *Entrepreneurship and Regional Development*, 13(3): 189–210.

Bellandi, M., and Caloffi, A. (2008). District internationalisation and trans-local development. *Entrepreneurship and Regional Development*, 20(6): 517–532.

Bellandi, M., and Caloffi, A. (2010). Forms of industrial development in Chinese specialized towns and types of challenges to European manufacturing SMEs: An Italian perspective. In H. Lenihan, B. Andreosso-O'Callaghan and M. Hart (eds.), *SMEs in a Globalised World. Survival and Growth Strategies on Europe's Geographical Periphery*. Cheltenham: Edward Elgar, pp. 113–132.

Belussi, F. (2010a). The evolution of a technologically dynamic district: The case of Montebelluna. In F. Belussi and A. Sammarra (eds.), *Business Networks in Clusters and Industrial Districts*. Abingdon: Routledge, pp. 90–113.

Belussi, F. (2010b). Transferring entrepreneurship: The making of the cluster of Timişoara. In F. Belussi and A. Sammarra (eds.), *Business Networks in Clusters and Industrial Districts*. Abingdon: Routledge, pp. 172–185.

Belussi, F., and Caldari, K. (2005). Fiducia e cooperazione nei processi di distrettualizzzione. *Sviluppo Locale*, 23–24: 52–81.

Belussi, F., and Pilotti, L. (2002). Knowledge creation, learning and innovation in Italian industrial districts. *Geografiska Annaler*, Series B, Human Geography, 84(2): 125–139.

Belussi, F., and Samarra, A. (2005). The opening of the industrial district value chain throughout inflow and outflow processes: How multinationals and international R&D co-operative networks have transformed the biomedical district of Mirandola. In F. Belussi and A. Samarra (eds.), *Industrial Districts, Relocation, and the Governance of the Global Value Chain*. Padova: Cleup, pp. 375–403.

Belussi, F., and Sammarra, A. (2010) (eds.), *Business Networks in Clusters and Industrial Districts*. Abingdon: Routledge.

Belussi, F., and Scarpel, M. (2002). L'evoluzione recente del distretto della Riviera del Brenta: Un approccio organizzativo. *Economia e Politica Industriale*, 115: 43–72.

Belussi, F., and Sedita, S.R. (2009). Life cycle vs. multiple path dependency in industrial districts. *European Planning Studies*, 17(4): 505–528.

Belussi, F., Sedita, S.R., Aage, T., and Porcellato, D. (2011). Inward flows of information and knowledge in low-tech industrial districts: Contrasting the 'few firms gatekeeper' and 'direct-peer' models. In P. Robertson and D. Jacobson (eds.), *Knowledge Transfer and Technology Diffusion*. Celtenham: Elgar.

Belussi, F., Sedita, S.R., and Caloffi, A. (2013). *Heterogeneity of MNEs Entry Modes in Industrial Clusters: An Evolutionary Approach Based on the Cluster Life Cycle Model*. Paper presented at the 35th DRUID Celebration Conference 2013, Barcelona, Spain, June 17–19.

Benito, G.R. (2005). Divestment and international business strategy. *Journal of Economic Geography*, 5(2): 235–251.

Biggiero, L. (2006). Industrial and knowledge relocation strategies under the challenges of globalization and digitalization: the move of small and medium enterprises among territorial systems. *Entrepreneurship and Regional Development*, 18(6): 443–471.

Birkinshaw, J. (2000). Upgrading of industry clusters and foreign investment. *International Studies of Management and Organization*, 30(2): 93–113.

Blomström, M., Globerman, S., and Kokko, A. (2000). *The Determinants of Host Country Spillovers from Foreign Direct Investment*. CEPR Discussion Paper 2350. London: Centre for Economic Policy Research.

Boari, C. (2001). Industrial Clusters, Focal Firms, and Economic Dynamism: A Perspective From Italy. Washington, DC: World Bank Institute.

Brenner, T. (2004). Local Industrial Clusters, Existence, Emergence and Evolution. London: Routledge.

Brown, R. (2000). Clusters, supply chains and local embeddedness in Fyrstad. *European Urban and Regional Studies*, 7(4): 291–305.

Brusco, S. (1986). Small firms and industrial districts: The experience of Italy. In D. Keeble and E. Wever (eds.), *New Firms and Regional Development in Europe*. London: Croom Helm, pp. 184–202.

Buciuni, G., and Pisano, G.P. (2015). Can Marshall's clusters survive globalization? *HBS Scholarly Articles*, n. 484, available at http://nrs.harvard.edu/urn-3:HUL.InstRepos:15548532. Accessed on June 2016.

Cantwell, J., and Mudambi, R. (2005). MNE competence-creating subsidiary mandates. *Strategic Management Journal*, 26(12): 1109–1128.

Cantwell, J., and Zhang, Y. (2011). Innovation and location in the multinational firm. *International Journal of Technology Management*, 54(1): 116–132.

Chen, S., and Karwan, K. (2008). Innovative cities in China: Lessons from Pudong New District, Zhangjiang high-tech park and SMIC village. *Innovation*, 10(2-3): 247–256.

Chen, Y.C. (2008). Why do multinational corporations locate their advanced R&D centres in Beijing? *The Journal of Development Studies*, 44(5): 622–644.

Chiarvesio, M., Di Maria, E., and Micelli, S. (2010). Global value chains and open networks: The case of Italian industrial districts. *European Planning Studies*, 18(3): 333–350.

Cornford, J., and Robins, K. (1992). Development strategies in the audiovisual industries: The case of North East England. *Regional Studies*, 26(5): 421–435.

Crone, M., and Roper, S. (2001). Local learning from multinational plants: Knowledge transfers in the supply chain. *Regional Studies*, 35(6): 535–548.

De Marchi, V., Lee, J., and Gereffi, G. (2014). Globalization, recession and the internationalization of industrial districts: Experiences from the Italian gold jewellery industry. *European Planning Studies*, 22(4): 866–884.

De Martino, R., Mc Hardy Reid, D., and Zygliodopoulos, S.C. (2006). Balancing localization and globalization: exploring the impact of firm internationalization on a regional cluster. *Entrepreneurship and Regional Development*, 18(1): 1–24.

Demirbag, M., and Glaister, K.W. (2010). Factors determining offshore location choice for R&D projects: A comparative study of developed and emerging regions. *Journal of Management Studies*, 47(8): 1534–1560.

Depner, H., and Bathelt, H. (2005). Exporting the German model: the establishment of a new automobile industry cluster in Shanghai. *Economic Geography*, 81(1): 53–81.

De Propris, L., and Driffield, N.L. (2006). The importance of cluster for spillover from FDI and technology sourcing. *Cambridge Journal of Economics*, 30(2): 277–291.

De Propris, L., Menghinello, S., and Sugden, R. (2008). The internationalisation of production systems: Embeddedness, openness and governance. *Entrepreneurship and Regional Development*, 20(6): 493–515.

Dunning, J.H. (1994). Multinational enterprises and the globalization of innovatory capacity. *Research Policy*, 23(1): 67–88.

Dunning, J.H. (1998). Location and the multinational enterprise: A neglected factor? *Journal of International Business Studies*, 29(1): 45–66.

Dunning, J.H. (2000). The eclectic paradigm as an envelope for economic and business theories of MNE activity. *International Business Review*, 9(1): 163–190.

Edgington, D., and Hayter, R. (2013). The in situ upgrading of Japanese electronics firms in Malaysian industrial clusters. *Economic Geography*, 89(3): 227–259.

Fang, T., and Lin, C. (2015). Minimum wages and employment in China. *IZA Journal of Labour Policy*, 4(22): 1–30.

Feldman, M. (2003). The locational dynamics of the US biotech industry: Knowledge externalities and the anchor hypothesis. *Industry and Innovation*, 10(3): 311–329.

Feldman, M.P., and Braunerhjelm, P. (eds.). (2007). *Cluster Genesis: Technology-based Industrial Development*. Oxford: Oxford University Press.

Finegold, D., Wong, P.K., and Cheah, T.C. (2004). Adapting a foreign direct investment strategy to the knowledge economy: the case of Singapore's emerging biotechnology cluster. *European Planning Studies*, 12(7): 921–941.

Fromhold-Eisebith, M. (2002). Regional cycles of learning: Foreign multinationals as agents of technological upgrading in less developed countries. *Environment and Planning A*, 34(12): 2155–2173.

Gereffi, G. (1999). International trade and industrial upgrading in the apparel commodity chain. *Journal of International Economics*, 48(1): 37–70.

Gereffi, G., and Bair, J. (2001). Local clusters in global chains: The causes and consequences of export dynamism in Torreon's blue jeans industry. *World Development*, 29(11): 1885–1903.

Gereffi, G., and Kaplinsky, R. (2001). The value of value chain: Spreading the gains from globalisation. *IDS Bulletin*, 32: 3.

Gereffi, G., and Korzeniewicz, M. (eds.). (1994). *Commodity Chains and Global Capitalism*. Westport: Praeger.

Gereffi, G., Humphrey, J., and Sturgeon, T. (2005). The governance of global value chains. *Review of International Political Economy*, 12(1): 78–104.

Giblin, M., and Ryan, P. (2012). Tight clusters or loose networks? The critical role of inward foreign direct investment in cluster creation. *Regional Studies*, 46(2): 245–258.

Giblin, M., and Ryan, P. (2015). Anchor, incumbent and late entry MNEs as propellents of technology cluster evolution. *Industry and Innovation*, 22(7): 553–574.

Giuliani, E., Pietrobelli, C., and Rabellotti, R. (2005). Upgrading in global value chains: Lessons from Latin American clusters. *World Development*, 33(4): 549–573.

Görg, H., and Greenaway, D. (2004). Much ado about nothing? Do domestic firms really benefit from foreign direct investment? *The World Bank Research Observer*, 19(2): 171–197.

Gugler, P., Keller, M., and Tinguely, X. (2015). The role of clusters in the global innovation strategy of MNEs: Theoretical foundations and evidence from the Basel pharmaceutical cluster. *Competitiveness Review*, 25(3): 324–340.

Harrison, B. (1994). Concentrated economic power and Silicon Valley. *Environment and Planning A*, 26(2): 307–328.

Hervas-Oliver, J.L., and Albors-Garrigos, J. (2008). Local knowledge domains and the role of MNE affiliates in bridging and complementing a cluster's knowledge. *Entrepreneurship and Regional Development*, 20(6): 581–598.

Hervas-Oliver, J.L., Albors-Garrigos, J., and Hidalgo, A. (2011). Global value chain reconfiguration through external linkages and the development of newcomers: A global story of clusters and innovation. *International Journal of Technology Management*, 55(1/2): 82–109.

Holm, U., Malmberg, A., and Sölvell, O. (2003). Subsidiary impact on host-country economies – The case of foreign-owned subsidiaries attracting investment into Sweden. *Journal of Economic Geography*, 3(4): 389–408.

Humphrey, J., and Schmitz, H. (2002). How does insertion in global value chains affect upgrading in industrial clusters? *Regional Studies*, 36(9): 1017–1027.

Iammarino, S., and McCann, P. (2010). The relationship between multinational firms and innovative clusters. In R. Boschma and R.L. Martin (eds.), *The Handbook of Evolutionary Economic Geography*. Cheltenham: Edward Elgar, pp. 182–204.

Ivarsson, I. (2002). Transnational corporations and the geographical transfer of localised technology: A multi-industry study of foreign affiliates in Sweden. *Journal of Economic Geography*, 2(2): 221–247.

Kearns, A., and Gorg, H. (2002). Linkages, agglomerations and knowledge spillovers in the Irish electronics industry: The regional dimension. *International Journal of Technology Management*, 24(7-8): 743–763.

Kenney, M., Massini, S., and Murtha, T.P. (2009). Offshoring administrative and technical work: New fields for understanding the global enterprise. *Journal of International Business Studies*, 40(6): 887–900.

Kim, J.Y., and Zhang, L. (2008). Formation of FDI clustering – A new path to local economic development? The case of electronics cluster in Qingdao City. *Regional Studies*, 42(2): 265–280.

Klepper, S. (2010). The origin and growth of industry clusters: The making of Silicon Valley and Detroit. *Journal of Urban Economics*, 67(1): 15–32.

Lazerson, M., and Lorenzoni, G. (1999). The firms that feed industrial districts: A return to the Italian source. *Industrial and Corporate Change*, 8(2): 235–266.

Lipsey, R.E. (2004). Home- and host-country effects of foreign direct investment. In R.E. Baldwin and L.A. Winters (eds.), *Challenges to Globalisation*. Chicago: Chicago University Press.

Lo, W., Niu, H.J., Yang, C., and Wang, Y.D. (2010). Determinants of manufacturing location in China: An examination of Taiwan-invested electronics assembly plants. *Journal of Contemporary Asia*, 40(4): 638–655.

Lomi, A., and Lorenzoni, G. (1992). Impresa guida e organizzazione a rete. In G. Lorenzoni (ed.), *Accordi, reti e vantaggio competitivo*. Milano: Etas.

Majocchi, A., and Presutti, M. (2009). Industrial clusters, entrepreneurial culture and the social environment: The effects on FDI distribution. *International Business Review*, 18(1): 76–88.

Manning, S. (2008). Customizing clusters: On the role of western multinational corporations in the formation of science and engineering clusters in emerging economies. *Economic Development Quarterly*, 22(4): 316–323.

Manning, S., Ricart, J.E., Rique, M.S.R., and Lewin, A.Y. (2010). From blind spots to hotspots: How knowledge services clusters develop and attract foreign investment. *Journal of International Management*, 16(4): 369–382.

Markusen, A. (1996). Sticky places in slippery space: A typology of industrial districts. *Economic Geography*, 72(3): 293–313.

Mason, CM., and Harrison, R.T. (2006). After the exit: Acquisitions, entrepreneurial recycling and regional economic development. *Regional Studies*, 40(1): 55–73.

McCann, P., and Mudambi, R. (2004). The location behaviour of the multinational enterprise: Some analytical issues. *Growth and Change*, 35(4): 491–524.

McCann, P., and Mudambi, R. (2005). Analytical differences in the economics of geography: The case of the multinational firm. *Environment and Planning A*, 37(10): 1857–1876.

McCann, P., Arita, T., and Gordon, I.R. (2002). Industrial clusters, transactions costs and the institutional determinants of MNE location behaviour. *International Business Review*, 11(6): 647–663.

Menghinello, S., De Propris, L., and Driffield, N. (2010). Industrial districts, inward foreign investment and regional development. *Journal of Economic Geography*, 10(4): 539–558.

Menzel, M., and Fornahl, D. (2010). Cluster life cycles. Dimensions and rationales of cluster evolution. *Industrial and Corporate Change*, 19(1): 205–238.

Morrison, A., Pietrobelli, C., and Rabellotti, R. (2008). Global value chains and technological capabilities: A framework to study learning and innovation in developing countries. *Oxford Development Studies*, 36(1): 39–58.

Mudambi, R. (2002). Knowledge management in multinational firms. *Journal of International Management*, 8(1): 1–9.

Mudambi, R., and Santangelo, G.D. (2016). From shallow resource pools to emerging clusters: The role of multinational enterprise subsidiaries in peripheral areas. *Regional Studies*, 50(12): 1965–1979.

Mudambi, R., and Santangelo, G.D. (2014). From shallow resource pools to emerging clusters: The role of multinational enterprise subsidiaries in peripheral areas. *Regional Studies*, 50(12): 1965–1979.

Mudambi, R., and Swift, T. (2012). Multinational enterprises and the geographical clustering of innovation. *Industry and Innovation*, 19(1): 1–21.

Nachum, L., and Keeble, D. (2003). Neo-Marshallian clusters and global networks: The linkages of media firms in Central London. *Long Range Planning*, 36(5): 459–480.

Nadvi, K., and Halder, G. (2005). Local clusters in global value chains: Exploring dynamic linkages between Germany and Pakistan. *Entrepreneurship and Regional Development*, 17(5): 339–363.

National Labour Committee. (2009). *High Tech Misery in China. The Dehumanization of Young Workers Producing Our Computer Keyboards*. Available at: www.globallabourrights.org/reports/HIGHTECH_MISERY_CHINA_WEB.pdf

OECD. (2000). *Main Determinants and Impacts of Foreign Direct Investment on China's Economy*. OECD Working Papers on International Investment, No. 2000/4, Paris: OECD.

Oliver, J.L.H., Garrigos, J.A., and Porta, J.I.D. (2008). External ties and the reduction of knowledge asymmetries among clusters within global value chains: The case of the ceramic tile district of Castellon. *European Planning Studies*, 16(4): 507–520.

Østergaard, R.C., and Park, E. (2015). What makes clusters decline? A study on disruption and evolution of a high-tech cluster in Denmark. *Regional Studies*, 49(5): 834–849.

Perez-Aleman, P. (2005). Cluster formation, institutions and learning: The emergence of clusters and development in Chile. *Industrial and Corporate Change*, 14(4): 651–677.

Phelps, N.A. (2008). Cluster or capture? Manufacturing foreign direct investment, external economies and agglomeration. *Regional Studies*, 42(4): 457–473.

Phelps, N., MacKinnon, D., Stone, I., and Braidford, P. (2003). Embedding the multinationals? Institutions and the development of overseas manufacturing affiliates in Wales and North East England. *Regional Studies*, 37(1): 27–40.

Po, L. (2006). Repackaging globalization: A case study of the advertising industry in China. *Geoforum*, 37(5): 752–764.

Potter, A., and Watts, H.D. (2011). Evolutionary agglomeration theory: Increasing returns, diminishing returns, and the industry life cycle. *Journal of Economic Geography*, 11(3): 417–455.

Raines, P., Turok, I., and Brown, R. (2001). Growing global: Foreign direct investment and the internationalization of local suppliers in Scotland. *European Planning Studies*, 9(8): 965–978.

Ramanauskas, G., Amdam, R.P., and Lunnan, R. (2007). FDI and the transformation from industry to service society in emerging economies: A Lithuanian-Nordic perspective. *Engineering Economics*, 1 (51): 22–28.

Rugman, A.M., and Verbeke, A. (2003). Multinational enterprises and clusters: An organizing framework. *Management International Review*, 43(3): 151–169.

Sajarattanochote, S., and Poon, J.P. (2009). Multinationals, geographical spillovers, and regional development in Thailand. *Regional Studies*, 43(3): 479–494.

Sammarra, A., and Belussi, F. (2006). Evolution and relocation in fashion-led Italian districts: Evidence from two case-studies. *Entrepreneurship and Regional Development*, 18(6): 543–562.

Sjöholm, F. (2002). The challenge of combining FDI and regional development in Indonesia. *Journal of Contemporary Asia*, 32(3): 381–393.

Sturgeon, T., Van Biesebroeck, J., and Gereffi, G. (2008). Value chains, networks and clusters: Reframing the global automotive industry. *Journal of Economic Geography*, 8(3): 297–321.

Tallman, S., and Fladmoe-Lindquist, K. (2002). Internationalization, globalization, and capability-based strategy. *California Management Review*, 45(1): 116–135.

Ter Wal, A.L., and Boschma, R. (2011). Co-evolution of firms, industries and networks in space. *Regional Studies*, 45(7): 919–933.

Teubal, M., Avnimelech, G., and Gayego, A. (2002). Company growth, acquisitions and access to complementary assets in Israel's data security sector. *European Planning Studies*, 10(8): 933–953.

Thompson, E.R. (2002). Clustering of foreign direct investment and enhanced technology transfer: Evidence from Hong Kong garment firms in China. *World Development*, 30(5): 873-889.

Tödtling, F., Sinozic, T., and Auer, A. (2017). Driving factors of cluster evolution: A multiscalar comparative perspective. In F. Belussi and J.L. Hervás-Oliver (eds.), *Unfolding Cluster Evolution*. London: Routledge.

Tong, X., and Wang, J. (2002). Global-local networking of PC manufacturing in Dongguan, China. In R. Hayter and R. Le Heron (eds.), *Knowledge, Industry and Environment: Institutions and Innovation in Territorial Perspective*. Aldershot: Ashgate, pp. 67–86.

Trippl, M., Grillitsch, M., Isaksen, A., and Sinozic, T. (2015). Perspectives on cluster evolution: Critical review and future research issues. *European Planning Studies*, 23(10): 2028–2044.

Van Winden, W., Van Der Meer, A., and Van Den Berg, L. (2004). The development of ICT clusters in European cities: Towards a typology. *International Journal of Technology Management*, 28(3-6): 356–387.

Whalley, J., and Xian, X. (2010). China's FDI and non-FDI economies and the sustainability of future high Chinese growth. *China Economic Review*, 21(1): 123–135.

Whitford, J. (2001). The decline of a model? Challenge and response in the Italian industrial districts. *Economy and Society*, 30(1): 38–65.

Wickham, J., and Vecchi, A. (2008). Local firms and global reach: Business air travel and the Irish software cluster. *European Planning Studies*, 16(5): 693–710.

Yang, C. (2009). Strategic coupling of regional development in global production networks: Redistribution of Taiwanese personal computer investment from the Pearl River Delta to the Yangtze River Delta, China. *Regional Studies*, 43(3): 385–407.

Yang, C., and Liao, H. (2010). Industrial agglomeration of Hong Kong and Taiwanese manufacturing investment in China: A town-level analysis in Dongguan. *The Annals of Regional Science*, 45(3): 487–517.

Yang, Y. (2006). *The Taiwanese Notebook Computer Production Network in China: Implication for Upgrading of the Chinese Electronics Industry*. WP Personal Computing Industry Center 02–01– 2006. Available at: https://escholarship.org/uc/item/9069n2sb.

Young, S., Hood, N., and Peters, E. (1994). Multinational enterprises and regional economic development. *Regional Studies*, 28(7): 657–677.

Zanni, L. (2004). *Leading Firms and Wine Clusters*. Milano: Franco Angeli.

Zhao, S.X., and Zhang, L. (2007). Foreign direct investment and the formation of global city-regions in China. *Regional Studies*, 41(7): 979–994.

Zhou, Y. (2005). The making of an innovative region from a centrally planned economy: Institutional evolution in Zhongguancun Science Park in Beijing. *Environment and Planning A*, 37(6): 1113–1134.

Zhou, Y., Sun, Y., Wei, Y.H., and Lin, G. (2011). De-centering 'spatial fix'—patterns of territorialization and regional technological dynamism of ICT hubs in China. *Journal of Economic Geography*, 11(1): 119–150.

Zhou, Y., and Xin, T. (2003). An innovative region in China: interaction between multinational corporations and local firms in a high-tech cluster in Beijing. *Economic Geography*, 79(2): 129–152.

6 Global value chains and the role of MNEs in local production systems

Mariachiara Barzotto, Giancarlo Corò and Mario Volpe

Introduction

In the last decades, economic activity has become international, not only in terms of the exchange of goods and services, but also in its organization (Gereffi et al., 2001). We have been witness to a reorganization of economic activities that has led to the fragmentation of production processes on a global scale and, accordingly, to the formation of GVCs.

The international fragmentation of production has emerged through the offshoring processes undertaken by MNEs. These processes consist of the transfer of activities in the value chain to regions with lower operating costs or specialized skills, and sometimes even to the widening of markets (Gereffi and Sturgeon, 2004). Many companies have moved lower value-added activities to low-labour cost countries, maintaining in the domestic market the upstream and downstream activities considered less replaceable and able to capture larger shares of economic value (see the literature on the smile curve, Everatt et al., 1999; Mudambi, 2008; for a critical perspective, see Buciuni et al., 2014). The extensive pursuit of this strategy of commoditizing manufacturing by companies in industrialized countries has produced effects on the resource endowment of the areas involved in GVCs, both in advanced and in emerging economies. Specifically, this labour division has led companies more open to international networks to drift progressively apart from their domestic productive ecosystem. In the territories in question, this move away from the domestic environment has generated a gradual dissipation of their "industrial commons" (Pisano and Shih, 2012); that is, the set of external economies of localization that companies in IDs widely employ, albeit often unconsciously, such as "R&D and manufacturing infrastructure, know-how process-development skills, and engineering capabilities embedded in firms, universities, and other organizations that provide the foundation for growth and innovation in a wide range of industries" (Pisano and Shih, 2012, p. 2). Indeed, relocation of operations to companies in emerging economies has led – in the domestic base – to the hollowing out of specialized supplier networks, competitors and qualified workforces, as well as experienced managers. The fading of this system of resources has accompanied the contraction of the knowledge spillovers (e.g. Capello and Lenzi, 2015) needed to keep the local manufacturing fabric engaged with production activities. The geographic separation from production activities seems to lead advanced economies to a severe reduction in the circulation of know-how necessary to create new products, to improve and innovate existing ones, and to be competitive in the long run (Berger, 2013; Ketokivi and Ali-Yrkkö, 2009).

The advantages arising from being part of a GVC, as well as the role of external economies for the competitiveness of firms and the overall ID, have been examined in the literature (e.g. De Marchi et al., 2014). However, the interplay between the local and global contexts is rather overlooked. Previous studies have started to shed light on the role of leading firms in fostering external knowledge diffusion at the district level (Morrison, 2008) and, more recently, on how the combination of local and non-local skills shapes new "cluster dependent" knowledge (Hervas-Oliver and Boix-Domenech, 2013, p. 1077). Nevertheless, there is still scant evidence for the link between companies' international presence and the reproduction of local factors embedded in the IDs sustaining manufacturing, such as home country employment and productivity growth (for an exception, see Castellani and Pieri, 2015; Elia et al., 2009). Exploring this relationship would provide policymakers with a deeper understanding of which externalities can positively affect the sustainability of the resources present in district areas as part of a globalized environment.

In light of this limitation of the existing literature, the following research questions emerge as interesting, and relevant, yet under-studied, issues: *Why do local companies which have grown into the global market still locate their main activities in district areas? Under what circumstances does the presence of MNEs engaging both in global and local connections play a supportive role in the development of district areas?*

This work aims to contribute to filling these gaps by providing empirical evidence to identify possible actions that an MNE can undertake to sustain the distinctive assets of an ID, those originally developed within a community of people and a population of firms in one naturally and historically bounded area (Becattini, 1990, p. 38). To address these issues, we focus on MNEs (three lead firms and seven specialized suppliers), as the emergence of large players in district systems has led to changes in the dynamics and relationships within the districts. Indeed, the use of local resources by MNEs potentially has a marked effect on the development of the industrial commons of the production systems in which they are embedded. Actions undertaken by MNEs can either strongly foster or equally strongly inhibit the reproduction of those assets that have enabled IDs to grow and become established over the years.

Industrial district and industrial commons: definitions and characteristics

Even though the division of labour in different production phases has traditionally enabled the thriving of small and medium companies, the evolutionary processes of the IDs show production systems characterized by the co-presence and the complementarities (Intesa Sanpaolo, 2015) of large, medium and small firms. Research has reported rising evidence of heterogeneity in terms of the size of companies populating an ID. As described by De Marchi et al. in Chapter 1 in this book, the presence of MNEs in the cluster has triggered new dynamics in the ID. To different extents, leading firms have moved both their business activities as well as their supply-chain relationships abroad by signing supply agreements and joint ventures in production, or alternatively by making proprietary investment in production plants or subsidiaries (De Marchi and Grandinetti, 2014). The presence of MNEs plays a crucial role in the knowledge diffusion within, as well as outside, the ID boundaries. In this respect, Morrison (2008) finds that MNEs as leading firms make significant efforts to search for and translate knowledge coming from external sources, including universities and sectoral research centres.

Over the last years, IDs have undergone a deep transformation. The dynamics brought about by an increasing heterogeneity of the ID fabric, along with globalization and technological changes, have had a considerable impact on the structure of the IDs. District firms – mainly medium and large ones – have increasingly established connections with actors located outside the district area, generating external economies that go beyond the cluster boundaries. The changes activated by firms based in districts in the geographical configuration of networks have led to the fading of the strong one-industry specialization originally peculiar to district areas. Nevertheless, a manufacturing supply infrastructure and know-how embedded in firms, the education system and public institutions can still be found in these territories to a certain extent. In light of the above-mentioned evolutionary processes, the concept of industrial commons seems to be more suitable to describe the resources currently present in district areas. Indeed, the definition of industrial commons coined by Pisano and Shih (2009) extends beyond the district dimension to the web of relationships among R&D and manufacturing infrastructures distinctive to an ID. Pisano and Shih (2009) define industrial commons as "the set of manufacturing and technical capabilities that support innovation across a broad range of industries" (2009, p. xii). It consists of "technological know-how, operational capabilities, and specialized skills that are embedded in the workforce, competitors, suppliers, customers, cooperatives R&D ventures, and universities and often support multiple industrial sectors" (2009, p. 13).

The ID concept constitutes the founding pillar to acknowledge the notion of industrial commons. It springs from the distinctive "industrial atmosphere" of IDs but goes beyond the circumscribed district areas to interpret the evolution of a geographically concentrated population of manufacturing and service companies, as well as the formation of inter-cluster innovation phenomena. The commons is constantly nourished by the knowledge flowing across companies through movements of employees, supplier-customer collaborations or formal and informal technology sharing. Knowledge spillover may occur amongst geographically proximate companies operating in different sectors but which are industrially complementary. As Pisano and Shih (2009) claim, these capabilities evolve over time and are likely to trigger the development of new products, both in the same industry and in new ones. Indeed, innovation in one industry is linked to development of other sectors; similarly, the decline of an industry commons is likely to damage other industries. Thus, bridging strong complementarities in capabilities with localized knowledge can pave the way to the flourishing of a specific industry, while inhibiting the development of others. As Pisano and Shih (2012) state, technical and operational capabilities to produce complex goods are strongly connected with a country's capacity to generate and capture value from innovation.

The international fragmentation of production, which gave rise to the creation of GVCs, has linked the industrial commons located in multiple countries as part of a same production ecosystem. The relocation of manufacturing activities to low labour-cost economies has undermined the sustainability of the industrial commons located in advanced countries due to the hollowing out of specialized supplier networks, competitors and qualified workforces, as well as experienced managers. Conversely, it has enabled the formation of commons in emerging countries by the creation of supplier infrastructures and, accordingly, local production systems.

The industrial commons can be classified as goods whose use is difficult to exclude from potential beneficiaries. These goods are also characterized by a certain degree of rivalry, especially when the allocation of these resources falls below a critical threshold. Given the nature of the positive externality of the industrial commons, two important aspects can be identified: first, the existence of a social benefit coming from the fact that the company can draw from the assets of the local commons without having to pay a price; second, the absence of property rights, which can easily give rise to a market equilibrium lower than the social optimum. Depending on the type of local resources, the imbalance arising from their under/over-exploitation can lead to the rapid disappearance of goods. The fact that people do not pay for the consumption of a common good leads them to use the resource at a higher rate than that at which it can be produced (over-exploitation imbalance of a tangible asset), eventually leading to its depletion. Hardin (1968) defines this phenomenon as a "tragedy of the commons". It might also be the case that common good under-use weakens the regeneration of the resource, determining its gradual disappearance. This is most likely to happen if the common good is an intangible resource, such as the industrial commons. Nevertheless, as shown in the masterful work of Elinor Ostrom (1990, 2010) we do not lack evidence nor models of successful governance of the use of the common goods, which have significant similarities with the system of local resources to which we refer.

This chapter explores what the industrial common assets are and why they keep local companies which have developed in the global market from locating their main activities outside the district areas. It then attempts to identify how MNEs can boost the regeneration of the industrial commons present in the district area in which the companies were founded, commons that have nourished their growth over the years. It investigates under what circumstances MNEs are able to sustain the local assets of their domestic bases through the simultaneous engagement with local industrial commons along with global ones, as part of the same production ecosystem. The exchange of resources between companies and the territory has a two-way structure: on the one hand, the locational context influences a firm's ability to compete in international markets; on the other, the features of this context are largely the outcome of enterprises' competitive strategies. Several local assets from which firms benefit constitute a common good produced by the interaction of a number of local actors, both public and private (Camagni, 2008). Consequently, entrepreneurial activities are essential in influencing the dynamics of agglomeration. It is the use of local assets by companies that can either reinforce or, on the contrary, weaken the formation of the industrial commons.

In our study, we focus on the analysis of immaterial assets, which emerge as the most critical ones in the literature on ID and industrial commons. We identify five local assets that are crucial for sustaining the development of an area and, accordingly, the innovation capabilities of the companies populating that territory: 1) labour pools and distinctive skills; 2) supplier and user networks; 3) education and research systems (including universities, higher education, lifelong education, public and private research centres); 4) public, private and associative institutions; and 5) the financial system and its ability to provide capital and information to companies.

Effects of companies' internationalization processes on the home-based industrial commons

Technological changes (mainly in digital innovation and integrated logistic developments) have enabled global openness in trading goods, services, information and production, giving manufacturing firms the "perception" of being "footloose" companies (Baldwin and Evenett, 2015). Supra-local organized relations (e.g. global networks of firms) might take place even in the absence of geographical proximity, as actors can collaborate by sharing rules and standards, as well as benefitting from the development of the long-distance mobility of individuals and information (Torre and Rallet, 2005). The implementation of new technologies has strongly impacted on the formation of production relationships. New technologies ease and strengthen the development of links outside the home-based industrial area, giving rise to the formation of GVCs.

Although the globalized economy might be seen as being characterized by an "increasing nomadism of firms" (Zimmerman, 1995), GVCs are not borderless and a-territorial networks. They are, instead, networks whose nodes are places where socio-economic-institutional activities are embedded (De Propris, 2010). Each area is endowed with specific commons, which are distinct from that of other socio-economic environments. The commons endowed in an area heavily affects the location decision of firms. In an increasingly global and competitive world, local territories become a key variable for the competitiveness of enterprises (OECD, 2001).

GVCs connect areas located in different countries that have territorial specialization – such as the ones occupied by IDs – in stages of the same production process. By reshaping the organization of economic activities through the creation of GVCs, globalization has led to a redefinition of the international networks of places, each of which is marked out by a specific economic task that still allows firms to exploit the competitive advantage of location (Baldwin and Evenett, 2015). The upgrading activities in emerging economies are undermining the competitive advantage of industrialized countries. Indeed, in high-income countries, the hollowing out of manufacturing activities has negatively impacted on their home-region productivity growth (Castellani and Pieri, 2015) and new job creation (Bailey et al., 2010). Globalization has strongly affected the firm population of IDs. It has weakened their socio-economic fabric and, accordingly, had a marked effect on their production structure, shrinking, amongst other things, the reproducibility of the entrepreneurial factor (De Marchi and Grandinetti, 2014). The drop in the critical mass of specific ties in the domestic socio-economic environment has contributed to the poorer performance of firms and their surrounding environment, a phenomenon known in the literature as the erosion of the industrial commons (Pisano and Shih, 2009). Firms in industrialized countries relocate their operations to emerging economies with the aim of intensifying resources in the development of activities with high-value added.

Contrary to expectations, the implementation of this strategy has led to an increasing volume of offshoring of functions requiring the involvement of highly-skilled workers (Blinder and Krueger, 2013). As shown by Pisano and Shih (2009) in their study on the offshoring of US industry, the economy runs the risk of weakening the foundation of skills and knowledge which support the most innovative activities (e.g. research) if the production system falls below a critical threshold of productive activity. Examining the effects of the transfer of production by multinational companies to foreign subsidiaries located both in low labour-cost countries and in industrialized ones, Elia et al. (2009) report three major production substitution effects on employment in foreign affiliates' domestic transfer: 1) a reduction in the domestic low-skilled workforce; 2) a loss of market share from local suppliers and the loss of the opportunity to learn and grow through the relationship with the leader firm; and 3) the sign-out of subcontracting agreements.

The depletion of the economic fabric in advanced economies has triggered significant reductions in knowledge circulation and, as a consequence, a shrinkage of knowledge spillovers. As widely shown by previous studies, knowledge externalities, informal knowledge and capabilities are crucial for the survival of innovative ecosystems (e.g. Anselin et al., 1997; Audretsch and Feldman, 1996; Ellison et al., 2007). Labour mobility and social networks (Agrawal et al., 2008; Breschi and Lissoni, 2009) have been identified as different mechanisms channelling knowledge flows, especially in the context of limited R&D intensity (Capello and Lenzi, 2015). The importance of informal knowledge flows amongst physically close, industrially complementary actors is even more critical in traditional sectors, such as low-tech manufacturing, where actors "rely more on technologies embodied in machinery and equipment" and "informal knowledge embedded in professionals" (Conte and Vivarelli, 2005 and Piergiovanni et al., 1997 as cited by Capello and Lenzi, 2015, p. 3).

The importance of engaging with global and local connections

The competitiveness of a company and the health of the communities around it are closely intertwined. As Porter and Kramer highlighted:

> A business needs a successful community, not only to create demand for its products but also to provide critical public assets and a supportive environment. A community

needs successful businesses to provide jobs and wealth creation opportunities for its citizens.

(Porter and Kramer, 2011, p. 6)

As this synergy occurs, territories need to connect local resources with non-local ones. Drawing on international business and economic geography literature, local companies could boost innovation and competitiveness by combining local and non-local knowledge, which generate unique repositories of knowledge or "knowledge domains" (Cooke, 2006). Given their international structure, MNEs emerge as pivotal actors that connect territories, convey information and knowledge amongst domestic and foreign actors, and articulate global pipelines.

As aforementioned, the intense reorganization of economic activity has been driven crucially by MNEs' offshoring strategies, which have led to the emergence of GVCs. MNEs have considered the creation of GVCs as an indispensable move in seeking to maintain their competitiveness vis-à-vis very price aggressive competitors, which has especially been the case in the manufacturing sector (Ramirez and Rainbird, 2010). Indeed, for lead firms in advanced economies, being involved in a GVC is a necessary condition for survival and, to a certain extent, their international presence is beneficial not just for the companies themselves, but also for home-region productivity. As the international business literature has shown, outward foreign direct investments (FDIs) are positively associated with sales increases for investing firms and their suppliers (Castellani and Pieri, 2015, p. 2). According to Castellani and Pieri (2010), FDIs show positive effects on regional productivity only up to a certain extent. If multinationals develop a "too" high volume of cross-border activities, the local supply chain slowly fades, forcing firms to turn to suppliers located outside the domestic base. Such a perspective threatens the sustainability of the growth process of the territory. To slow down this phenomenon, companies need to activate the production relationship with the actors populating their home-country territory. In the ID literature, scholars (e.g. Chiarvesio et al., 2010) have shown how some leading firms in ID have started acting as an "open network". These open network companies have extended their value chain beyond district borders and managed global networks in a completely different way with respect to the traditional model of industrial district firms, which is mainly organized on a local basis. Therefore, it is important to re-think the role of MNEs and how they could sustainably use their local and global networks. IDs can benefit from involvement in GVCs by, for instance, learning from the strategies applied by global buyers (e.g. Schmitz and Knorringa, 2000; Bair and Gereffi, 2001). Both MNEs and their domestic bases would benefit from the simultaneous use of global and local connections. In the results and discussion sections we present some of the possible simultaneous uses of global and local connections undertaken by lead firms, which would benefit the MNEs themselves, as well as the economic environment surrounding them.

Manufacturing and offshoring trends in Italy and specifically in the Veneto region

The manufacturing share of western European economies has been decreasing since 2000, falling by 3.3 percentage points of Gross Domestic Product (GDP) over the period 2000 to 2012. With an increase of 0.1 percentage points, Germany was the only western European country showing a manufacturing share of gross value added higher in 2012 compared to 2000. In the same period (2000–12), Finland reported the largest decrease in Western Europe (−10.2 percentage points), followed by Belgium (−5.9 percentage points), the United Kingdom (−5.6 percentage points), Sweden (−5.6 percentage points), France (−5.2 percentage points),

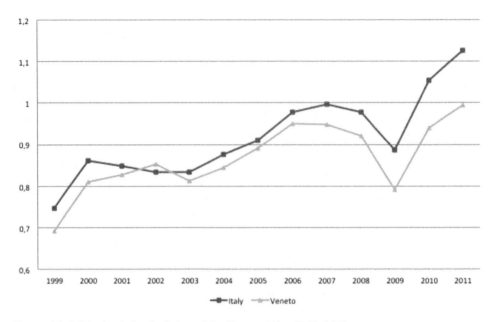

Figure 6.1 Offshoring index for Italy and the Veneto region 1999–2011

Source: Computation by Corò et al. (2013) based on Trade Statistics available from Istat, www.coeweb.it.

Denmark (−4.7 percentage points), Spain (−4.6 percentage points) and Italy (−4.5 percentage points) (Heymann and Vetter, 2013).[1]

International fragmentation has affected many production activities. In particular, with respect to the case of Italy, outsourcing has been crucial in the economic systems of the north-eastern region of Veneto, as well as the whole country, since 1999. As shown by Corò et al. (2013), in the period 1999–2011 the offshoring index, defined as the share of imports of manufacturing goods over value added in manufacturing, exhibited an upward trend (except in 2009) both at the national level and in Veneto itself (Figure 6.1). Corò et al. (2013) claim that the lower value of the index in Veneto compared to the value reported in Italy can be explained by the strong specialization of Veneto in manufacturing sectors. Manufacturing production in Veneto is mainly based in the industrial districts in the Made in Italy sectors. Indeed, this region hosts 28 industrial districts operating in these sectors, accounting for 62% of the districts in the north-eastern macro-area, and for about 20% of all districts in Italy. They are specialized in medium-high technology (mechanics: 43%), and low-technology sectors (home furniture: 25%; textile and clothing: 18%; leather and shoes: 7%; food and jewellery: 4% each) (ISTAT, 2015).

Notwithstanding the fact that the manufacturing industry is the sector that has mainly suffered from the impact of offshoring processes, the importance of this industry is still particularly relevant in advanced economies. For instance, in Europe the manufacturing sector accounts for over 15% of GDP (EU-27), but the overall impact on the economy is much greater, especially in terms of jobs. Rueda-Cantuche et al. (2012) have estimated that for every new job in manufacturing up to two jobs in other sectors will be created in Europe. Indeed, a solid industrial base not only generates the need for highly skilled workers, but also fosters labour markets in other sectors by inducing demand for related business functions and services. Moreover, a strong manufacturing industry contributes to sustaining, as well as stimulating, new export channels, as manufacturing exports on average account for over 50% of total exports in Western Europe (Kroker and Lichtblau, 2013 as cited by Heymann and Vetter, 2013, p. 2).

A balanced economy may be a powerful tool to better face economic downturns, and for this reason European policymakers are promoting a manufacturing renaissance by: 1) establishing "an industrial policy creating the best environment to maintain and develop a strong, competitive and diversified industrial base in Europe [. . .]" (EU Commission, 2010); and 2) reversing the declining role of industry in Europe by targeting an increasing share of the manufacturing sector of up to 20% of GDP by 2020 (EU Commission, 2012).

In 2012, Italy was the second-largest industrial country in the EU, after Germany. In the same year, it generated 12.5% of the total industrial gross value-added (GVA) within the EU, preceded only by Germany, with 30.5% of the total EU GVA (Eurostat, as cited by Heymann and Vetter, 2013).

Despite the decline in the manufacturing sector and the job losses, the northern Italian region of Lombardia (including the city of Milan) and the French capital city region of Île de France recorded the highest number of workers employed in manufacturing in 2012 at the NUTS-2 level within the EU-28. The regions with the next largest manufacturing workforces were Stuttgart (Germany) and the north-eastern Italian region of Veneto, with just over half a million people employed in manufacturing (Eurostat, 2016). In 2012, among the top 20 regions with the highest workforce share in the manufacturing sector, Eurostat (2016) reports eight German regions, followed by five in Italy, three in Poland, two in France, and one each in Spain and Portugal.

Methodology

Building on Yin's (2003) work, we adopt a multiple case study approach, as this represents a suitable research method given the exploratory nature of the analysis (Hartley, 1994; Silvi and Cuganesan, 2006). The in-depth investigation implied in this method allows the researcher to acquire a finer understanding of the specific phenomenon under analysis (Eisenhardt, 1989; Yin, 2003) and at the same time provides grounded evidence for whether the findings are idiosyncratic to a single case or generalizable, as they are consistently replicated in several cases (Eisenhardt, 1989). Thus, drawing on previous qualitative studies underlining the need to examine cases showing differences (Eisenhardt and Graebner, 2007), we have selected 10 manufacturing MNEs located in Veneto which differ in sector, internationalization process and the GVC to which they belong.

The 10 companies have been chosen primarily on the basis of four criteria:

1 They operate in industries that have faced considerable pressure from the global opening up processes in the last decades;
2 They are based in Italy and, in particular, in the Veneto region. The rationale for this choice is four-fold. First, Italy is the second-largest industrial country in the EU and Veneto recorded the highest number of workers employed in the manufacturing sector in 2012. Second, Italy has a long and renowned worldwide tradition in manufacturing, as above reported. Third, focusing on this manufacturing region allows us to explore the role played by MNEs in the emergence of new sectors stemming from the combination of know-how embedded in different IDs (inter-cluster innovation). Finally, keeping the industrial location constant (Navas-Alemán, 2011) enables us to control for legal, cultural, and socio-economic frameworks;

3   The selected companies operate in sectors in which Italy, and in particular Veneto, traditionally has a competitive advantage; for example, 1) high-quality mechanical engineering, automation and pharmaceuticals in the field of technology-intensive and medium-tech industries; and 2) textiles, apparel and furniture, with regard to traditional manufacturing industries.

4   The sampled companies are multinationals, as they are, by definition, multi-located. Hence, these companies have tools available to evaluate where to carry out their activities and how to undertake strategies of integrated production. This allows us to investigate to what extent the assets of the industrial commons present in Veneto are key resources for the companies.

To explore whether the ownership of the company could make a difference in sustaining the development of the local assets, we have considered firms that are both domestically and foreign owned. All the ten analysed companies are home-grown, but three of them have been acquired by foreign companies. Two of the three owned by foreign companies are controlled by investment funds, the other by an MNE operating in the same sector as the firm acquired. The high-level competencies of the Italian companies represent the main rationale of the foreign direct investments. The sampled firms differ in terms of type of governance and position in the GVC. Three of them are lead firms present in captive GVCs, whilst the remainder are specialized suppliers (six relational suppliers and one full-package supplier in a modular GVC). Notwithstanding their different roles, they all play the function of leading firms in the territory in which they are located. None of the companies analysed is a dominant player for the entire ID to which it belongs, but all of them are key leaders in their district area. The ten companies have kept R&D, logistics, ICT and corporate activities in-house, whilst they have undertaken different strategies in terms of the location of operations. Some of them decided not to move production from the Veneto base; others moved completely or partially abroad. Table 6.1 indicates the main economic features of the case studies and their position in the GVC in which they are involved. To guarantee the anonymity of the ten companies, we list them under pseudonyms.

The in-depth study of the ten cases is the result of the collection of primary and secondary data, through semi-structured interviews and archival research. Specifically, the archival research aimed to collect quantitative data through analysis of published corporate reports, financial reports, and companies' websites. The information gathered was subsequently supplemented by qualitative data obtained through in-depth interviews, mainly with human resource (HR) managers or Chief Executive Officers (CEOs). During the interviews we obtained information on the organization's international production activities, as well as the business functions that the company performs and where they take place. The specific links the company has established with the home-based socio-economic environment in which it is embedded were also investigated.

Results and discussion

Industrial commons strategic assets

The evidence collected clearly shows that the presence of critical skills, suppliers, and educational/training programs play an important role for companies and, in general, for their home-based production system.

Table 6.1 Case study main characteristics

Company	Industry	Turnover size class	Employment size class	Ownership	District	Type of governance and position in the GVC
Company One	Electric motors	5	5	Domestically owned	Mechatronics and innovative mechanical (M&iM) technologies (meta-district)	Relational supplier
Company Two	Glass installation	1*	4	Domestically owned	Vicenza gold district and furniture	Lead firm in a captive GVC
Company Three	Sportswear and protections	2*	2*	Foreign owned since 2014	Vicenza leather-tanning and Montebelluna sportsystem	Lead firm in a captive GVC
Company Four	Pharmaceuticals	1	2	Foreign owned since 2000	Area with high presence of pharmaceutical industry	Relational supplier
Company Five	Motors and generators	2	4	Foreign owned since 2013	M&iM technologies	Relational supplier
Company Six	Glass packaging and forming technology	4	5	Domestically owned	M&iM technologies	Full-package supplier
Company Seven	Apparatus and power systems	4	5	Domestically owned	M&iM technologies	Lead firm in a captive GVC
Company Eight	Machines and systems	4	5	Domestically owned	M&iM technologies	Relational supplier
Company Nine	Fashion	3	2	Domestically owned	Schio – Thiene – Valdagno textile and clothing	Relational supplier
Company Ten	Heating and electrical system	3*	5	Domestically owned	Conegliano electronic appliances	Relational supplier

Source: AIDA database by Bureau van Dijk and company reports.

Note: Turnover size class depending on annual turnover, in millions of Euros: 1 (less than 50); 2 (50–100); 3 (100–250); 4 (250 or more). Employment size depending on number of employees: 1 (1–99); 2 (100–249), 3 (250–499), 4 (500–999); 5 (1000 or more). Data refers to 2013.

* Unconsolidated

Labour pool

The know-how circulating in the ID area allows enterprises to source workers from a pool of people whose skills are tailored to enterprises' demands. The match between skills demand and supply, particularly those necessary for operations management, has allowed companies to develop high-quality products, customizing the offering according to demand needs and maintaining control over the innovation processes. As claimed by Company Ten's General Manager:

> The territory in which the company was founded ["Inox Valley" ID²] and has grown is endowed with such a strong and qualified human capital that it has allowed the company to reach its goal over time. He continues that "there is no application area in which we operate that cannot be supplied with the local human resources."

The human capital present in the local labour market prevents MNEs from making the decision to move production to more economically convenient areas. The technical skills of the people educated in the area match well the competencies needed by the firms, especially in operations.

> *We find these competencies ready in the market. Fortunately, here [in this area] the pool is broader than in other Italian regions and/or in other countries"*. Company Five's Chief HR and Organization Officer continues by saying *"here the walls exude electrical engineering.*
>
> (Company Five's Chief HR and Organization Officer)

> *In the territory, you can easily find the technical skills needed for operations.*
>
> (Company Eight's HR Manager)

Education system

From this perspective, an important role is played by the technical and vocational educational system, in which companies recognize the ability to have created a pool of technical skills and attitudes necessary to constantly develop new viable products.

> *We benefit from a local higher education (as well as vocational) presence which is extremely qualified. For instance, the local university shapes a pool of knowledgeable graduates. There is no obstacle in employing a mechanical engineer; the university prepares professional profiles that absolutely meet our needs.*
>
> (Company Seven's HR Manager)

> *If we talk about technical competencies, we are very strong as we have a great tradition in our universities and other educational institutions.*
>
> (Company Five's Chief HR and Organization Officer).

> *Chemists, chemical engineers and pharmacists come mainly from the [City] University. Here there is a long tradition of organic chemistry. If I want to find a chemist with a doctorate degree and a specific curriculum I can easily find one.*
>
> (Company Four's General Manager)

Supplier networks

Over the years, supply networks have become increasingly global. In particular, the proximity of original equipment manufacturer (OEM) suppliers is now defined in terms of macro-areas. The Italian bases of the investigated companies mainly use OEM suppliers located in Europe. The cases in which companies use local suppliers refer to a few special needs, such as commodities (for example, standard solvents used in the chemical industry in Company Four's case) or goods, which involve an intensive interchange between producer and consumer.

> *"The district is fundamental for our supply, for two main reasons: first, the typology of the product they make; second, which is the most important, they have a distinctive competence in the treatment of the raw material that nobody else in the world has. We have to buy this product here because of their knowledge."*
>
> (Company Three's CEO)

The type of OEM suppliers the interviewed companies deal with has been changing over time. The local suppliers have evolved into global suppliers; that is, they have spread their presence through production facilities at the international level:

> *In the past, we had local suppliers. Now we have begun to have global suppliers, but with a base in Italy. [. . .] Because our activities require special designs and pieces, local control is quite important. There is the risk that a supplier mistakenly produces a piece and we cannot have a supplier that is a thousand kilometres away. [. . .] The relationship with the supplier is built on a constant interchange, which needs not only a common technical language, but also trust.*
>
> (Company Eight's HR Manager)

> *An important share of our key suppliers is located close to our headquarters. We have established a medium/long-term relationship with them, based on a win-win client-supplier exchange.*
>
> (Company Six's Supply Chain Manager)

The presence of local suppliers, whether they are global suppliers or not, is a necessary condition for the local production system to be dynamic and innovative, as it simultaneously slows down the fading of the local supply chain, which enables the development of the home-based industrial commons.

Institutions and financial system

The institutional environment, as well as the financial system, represents local assets which are important for the sampled companies; both of them enable and empower companies to carry out their activities. However, their relevance emerges as secondary with respect to the local workforce skills, education system and supplier network.

> *We have relationships with local institutions, more specifically with the industrial association of our province. We have activated collaboration with both public and private organizations, which have supported our internationalization process over several stages, such as scouting, analysis and settlement in foreign markets.*
>
> Company Six's Accounting Manager continues by saying

> *Our group cultivates relationships both with local, national and global financial institutions. We avail ourselves of the support of the local financial system, in particular of that provided by the local banking system. Amongst our partners we count financial institutions, characterized by strong local vocations, that have gone along and still go along with our group, fostering our business growth.*

With regard to the financial system, the access to credit does not emerge as a critical local asset. The majority of the sampled companies source complex financial services from suppliers located in national or international financial centres.

The institutional environment could potentially be considered a key asset by the companies, just as local workforce skills, the education system and supplier network are. Yet, according to the sampled firms, there is scope for improvement in building fruitful relationships with local public administration. Managers from Company Ten and Company One suggested some concrete examples:

> *It would be useful if the local institutional body could help boost companies based in its territory, through actions supporting firms' presence abroad. For instance, in the exhibition [omitted], a country like [omitted] promotes goods produced in its country and assists its companies on a systematic basis, through marketing actions and technical support (i.e. supplying firms with timely technical reports on-demand during the exhibitions).*
>
> (Company Ten's General Manager)

> *Public administration should improve the territorial attractiveness by developing infrastructures and contributing to creating more lively cities; this would help companies to be more appealing for workers.*
>
> (Company One's HR Manager)

The role of MNEs in supporting ID assets

Local assets and MNE actions are strictly connected. On the one hand, local assets influence MNEs' performance (according to the mechanisms mentioned in the section "Industrial commons strategic assets"); on the other hand, the activities undertaken by MNEs contribute to the generation of a set of local assets. The actions that the companies investigated have taken in favour of the industrial commons present in their home base are different, although very often it is an indirect effect (outcome), not intentionally directed to that scope.

Empirical evidence highlights the pivotal role that MNEs may play in sustaining and fostering knowledge specialization and resource agglomeration. More specifically, all the companies interviewed have acted as "anchor tenant" (Feldman, 2003), triggering positive externalities by attracting a critical mass of suppliers as well as a skilled labour force. According to the anchor tenant hypothesis proposed by Feldman (2003, p. 323),

> a large firm may be a better anchor, in terms of economic success, for a developing industry than an equivalent number of small firms. Even if the stock of skilled employees were equal under each regime, the large firm may exert a stronger influence.

Indeed, large established firms are more likely to generate an agglomeration of skilled labour, demand for specialized inputs, and the presence of potential entrepreneurs who may generate spin-offs from the established anchor and set up new firms (Klepper, 2001).

The evidence shows that when MNEs perceive the district areas in which have grown as a strategic base performing high added value business functions, they further stimulate the agglomeration of investments, expertise and specialized companies. As shown in the interviews, Italian plants are places dedicated to the development of strategic products.

> *We have made significant investments in Italy to develop [new equipment]. Last year we increased investment to strengthen the group's innovative capacity by enlarging the testing room for new high-technological products.*
>
> (Company Five's Chief HR and Organization Officer)

The analysis reports that local assets benefit from the presence of the "anchor tenant", the MNE leader at the international level, in the sector in which they operate. Indeed, the "catalyst" (Feldman and Lowe, 2008) function performed by the anchor tenant also clearly arose during the interviews with Company Ten's General Manager and Company Eight's HR Manager.

> *We manufacture our product in Italy and, moreover, we approved a further expansion in this territory. [. . .] We will employ more than 150 workers (both low- and high-skilled profiles) to supply one of the biggest automobile players. [. . .] We absorb workers from those companies located in this territory that experienced a downshift.*
>
> (Company Ten's General Manager)

Company Eight's HR manager states that the company attracts high-qualified workers thanks to the role of technological leader that it plays in the sector.

In a few cases, the MNEs we interviewed act as an anchor tenant intentionally, with the final aim of being loyal to the territory and of supporting the accumulation of knowledge as well as expertise. Building on the historical specialization of the socio-economic environment in which the company is set, Company Seven supports the accumulation of knowledge and the agglomeration of expertise by training future workers. Indeed, the company continuously employs intern students enrolled at local technical schools. According to the company's HR Manager, Company Seven decided to undertake this action as a tribute to the territory that has allowed (and still allows) it to become (and be) an international player.

MNEs do not only act as anchor tenant, but may undertake an "anchoring role" to "dovetail the local circuits of embedded and cumulative competences and specializations with the global circuit knowledge creation and transfer" (De Propris and Crevoisier, 2011, p. 171). According to the definition of De Propris and Crevoisier (2011), anchoring can have a different meaning to that of Feldman, which is related to the anchoring to the locally embedded nature of tacit knowledge and learning in firms' and regions' innovation processes. De Propris and Crevosier propose an alternative concept of anchoring; that is, deep and complex roots that businesses have in a local context whilst simultaneously engaging in open, multi-local networks. Anchoring refers to the fact there are forms of linkages and relations that can occur between a context of localized knowledge, like the one present in district areas, and those that are outside them.

MNEs at the same time engage in both local assets and global networks, enabling the pollination of the local socio-environment with new inputs, ideas and innovations (Giblin, 2011). The following quotation reveals three ways (passive internationalization, foreign collaboration and active internationalization, respectively) according to which district territories can benefit from having MNEs undertaking an anchoring role, which allows them to be able to float in the global network while being rooted in the district:

> *Thanks to the investment fund that acquired us, we have been able to absorb the exper-*
> *tise of international sales as well as use their knowledge and network to penetrate new*
> *markets. [. . .] The financial resources and know-how of international markets provided*
> *by the fund have enabled us to boost our locally grounded technical competencies and*
> *become one of the major international players in our sector.*
>
> (Company Five's Chief HR and Organization Officer)

To complement and foster local resources with global ones, Company Eight and Company Six employ foreign technicians in R&D activities within their Italian branches in order to facilitate the activation of collaborations with research institutions abroad, integrating and thus increasing the knowledge stock in the area. New inputs and innovations also arise from the collaboration on a continuous basis with international universities and research centres (e.g. Company Three), and with international artists (leading architects and designers) in the case of the fashion/design sector (Company Two).

> *We signed partnerships with several international research centres and universities. We*
> *collaborated with and for [omitted] university [in the USA]. They paid us to develop*
> *[clothes for specific activities]. A small group of students came here to work with our*
> *experienced modelers.*
>
> (Company Three's CEO)

Following a technology-seeking strategy, MNEs may acquire companies in related sectors to upgrade their products and boost parent company innovation capabilities, as occurred in Company Seven and Company Ten.

> *Our acquisitions have been the outcome of a strategic choice, aiming to become an inter-*
> *national player. [. . .] In Europe and other advanced markets, the goal of acquisitions*
> *was to internalize specific technologies. The acquisition path has been coherent with our*
> *core business, to complement our know-how and develop new strategic products.*
>
> (Company Seven's CEO)

MNEs are one of the territorial actors that can play the role of anchor tenant in a regional system of innovation; universities and public laboratories might also assume this role (Feldman, 2003). The exploitation of synergies and interdependencies amongst the business community, government and universities (the triple helix; see Etzkowitz and Leydesdorff, 2000) would enhance the sustainability of the regional innovation systems (De Propris and Crevoisier, 2011). Thus, the impact of an MNE acting as "anchor tenant" on the reproduction of the local resources system can be fostered by initiating partnerships between companies and technical institutes/universities in the region. The companies investigated have implemented several local channels to constantly increase workers' skills endowment, in an attempt to integrate the technical knowledge that employees already own thanks to the local education system, with managerial skills and behavioural ones. The partnerships with universities are mostly made with institutions located close to the companies, in the same region and/ or neighbouring regions. The partnerships established with technical schools highlight a more pronounced local nature; they tend to be created within the same region, and often the same province or district. The collaborations between the companies investigated and the educational system are heterogeneous. They differ in terms of intensity and duration, as well as in the types of programs. In Company Four, Company Five and Company Eight the collaborations with universities are structured and continuous. Collaborations established to meet specific company needs are more common. A possible result of the synergy between higher education institutes and companies is evidenced by the experience, revealed by Company Five's Chief HR and Organization Officer, of actions undertaken by the firm to develop its corporate workforces. Company Five has established a continuous collaboration with at least one Italian university. In their plants and offices, courses are continuously organized for high-skilled workers in order to enrich and complement their soft skills to enable the company to be more efficient and integrated at the international level.

Finally, actions taken by the companies show how MNEs can sustain the regeneration of the industrial commons by recombining specificities of geographically close IDs, enabling them to create new products and/or new sectors. Indeed, MNEs can play a key role in the emergence of new sectors, stemming from the combination of know-how embedded in different IDs (inter-cluster innovation). Two interviewed MNEs (namely Company Two and Company Three) have developed new products and created new market niches by using the web of relationships located in the two different IDs. Company Two was able to couple expertise embedded in the gold jewellery district with the furniture district, becoming international leader in providing customized solutions for interior and outdoor design projects. At the same time, by blending knowledge flow in the Montebelluna sportsystem district with that circulating in the leather-tanning Arzignano district, Company Three has triggered the development of new products within the fields of sportswear and protective clothing. Such joint use of expertise belonging to different IDs has nourished a critical mass of talented labour, educational/research centres and specialized firms, ensuring the regeneration of the ID capabilities and the flourishing of a specific industry.

Conclusions

The aim of this research was to shed light on the relationship between MNEs' internationalization processes and the use of industrial commons embedded in district areas. The analysis helps to explore what the critical factors in upgrading the manufacturing base in advanced countries are, as well as in maintaining the attractiveness and competitiveness of these countries in the new global division of labour. To investigate this phenomenon, we devote particular attention to the expertise and networks of inter-organizational relationships developed in the district areas located in the Veneto region (Italy), as an expression of the local engines that have enabled Italian economic growth and contributed to its presence in international markets.

Comparing previous studies on international business, ID and GVC, there emerges a need to balance local and global involvement. Being at the edges of the local and global continuum might generate detrimental effects. Delocalizing many business functions might lead to losing core knowledge; conversely, sharing many proximity dimensions can be disadvantageous, because being too involved in a territory can inhibit cross-pollination through "lock-in". The information collected confirms that local relationships are not an alternative to global ones. Conversely, the ability of a manufacturing company to develop strong links with the local labour market and supplier networks is a condition to increase its international projection. The intense use of local resources integrated with external factors eases the maintenance of the home-based industrial commons, which in turn contributes to improving both companies' competitiveness and local resource quality. The influence of local assets in supporting the strategies of internationalization has been clearly shown in all the investigated companies, in particular in the matching of supply/demand in the labour market, in local supplier networks and the education system. The programs provided by the education system have been evaluated to correspond to company needs. Knowledge and skills, both technical and manufacturing in nature, seem to be the factors that have greater territorial impact on the companies' results and, more specifically, on the conditions that make it possible to maintain some degree of GVC governance. Evidence from the present work highlights how local supplier networks continue to be relevant factors in the territory, especially when there is a need for a company to exchange strategic information continuously and with high frequency.

The results show some examples of how territorial competitiveness can rely on local capacity to be part of long-distance interactions, through foreign investments carried out by MNEs, their actions as anchor tenants and their anchoring role. Companies can contribute to the development of the home-based industrial commons even through their foreign investment decisions. Indeed, to a certain extent foreign investment decisions by local companies could be beneficial for the development of local assets. They are desirable if MNEs undertake them not to weigh anchor but to leverage the domestic-based resources. The presence of MNEs acting, either intentionally or not, as anchor tenants in the territory and representing international excellence is an extraordinary factor in attracting talent and resources from outside the local system. Moreover, thanks to the "anchoring role" performed by these companies, the local dimension can take advantage of the diversity and complementarity of these external inputs, integrating them with the existing "local circuits of embedded and cumulative competences" (De Propris and Crevoisier, 2011, p. 175).

As our evidence has shown, MNEs can also sustain the regeneration of the ID production fabric by re-combining the specificities of geographically close IDs, which lead, in turn, to the creation of new products and/or the development of new sectors. The capability of MNEs to exploit and re-combine the industrial commons present in two different districts has first enabled them to penetrate international markets; second to nourish a critical mass of talented labour, educational and research centres, and specialized firms; and third, to ensure the regeneration of ID capabilities as well as the flourishing of a specific industry.

The findings also provide suggestions on the conceptualization of sustainable growth models, which enable territories to attract and retain specialized workers and "deeply-rooted firms" (Magnani, 2016). Better knowledge of local resources affecting the competitive advantage of firms willing to engage with global networks is a condition for defining the most appropriate interventions for local development policy and, more generally, for industrial policy intervention. To enhance MNEs' anchoring role, it is necessary to increase companies' awareness of the critical function played by the industrial commons in sustaining their growth and innovation capability. Only some of the investigated companies are aware of the critical role played by the local resources system. Paradoxically, foreign companies or foreign funds acquiring Italian firms have a better perception of this economic value. The value can be expressed by a certain degree of local stickiness in terms of manufacturing activity, which is the maintenance of, or the increase in, specialized manufacturing activities in the Italian base, as an implicit acknowledgement of the importance of the local industrial commons. To conclude, the chapter focuses on possible actions that the main private economic players, such as MNEs, can undertake to foster successful governance of the industrial commons. To increase this awareness, the territory should be considered as one of the company's stakeholders. Concepts such as "territorial loyalty" should be promoted by a supportive political system or, as suggested in Ostrom's work, by the resource users (not only companies, but also institutions and local communities). That means complex relationships between different actors; not only MNEs, but also institutions and local communities, all involved in maintaining a shared value. Further analysis needs to be made to establish precise policy interventions; there is need for further evidence on institutional behaviour, identifying institutional designs of sustainable use of the local industrial commons, investigating institutional regularities in effectively managing the local and global value chains involvement, and finally suggesting possible governance models. The findings of this research suggest that another promising research line is to study models of "synergistic governance" as sustainable ways of upgrading, both economically and socially (Gereffi and Lee, 2016).

Notes

1 Further details can be found at Eurostat (2016). Industrial production (volume) index overview. European Commission.
2 The "Inox Valley" [Stainless Steel Valley] is an ID of household appliances, small household appliances, large plants or food service equipment, non-food service equipment and sanitary plants.

References

Agrawal, A., Kapur, D., and McHale, J. (2008). How do spatial and social proximity influence knowledge flows? Evidence from patent data. *Journal of Urban Economics*, 64(2): 258–269.

Anselin, L., Varga, A., and Acs, Z. (1997). Local geographic spillovers between university research and high technology innovations. *Journal of Urban Economics*, 42(3): 422–448.

Audretsch, D.B., and Feldman, M.P. (1996). R&D spillovers and the geography of innovation and production. *The American Economic Review*, 43(2): 630–640.

Bailey, D., Bellandi, M., Caloffi, A., and De Propris, L. (2010). Place-renewing leadership: Trajectories of change for mature manufacturing regions in Europe. *Policy Studies*, 31(4): 457–474.

Bair, J., and Gereffi, G. (2001). Local clusters in global chains: The causes and consequences of export dynamism in Torreon's blue jeans industry. *World Development*, 29(11): 1885–1903.

Baldwin, R.E., and Evenett, S.J. (2015). Value creation and trade in 21st century manufacturing. *Journal of Regional Science*, 55(1): 31–50.

Becattini, G. (1990). The Marshallian industrial district. In F. Pyke, G. Becattini and W. Sengenberger (eds.), *Industrial Districts and Inter-firm Cooperation in Italy*. Geneva: International Institute for Labour, pp. 37–51.

Berger, S. (2013). *Making in America: From Innovation to Market*. Cambridge, MA: The MIT Press.

Blinder, A.S., and Krueger, A.B. (2013). Alternative measures of offshorability: A survey approach. *Journal of Labour Economics*, Part 2, 31(2): 97–127.

Breschi, S., and Lissoni, F. (2009). Mobility of skilled workers and co-invention networks: An anatomy of localized knowledge flows. *Journal of Economic Geography*, 9 (4): 439–468.

Buciuni, G., Corò, G., and Micelli, S. (2014). Rethinking the role of manufacturing in global value chains: An international comparative study in the furniture industry. *Industrial and Corporate Change*, 23(4): 967–996.

Camagni, R. (2008). Regional competitiveness: Towards a concept of territorial capital. In R. Camagni, R. Capello, B. Chizzolini and U. Fratesi (eds.), *Modelling Regional Scenarios for the Enlarged Europe*. Springer Berlin Heidelberg, Berlin, pp. 33–47.

Capello, R., and Lenzi, C. (2015). The knowledge – Innovation nexus: Its spatially differentiated returns to innovation. *Growth and Change*, 46(3): 379–399.

Castellani, D., and Pieri, F. (2010). Investimenti esteri e produttività: Le regioni italiane nel contesto europeo. In A. Zazzaro (eds.), *Reti Di Imprese E Territorio*. Il Mulino, Bologna.

Castellani, D., and Pieri, F. (2015). Outward investments and productivity: Evidence from European regions. *Regional Studies*, 50(12): 1945–1964.

Chiarvesio, M., Di Maria, E., and Micelli, S. (2010). Global value chains and open networks: The case of Italian industrial districts. *European Planning Studies*, 18(3): 333–350.

Conte, A., and Vivarelli, M. (2005). *One or Many Knowledge Production Functions?* Mapping Innovative Activity Using Microdata, IZA Discussion Papers: 1878.

Cooke, P. (2006). Global bioregions: Knowledge domains, capabilities and innovation system networks. *Industry and Innovation*, 13(4): 437–458.

Corò, G., Schenkel, M., and Volpe, M. (2013). International offshoring, local effects: An inquiry on Italian firms. *Symphonya. Emerging Issues in Management*, 2: 1–13.

De Marchi, V., and Grandinetti, R. (2014). Industrial districts and the collapse of the Marshallian model: Looking at the Italian experience. *Competition and Change*, 18(1): 70–87.

De Marchi, V., Lee, J., and Gereffi, G. (2014). Globalization, recession and the internationalization of industrial districts: Experiences from the Italian gold jewellery industry. *European Planning Studies*, 22(4): 866–884.

De Propris, L. (2010). *Re-Territorialising Production: Global Value Chains*. Paper presented at the Annual Meeting of the SASE Annual Conference, Philadelphia, PA, USA.

De Propris, L., and Crevoisier, O. (2011). From regional anchors to anchoring. In P. Cooke, B.T. Asheim, R. Boschma, R. Martin, D. Schwartz and F. Tödtling (eds.), *Handbook of Regional Innovation and Growth*. Edward Elgar Publishing, Cheltenham (UK).

Eisenhardt, K.M. (1989). Building theories from case study research. *Academy of Management Review*, 14(4): 532–550.

Eisenhardt, K.M., and Graebner, M.E. (2007). Theory building from cases: Opportunities and challenges. *Academy of Management Journal*, 50(1): 25–32.

Elia, S., Mariotti, I., and Piscitello, L. (2009). The impact of outward FDI on the home country's labour demand and skill composition. *International Business Review*, 18(4): 357–372.

Ellison, G., Glaeser, E.L., and Kerr, W. (2007). *What Causes Industry Agglomeration? Evidence From Coagglomeration Patterns*. NBER Working Paper No. 13068. National Bureau of Economic Research. Available at: www.nber.org/papers/w13068.

Etzkowitz, H., and Leydesdorff, L. (2000). The dynamics of innovation: From national systems and 'mode 2' to a triple helix of university – Industry – Government relations. *Research Policy*, 29(2): 109–123.

European Commission. (2010). Europe 2020: A Strategy for Smart, Sustainable and Inclusive Growth. Brussels.

European Commission. (2012). *Industrial revolution brings industry back to Europe*. IP/12/1085. Available at: http://europa.eu/rapid/press-release_IP-12-1085_en.htm?locale=en

Eurostat. (2016). *Manufacturing Statistics – NACE Rev. 2 – Data Extracted in November 2015*. ISSN 2443–8219. Last modified on 24 February 2016. Available at: http://ec.europa.eu/eurostat/statistics-explained/index.php/Manufacturing_statistics_-_NACE_Rev._2

Everatt, D., Tsai, T., and Cheng, B. (1999). *The Acer Group's China Manufacturing Decision*. Version A. Ivey Case Series #9A99M009, Richard Ivey School of Business, University of Western Ontario.

Feldman, M. (2003). The locational dynamics of the US biotech industry: Knowledge externalities and the anchor hypothesis. *Industry and Innovation*, 10(3): 311–329.

Feldman, M., and Lowe, N. (2008). Consensus from controversy: Cambridge's biosafety ordinance and the anchoring of the biotech industry. *European Planning Studies*, 16(3): 395–410.

Gereffi, G., Humphrey, J., Kaplinsky, R., and Sturgeon, T.J. (2001). Introduction: Globalisation, value chains and development. *IDS Bulletin*, 32: 1–8.

Gereffi, G., and Lee, J. (2016). Economic and social upgrading in global value chains and industrial clusters: Why governance matters. *Journal of Business Ethics*, 133(1): 25–38.

Gereffi, G., and Sturgeon, T.J. (2004). *Globalization, Employment, and Economic Development: A Briefing Paper*. Sloan Workshop Series in Industry Studies. Rockport, Massachusetts.

Giblin, M. (2011). Managing the global – Local dimensions of clusters and the role of 'lead' organizations: The contrasting cases of the software and medical technology clusters in the west of Ireland. *European Planning Studies*, 19(1): 23–42.

Hardin, G. (1968). The tragedy of the commons. *Science*, 162(3859): 1243–1248.

Hartley, J. (1994). Case studies in organizational research. In C. Cassell and G. Symon (eds.), *Qualitative Methods in Organizational Research*. London: Sage, pp. 208–229.

Hervas-Oliver, J.L., and Boix-Domenech, R. (2013). The economic geography of the meso-global spaces: Integrating multinationals and clusters at the local – Global level. *European Planning Studies*, 21(7): 1064–1080.

Heymann, E., and Vetter, S. (2013). *Europe's Re-Industrialisation: The Gulf Between Aspiration and Reality*. Frankfurt: Deutsche Bank EU Monitor.

Intesa Sanpaolo. (2015). *Economia e finanza dei distretti industriali*. Annual Report – N. 8, Direzione Studi e Ricerche, December.

ISTAT. (2015). Rapporto Annuale 2015. La situazione del Paese. ISTAT, Rome.

Ketokivi, M., and Ali-Yrkkö, J. (2009). Unbundling R&D and manufacturing: Postindustrial myth or economic reality? *Review of Policy Research*, 26(1–2): 35–54.

Klepper, S. (2001). *The Evolution of the U.S. Automobile Industry and Detroit as Its Capital*. Carnegie Mellon University Working Paper, November.

Kroker, R., and Lichtblau, K. (2013). 'Industrieland Europa': Die europäische Industrie im internationalen Vergleich. In Cologne Institute for Economic Research (ed.), *Die Zukunft der Industrie in Deutschland und Europa*. IW-Analysen No. 88. Cologne: Cologne Institute for Economic Research.

Magnani, M. (2016). Terra e buoi dei paesi tuoi: Scuola, ricerca, ambiente, cultura, capitale umano: quando l'impresa investe nel territorio. Utet Libri, Novara.

Morrison, A. (2008). Gatekeepers of knowledge within industrial districts: Who they are, how they interact. *Regional Studies*, 42(6): 817–835.

Mudambi, R. (2008). Location, control and innovation in knowledge-intensive industries. *Journal of Economic Geography*, 8(5): 699–725.

Navas-Alemán, L. (2011). The impact of operating in multiple value chains for upgrading: The case of the Brazilian furniture and footwear industries. *World Development*, 39(8): 1386–1397.

OECD. (2001). *Territorial Outlook 2001*, p. 15. DOI:10.1787/9789264189911-en

Ostrom, E. (1990). Governing the Commons: The Evolution of Institutions for Collective Action. Cambridge: Cambridge University Press.

Ostrom, E. (2010). Beyond markets and states: Polycentric governance of complex economic systems. *American Economic Review*, 100(3): 641–672.

Piergiovanni, R., Santarelli, E., and Vivarelli, M. (1997). From which source do small firm derive their innovative inputs? Some evidence from Italian provinces. *Review of Industrial Organization*, 12: 243–258.

Pisano, G.P., and Shih, W.C. (2009). Restoring American competitiveness. *Harvard Business Review*, 87(7–8): 114–125.

Pisano, G.P., and Shih, W.C. (2012). *Producing Prosperity: Why America Needs a Manufacturing Renaissance*. Boston: Harvard Business School Press.

Porter, M.E., and Kramer, M.R. (2011). Creating shared value. *Harvard Business Review*, 89(1/2), 62–77.

Ramirez, P., and Rainbird, H. (2010). Making the connections: Bringing skill formation into global value chain analysis. *Work, Employment and Society*, 24(4): 699–710.

Rueda-Cantuche, J.M., Sousa, N., Andreoni, V., and Arto, I. (2012). *The Single Market as an Engine for Employment Growth Through the External Trade*. Joint Research Centre, IPTS, Seville.

Schmitz, H., and Knorringa, P. (2000). Learning from global buyers. *Journal of Development Studies*, 37(2): 177–205.

Silvi, R., and Cuganesan, S. (2006). Investigating the management of knowledge for competitive advantage: A strategic cost management perspective. *Journal of Intellectual Capital*, 7(3): 309–323.

Torre, A., and Rallet, A. (2005). Proximity and localization. *Regional Studies*, 39(1): 47–59.

Yin, R.K. (2003). *Case Study Research: Design and Methods*. Newbury Park, CA: Sage Publications, 3/e.

Zimmermann, J.B. (1995). L'ancrage territorial des activités industrielles et technologiques: Une approche méthodologique. Commissariat Général du Plan, Paris.

7 Knowledge, systemic contribution and brokerage in industrial clusters

Francesc Xavier Molina-Morales, Luis Martínez-Cháfer and José Antonio Belso-Martínez

Introduction

There is widespread consensus on the role of geographical proximity as a facilitator of knowledge sharing, diffusion and consequently innovation (Maskell and Malmberg, 1999; Tallman et al., 2004). Although the literature on geographical clusters has traditionally assumed a high degree of homogeneity in cluster firms (Becattini, 1990; Becattini, 1979; Signorini, 1994; Paniccia, 1998), such reductionist view has been recently questioned. Innovation-related knowledge is actually selectively and unevenly exchanged in clusters (Boschma and Ter Wal, 2007; Giuliani, 2007).

Different types of knowledge flows can be identified in clusters, including technological, market or managerial knowledge (Sammarra and Biggiero, 2008). Largely, access to these knowledge flows depends on firm's specific position within the network. Particularly interesting are the knowledge brokerage activities and positions in cluster networks (Alberti and Pizzurno, 2015; Boschma and Ter Wal, 2007). Knowledge brokers are defined as intermediaries that aim to develop relationships and networks with, among, and between producers and users of knowledge by providing linkages and resources to them, playing diverse roles (Gould and Fernandez, 1989).

Based on the above arguments our research addresses the following key question: What is the impact of firms' brokerage activities on the clusters' systemic innovation in the context of the Global Value Chain (GVC)? In order to address this question, we have carried out a comparative study of two clusters located in the Valencian region (Spain): the ceramic tile cluster, in the province of Castellón, and the toy cluster, Alicante. Since the empirical setting described two clusters considered as low- and medium-tech industries, this choice is consistent with certain claims that emphasize the importance of studying these contexts in contrast with a dominant focus on high-tech studies in this specific literature (Sciascia et al., 2014).

Using social networks and econometric analysis on a representative sample, we confirmed our expectations about firms' contribution to cluster's innovation according to the specific type of brokerage activity (Gould and Fernandez, 1989), the relevance of external links of the local firms (McEvily and Zaheer, 1999) and the contingency of our results on the specific characteristics of the cluster and the type of knowledge shared. These findings relevantly add to the cluster literature and the promising line of investigation on brokerage activities in firms (Alberti and Pizzurno, 2015; Boari and Riboldazzi, 2014).

Theoretical framework

Knowledge exchanges in clusters: origin and diversity

Clusters are geographical concentrations of related companies, organizations and institutions in a particular field, all united by common elements and complementarities (Porter,

2000). The overlapping of territory and linkages between different actors, such as customers, competitors, suppliers, supporting organizations and local institutions (Piore, 1990), has promoted their conceptualization as networks (Inkpen and Tsang, 2005; Porter, 1998; Tallman et al., 2004). Geographical proximity and a strong sense of membership characterizing clusters facilitate these types of relationships which are often based on shared norms and values such as trust and reciprocity (Antonelli, 2000).

Recent works on industrial clusters have led researchers to reconsider firms' resources and internal capabilities as the main drivers of cluster innovation (Hassink, 2005). In this regard, our theoretical proposal acknowledges the internal heterogeneity of the cluster, thereby affording a prominent role to the characteristics of the individual firm (Giuliani, 2007; Boschma and Ter Wal, 2007).

Additionally, we assume the potential importance of the portfolio of a firm's relationships in the cluster that determine its position in the cluster network and the cluster external networks (Capaldo, 2007; Molina-Morales and Martínez-Fernández, 2009; Boari, Odorici, and Zamarian, 2003). This portfolio of activities in the context of the GVC has been conceptualized using different terms. According to Gereffi (2005, p. 168) "a variety of overlapping terms has been used to describe the complex network relationships that make up the global economy". Finally, we consider that the degree of affinity of these firms in both cognitive and cultural terms, such as the extent to which network members share aims and have similar ideas on local interactions, allow the positive effects of both internal and external resources to be amplified (Inkpen and Tsang, 2005).

Inside the cluster, firms exchange different types of knowledge in different forms. Distinction among different flows is a relevant issue since each of them presents specific characteristics and pursues different goals. A well-known distinction used by scholars in this respect is between market and technological knowledge (Alberti and Pizzurno, 2015; Chiesa et al., 2007). Sammarra and Biggiero (2008) added a further type of knowledge (managerial). Other authors like Giuliani (2007), Morrison (2008) or Morrison and Rabellotti (2009) establish two types of networks in this context: the business information network and the technical knowledge network.

They found that differences in exchanges are multiple – distinctive knowledge exchanges involve particular firms, which adopt diverse knowledge-sourcing strategies. Knowledge flows in these networks unevenly affect specific groups of actors (Breschi and Lissoni, 2001; Boschma and Frenken, 2006; Lissoni, 2001). In this context we can consider the business/ market information network based on the transmission of declarative knowledge that is mainly codified, while the technological knowledge network that focuses on the transmission of knowledge, new technologies and knowledge that is primarily tacit (Lissoni, 2001).

Besides intra-cluster considerations, considerable attention has been paid to cluster external connections. Previous research has identified cluster gatekeepers as bridges between cluster external and internal organizations. These mediating positions have access to potentially more diverse knowledge which enhances their creativity and innovation (McEvily and Zaheer, 1999; Zaheer and Bell, 2005). Access to innovation-related knowledge that frequently comes from outside the cluster (Asheim and Belussi, 2007; Boschma and Ter Wal, 2007; Maskell et al., 2006) allows them to outperform their local counterparts.

Knowledge brokerage activities in clusters

The transfer of valuable information across firm boundaries fosters the creation of knowledge and innovation (Phelps et al., 2012; Powell et al., 1996). Certain strategic positions within knowledge networks allow higher performance (Zaheer and Bell, 2005) or ease the access to external knowledge sources (Buckley et al., 2009). Consequently, the capacity of innovation appears dependent on firm's position within the heart of the network. By being located in strategic network positions, actors receive better information related to innovation that other actors in less favourable locations tend to miss out (Becker, 1970).

Brokerage positions are one of these strategic positions in networks through which an actor facilitates interactions between other members of the network who lack access to or trust in one another (Marsden, 1982). Therefore, any exchange arising from the process of brokerage involves a relationship that comprises three actors, two of whom carry out the transaction and a third who mediates. Particularly in knowledge networks, a broker facilitates valuable information transfers through interactions, attains privileged access to information, enjoys advantages for identifying arbitrage opportunities and can better capitalize on existing capabilities (Burt, 1997; Hargadon and Sutton, 1997; Zaheer and Bell, 2005). According to Hargadon (1998), there are three mechanisms through which knowledge brokers generate and transfer knowledge: the systematic exploration of new territories, the creative reconsideration of past experiences and the proposal of synergistic combinations of internal resources and external sources for knowledge.

Brokers in knowledge networks may not only connect and foster information flows between particular actors but also among different communities (Hargadon, 1998; Boari and Riboldazzi, 2010). In this vein, Galunic and Rodan (1998), drawing on a work undertaken by Hargadon and Sutton (1997), found that a firm located at the convergence of several industries was able to broker the knowledge generated from multiple sectors and create innovative business behaviours. Knowledge transmission trough mediators has been proved crucial to generate innovation (Uzzi and Spiro, 2005; Boari and Riboldazzi, 2010).

Within social structures, actors can be categorized according to their activities or interests in such a way that exchanges between actors can have contrasting meanings for other different actors. In other words, the existence of homogeneous categories implies that communication flows within these subgroups ought to be distinguished from those produced between each other. By taking this distinction and the direction of knowledge transfer into account, Gould and Fernandez (1989) outline five possible triadic structures of linkages: coordinator, representative, gatekeeper, consultant and liaison. The added value of this taxonomy derives from the delineation of knowledge flows between groups versus knowledge flows within groups.

The *Coordinator* role occurs when the three actors belong to the same subgroup or category in such a way that the brokerage takes place between members of the same category. *Representative* is the role that appears when a member of a specific category delegates to another member the responsibility for communicating or negotiating the exchanges with a different group. *Gatekeepers* are brokers that selectively filter the access of external actors to the rest of members in the same category. *Consultant* mediates between two members of the same group, but being part of an external group to either the issuer or recipient. The *liaison* role arises when the broker is an agent that belongs to neither the issuer nor the recipient's group. In other words, the liaison connects members of different groups to which it does not belong.

During the last decade, network studies in clusters have thrown light on what cluster-based relational structures look like. In this vein, cluster members apparently differ in their connectedness and position in the local network as a function of their cognitive assets and social relations (Giuliani and Bell, 2005; Morrison, 2008; Morrison and Rabellotti, 2009). Such asymmetries redound in uneven participation in local knowledge exchanges (Giuliani, 2007; Morrison, 2008).

In-between positions within the local network provide opportunities for knowledge creation, transformation and transmission (Howells, 2006) whose loss would seriously affect intra-cluster knowledge circulation. The sum of flows from unconnected partners represents an important part of the broker learning process through which new opportunities are discovered, knowledge base augmented, and new competences are developed by blending existing and novel knowledge. Empirical research endorses that knowledge brokers are more innovative than other firms (Belso-Martínez et al., 2015; McEvily and Zaheer, 1999; Zaheer and Bell, 2005).

To operationalize the above presented brokerage structures, Gould and Fernandez (1989) classified a network of organizations according to their public, private or non-profit nature. However, cluster literature offers different options to categorize local actors. For instance, Alberti and Pizzurno (2015) considered four groups: large, small companies, universities and research centres and institutions for collaboration. The cluster value chain may also represent an interesting alternative to split network members in homogeneous factions

Industrial clusters are characterized by a high degree of specialization and complementarity. The fragmentation of the production process leads individual companies to focus on specific industrial activities ranging from the manufacture of inputs to final products, and engenders bidirectional knowledge flows (Sammarra and Biggiero, 2008). Over time, systemic competences accumulate across the stages of the production process (De Propris and Driffield, 2006).

Although mediating positions affect firm's opportunities for knowledge exchange (Burt, 1997; Provan and Human, 1999) and hence its success in developing innovations (Graf and Kruger, 2011; Noteboom, 1999; Tsai, 2001), brokers' innovation potential depends on the accessible knowledge. The spectrum of reachable knowledge by each broker shapes its specific knowledge generation, learning dynamics and contribution. Accordingly, knowledge diversity increases the innovative potential (Garcia-Vega, 2006; Quintana-García and Benavides-Velasco, 2008) through maintaining the availability to a broader set of alternative recombinations (Carnabuci and Bruggeman, 2009).

Research questions

Brokerage positions and the different stages of cluster value chain

Mutual learning and knowledge sharing within the cluster value chain are at the heart of the build-up of innovative capabilities that underlie the cluster-specific advantages (Bathelt et al., 2004; Gordon and McCann, 2000; Malmberg and Maskell, 2002; Maskell and Malmberg, 2007). Both vertical and horizontal knowledge interactions and diffusion contribute to the local innovation system (Malmberg and Maskell, 2002) and play a distinct role in the innovation process (Zeng et al., 2010). While the vertical dimension encompasses collaborators providing related activities that possess knowledge useful for undertaking dissimilar but complementary activities, the horizontal dimension includes firms engaged in comparable activities leading to cognitive communalities that enable efficient communication and mutual learning (Cantner and Meder, 2007). Nevertheless, high levels of cognitive overlap may hinder learning and innovation (Boschma, 2005; Boschma and Frenken, 2009).

The contribution of brokerage positions on innovation would depend on the knowledge diversity, and subsequently on the involved subgroups across the cluster value chain. A priori, mediating within a particular stage of the cluster value chain implies exchanges of similar knowledge resources. Partners present high degree of cognitive overlap, so the mutual enlargement of their respective knowledge bases appears limited to slight refinements or simply non-existent (Nooteboom et al., 2007). In this vein, horizontal relationships have been proven not to be as important (Tomlinson, 2010), possibly due to the fear of undesirable imitation by competitors, (Boschma and Ter Wal, 2007).

On the contrary, incoming knowledge resources from partners operating in different stages of the cluster value chain create more opportunities for recombination due to assumable diversity. Consistently, empirical evidences support how vertical ties accelerate knowledge transfers, foster the potential of new innovative combinations and simplify innovation process (Von Hippel, 1987; Yli-Renko, Autio, and Sapienza, 2001) and foster firm's performance (Lorenzoni and Lipparini, 1999).

Brokers operate in the midst of users and producers of knowledge (Smedlund, 2006), putting together intra-cluster members to work collectively on a diversity of innovation related practices and knowledge processes. A priori, dipping in such diversity enhances broker's creativity and innovation (McEvily and Zaheer, 1999; Zaheer and Bell, 2005). Regardless, Giuliani (2008) points out that the advantages of mediating positions may vanish in clusters because the degree of knowledge diversity is sometimes scarce due to the narrow scope of the local knowledge sources.

Consistently with the vertical vs. horizontal linkages previously presented, we presume that different types of brokers facilitate diverse types of learning and knowledge exchanges, which take place in distinctive contexts. We expect a certain degree of duplication and knowledge overlap in triads within sub-groups populated by similar firms in traditional clusters (horizontal relationships). In view of previous literature on knowledge diversity (Broekel and Boschma, 2012; Gilsing et al., 2008), the performance and contribution of in-between positions would be moderated or even absent due to redundancies. On the opposite, firms of different sub-groups bring distinct pieces of knowledge within the cluster network which can be recombined in new and original way (Nooteboom et al., 2007). Therefore, brokers connecting members of different sub-groups (vertical relationships) experience less degree of knowledge overlap and greater diversity, which redounds in originality and higher innovation results contribution. Therefore, we expect that brokerage positions across different stages will generate greater innovation results compared to brokerage positions within the same stage of the cluster value chain.

Brokerage positions and the different types of flows of knowledge

As previously mentioned, cluster literature suggested the existence of different knowledge flows in local agglomerations (Boschma and Frenken, 2006; Breschi and Lissoni, 2001; Lissoni, 2001; Malmberg and Maskell, 2002). Among various flows of different types of knowledge, we distinguish between the business (market) knowledge and the technical knowledge. The distinction of both types of knowledge induced the separation between the so-called business network of relations and the knowledge network of relations in a cluster (Boschma and Ter Wal, 2007; Giuliani, 2007; Morrison and Rabellotti, 2009; Sammarra and Biggiero, 2008).

What we defined as technical knowledge can be assumed to be mainly personal, contextual, harder to be formalized and difficult to communicate (Nonaka and Takeuchi, 1995). On the contrary, business or market knowledge is always more subject to be coded and easily transferable in form of documents. It mainly refers to market related issues that resides in organizational members and can be uttered in form of e-mails or written documents. Developments in knowledge management literature emphasize this point (Gebert et al., 2003; Troilo, 2006).

Under this framework, these cluster network structures are contingent to the type of knowledge shared. Business networks appear to be denser than knowledge networks (Boschma and Ter Wal, 2007; Giuliani, 2007), but exhibit lower levels of reciprocity (Morrison and Rabellotti, 2009). Networks characterized by trust and reciprocity facilitate transfers of complex knowledge of tacit nature (Zander and Kogut, 1995). Comparatively, declarative knowledge such as market related information does not require specific skills for its successful internalization (Kogut and Zander, 1992) and travels across organizations more effortlessly (Nonaka, 1994). In view of these arguments, it seems that the business information network is more based on the transmission of declarative knowledge that is mainly codified, while the technological knowledge network focuses on the transmission of knowledge that is primarily tacit. We can expect a significant difference in the knowledge contribution according to the type of knowledge they exchange. Brokerage positions and effects are, therefore, contingent on the properties of the knowledge channelled by reason of the differential prerequisites related to tacit knowledge. In this vein, the contribution of brokerage positions to innovation will be contingent on the type of knowledge network in which clustered firms are involved.

Brokerage positions and cluster external relations

All of the brokerage roles analysed in the previous section correspond to internal cluster interactions. However, the cluster network is not an isolated space; conversely, internal actors in the cluster network can interact and maintain on-going relationships with external actors. In fact, previous research on cluster gatekeepers has explained this role as an intermediary between cluster external and internal agents (Giuliani, 2011). Empirical research mainly supports that cluster members in brokerage positions between inside and outside actors have access to potentially more diverse knowledge which enhances their creativity and innovation (McEvily and Zaheer, 1999; Zaheer and Bell, 2005). In fact, a number of authors have already suggested that much of the innovation in clusters may derive from outside of the cluster (Asheim and Belussi, 2007; Boschma and Ter Wal, 2007; Maskell et al., 2006). Even, it is argued that without such external interactions the cluster may accelerate its decline (De Martino et al., 2006).

In consequence, cluster firm innovations, and even more, the survival of many local firms and the entire cluster to some extent may depend on their ability to capture and adjust to external changes and developments (Robertson et al., 2008). At this point, the role of the GVC becomes important when companies can harness potential opportunities which also exist in the globalization context (Gereffi, 2005).

Cluster firms can detect and react to external changes through suitable non-local channels of communication, avoiding, for instance, the so-called myopia of success (Alberti, 2006). Accordingly, rather than focus on alternatively close or distant contacts, authors seem to suggest firms to combine both categories of ties. In fact, Boschma (2005) suggested that learning and innovation are detrimental when firms are too near or too far. At the end, if distance can evolve over time, a link between the issues of proximity and life cycle can be clearly suggested (Robertson et al., 2008). Therefore, brokerage positions connecting cluster external and internal actors will positively affect the systemic innovation contribution.

Empirical study

Context of the investigation

The toy valley cluster

The Spanish toy industry is a fine example of how technical and managerial innovation is able to facilitate survival of the sector within a competitive environment that is dominated by large corporations and manufacturers that belong to the GVC, especially from Far East countries (see Table 7.1). Although 61% of the companies operate in overseas markets,

Table 7.1 Overview of the ceramic tile and toy valley clusters in the GVC

	Ceramic tile cluster	*Toy Valley cluster*
Product	Wall and floor ceramic tiles	Traditional toys such as dolls, cars and miniatures
ID position in the GVC	The cluster conducts several activities such as manufacturing the final products and raw materials that are sold worldwide. Also intangible activities (Design, R&D and logistics)	The cluster conducts both tangible (manufacturing) and intangible activities/functions (design, R&D, marketing and logistics).
GVC key actors	China is the world's leading producer (47,8% of the world production) followed by Brazil and India. Spain is the fifth country and Italy the seventh. Spain is the leader of frits and glazes production while machinery engineering has a shared leadership between Spain and Italy.	China is by far the world's leading producer, although global brands (Mattel, Hasbro, Lego and Bandai Namco Group) dominate the industry. Some relevant domestic players also exist (Giochi Preziosi or Guandong Alpha)
ID firms and employment	The cluster comprises 95% of Spanish production. According to the major trade association the cluster has 15500 direct employees and 7000 indirect ones. Small and Medium enterprises predominate.	Cluster comprises 40% of the 158 Spanish manufacturers. Micro, small and medium enterprises largely predominate (98%).
ID Export propensity	Nowadays the cluster exports around 80% of the total production with total sales of €3075 million on 2015. The cluster products are present in 186 countries.	Toy exports have grown steadily since 2009 up to 197 million euros, representing 24% of the Spanish toy industry. France, Greece and Italia account for 58% of the foreign sales.
ID Supporting industries	Most of the supporting industries involved on the ceramic process are in the cluster: glazes and frits, machinery and additives. Additionally, there are logistic operators, consulting firms, financing institutions, furniture manufacturers for expositions, marketing services etc.	Supply of components and raw materials: metal products, electronics, textiles and garments for dolls, chemicals (paints and coatings), moulds, plastics, injected and blowing plastic components.
ID Local institutions	Technological ceramic institute (ITC), Business associations (ASCER, ASEBEC, ANFFECC), Universitat Jaume I (UJI)	Technological centre (AIJU), Business association (AEFJ), University Miguel Hernandez, University of Alicante, Polytechnic University of Valencia.
ID Major transformations	Innovations on the production process like single fire ovens and the latest major radical innovation, the inkjet technology. Developed by a local machinery company this is now the main standard for tiles decoration all over the world.	Smart specialization showing the openness and insertion into global value chains. The coalescence of traditional and new technologies or the entry of foreign MNEs favoured the sophistication of the toy offer and diversification towards other sectors.

with sales exceeding 400 million euros, the Spanish toy industry is not a major player on the world stage. In fact, Spain ranks 10th with 4% of the total European exports. Production is primarily concentrated in the Valencia region, where 41.3% of jobs (and 38.4% of total sales) are generated. Built around four towns in the southern part of the area (Ibi, Onil, Castalla and Tibi), the toy valley cluster concentrates 98% of the sector's activity in this region thanks to a diversified production that addresses different market niches.

The genesis and development of the current productive system is based on consolidating an SME network as well as the increasing role of a range of local organizations that have boosted collective efficiency and competitiveness. During the first half of the 20th century, the absorptive capacity with respect to external knowledge underpinned the transformation of artisan tinsmiths into toymakers. The availability of raw materials and skilled workers allowed local entrepreneurs to drive the manufacture of miniatures or dolls in the towns of Ibi and Onil. Structural changes induced by the implementation of new materials and technology (e.g. plastic and injection moulding) along with the flourishing of a thriving auxiliary industry, led to a substantial period of growth during which spin-offs or innovative marketing strategies bore their fruits. Even though increasing globalization has hindered the materialization of many of these projects and even threatened sustainability on the part of manufacture, the intensification of innovation practices and new strategies (such as offshoring, licensing, diversification) have managed to halt the decline in local activity.

Proximity and particularly support organizations have been key factors in the revitalization of the cluster. Local firms have strengthened their technological expertise and innovation capabilities through collaborative practices and well-designed programs (Albaladejo, 2005). On providing specific services at a reasonable cost, the technological institute (AIJU) plays a pivotal role in capacity-building at a company level and systemic capacities (Holmström, 2006). Moreover, it serves as a valuable repository of the latest knowledge and fosters innovation, contributing to areas such as product development, manufacture or training (Holmström, 2006). Together with the institute, the business association (AEFJ) has also driven innovation as an advanced service provider, and a real forum where valuable experiences are shared.

The ceramic tile cluster of Castellón

Although the ceramic tile cluster is globally spread out (China, Italy, Brazil, Portugal among others), our empirical study is based on the Spanish ceramic tile industry. Generally speaking, the sector presents increasing dynamism and intensity in terms of knowledge with a growing number of technological advances concentrated particularly in process and product (Russo, 1985). However, the industry shows a high dependence on construction sector cycles, which has become more apparent in the context of the current recession (Fernandez de Lucio, Gabaldón, and Gómez, 2005).

This industry includes the production of ceramic floors, tiles and other related activities, such as the production of decorative pieces, chemical additives, frits and glazes, machinery and equipment, and suppliers of atomized clay, among others. Over the last two decades, the ceramic tile industry has changed drastically because of the increasing sophistication of the global demand that requires value-added ceramic products obtained through efficient and flexible technologies with a moderate environmental impact (Budí-Orduña, 2008).

The mechanisms for the dissemination of knowledge (spin-offs, mobility of human resources or informal channels) allow a solid transmission of specialized knowledge in terms of technology or business strategy (Molina-Morales, 2002). Perhaps one of the fundamental driving factors in the generation of knowledge is a highly competitive auxiliary industry, able to provide a sales differential to the overall Castellón cluster (Hervas-Oliver, 2004). Generally speaking, suppliers share information and knowledge generated internally or collaboratively with their customer portfolio, which basically means an improvement in resources and capacities at a systemic level. This has also and impact on the GVC due to the fact that some activities of the cluster value chain, as frits and glazes production, are performed by locally born multinational companies that have customers all around the world. Once more, we have a traditional case where innovative activity is driven by a supplier base that controls the main sources and determines the direction of technological change.

The cluster comprising the geographical areas of Plana Alta, Plana Baixa and Alcalatén, has over 90% of the national ceramic tile production concentrated in a 20-km radius. This concentration of business activity along with the existence of a group of supporting organizations that are key in knowledge transmission (Molina-Morales, 2005) has been of the "Marshallian" industrial area (Boix, 2009; Boix and Galletto, 2006). In the literature on clusters, Porter (2000) particularly underlines the existence of this Spanish productive cluster in his description of the case of international competitors to the Italian ceramic tile industry.

Questionnaire and data collection

The data for this study was gathered throughout 2011 in both clusters. In the first stage, personal interviews, held with manufacturers and key institutions, enabled us to gather information on different aspects of the clusters. The information obtained and a review of relevant literature provided the basis for designing the questionnaire and discussing the results obtained. Following a pilot test carried out with representatives of the academic and business community, the final tool was used with the totality of business people located within each cluster.

The profile of data required for the study and the population characteristics, led us to opt for the "Roster-Recall" methodology as the most appropriate for identifying relationships between firms (Boschma and Ter Wal, 2007; Giuliani and Bell, 2005; Morrison and Rabellotti, 2009). Each interviewee rated the relationship maintained with a list of manufacturers and local suppliers with whom technical or business/market knowledge was either obtained or delivered. The respective lists were compiled on data provided by technical institutes or business associations in each cluster. Furthermore, the respondents were invited to add further companies (competitors, customers or suppliers) with whom they had maintained contact but were not included in the list.

Finally, a total of 166 and 75 end-product manufacturers and suppliers in the clusters of Castellón and Foia de Castalla took part in the study, reaching a response rate of between 70% and 96%. Peer debriefing with local experts confirmed that all relevant actors were interviewed. Given the size of both clusters, the number of interviews can be considered appropriate for a network analysis. Table 7.2 presents the characteristics at a company level: size and industrial activities. Moreover, it offers information regarding membership of local organizations and the main business activity.

An expert, with experience in innovation programs and work experience in business organizations, made the interviews of between 40 and 50 minutes, to owners or top company executives. The relational data gathered determined the importance of contact according to the interviewees. The questions made, allowed to establish the existence of the transfer of technological and business knowledge. The respective questions read as follows: 1) Which of the following firms on the list have you regularly asked for technical (business)

Table 7.2 Sample firms' profile

	Ceramic tile cluster	*Toy Valley cluster*
Company size		
Small	13.25%	86.7%
Medium	55.42%	10.7%
Large	31.33%	2.7%
Sample size	166/240	75/78
Industrial activities	• End-product firms • Frits and Glazes • Machinery and equipment • Special and decorative pieces • Atomized clay • Ceramic additives	• Toy manufacturers • Auxiliary industry • Suppliers of raw materials • Others

information over the last three years; 2) Which of the following firms on the list have contacted you to request technical (business) information over the last three years?

Methodology

Social Network Analysis (SNA) allows one to map out and measure relationships and flows between people, groups, organizations or any other entity that can process information/ knowledge (Hanneman and Riddle, 2005). It contemplates a group of actors that are located in or form part of an extensive network, and individual relations whose aggregation allows establishing global patterns. An approximation to the whole network enables an analysis on the way in which an actor fits in within a relational structure, that at the same time emerges from the specific micro-relations of the different actors (Hanneman and Riddle, 2005). In our case, the use of SNA allows us to determine the cluster's knowledge map, thereby facilitating an audit process of knowledge.

Within the network, those actors connected to unrelated third parties exercise substantial advantages in terms of control and access to knowledge. Thanks to the use of specialized software and the allocation of actors to groups established on the basis of criteria such as activity or position in the cluster value chain, makes it possible to define different measurement profiles. Precisely, Gould and Fernández (Gould and Fernandez, 1989) build up a typology of brokerage according to whether the actors involved belong to the same or different groups. Such a classification enhances the study of the brokerage role in innovation, since there are considerable differences in the knowledge shared between peers (all actors carrying out the same activity) or between members of different groups. As we can observe in Figure 7.1, the coordinator mediates between another two companies that carry out the same activity within the same stage of cluster value chain. Those firms that act as a consultant or liaison mediate between two actors that develop activities that are different to theirs. Finally, the gatekeeper and the representative act as intermediaries between companies carrying out the same activity as theirs and a third that belongs to a different group in the cluster value chain.

Once we calculated the indicators related with the brokerage activity we introduced these independent variables along with the control ones in our model. We also calculated separated OLS Regressions for each network analyzing the effect of brokerage activities on two types of systemic contribution: The technical contribution and the business/ market contribution (Table 7.3).

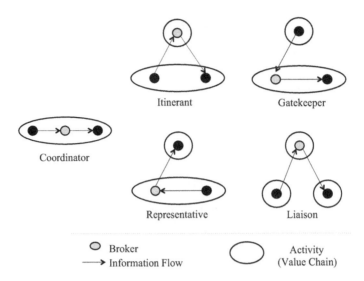

Figure 7.1 Types of brokerage

Table 7.3 Dependent, independent and control variables

Type	Variable	Items
Dependent variable	Technical innovation contribution	Has your company introduced any of the following innovations in the last three years (1 = no, 2 = yes)? • New or improved methods for the production of goods or services. • New or improved logistics systems or delivery methods. • New or improved support activities for production processes Cronbach Alpha > 0.7.
	Business innovation contribution	Has your company introduced any of these innovations in the last three years? (1 = no, 2 = yes). • New practices in work procedures and organization. • New structure in work organization. • New management systems to improve the application, exchange and compilation of knowledge. Cronbach Alpha > 0.7.
Independent variables	External links with the GVC	Extra-cluster links with members of the GVC like: end-product manufacturers, suppliers, research centres or universities. Dichotomous variable (1 = No; 2 = Yes)
	Coordinator	Total number of times acting as a coordinator divided by the expected result as coordinator (under a probability model).
	Consultant	Total number of times acting as a consultant divided by the expected result as consultant (under a probability model)
	Gatekeeper	Total number of times acting as a gatekeeper divided by the expected result as gatekeeper (under a probability model)
	Representative	Total number of times acting as a representative divided by the expected result as representative (under a probability model)
	Liaison	Total number of times acting as a liaison divided by the expected result as liaison (under a probability model)
Control variables	Absorptive capacity	Factor that combines replies about activities related to innovation in the last three years.
	Size	Factor that combines replies related to sales and the average number of employees in the company over the last three years.

Results

Below we report the results obtained in our econometric analysis. We will see how the extent of brokerage activities, portrayed in its different roles, has an influence on the systemic contribution of the clusters studied. As reported above in the empirical section, we have differentiated between two types of contribution depending on the technical or business bases. Accordingly, the tables showing our results present two regressions for each cluster analysed (See Tables 7.4 and 7.5). Moreover, the role played by the other variables considered: size, external links (GVC) and absorptive capacity could be verified in all the models.

Table 7.4 Results for the toy sector

	Technical contribution (KN)		Business contribution (IN)	
	B (Standard Error)	p-value	B (Standard Error)	p-value
(Constant)	−8.566 (3.825)	**.028	0.296 (4.9347)	.952
Size	.431 (.136)	.748	1.147 (1.6368)	.486
External links (GVC)	3.207 (1.467)	**.032	−2.975 (1.8215)	*.107
Absorptive capacity	1.524 (1.382)	.274	0.652 (1.6667)	.697
Coordinator	−3.482 (1.486)	*.022	−0.203 (1.4194)	.886
Consultant	.611 (1.781)	.732	2.724 (1.2653)	**.035
Gatekeeper	−1.592 (1.480)	.286	−0.664 (1.662)	.691
Representative	.981 (1.067)	.361	−2.612 (1.7763)	.146
Liaison	−0.383 (1.481)	.797	−1.130 (1.3294)	.398
Multiple R-squared	0.378		0.455	
Adjusted R-squared	0.292		0.291	
F Statistic	4.393***		6.028***	

Table 7.5 Results for the ceramic tile sector

	Technical contribution (KN)		Business contribution (IN)	
	B (Standard Error)	p-value	B (Standard Error)	p-value
(Constant)	0 (0.073)	1.000	0 (0.069)	1.000
Size	−0.109 (0.087)	0.211	0.259 (0084)	***.002
External links (GVC)	0.389 (0.084)	***.000	−0.024 (0.081)	0.768
Absorptive capacity	−0.108 (0.083)	0.198	0.115 (0.079)	0.145
Coordinator	−0.006 (0.08)	0.942	−0.122 (0.091)	0.179
Consultant	0.09 (0.077)	0.245	0.149 (0.077)	0.23
Gatekeeper	−0.131 (0.088)	0.137	0.083 (0.084)	0.493
Representative	0.035 (0.09)	0.697	−0.052 (0.076)	*0.054
Liaison	0.045 (0.08)	0.577	0.211 (0.081)	***0.010
Multiple R-squared	0.153		0.255	
Adjusted R-squared	0.110		0.217	
F Statistic	3.553***		6.713***	

Initially, we hypothesized that brokerage positions across different stages of the cluster value chain will generate greater innovations compared to firms broker knowledge between similar. In the two technical knowledge networks, none of the mediating positions across different stages of the cluster value chain analysed achieved statistical relevance. Conversely, when we turn to the business information network, the consultant role in the toy valley and the liaison role in the tile cluster become significant at p-value $< .05$ and p-value $< .01$, respectively. Regarding brokerage positions where incoming knowledge from competitors predominate, the coordinator role presents a significant negative value in the technical network of the toy cluster (p-value $< .01$), while the representative role provokes similar consequences within the business network of the tile cluster (p-value < 0.1). In view of these positive and negative effects obtained, our main expectations are supported.

Tightly linked with our previous conjecture, the systemic contribution of brokerage positions to innovation were expected to depend on the type of knowledge shared within each network. As mentioned above, the consultant and the liaison roles exert positive effect in both business information networks. On the contrary, both the coordinator role in the technical network of the toy valley and the representative role in business network of the toy valley generate harmful effects in terms of systemic contribution. To put it differently, brokerage between different stages matters only in the business network, while positions mediating incoming knowledge from similar companies are relevant in both the technical and the business network. Therefore, our expectations are only partially corroborated.

We expect that brokerage positions connecting external and internal actors boost cluster knowledge base through a solid systemic contribution. In both the toy cluster and the tile cluster technical networks, findings obtained clearly endorse our expectations at p-value $< .05$ and p-value $< .01$ respectively. Unexpectedly, these positive and significant effects do not hold for any of our business knowledge networks. Even more, although barely significant (p-value $< .10$), external links (GVC) shows a negative effect in the toy valley case. Thus, we only confirmed our beliefs in the technical knowledge network.

Conclusions

In this work, we have analysed the influence that cluster firms' brokerage has on their systemic contribution in terms of technical knowledge and business-related information. In order to carry out this study, we examined two economic realities, namely the ceramic tile and toy clusters, both located in the Valencia region in Spain. By comparing the effects of five different brokerage roles on the technical and business network of two different clusters, the paper represents a step forward on the state of the art. Despite of the complexity of the analysis, a clear message particularly came out. Brokerage positions are not systematically benign for the systemic contribution and innovation. The structure of the network, the shared knowledge, the composition of the triads or the specific nature of the cluster analysed determines the brokerage effect.

Within the cluster boundaries, it appears that only brokerage positions providing access to diverse repositories of knowledge provides valuable systemic contribution compared to the absent or even the detrimental effect generated when knowledge proceeds from competitors. This may obviously reflect certain overlapping of knowledge between firms from the same stage of the cluster value chain consequence of shared experiences and apprenticeships mechanisms prolonged in time. This result seems partially consistent with Giuliani (2008). However, our findings provide a more refined picture, as the advantages mediating positions in clusters may not vanish if knowledge sources present certain doses of diversity.

The stickiness and tacitness of the technical knowledge can be seen on the basis of the asymmetric contribution of brokerage positions. Pervasive interactions necessary for exchanges of tacit technological knowledge progressively narrow the scope of the local knowledge sources by bringing closer firm's cognitive maps, and diminish the benefits of brokerage. In contexts where knowledge is more easily accessed and transferred, such as in the business network, firms may frequently renew their knowledge stock and share it with its local partners. However, this argument does not hold for horizontal relationships possibly due to competition.

As far as knowledge overlapping and redundancies emerge, a replacement process of knowledge sources through the establishment of trans-local linkages is triggered. In line with (Morrison, 2008) or (Giuliani, 2011), local firms catalysing extra-cluster knowledge into the local milieu not only reinforce their own knowledge base but also generate a crucial systemic contribution. Conversely, having external links with members of the GVC does not seem to be relevant when the contribution is considered in business-related aspects. Perhaps, this may be due to the higher permeability of local actors to market information that can be obtained through a wide number of local sources due to higher levels of codification.

Firms that acquire valuable new information through links with actors that are not related to the cluster, beyond local boundaries in the context of global value chain, are the main contributors to the system. This evidence highlights the role of external gatekeepers on the absorption of complex technological knowledge from non-local actors. However, the codified nature of business-related knowledge minimizes the prominent role of these external gatekeepers in the systematic internalization of external knowledge.

Furthermore, our work shows how brokerage between members of a same group does not end up benefitting the systemic contribution of clusters. In fact, the coordinator role does not have a positive effect on innovation in any of our models and only presents one significant but negative relationship in the toy sector. This highlights the importance of studying the dynamics of cooperation-competition that exist in clusters, particularly in settings such as those studied that are characterized by a high degree of maturity in evolution and industrial context as well as the life cycle of the products they offer. This argument is substantiated to a certain extent by observing the results offered by some roles that involve companies that carry out different activities in both stages cluster value chains. In fact, brokers that mediate between firms belonging to different stages of the cluster value chain make a more relevant contribution. This may be because codified information flows easily between non-rival companies that manage different knowledge bases. This finding reinforces our expectations on the increasing relevance of competition on explaining cooperation at a micro level.

Finally, this research contributes to the existing literature on clusters and in particular, to the work on brokerage that makes a case for the existence of a specific type of knowledge that arises from such activity. Brokers transfer valuable knowledge, connect different audiences and carry out several brokerage roles simultaneously (both internally and externally). On carrying out this type of activity, brokers perform a myriad of functions such as investigation, connection, information processing and the transfer of knowledge in such a way that it can be successfully applied. Therefore, our results suggest that brokerage activities combined with a strategic position within networks offer opportunities for improving the resources of clusters in accordance with the type of knowledge exchanged.

This study is not without certain limitations that ought to be addressed and modified as far as possible in future lines of investigation. First, our sample is based on data that we gathered from two clusters during a mature stage in their life cycle. Therefore, this limitation ought to be taken into account when examining the results obtained and their possible implications. We should be particularly cautious in the generalization of conclusions to other contexts. Moreover, the study undertaken is a static view that captures the essence of the brokerage phenomenon at a particular time, but of course, relationships evolve over time. In fact, a possible continuation of this work would be to replicate the fieldwork so that the long-term effects of roles and their possible evolution can be known.

As regards the context of the study, we have focused on relationships that arise within the clusters themselves. This limits the study of brokerage roles by conditioning their calculation to the possibilities of sub-divisions in each cluster. A more complete study must include the analysis of brokerage activities that involve firms located outside the cluster. Finally, another possibility for future research is to investigate the conditions that explain the distinctive effects and the consequences of each brokerage role and their possible combination, in greater depth.

Acknowledgements

Financial support provided by the Spanish Ministry of Economy and Competitiveness (Project number ECO2015–67122-R).

References

Albaladejo, M. (2005). A service centre approach to local innovative SMEs: The case of the Spanish toy valley cluster. *The IUP Journal of Applied Economics*, 4: 13–29.

Alberti, F.G. (2006). The decline of the industrial district of Como: Recession, relocation or reconversion? *Entrepreneurship & Regional Development*, 18: 473–501.

Alberti, F.G., and Pizzurno, E. (2015). Knowledge exchanges in innovation networks: Evidences from an Italian aerospace cluster. *Competitiveness Review*, 25: 258–287.

Antonelli, C. (2000). Collective knowledge communication and innovation: The evidence of technological districts. *Regional Studies. Journal of Regional Studies Association*, 34: 535–547.

Asheim, B., and Belussi, F. (2007). *Industrial Districts and Globalisation: Learning and Innovation in Local and Global Production and Innovation Systems*. EIBA (European International Business Academy) Annual Conference on 'International Business, Local Development and Science-Technology Relationships', Catania, Italy.

Bathelt, H., Malmberg, A., and Maskell, P. (2004). Clusters and knowledge: Local buzz, global pipelines and the process of knowledge creation. *Progress in Human Geography*, 28: 31–56.

Becattini, G. (1979). Dal settore industriale al distretto industriale. *Rivista Di Economia E Politica Industriale,* 1: 1–8.

———. 1990. The Marshallian industrial district as a socio-economic notion. In F. Pyke (ed.), *Industrial Districts and Local Economic Regeneration*. Ginebra: International Institute for Labour Studies.

Becker, M.H. (1970). Sociometric location and innovativeness: Reformulation and extension of the diffusion model. *American Sociological Review*, 35: 267–282.

Belso-Martínez, J.A., Molina-Morales, F.X., and Martínez-Cháfer, L. (2015). Contributions of brokerage roles to firms' innovation in a confectionery cluster. *Technology Analysis & Strategic Management*, 27: 1014–1030.

Boari, C, Odorici, V., and Zamarian, M. (2003). Clusters and rivalry: Does localization really matter? *Scandinavian Journal of Management*, 19(4): 467–89.

Boari, C, and Riboldazzi, F. (2010). Innovare nei cluster geografici: Origine e sviluppo di un knowledge broker. In C. Boari (ed.), *Dinamiche Evolutive Nei Cluster Geografici Di Imprese*. Bologna: Il Molino.

Boari, C., and Riboldazzi, F. (2014). How knowledge brokers emerge and evolve: The role of actors' behaviour. *Research Policy*, 43: 683–695.

Boix, R. (2009). The empirical evidence of industrial districts in Spain. In G. Becattini, M. Bellandi, and L. De Propris (eds.), *A Handbook of Industrial Districts*. Cheltenham: Edward Elgar.

Boix, R, and Galletto.V. (2006). El nuevo mapa de los distritos industriales de España y su comparación con Italia y el Reino Unido. Documento de trabajo 06.04. Departament d'Economia Aplicada. Universitat Autònoma de Barcelona.

Boschma, R.A. (2005). Role of proximity in interaction and performance: Conceptual and empirical challenges. *Regional Studies*, 39: 41–45.

Boschma, R.A., and Frenken, K. (2006). Why is economic geography not an evolutionary science? Towards an evolutionary economic geography. *Journal of Economic Geography*, 6: 273–302.

Boschma, R.A., and Frenken, K. (2009). Some notes on institutions in evolutionary economic geography. *Economic Geography*, 85: 151–158.

Boschma, R.A., and Ter Wal, A.L.J. (2007). Knowledge networks and innovative performance in an industrial district. *Industry and Innovation*, 14: 177–199.

Breschi, S., and Lissoni, F. (2001). Knowledge spillovers and local innovation systems: A critical survey. *Industrial and Corporate Change*, 10: 975–1005.

Broekel, T., and Boschma, R. (2012). Knowledge networks in the Dutch aviation industry: The proximity paradox. *Journal of Economic Geography*, 12: 409–433.

Buckley, P.J., Glaister, K.W., Klijn, E., and Tan, H. (2009). Knowledge accession and knowledge acquisition in strategic alliances: The impact of supplementary and complementary dimensions. *British Journal of Management*, 20: 598–609.

Budí-Orduña, V. (2008). El distrito de la cerámica de Castellón. *Mediterráneo Económico*, 13: 383–407.

Burt, R.S. (1997). Contingent value of the social capital. *Administrative Science Quarterly*, 42: 339–365.

Cantner, U., and Meder, A. (2007). Technological proximity and the choice of cooperation partner. *Journal of Economic Interaction and Coordination*, 2: 45–65.

Capaldo, A. (2007). Network structure and innovation: The leveraging of a dual network as a distinctive relational capability. *Strategic Management Journal*, 28(6): 585–608.

Carnabuci, G., and Bruggeman, J. (2009). Knowledge specialization, knowledge brokerage and the uneven growth of technology domains. *Social Forces*, 88: 607–641.

Chiesa, V., Frattini, F., Gilardoni, E., Manzini, R., and Pizzurno, E. (2007). Searching for factors influencing technological asset value. *European Journal of Innovation Management*, 10: 467–488.

De Martino, R., Mc Hardy Reid, D., and Zygliodopoulos, S.C. (2006). Balancing localization and globalization: Exploring the impact of firm internationalization on a regional cluster. *Entrepreneurship and Regional Development*, 18: 1–24.

De Propris, L., and Driffield, N. (2006). The importance of clusters for spillovers from foreign direct investment and technology sourcing. *Cambridge Journal of Economics*, 30: 277–291.

Fernandez de Lucio, I., Gabaldón, D., and Gómez, C. (2005). La innovación en el sector de pavimentos y revestimientos cerámicos de la Comunidad Valenciana. In Alto Consejo Consultivo en I+D de la Presidencia de la Generalitat Valenciana. Valencia.

Garcia-Vega, M. (2006). Does technological diversification promote innovation?: An empirical analysis for European firms. *Research Policy*, 35: 230–246.

Gebert, H., Geib, M., Kolbe, L., and Brenner, W. (2003). Knowledge-enabled customer relationship management: Integrating customer relationship management and knowledge management concepts [1]. *Journal of Knowledge Management*, 7: 107–123.

Gereffi, G. (2005). The global economy: Organization, governance, and development. In N.J. Smelser and R. Swedberg (eds.), *The Handbook of Economic Sociology*. New York: Princeton University Press, pp. 160–182.

Gilsing, V., Nooteboom, B., Vanhaverbeke, W., Duysters, G., and van den Oord, A. (2008). Network embeddedness and the exploration of novel technologies: Technological distance, betweenness centrality and density. *Research Policy*, 37: 1717–1731.

Giuliani, E. (2007). The selective nature of knowledge networks in clusters: Evidence from the wine industry. *Journal of Economic Geography*, 7: 139–168.

Giuliani, E. (2008). *What Drives Innovative Output in Emerging Clusters? Evidence From the Wine Industry*. Science and Policy Research Unit (SPRU) Working Paper Series.

Giuliani, E. (2011). Role of technological gatekeepers in the growth of industrial clusters: Evidence from Chile. *Regional Studies*, 45: 1329–1348.

Giuliani, E., and Bell, M. (2005). The micro-determinants of meso-level learning and innovation: Evidence from a Chilean wine cluster. *Research Policy*, 34: 47–68.

Gordon, I.R., and McCann, P. (2000). Industrial clusters: Complexes, agglomeration and/or social networks? *Urban Studies*, 37: 513–532.

Gould, R.V., and Fernandez, R.M. (1989). Structures of mediation: A formal approach to brokerage in transaction networks. *Sociological Methodology*, 19: 89–126.

Graf, H., and Kruger, J.J. (2011). The performance of gatekeepers in innovator networks. *Industry and Innovation*, 18: 69–88.

Hanneman, R. A, and Mark R. (2005). *Introduction to Social Network Methods*. Riverside (CA): Department of Sociology, University of California.

Hargadon, A.B. (1998). Firms as knowledge brokers: Lessons in pursuing continuous innovation. *California Management Review*, 40(3): 209–27.

Hargadon, A.B., and Sutton, R.I. (1997). Technology brokering and innovation in a product development firm. *Administrative Science Quarterly*, 42: 716–749.

Hassink, R. (2005). How to unlock regional economies from path dependency? From learning region to learning cluster. *European Planning Studies*, 13: 521–535.

Hervas-Oliver, J.L. (2004). *Heterogeneidad Estratégica En Un Cluster. Evidencia Empírica de La Identificación de Grupos Estratégicos a Través de La Cadena de Valor Y Su Impacto En La Performance En El Sector Industrial Cerámico*. Valencia: Polytechnic University of Valencia.

Holmström, M. (2006). Globalisation and good work: Impiva, a Spanish project to regenerate industrial districts. *Tijdschrift voor economische en sociale geografie*, 97: 491–502.

Howells, J. (2006). Intermediation and the role of intermediaries in innovation. *Research Policy*, 35: 715–728.

Inkpen, A.C., and Tsang. E.W.K. (2005). Social capital, networks, and knowledge transfer. *The Academy of Management Review*, 30:146–65.

Kogut, B., and Zander, I. (1992). Knowledge of the firm, combinative capabilities, and the replication of technology. *Organization Science*, 3: 383–397.

Lissoni, F. (2001). Knowledge codification and the geography of innovation: The case of Brescia mechanical cluster. *Research Policy*, 30: 1479–1500.

Lorenzoni, G, and Lipparini, A. (1999). The leveraging of interfirm relationships as a distinctive organizational capability: A longitudinal study. *Strategic Management Journal*, 20(4): 317–38.

Malmberg, A., and Maskell, P. (2002). The elusive concept of localization economies: Towards a knowledge-based theory of spatial clustering. *Environment and Planning A*, 34: 429–450.

Marsden, P.V. (1982). Brokerage behavior in restricted exchange networks. In P.V. Marsden and L. Nan (eds.), *Social Structure and Network Analysis*. Beverly Hills: Sage, pp. 201–218.

Maskell, P., Bathelt, H., and Malmberg, A. (2006). Building global knowledge pipelines, the role of temporary clusters. *European Planning Studies*, 14: 997–1013.

Maskell, P., and Malmberg, A. (1999). Localized learning and industrial competitiveness. *Cambridge Journal of Economics*, 23: 167–185.

Maskell, P., and Malmberg, A. (2007). Myopia, knowledge development and cluster evolution. *Journal of Economic Geography*, 7: 603–618.

McEvily, B., and Zaheer, A. (1999). Bridging ties: A source of firm heterogeneity in competitive capabilities. *Strategic Management Journal*, 20: 1133–1156.

Molina-Morales, F. X. (2002). Industrial districts and innovation: The case of the Spanish ceramic tiles industry. *Entrepreneurship & Regional Development*, 14 (4): 317–35.

————. (2005). "Estrategias de exploración y explotación en las aglomeraciones territoriales de empresas: Una aproximación desde la perspectiva del capital social. *Revista Valenciana de Economía Y Hacienda*, 13(2005): 157–84.

Molina-Morales, F. X., and Martínez-Fernández, T. (2009). Too much love in the neighborhood can hurt: How an excess of intensity and trust in relationships may produce negative effects on firms. *Strategic Management Journal*, 30(9): 1013–23.

Morrison, A. (2008). 'Gatekeepers of knowledge' within industrial districts: Who they are, how they interact. *Regional Studies*, 42: 817–835.

Morrison, A., and Rabellotti, R. (2009). Knowledge and information networks in an Italian wine cluster. *European Planning Studies*, 17: 983–1006.

Nonaka, I. (1994). A dynamic theory of organizational knowledge creation. *Organization Science*, 5: 14–37.

Nonaka, I., and Takeuchi, H. (1995). *The Knowledge-creating Company*. Oxford: Oxford University Press.

Nooteboom, B., Van Haverbeke, W., Duysters, G., Gilsing, V., and Van Den Oord, A. (2007). Optimal cognitive distance and absorptive capacity. *Research Policy*, 36: 1016–1034.

Noteboom, B. (1999). Innovation, learning and industrial organization. *Cambridge Journal of Economics*, 23: 127–150.

Paniccia, I. (1998). One, a hundred, thousands industrial districts. Organizational variety of local networks of SMEs. *Organizational Studies*, Special Is (4): 667–700.

Phelps, C., Heidl, R., and Wadhwa, A. (2012). Knowledge, networks, and knowledge networks a review and research agenda. *Journal of Management*, 38: 1115–1166.

Piore, M. (1990). Work, labour and action: Work experience in a system of flexible production. In F. Pyke, G. Becattini, and W. Sengenberger (eds.), *Industrial Districts and Inter-Firm Cooperation in Italy*. Ginebra: International Institute for Labour Studies.

Porter, M E. (1998). Clusters and the new economics of competition. *Harvard Business Review*, December: 77–90.

————. (2000). Location, competition and economic development: Local clusters in a global economy. *Economic Development Quarterly*, 14(1): 15–34.

Powell, W.W., Koput, K.W., and Smith-Doerr, L. (1996). Interorganizational collaboration and the locus of innovation: Networks of learning in biotechnology. *Administrative Science Quarterly*, 41: 116–145.

Provan, K.G., and Human, S.E. (1999). Organizational learning and the role of the network broker in small-firm manufacturing networks. In A. Grandori (ed.), *Interfirm Networks: Organization and Industrial Competitiveness*. London: Routledge, pp. 185–207.

Quintana-García, C., and Benavides-Velasco, C.A. (2008). Innovative competence, exploration and exploitation: The influence of technological diversification. *Research Policy*, 37: 492–507.

Robertson, P.L., Jacobson, D., and Langlois, R.N. (2008). Innovation processes and industrial districts. *Economics Working Papers*. 200803. Available at:
http://digitalcommons.uconn.edu/econ_wpapers/200803

Russo, M. (1985). Technical change and the industrial district: The role of interfirm relations in the growth and transformation of ceramic tile production in Italy. *Research Policy*, 14(6): 329–43.

Sammarra, A., and Biggiero, L. (2008). Heterogeneity and specificity of inter-firm knowledge flows in innovation networks. *Journal of Management Studies*, 45: 800–829.

Sciascia, S., D'Oria, L., Bruni, M., and Larrañeta, B. (2014). Entrepreneurial orientation in low-and medium-tech industries: The need for absorptive capacity to increase performance. *European Management Journal*, 32: 761–769.

Signorini, L.F. (1994). Una verifica quantitativa dell'effetto distretto. *Sviluppo Locale*, 1(1): 31–70.

Smedlund, A. (2006). The roles of intermediaries in a regional knowledge system. *Journal of Intellectual Capital*, 7: 204–220.

Tallman, S., Jenkins, M., Henry, N., and Pinch, S. (2004). Knowledge, clusters, and competitive advantage. The Academy of Management Review, 29: 258–271.

Tomlinson, Philip R. (2010). Co-operative ties and innovation: Some new evidence for UK manufacturing. *Research Policy*, 39(6): 762–75.

Troilo, G. (2006). Marketing Knowledge Management: Managing Knowledge in Market Oriented Companies. Cheltenham, UK: Edward Elgar.

Tsai, W. (2001). Knowledge transfer in intraorganizational networks: Effects of network position and absorptive capacity on business unit innovation and performance. *Academy of Management Journal*, 44: 996–1004.

Uzzi, B., and Spiro J. (2005). Collaboration and creativity: The small world problem. *American Journal of Sociology*, 111(2): 447–504.

Von Hippel, E. (1987). Cooperation between rivals: Informal know-how trading. *Research Policy*, 16(6): 291–302.

Yli-Renko, H., Autio E., and Sapienza, H.J. (2001). Social capital, knowledge acquisition, and knowledge exploitation in young technology-based firms. *Strategic Management Journal*, 22(6–7): 587–613.

Zaheer, A., and Bell, G.G. (2005). Benefiting from network position: Firm capabilities, structural holes, and performance. *Strategic Management Journal*, 26: 809–825.

Zander, U., and Kogut, B. (1995). Knowledge and the speed of the transfer and imitation of organizational capabilities: An empirical test. *Organization Science*, 6: 76–92.

Zeng, S.X., Xie, X.M., and Tam, C.M. (2010). Relationship between cooperation networks and innovation performance of SMEs. *Technovation*, 30: 181–194.

8 Local liabilities between immigrant and native entrepreneurship in clusters and global value chains

Simone Guercini

Introduction

The chapter proposes the new concept of "local liabilities" for a better understanding of the link between immigrant entrepreneurship in industrial districts (IDs) and global value chains (GVCs). Local liabilities, in which the term "local" refers to social space, emerges in settings where two (or more) separate communities (of persons and firms) exist: the greater the separation between the communities, the larger the local liabilities. This new form of liability has not yet found a place in the business literature. The term "liability" refers to conditions of disadvantage experienced by certain business actors. It has been widely addressed both in international business studies (the liability of foreignness, the liability of outsidership – Johanson and Vahlne, 1977, 2009; Johanson and Wiedersheim-Paul, 1975), as well as in studies on the role of the age and size of enterprises in determining conditions for success (liability of newness, liability of smallness – Stinchcombe, 1965; Freeman et al., 1983; Aldrich and Auster, 1986). The chapter proposes and elaborates on the concept of "local liabilities", specifically with regard to the problems associated with changes to clusters of originally district-based enterprises (Becattini, 1990; Varaldo and Ferrucci, 1996), a phenomenon which has been contextually observed during the development of immigrant entrepreneurship (Waldinger, 1986; Aldrich and Waldinger, 1990).

The concept of local liability is moreover addressed in relation to communities of enterprises and people, both in local settings and in the global value chains to which the enterprises belong (Gereffi, 1999). The separation between different communities of people and enterprises does not exclude the presence of even significant transactions between immigrant and native entrepreneurship. Such separation, however, reduces the possibilities for interaction, thereby creating not only weak bonds (that could have positive effects – Granovetter, 1973), but limiting the contact between the actors associated with different communities of people (Guercini and Ranfagni, 2016). Local liability thus represents a barrier to the development of trust and reciprocal learning (Camuffo and Grandinetti, 2011; Grandinetti, 2011) and business interaction (Håkansson, 1982; Guercini and Runfola, 2015).

The relation between native and immigrant entrepreneurship and their respective value chains is examined with regard to the consequences of the local liabilities that may emerge in industrial clusters. The possibilities for interaction are influenced by the different characteristics of the relationships between the industrial cluster's enterprises and the actors in their respective value chains. A division of these relationships is proposed, according to whether the native and immigrant enterprises belong to the same or different global value chains (Gereffi, 1999; Cattaneo et al., 2010). The fact that the enterprises belong to different value chains likely plays an important role in fostering the survival of the two (or more) communities of people and enterprises, despite the disrupting influence of local liabilities

(Humphrey and Schmitz, 2002). For example, there are different value chains when companies of the two (or more) communities evolve in very different ways and times in the shift from "producer-driven" to "buyer-driven" commodity chains (Gereffi, 1994) and the business of the different communities interact with different and separate groups of customers and suppliers both locally and globally. Moreover, relationships with actors in the global value chain can aid both the native as well as the immigrant business, even in the presence of local liabilities (Dei Ottati, 2016). However, when faced with change, the separation between the enterprises reduces the possibilities for learning and development within the local setting. A potential way to overcome such local liability is by strengthening the interaction capacities of both the native and immigrant enterprises (Guercini and Runfola, 2015).

The chapter takes a general approach, developing a number of concepts that are not specific to any individual enterprise, value chain or industrial district. However, methodologically it is based for the most part on nearly 20 years' experience studying Chinese immigrant entrepreneurship in the Prato industrial cluster, a fashion production area located near Florence known as one of Italy's largest and most important industrial district (Becattini, 1990; Dei Ottati, 1994; Guercini, 2004).

Liabilities in internationalization and global value chain

In the management and business economics literature, the concept of "liability" is associated to the difficulties, additional costs or probability of failure consequent to a certain condition in which an enterprise finds itself with respect to other competing firms. The type of condition determines the type of liability. For example, the "liability of newness" (Stinchcombe, 1965) hinders newly established enterprises, which thus experience greater mortality than already established firms because they are still unable to compete effectively and enjoy a lesser degree of legitimacy. Instead, one consequence of the "liability of smallness" is that new large-sized enterprises have a greater chance of survival than smaller ones (Freeman et al., 1983; Aldrich and Auster, 1986).

The concept of liability has been widely used in the international business literature (Zaheer, 1995; Johanson and Vahlne, 2009) with regard to the conditions of disadvantage that may be associated to operating in a market other than one's own domestic one. Such issue has been addressed within the theory of multinational enterprise, which maintains that firms doing business abroad face greater costs (Hymer, 1976; Kindleberger, 1969). The reasons for such costs are various, including the foreign country's language, economy, laws and politics, which all told put a greater burden on foreign firms in comparison to national ones (Hymer, 1976), in that they must sustain additional costs in order to face: 1) the reduced availability of information on how to do business; 2) discrimination from the government, the consumers and/or the suppliers; 3) foreign exchange risk. Moreover, in a multinational network 4) the lines of communications are longer and hence the risks of information loss and/or distortion represent a source of disadvantage in comparison to domestic firms (Kindleberger, 1969).

In the Uppsala School model (U-model) the greater costs of doing business abroad is linked to "psychic distance" (Johanson and Vahlne, 1977), defined as "the sum of factors preventing the flow of information from and to the market. Examples are difference in language, education, business practices, culture and industrial development" (Johanson and Vahlne, 1977, p. 24). This model has been developed beginning with the empirical research conducted on internationalization through a database of Swedish enterprises (Johanson and Wiedersheim-Paul, 1975; Carlson, 1970). Distance imposes a gradual process of internationalization, which is described by a so-called "establishment chain" (Cavusgil, 1980). Such establishment chain proceeds step by step at the same pace as the enterprise's learning processes (Grandinetti and Rullani, 1996; Forsgren, 2002). The model includes interacting aspects of state and change in the internationalization process. The concept of psychic distance is then compared with that of cultural distance, including measures of the two constructs (Sousa and Bradley, 2006).

The U-model has been compared with other, previously formulated models, starting with internationalization models based on the role of technology and innovation (I-model – Vernon, 1966; Gruber et al., 1967). In this case the power of superior technology developed in the framework of the enterprise's national base could provide impetus to an express process of internationalization to expand the technology's market base (Lorenzoni, 1987), and hence the "costs of doing business abroad" lose importance. Later, further criticisms were also levelled at the U-model due to the empirical observation that the predicted gradualism is lacking in phenomena such as "born global" (Knight and Cavusgil, 1996). The role played by outsidership with regard to the relevant networks in internationalization processes has also been subjected to criticism (Vahlne and Johanson, 2013).

The costs of doing business abroad and psychic distance are associated with the concept of the liability of foreignness (LOF), as first defined by Zaheer (1995). The attention here has always been focused on subsidiaries of multinational enterprises. Zaheer links foreignness to the following factors that engender extra costs for foreign subsidiaries in comparison to domestic firms: 1) spatial distance between parent company and subsidiaries; 2) lack of familiarity with the host-country environments; 3) nationalism and lack of legitimacy in the host country (Zaheer, 1995). Differences in culture and language, economic and political regulations, spatial distance and its consequences on communication processes are all sources of LOF (Matsuo, 2000). Although some of these costs must also be sustained by domestic firms, they are substantially greater for foreign firms (Mezias, 2002). This leads to considering other factors that may generate LOF, hence broadening the definition of the construct itself.

The existence of LOF "explained why a foreign investor needed to have a firm-specific advantage to more than offset this liability . . . the larger the psychic distance, the larger is the liability of foreignness" (Johanson and Vahlne, 2009, p. 1412). In recent years the factors generating costs associated with doing business abroad seem to have lost importance in comparison to other factors. Zaheer (2002) focuses on the differences between the "cost of doing business abroad" and LOF, highlighting that the former is an "economic concept", based on quantification of costs connected to the market and linked to physical distance, while the latter is a "sociological concept", linked to legitimacy and the relationship between the actor and the host society.

LOF has been object of extensive debate in the literature of the last few decades, as demonstrated by the fact that academic journals have devoted special editions to the issue (see the *Journal of International Management*, vol. 8, n. 3, 2002). The concept of outsidership consistently emerges from studies of multinational enterprises (Eden and Miller, 2001). LOF is generally subdivided in two types of hazards that foreign enterprises, and not national enterprises, have been found to face in the host market: 1) unfamiliarity hazards, due to a lack of knowledge and experience in the foreign market; 2) discrimination hazards due to the unfair treatment that may be reserved for foreign firms in comparison to local enterprises. While the first aspect is linked to the issue of knowledge and experience, and can be overcome by the enterprise through learning, the second has to do with the attitudes of the actors in the host country and can be tackled by fostering relationships and the ability to develop insidership in the relevant networks.

In recent years the same authors that developed the U-model have examined other aspects associated with the positions of different actors within relevant networks operating in global markets, as such positions may be related to the liability of outsidership (LOO). Markets are "networks of relationships, in which firms are linked to each other in various, complex and, to a considerable extent, invisible patterns . . . insidership in relevant network(s) is necessary for successful internationalization, and so by the same token there is a liability of outsidership" (Johanson and Vahlne, 2009, p. 1411).

Moreover, "relationships offer potential for learning and for building trust and commitment, both of which are preconditions for internationalization" (Johanson and Vahlne, 2009, pp. 1411–1412). LOO affects firms that enter a business environment as outsiders in the relevant networks, without knowing who the business actors are, or how they are connected to each other. In order to overcome LOO it is necessary to become a member of the relevant networks, in other words, become an insider through processes of observation, construction and maintenance of networks (Hilmersson and Jansson, 2012).

The concept of LOO provides a link between the interpretative model of internationalization processes and models studying buyer-supplier relationships in business networks. It has emerged from the Nordic School of Industrial Marketing, in particular the approach of the so-called IMP Group, which studies interactional and relational processes and industrial networks (Håkansson, 1982; Håkansson and Snehota, 1995).

Global value chain literature highlights the importance of transnational business networks, cross-border but often inside the same national groups, overcoming both LOF and LOO, as in the case of overseas Chinese business groups in Vietnam or the Philippines, (and elsewhere), which were tapped by Hong Kong and Taiwanese firms in creating triangle manufacturing networks in apparel and other industries (Gereffi, 1999).

One important aspect regarding the relation between internationalization theory and the study of interactions and networking is the promotion of learning at the inter-organizational level (Håkansson et al., 2009). Access to the relevant networks modifies the costs of doing business abroad, and hence leads to a rethinking of the processes necessary to overcome the underlying liabilities, LOO in particular. The dynamics of learning through dyadic interactions can also take on significant importance for industrial clusters in local systems (Guercini and Runfola, 2015) and probably also in the national contexts in which the enterprises are embedded.

Studying models of business networks in industrial marketing offers some important insights for understanding inter-organizational dynamics within global value chains. In these latter, changes in the relations between industry and distribution leads in the last decades to a strengthening of the power of the distribution side, contributing to the emergence of the distinctive features of the globalization process seen in recent decades (Gereffi, 1994; Humphrey and Schmitz, 2002; Gereffi et al., 2005).

A number of actors, especially in particular industries, emerge and base their activities on the processes of design, marketing and distribution, outsourcing operations. Historically, the issue of internationalization has assumed particular importance in the apparel industry: beginning in the 1980s and continuing throughout the 1990s and better part of the subsequent decade, a global shift of manufacturing occurred from the oldest industrialized countries to the emerging ones, foremost amongst which was China (Jones, 2002).

This global shift in production has not, however, eliminated the presence of developed nations' enterprises in the textile and apparel industries, both because there remained a number of firms acting as focal enterprises, concentrating their efforts on design, marketing and distribution, and also because some enterprises can continue to carry out an important role as suppliers of semi-finished goods and services to the focal enterprises (also given the variety of different business models adopted). For example, the development of fast fashion in Europe and North America has favoured the search for suppliers to form a "regional supply chain" (Barrientos et al., 2011; Rossi, 2013), in contrast to the "global supply chain" associated with manufacturing in emerging countries, which clearly could not meet the logistics demands of fast fashion (Gereffi and Memedovic, 2003; Guercini, 2008).

The case of native and immigrant entrepreneurship in Prato

Regarding the issue of internationalization of enterprises and supply chains, one particularly interesting case is represented by the firms located in the area of the city of Prato in Tuscany, Italy, whose evolution (which in some respects is quite surprising given the available study models for Italian industrialization) has led some to speak of a "black swan" phenomenon (Milanesi et al., 2016).

The Prato area is the site of the development of one of Italy's largest industrial districts (Becattini, 1990; Dei Ottati, 1994), which is specialized in the production of semi-finished woollen textile goods (fabrics and yarns). The term "industrial district" refers "to a particular form of socio-economic organization in which small and medium-sized businesses, most often specialized in a particular production sector and related activities, tend to cluster together in a given area . . . there is a notable level of exchange (market) relations among these businesses, but exchange typically takes place between persons belonging to the same social group, whose members share implicit rules of reciprocal cooperation (community)" (Dei Ottati, 2016, p. 56).

In the specific case of Prato, the history of the industrial district is linked to local entrepreneurship that has benefitted from extensive immigration from other regions of Italy. Thus, the district grew to considerable size in the late 1900s, culminating in Prato becoming one of the largest textile-producing areas in the world (Becattini, 2000). At the time, the area was the destination of many immigrants, for the most part from other Italian regions, and was characterized by a high capacity to integrate the new arrivals into the socio-economic fabric of the local system.

With the growing phenomenon of immigration from other countries, in recent decades Italy has also witnessed a substantial growth in the immigration of people and immigrant entrepreneurs. In particular, in recent years a considerable number of enterprises have been established by Chinese immigrants in Italian industrial clusters and in major metropolitan area. This, in an overall backdrop of the spread of such entrepreneurship throughout Europe (Baldassar et al., 2015) and a general transformation of its industrial districts (De Marchi and Grandinetti, 2014; Di Maria and Micelli, 2006). The Prato area has experienced extensive immigration of Chinese nationals, mainly with origin from the municipality of Whenzhou in Zhejiang, with the first arrivals in the late 1980s and a rapidly increasing influx during the subsequent decade, accompanied in parallel by a growing number of immigrant Chinese firms active in the apparel sector in Prato (Colombi, 2002; Guercini, 1999, 2002; Dei Ottati, 2009). The economics literature has devoted an extensive body of work to the case of Prato for the last 10 to 15 years, when the growth of Chinese entrepreneurship in the apparel industry was co-occurring with the contraction of the textile manufacturing activities conducted in the traditional industrial district (Dei Ottati, 2016).

Data from the Prato Chamber of Commerce from the late 1990s already reported a community of about 9,000 registered Chinese legal aliens and over a thousand enterprises, of which about 80% were in the clothing business, figures that more than doubled over the subsequent 10 years. During the 1990s the immigrant firms represented mostly sub-contracting suppliers for the apparel industry, and could at that time count on certain advantages with respect to native firms in similar positions as subcontractors, namely, lower labour costs and very rapid response times (Guercini, 2002). Their Italian client enterprises at this stage were ready-fashion knitwear and clothing manufacturers that in some cases grew during these years through the creation of brands and new distribution policies (Guercini, 2001). At the time, clothing firms (both native and immigrant) had a relatively marginal role in comparison to Prato's native textile firms, from whom some would acquire fabrics, though in limited quantities because the main final firms in the textile district worked mainly for a national and international clientele represented by enterprises in programmed fashion and large international department stores, with sourcing needs that were different from fast fashion stores (Guercini, 2004).

Though this was the situation in the 1990s, the following decade opened up a wholly new stage of development, during which some of the immigrant clothing firms acquired the capacity to complete the entire apparel manufacturing cycle (Guercini et al., 2013; Dei Ottati, 2016). This was a very important transition from a global value chain point of view, since local apparel immigrant firms in Prato became "full-package suppliers" (Gereffi, 1999). In some cases, their clients closed down, while in others, they gave up the manufacturing stages and invested increasingly in branding and distribution. The old Chinese subcontractors, or at least some of them, became final manufacturers, and other Chinese firms became subcontractors for other immigrant clothing firms. At the same time, a part of the Italian native apparel firms (a minority in comparison with the native textile firms) were externalizing manufacturing focusing on design, marketing and especially retailing their (new) brands; another part of the Italian apparel manufacturers were pushed out from the market by competition with local immigrant firms, or moved toward the upper segment of clothing manufacturing services, working with national and global luxury brands as main customers. In this stage, they had already integrated some of their client firms' resources, including native human resources (Ceccagno, 2004). Their advantage over their former client enterprises stemmed partly from what they learned from the host country, partly from easy access to both the supply market in their country of origin and the resources of the host country (services, "made in"), aspects that together have equipped them with distinctive capacities in global supply chains (Guercini et al., 2013).

At the same time that Chinese enterprises were on the rise, the Italian-owned textile enterprises of the Prato district were in dire straits, and their number progressively fell significantly after 2001, and then even more precipitously afterwards, with a consequent decrease in the exportation of textile products. The recent evolution of the immigrant and native data on entrepreneurship in the Prato confirms the trends already mentioned, which are accentuated in the last decade (see Table 8.1). Nevertheless, it is important to claim that natives'

Table 8.1 Native and immigrant firms in textile and clothing in the local Prato area (2002–14)

(a) Native and immigrant firms in the province of Prato[1]

Firms by origin of the entrepreneur	*2002*	*2010*	*2011*	*2012*	*2013*	*2014*	*2014/2002*
Immigrant	2,194	7,028	6,954	7,139	7,477	7,801	+255%
– Chinese	1,537	4,808	4,700	4,803	5,023	5,230	+240%
– Others	657	2,245	2,254	2,336	2,454	2,571	+291%
Mix of immigrant-immigrant	13	25	27	26	26	21	+61%
Mix of immigrant-native (national)	465	458	432	436	438	447	−4%
Native (national)	23,707	21,876	21,756	21,466	21,239	20,707	−13%
– Native/immigrant	10,8	3,1	3,1	3,0	2,8	2,7	−75%
– Native/immigrant Chinese	15,4	4,5	4,6	4,5	4,2	4,0	−74%
Total	26,379	29,387	29,169	29,067	29,180	28,976	+10%

[1] The figure is at December 31 of each year, firms in the "active".

Source: Author's elaboration on data of Chamber of Commerce of Prato

(b) Clothing industry and textile industry – Native and immigrant firms in the province of Prato[1]

Firms by origin of the entrepreneur	2002	2010	2011	2012	2013	2014	2014/2002
Total (foreigners and natives)							
– textile firms	4,454	2,448	2,353	2,274	2,256	2,212	−50%
– clothing firms	1,910	4,029	4,003	3,928	3,963	3,984	+109%
Chinese (immigrant and mixes)[2]							
– textile firms	45	243	242	264	320	339	+653%
– clothing firms	1,131	3,364	3,165	3,200	3,255	3,304	+192%
Natives (national)[3]							
– textile firms	4,396	2,143	2,056	1,947	1,874	1,815	−59%
– clothing firms	767	630	804	696	676	643	−16%
Share of Italian native in textile	98,7%	87,5%	87,4%	85,6%	83,1%	82,1%	−17%
Share of Chinese in clothing	59,2%	83,5%	79,1%	81,5%	82,1%	82,9%	+40%

[1] The figure is at December 31 of each year, firms in the "active".

[2] The data about "Chinese textile" and "Chinese clothing" firms includes the firms with Chinese in the mix immigrant-immigrant and in the mix immigrant-native including Chinese (national).

[3] The data about the "native" is calculated as the total minus the total with foreigners (immigrants and mixed).

Source: Author's elaboration on data of Chamber of Commerce of Prato.

(c) Fashion firms in the area of Prato[1]

Fashion industries in the Prato area	2002	2010	2011	2012	2013	2014	2014/ 2002
– Textiles	7,276	3,143	3,027	2,918	2,876	2,815	−61%
– Clothing	2,529	4,476	4,438	4,347	4,371	4,379	+73%
– Leather goods and shoes	Nd	422	474	530	539	557	+32%*
Total	9,805	8,041	7,939	7,795	7,786	7,751	

[1] The "Prato area" is larger than the Province of Prato and corresponds to the area of the "industrial district of Prato", including territory of the municipalities of Cantagallo, Carmignano, Montemurlo, Poggio a Caiano, Prato, Vaiano, Vernio, Agliana, Montale, Quarrata, Calenzano, Campi Bisenzio. The figure is at December 31 of each year; the data or 2002 is in part different because of a different classification of "textiles" and "clothing" firms; for example, the knitwear firms, 1,126 in 2002, 514 in 2010 and 441 in 2014, in 2002 where classified in the "textiles" and in 2010–2014 were classified in "clothing".

* For the Leather goods and shoes the change is in the period 2014/2010.

Source: Author's elaboration on data of Chamber of Commerce of Prato.

(Continued)

Table 8.1 Continued

(d) Number of textile and clothing firms (immigrant Chinese and native Italians) in the province of Prato by year

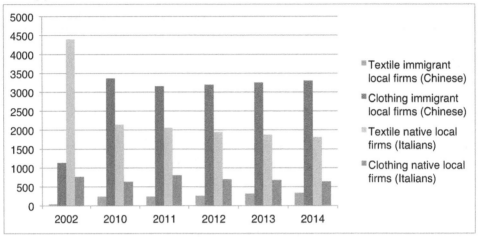

Source: Author's elaboration on data of Chamber of Commerce of Prato.

firms are still the main component in the local textile industry, while Chinese immigrants' firms are prevalent in the local clothing industry (Table 8.1).

There are two possible interpretations of this stage, as highlighted by Dei Ottati (2016). Some hold that the Prato system profited from immigrant Chinese entrepreneurship, both because the textiles utilized by the Chinese firms were bought locally, and because local human resources were employed (Ceccagno, 2009). Others instead view the Prato district as falling prey to the Chinese entrepreneurs because the fabrics they used were imported (Pieraccini, 2009). Indeed, the supply of textile materials represents a key question in this regard: are the Chinese enterprises supplied by local enterprises or foreign ones? Unfortunately, the data on this point are misleading: even when the Chinese firms buy locally, statistics on textile importation to the Prato area show increases, which would confirm their foreign origin.

The research on textile and clothing industry in Central America gave an additional dimension to the problem. That research shows that the Asian textiles (from Korea, Taiwan or Hong Kong) had greater variety, which was better suited to women's wear and children garments, compared to the cotton-based textile imports from American firms, which were targeted to the more standardized men's wear segment (Gereffi, 1994, 1999; Frederick et al., 2015; Bair and Gereffi, 2014; Frederick and Gereffi, 2011). This does not seem to be the case of the Italian textile firms in Prato. Research on fabrics and yarn producers has always highlighted the huge variety of items offered by the Italian textile companies, that survive despite their high prices thanks to this variety and the ability to meet many small demand segments (niches) (Guercini, 2004; Guercini and Runfola, 2012). Actually, the dynamics of the Prato district textile enterprises are determined by the competition between global supply chains, and the role of immigrant enterprises present in the Prato area must be considered within a more complex scenario. The native textile and the immigrant Chinese enterprises belong to different global value chains, whose evolution varies with changes in business models and consumption in the global market. The global value chains are different because they are targeting different market segments (respectively, low-price fast fashion and the medium-high fashion and luxury apparel) in similar geographic markets. However, different supply relations existed during the same period, as schematized in Table 8.2 (first and second stages, respectively in the 1990s and in the 2000s-last decade).

Table 8.2 Evolution of the positions covered by native and immigrant local firms of Prato in their global value chain

(a) Components covered in the fast fashion value chain by the Chinese immigrant firms[1]

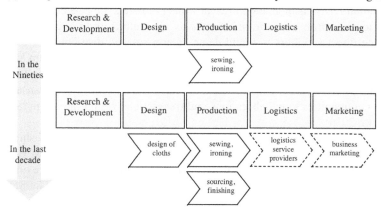

(b) Components covered in the textile value chain by the Italian native firms[1]

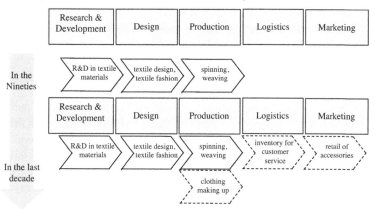

(c) Upgrading of the position of the Chinese immigrant local firm in the fast fashion global value chain with "relational" governance type[2]

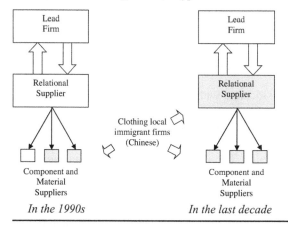

[1] The boxes in dotted line correspond to the parts of the supply chain less frequently covered.
[2] The grey background marks the Chinese immigrant actors in the value chain

Source: Author's elaboration and adaptation from Gereffi et al. (2005).

The case of Prato highlights the local level liabilities that may confront enterprises. In particular, significant learning processes occurred (primarily) in the former Chinese sub-contractors for the Italian ready-fashion and knitwear firms (Table 8.2.a). This enabled the Chinese enterprises to grow from their original status as subcontractors to one of OEM enterprises, and hence direct suppliers to brand-name enterprises and distributors. Obviously, not all the Chinese enterprises were able to enhance their positions downstream and become final firms. Many remained as subcontractors, often transitioning from serving Italian firms to serving the Chinese ones that had made the "leap", and switching from transactions across the two communities to collaborations and transactions within the immigrant community (Dei Ottati, 2016).

The learning processes activated by some of the former Italian clients of the fast-fashion supply chains in China clearly seem to have been inadequate (actually, for the most part they were lacking altogether). The Prato textile firms operated in supply chains where only few firms managed to implement downstream integration in the production of manufactured clothing articles by exploiting the capacities of Chinese enterprises. Naturally, there are a number of reasons such a process did not come about. In particular, while the local native enterprises produced primarily textiles for the manufacture of apparel based on the pro-grammed fashion business model, the strong points of the Prato immigrant firms were precisely their competencies in the manufacture of apparel according to the fast-fashion model (Milanesi et al., 2016). Such strong points included rapid production times and proximity to European consumer markets. Actually, this lack of learning on the part of native firms was not absolute, as some of these enterprises began more or less successful operations in China, first resource seeking, then market seeking.

The second stage (in the last decade) is characterized by limited interaction between native and immigrant entrepreneurship in comparison to the first stage. The Chinese immigrant firms in the early years had as customers Italian and international clothing companies that outsourced sewing and later the entire manufacturing. In some cases the Chinese suppliers replaced failed Italian native apparel producers. There is no doubt that the enterprises in the two groups did utilize the resources of the other, though they did it mainly through transactions and/or asymmetrical learning.

Apart from the lack of familiarity, the immigrant and native firms also had to face discrimination hazards (Eden and Miller, 2001). Particularly in the first stage these problems likely affected the immigrant firms almost exclusively, though in the 2000s, with the progressive growth of the Chinese firms' influence and power, it became more and more likely that native enterprises also had to face discrimination, and hence suffered the consequences of the lack of relationships and collaboration between the two communities, and the existence of two parallel districts with different and separate positions in their global value chain (GVC) (Table 8.3).

The growth of the immigrant firms, associated with the rise of fast fashion (Guercini, 2001; Barnes and Lea-Greenwood, 2010), has now entered a new, "mature" stage, as the Prato Chinese community has given rise to many Chinese second-generation entrepreneurs. In addition, their positions with respect to the China market in comparison to the host country market have changed over these decades. The immigrant community can moreover count on a network of relationships with the Chinese diaspora in many other countries, including China, France and Southeast Asia (Baldassar et al., 2015). For this reason, the growth of demand in the Chinese market and the evolution of international scenarios seem to have recently opened up new prospects for the relations between immigrant and native entrepreneurship. These regard the possibility for the immigrant Chinese firms to play a

Table 8.3 Overview of Prato Italian-native and Chinese-immigrant clusters in the GVC

	Prato Italian native district	*Prato Chinese immigrant district*
Product	Fabric, yarns and other textiles	Fast-fashion clothing and accessories
ID Position in the GVC	Design and production of semi-finished products for national and global apparel producers and retailers	Production and design of finished goods mainly for national and European fast-fashion retailers and producers
GVC key actors	Branded apparel manufacturer and retailers (department stores) in luxury and the high and medium fashion segment	Fast-fashion retailer and producer in the medium positioned segment (including branded) and unbranded low-cost segment
ID Export propensity	Very high propensity to export – 59.5% turnover (€1.622 billion in textile export on a turnover of €2.728 billion in 2014), mainly to Europe and North America	Very high propensity to export – 58.9% (€862 million in apparel and accessories export on a turnover of €1.464 billion in 2014), mainly to European countries
ID # of firms/ employees	2,458 firms with about 20,000 employees at the end of 2014	3,643 firms with about 18,000 employees at the end of 2014
ID Local firms	Mainly OBMs and OEMs of textiles (semi-finished products), textile design, phase suppliers and specialized suppliers for local and global customers, including textiles finishing	OEMs of clothing for fast-fashion retailers and designers, and mainly stage suppliers for local producers (sewing, ironing etc.); more recently, OBMs of fast-fashion products and import-export trading
ID Supporting industries	Textile machinery and components; finishing industry; logistics and commercial professional services (textile trading, logistics)	Semi-finished textiles and accessories trade and production; commercial professional services (trading, design, logistics)
ID Local institutions	Textile business associations (industry, artisans), technical institutes of higher education, cultural associations, close relationships with local institutions such as municipalities, Chamber of Commerce, and universities	Cultural association of Chinese immigrants, present in local textile and clothing business associations (mainly artisans), and local and trans-local Guanxi; some/few relationships with local institutions such as municipalities, Chamber of Commerce, and universities
ID Major recent transformations	Progressive reduction in the number of enterprises, employees and turnover. The role of exports is still important. The crisis has not led to concentration, as it involves large companies as well as small ones. Some have expanded into integrated production of clothing and accessories. The largest textile firm has a turnover of just over €50 million.	The number of companies, employees and the turnover volume grew rapidly until the end of the last decade. Businesses have gone from simple phase suppliers to OEMs and in some cases OBMs. Some companies have invested in the creation of brands. There are cases of diversification into other sectors, including non-manufacturing (trade, agriculture)

Source: Author's elaboration.

crucial role in the export chains of Italian products in various sectors of the Chinese market, with a further increase in the complexity and diversification of their business models. This also makes their continued presence in Italy "sustainable", in that second-generation Chinese-Italians have developed strong ties to Italy (Zhang and Zhang, 2016).

During interviews with Chinese immigrant entrepreneurs conducted within the framework of our research, some new types of relationships between native and immigrant entrepreneurship emerged. These are no longer limited to simple transactions and include not only greater integration between the clothing business enterprises in the two communities (first example), but also establishing a business for the production and marketing in China of Italian agricultural products, and the commercial real estate plans of a well-known immigrant Chinese entrepreneur to build, together with Italian partners, showrooms in China for the presentation of products "Made in Italy" (second example). These two examples correspond to actually emerging cases of interaction between native and immigrant entrepreneurship in Prato, but the number of cases is not high.

An emerging theory on local liabilities

The case of Prato is interesting in its evolution and the implications for the study of the relations between global value chains and local system enterprises. Comparison of the international business literature and the case of Prato's native and immigrant enterprises highlights some types of liabilities strictly associated with the globalization process, immigration and entrepreneurship in local contexts and their relations with global value chains.

The case of Prato clearly underlines that the phenomena associated with the liabilities typical of internationalization processes (LOF and LOO) do not affect only firms outside their national borders, but domestic firms as well. The typical difficulties of foreignness and outsidership are experienced not only by immigrant enterprises, but also by native firms. As we have seen, the literature has already revealed that even domestic enterprises can come up against some of the phenomena associated with LOF (Mezias, 2002), though they clearly affect foreign firms more heavily. However, the case examined herein regards the conditions determining the LOF and LOO impacting both native and immigrant entrepreneurship operating in the same local setting. Such liabilities can hinder both groups and limit their (potential of) competitive capacity. But seen from another angle, these liabilities can be converted to opportunities, if industrial district and global value chain linkages are developed more fully by both Chinese and Italian firms working together in new ways (Guercini et al., 2017).

The conditions in question include the relative unavailability of information on how to do business in local market segments dominated by the other community, problems recruiting suppliers from the other community, asymmetry in interpreting and following the rules defined by the local and national governments of the host country, the effects of policies adopted by the government of the immigrants' country of origin and asymmetrical regulations on international commerce. Local liabilities do not affect the immigrant and native firms equally in every phase. Today the latter may experience greater difficulty due to both "unfamiliarity hazards", as they lack knowledge and experience of the possibilities offered by the value chains in which the immigrant firms participate, and "discrimination hazards" (Eden and Miller, 2001), because, due to language and cultural barriers or discriminatory choices against them, they remain outsiders with respect to immigrant community networks (Ong et al., 2016).

Based on the foregoing, we can therefore propose a definition of these types of liabilities, which have not to date been addressed in the literature, but that represent important elements in the case analysed. *Local liabilities (LLs) are produced in local contexts where two (or more) separate communities (of persons and firms) exist. The term "local" refers to a social space. The larger is the separation between the communities, the larger are the local liabilities.* The phenomenon of LLs stems from the processes of globalization and may arise where situations similar to those in Prato exist. Globalization does not only build "bridges" between distant contexts, it also creates these sorts of liabilities at the local level (Guercini et al., 2017). Anyway, it is only one side of the LLs issue and, as indicated here,

Table 8.4 Liability of foreignness, liability of outsidership and local liabilities

Liabilities	Entry abroad	Local context
Psychic distance	Liability of foreignness	Local liabilities
Link to relevant business networks	Liability of outsidership	

Overcoming liabilities	Entry abroad	Local context
Interactions inside the same community	Leveraging on actors of the same community in the target market	Leveraging on the local actors belonging to the same community
Interactions across communities	Leveraging on the easy access to partner of another culture in the country of origin	Leveraging on the growth of externalities in the local context

Source: Author's elaboration.

globalization indeed can also be a bridge to upgrading in the Prato district, for example if new external markets (like China) are brought into the picture.

Rather than a single liability, LLs constitute a set of liabilities that can be set in relation to both LOF and LOO (Table 8.4). Indeed, local enterprises may be affected as much by "psychic distance" as by the lack of connections to relevant business networks, that is to say, by "outsidership." For local enterprises LLs determine analogous conditions to those studied with regard to LOF and LOO, without however their operating at the international level. Such conditions impact both immigrant as well as native firms, though their effects may be greater for the former or for the latter depending on the potentials in time of the business network as a market and the values chain to which the firms belong. The equilibrium among the various LLs experienced by one a group or the other also depends partly on other sources of liabilities, such as company size or age (liabilities of smallness and newness). LLs are an effect of globalization that contributes to enhancing the processes of global competitive selection at local level, though, as seen, they also act on enterprises operating only locally.

The emergence of LLs in any business setting is strictly related to the separation between the different communities within that setting. In order to see how the LLs may evolve (or resolve), it is necessary to determine what separates the local communities and how such separation can be overcome. In some respects, separation is a force opposing those that led to the emergence of industrial districts. Although it is a source of liabilities for the immigrant entrepreneur (Waldinger, 1986), given globalization, cross-border community bonds may be more relevant than local ones, by which the effects of LLs also apply to native firms. In order to overcome such liabilities, it should be borne in mind that such "separation" is merely one aspect of the complex process of acculturation, which is accompanied by "integration", "assimilation" and "marginalization" (Berry et al., 1987), but the condition of "separation" is typical of LLs (Guercini et al., 2017). In the condition of "integration" the LLs tend to be overcome, while in that of "marginalization" and "assimilation" the LLs lose their importance.

The above appeal to the concept of acculturation underscores the complexity of the phenomena at play in LLs. Such phenomena are closely linked to the evolution of the local setting, including, for example, generational transition, which can lead to entrepreneurial behaviours quite distinct from those of the first-generation immigrants, let alone the second and third generations (Baldassar et al., 2015). In the long term, the position of the immigrant community may evolve from one state to another in the acculturation matrix proposed

Table 8.5 Overcoming "local liabilities": an adaptation from the Uppsala Model

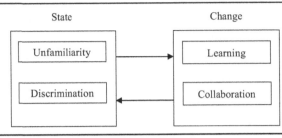

Liability sources	Tools	Political process
Unfamiliarity	Knowledge, experience	Learning, experiencing
Discrimination	Insidership	Collaboration, socialization

Upgrading	Economic	Social
Learning about technical processes	Upgrading in the business network in the GVCs	Upgrading status in the community and local society
Learning about the other culture	Upgrading access to local externalities	Upgrading collaboration and institutions

Source: Author's elaboration on Johanson and Vahlne (2009), Eden and Miller (2001) and Barrientos et al. (2011).

by Berry and colleagues, and this is one mechanism that can convert LLs to opportunities (Berry et al., 1987). To complicate matters, public policy-makers may promote initiatives aimed at favouring integration between immigrant and native firms, an issue that appears to be ever more important and topical in our societies, and which is also relevant to global value chains and the evolution of business environments.

The subject is also of importance for company policies makers, given the implications of LL effects on business. Overcoming LLs thus becomes an important goal for enterprises that intend to enter foreign economies. What contributions can international business theory make in this regard? Herein we propose a model that adopts the distinction between state aspects and change aspects made in the U-model, both in its original formulation and the more recently re-worked version. In the model's original formulation, enterprises tackle "psychic distance" (Johanson and Vahlne, 1977, p. 26), and therefore LOF, by comparing market knowledge and market commitment (state aspects) with commitment decisions and current activities (change aspects). Instead, the second version sees enterprises tackling LOO by comparing knowledge opportunities and network position (state aspects) with relationship commitment decisions, learning, creating and trust building (change aspects). On the basis of these two models, we propose a third model that sets forth a process for overcoming the LLs existing between native and immigrant actors, firstly, by exchanging knowledge and experience in order to overcome unfamiliarity, and secondly, through insidership commitment to overcome discrimination through learning, experiencing, socialization and collaboration (Table 8.5).

Local liabilities and global value chains: some conclusions

The case of Prato highlights how the relations between native and immigrant entrepreneurship can affect (and be affected by) the evolution of (local, regional and) global value chains

(Gereffi et al., 2005). However, it also serves to demonstrate that any given enterprise's position in the value chain is not stable, and the evolution of such a position can be interpreted in light of the manner in which the firm addresses LLs above and beyond external factors such as business evolution and competitive environment.

The local liabilities arising from globalization are an aspect to be considered attentively in studying global value chains, in that the presence of immigrant firms at the local level can open up new challenges and opportunities for native firms that cannot be understand by considering the local dimension alone. Learning processes, the separation between the native and immigrant communities, transactions aiming to access local and global resources, and the interactions between enterprises all contribute in complex ways to business networks and their evolution. The case of Prato's native and immigrant firms offers a prime example of this.

Globalization does not produce only bridges between distant places, with enterprises developing capacities to address, as never before, the liabilities associated with the processes of internationalization. For a small enterprise, the separation between communities produces within the local setting a number of phenomena associated with "doing business abroad", such as "foreignness" and "outsidership", which we have examined herein under the term "local liabilities" (LLs). The presence of LLs hinders the emergence at the local level of those external effects that figure crucially in the Italian industrial district model, thereby contributing to altering the correspondence between the theoretically hypothesized conditions and the actual reality.

In the case of the Prato industrial cluster, the evolution of the relationships between immigrant clothing firms and native textile firms is strictly linked to that of the changing global value chains to which they belong. Initially, the immigrant firms' role was that of subcontractors for the local fast fashion industry, which underwent rapid growth during the 1990s. At the time, immigrant firms represented a valid response to the demands for reduced production times, proximity for logistics and cost containment. In this initial stage, immigrant firms provided the needed support to the local and regional value chain of the ready fashion and knitwear industries (Guercini, 2008), which were in competition with the global value chain that could exploit low-cost production in the emerging countries. The native textile firms of the Prato industrial district were instead important components in global supply chains, especially in programmed medium- and high-end fashion goods, destined for tough competition with products manufactured directly in the emerging countries, particularly China. The national knitwear and packaging enterprises did not form the "core" of the district's activities, which were focused instead on textiles for the regional and global value chain of middle- to high-range attire and the luxury market (Gereffi, 1999).

In a subsequent stage the immigrant firms were able to replace their former clients by conducting the entire manufacturing cycle up to and including offering finished products for distribution. This was also a consequence of a change in the activities of their clients, who in some cases were engaged in disinvesting from manufacturing to invest in distribution activities in foreign markets (Guercini and Runfola, 2016; Runfola and Guercini, 2013). At the same time, the crisis in the textile and apparel market led to the closing of parts of these enterprises.

Even more recent times brought about further changes in business conditions: the increasing maturity of the fast fashion business and the generational exchange further stimulated interest on the part of the immigrant entrepreneurship in investing "downstream", toward branding and distribution (vertical integration) or even in other business fields (diversification). For their part, Italian entrepreneurs are going through a transition phase in relation to the outcome of the crisis in the textile firms of the traditional industrial district. This phase, also linked to the advent of new generations, may provide the impetus to overcome the LLs, at least in part, by formulating hypotheses according to which, as has occurred in some cases, members of the two communities can exploit certain forms of integration to operate successfully in new global value chains.

The case of the immigrant and native firms in the Prato industrial district shows how things can change due to various factors that happen to act contemporaneously. The positions of the enterprises in local, regional and global value chains are not nearly as stable as they might appear through a static perspective. In a dynamic perspective, instead, enterprises' positions can become contestable through asymmetrical processes of learning and the capacity to overcome conditions of outsidership, as well as due to changes in the relevant networks, the market setting and the environment in general. This is clearly of significant import to both single enterprises and local clusters, as the case of Prato underscores.

Acknowledgements

The author thanks Gabi Dei Ottati, Matilde Milanesi, Anna Marsden, Susan Freeman, Xander Ong, and Alexandra Waluszewski for the fruitful exchange of ideas gained over the years on the subject of Chinese entrepreneurship in Prato.

References

Aldrich, H.E., and Auster, E.R. (1986). Even dwarfs started small: Liabilities of age and size and their strategic implications. *Research in Organizational Behavior*, 8: 165–186.

Aldrich, H.E., and Waldinger, R. (1990). Ethnicity and entrepreneurship. *Annual Review of Sociology*, 16: 111–135.

Bair, J., and Gereffi, G. (2014). Toward better work in Central America: Nicaragua and the CAFTA context. In A. Rossi, A. Luinstra and J. Pikles (eds.), *Toward Better Work: Understanding Labour in Apparel Global Value Chains*. Basingstoke: Palgrave.

Baldassar, L., Johanson, G., McAuliffe, N., and Bressan, M. (eds.). (2015). *Chinese Migration to Europe*. London: Palgrave Macmillan.

Barnes, L., and Lea-Greenwood, G. (2010). Fast fashion in the retail store environment. *International Journal of Retail and Distribution Management*, 38(10): 760–772.

Barrientos, S., Gereffi, G., Rossi, A. (2011). Economic and social upgrading in global production networks: A new paradigm for a changing world. *International Labour Review*, 150(3–4): 319–340.

Becattini, G. (1990). The Marshallian industrial district as a socio-economic notion. In F. Pyke, G. Becattini and W. Sengenberger (eds.), *Industrial Districts and Inter-firm Co-operation in Italy*. Geneva: ILO Publications, pp. 37–51.

Becattini, G. (2000). *Il bruco e la farfalla. Prato: Una storia esemplare dell'Italia dei distretti*. Firenze: Le Monnier.

Berry, J.W., Kim, U., Minde, T., and Mok, D. (1987). Comparative studies of acculturative stress. *International Migration Review*, 21(3): 491–511.

Camuffo, A., and Grandinetti, R. (2011). Italian industrial districts as cognitive systems: Are they still reproducible? *Entrepreneurship and Regional Development*, 23(9–10): 815–852.

Carlson, S. (1970). *How Foreign Is Foreign Trade? A Problem in International Business Research*. Uppsala: Acta Universitatis Upsaliensis, Studia Oeconomiae Negotiorum 11.

Cattaneo, O., Gereffi, G., and Staritz, C. (eds.). (2010). *Global Value Chains in a Postcrisis World: A Development Perspective*. Washington, DC: The World Bank.

Cavusgil, S.T. (1980). On the internationalization process of firms. *European Research*, 8(November), 273–281.

Ceccagno, A. (2004). *Giovani migranti cinesi: La seconda generazione a Prato*. Milano: Franco Angeli.

Ceccagno, A. (2009). Chinese migrants as apparel manufacturers in an era of perishable global fashion: New fashion scenarios in Prato. In G. Johanson, R. Smyth and R. French (eds.), *Living Outside the Walls: The Chinese in Prato*. Newcastle upon Tyne: Cambridge Scholars.

Colombi, M. (ed.). (2002). *L'imprenditoria cinese nel distretto industriale di Prato*. Firenze: L. Olschki.

Dei Ottati, G. (1994). Trust, interlinking transactions and credit in the industrial district. *Cambridge Journal of Economics*, 18: 529–546.

Dei Ottati, G. (2009). An industrial district facing the challenges of globalization: Prato today. *European Planning Studies*, 17(12): 1817–1835.

Dei Ottati, G. (2016). Chinese immigrant businesses in the industrial districts of Prato and their interpretation. In M. Sanfilippo and A. Weinar (eds.), *Chinese Migration and Economic Relations With Europe*. London: Routledge.

De Marchi, V., and Grandinetti, R. (2014). Industrial districts and the collapse of the Marshallian model: Looking at the Italian experience. *Competition and Change*, 18(1): 70–87.

Di Maria, E., and Micelli, S. (2006). *District Leaders as Open Networks: Emerging Business Strategies in Italian Industrial Districts*. Working Paper, University of Padua, Padua.

Eden, L., and Miller, S. (2001). Opening the back box: Multinationals and the costs of doing business abroad. *Academy of Management Proceedings*, 16(1): C1–C6.

Forsgren, M. (2002). The concept of learning in the Uppsala internationalization process model: A critical review. *International Business Review*, 11(3): 257–277.

Frederick, S., Bair, J., and Gereffi, G. (2015). Regional trade agreements and export competitiveness: The uncertain path of Nicaragua's apparel exports under CAFTA. *Cambridge Journal of Regions, Economy and Society*, 8(3): 403–420.

Frederick, S., and Gereffi, G. (2011). Upgrading and restructuring in the global apparel value chain: Why China and Asia are outperforming Mexico and Central America. *International Journal of Technological Learning, Innovation and Development*, 4(1/2/3): 67–95.

Freeman, J., Carroll, G.R., and Hannan, M.T. (1983). The liability of newness: Age dependence in organizational death rates. *American Sociological Review*, 48(5): 692–710.

Gereffi, G. (1994). The organization of buyer-driven global commodity chains: How US retailers shape overseas production networks. In G. Gereffi and M. Korzeniewicz (eds.), *Commodity Chains and Global Capitalism*. Westport, CT: Praeger.

Gereffi, G. (1999). International trade and industrial upgrading in the apparel commodity chain. *Journal of International Economics*, 48(1): 37–70.

Gereffi, G., Humphrey, J., and Surgeon, T. (2005). The governance of global value chains. *Review of International Political Economy*, 12(1): 78–104.

Gereffi, G., and Memedovic, O. (2003). *The Global Apparel Value Chain: What Prospects for Upgrading by Developing Countries*. Vienna: United Nations Industrial Development Organization, pp. 1–40.

Grandinetti, R. (2011). Local/global cognitive interfaces within industrial districts: An Italian case study. *The Learning Organization*, 18(4): 301–312.

Grandinetti, R., and Rullani, E. (1996). *Impresa transnazionale ed economia globale*. Rome: La Nuova Italia Scientifica.

Granovetter, M. (1973). The strength of weak ties. *American Journal of Sociology*, 78(6): 1360–1380.

Gruber, W., Mehta, R., and Vernon, R. (1967). The R&D factor in international trade and international investment of the United States. *Journal of Political Economy*, 75(1): 20–37.

Guercini, S. (1999). L'impresa con vertice di nazionalità cinese nel distretto pratese: Caratteri, processi di sviluppo e politiche di mercato. Proceedings of the Conference "Il futuro dei distretti", Università di Padova, Vicenza, June.

Guercini, S. (2001). Relation between branding and growth of the firm in new quick fashion formulas: Analysis of an Italian case. *Journal of Fashion Marketing and Management*, 5(1): 69–79.

Guercini, S. (2002). profilo del vertice, processi di sviluppo e politiche di mercato dell'impresa cinese a Prato. In M. Colombi (ed.), *L'imprenditoria cinese nel distretto industriale di Prato*. Firenze: Leo S. Olschki Editore.

Guercini, S. (2004). International competitive change and strategic behaviour of Italian textile-apparel firms. *Journal of Fashion Marketing and Management*, 8(3): 320–329.

Guercini, S. (2008). Matching format strategy and sourcing strategy in clothing retail: A conceptual representation. *International Journal of Process Management and Benchmarking*, 2(3): 185–196.

Guercini, S., Dei Ottati, G., Baldassar, L., and Johanson, G. (eds.). (2017). Native and Immigrant Entrepreneurship: Lessons for Local Liabilities in Globalization From the Prato Case Study. New York: Springer.

Guercini, S., Milanesi, M., and Dei Ottati, G. (2013). *Global and Local Business Networks in the Growth of the Chinese Firm in Prato*. 6th Chinese in Prato and 4th Wenzhouese Diaspora Symposia on "Chinese Migration Entrepreneurship and Development in the New Global Economy", 28–30 October.

Guercini, S., and Ranfagni, S. (2016). Conviviality behavior in entrepreneurial communities and business networks. *Journal of Business Research*, 69(2): 770–776.

Guercini, S., and Runfola, A. (2012). Relational paths in business network dynamics: Evidence from the fashion industry. *Industrial Marketing Management*, 41(5): 807–815.

Guercini, S., and Runfola, A. (2015). Actors' roles in interaction and innovation in local systems: A conceptual taxonomy. *Journal of Business and Industrial Marketing*, 30(3/4): 269–278.

Guercini, S., and Runfola, A. (2016). How western marketers respond to the new middle class in emerging market cities: The case of Italian Fashion Marketers. *International Business Review*, 25(3): 691–702.

Håkansson, H. (ed.). (1982). *International Marketing and Purchasing of Industrial Goods*. Chichester: IMP Project Group, Wiley.

Håkansson, H., Ford, D., Gadde, L.-E., Snehota, I., and Waluszewski, A. (2009). *Business in Networks*. Chichester: Wiley.

Håkansson, H., and Snehota, I. (1995). *Developing Relationships in Business Networks*. Chichester: Wiley.

Hilmersson, M., and Jansson, H. (2012). International network extension processes to institutionally different markets: Entry nodes and processes of exporting SMEs. *International Business Review*, 21(4): 682–693.

Humphrey, J., and Schmitz, H. (2002). How does insertion in global value chains affect upgrading in industrial clusters? *Regional Studies*, 36(9): 1017–1027.

Hymer, S.H. (1976). *The International Operations of National Firms: A Study of Direct Foreign Investment*. Cambridge: MIT Press.

Johanson, J., and Vahlne, J.-E. (1977). The internationalization process of the firm – A model of knowledge development and increasing foreign market commitments. *Journal of International Business Studies*, 8(1): 23–32.

Johanson, J., and Vahlne, J.-E. (2009). The Uppsala internationalization process model revisited: From liability of foreignness to liability of outsidership. *Journal of International Business Studies*, 40(4): 1411–1431.

Johanson, J., and Wiedersheim-Paul, F. (1975). The internationalization of the firm: Four Swedish cases. *Journal of Management Studies*, 12(3): 305–322.

Jones, R.M. (2002). *The Apparel Industry*. Oxford: Blackwell.

Kindleberger, C.P. (1969). *American Business Abroad: Six Lectures on Direct Investment*. New Haven, CT: Yale University Press.

Knight, G.A., and Cavusgil, S.T. (1996). The born global firm: A challenge to traditional internationalization theory. *Advances in International Marketing*, 8: 11–26.

Lorenzoni, G. (1987). Le nuove imprese nei settori ad alta tecnologia. *Kybernetes*, 6, April: 20–32.

Matsuo, H. (2000). Liability of foreignness and the uses of expatriates in Japanese multinational corporations in the United States. *Sociological Inquiry*, 70(1): 88–106.

Mezias, J. (2002). How to identify liabilities of foreignness and asses their effects on multinational corporations. *Journal of International Management*, 8(3): 265–282.

Milanesi, M., Guercini, S., and Waluszewski, A. (2016). A Black Swan in the district? An IMP perspective on immigrant entrepreneurship and changes in industrial districts. *IMP Journal*, 10(2): 243–259.

Ong, X., Freeman, S., Cooper, B., and Guercini, S. (2016). *Challenges and Opportunities Created by Ethnic Networks: The Liability of Outsidership.* Working Paper.

Pieraccini, S. (2009). L'assedio cinese: Il distretto parallelo del pronto moda di Prato. Milano: Il Sole 24 Ore.

Rossi, A. (2013). Does economic upgrading lead to social upgrading in global production networks: Evidence from Morocco. *World Development*, 46: 223–233.

Runfola, A., and Guercini, S. (2013). Fast fashion companies coping with internationalization: Driving the change or changing the model? *Journal of Fashion Marketing and Management: An International Journal*, 17(2): 190–205.

Sousa, C.M.P., and Bradley, F. (2006). Cultural distance and psychic distance: Two peas in a pod? *Journal of International Marketing*, 14(1): 49–70.

Stinchcombe, A.L. (1965). Social structure and organizations. In J.G. March (ed.), *Handbook of Organizations*. Chicago: Rand Mc Nally, pp. 142–193.

Vahlne, J.E., and Johanson, J. (2013). The Uppsala model on evolution of the multinational business enterprise – From internalization to coordination of networks. *International Marketing Review*, 30(3): 189–210.

Varaldo, R., and Ferrucci, L. (1996). The evolutionary nature of the firm within industrial districts. *European Planning Studies*, 4(1): 27–34.

Vernon, R. (1966). International investment and international trade in the product cycle. *The Quarterly Journal of Economics*, 80(2): 190–207.

Waldinger, R. (1986). Immigrant enterprise: A critique and reformulation. *Theory and Society*, 15: 249–285.

Zaheer, S. (1995). Overcoming the liability of foreignness. *Academy of Management Journal*, 38(2): 341–363.

Zaheer, S. (2002). The liability of foreignness, redux: A commentary. *Journal of International Management*, 8(3): 351–358.

Zhang, Y., and Zhang, M. (2016). Can overseas migrants develop sustained entrepreneurship? Multiple case studies of Wenzhou migrants in Italy. *Journal of Chinese Sociology*, 3(4): 1–23.

Part III

Value chain activities

Rethinking the role of manufacturing and innovation

9 Manufacturing, where art thou? Value chain organization and cluster-firm strategies between local and global

Marco Bettiol, Maria Chiarvesio,
Eleonora Di Maria and Stefano Micelli

Introduction

A growing set of studies describes the massive international relocation of manufacturing activities from Western to low-cost countries. According to the "smile" approach (Mudambi, 2007) this phenomenon is particularly related to the low value associated with manufacturing activities that can be standardized and controlled – in the global value chain (GVC) approach – through the power of lead firms (Gereffi et al., 2005). On the contrary, serviced-based activities such as R&D and marketing contribute toward supporting the (Western) firms' competitive advantage and sustain value creation.

Recently, scholars have increased their attention on the positive linkages between innovation and manufacturing management. Through learning-by-doing processes and interdependence between design and manufacturing activities, firms can produce additional knowledge useful to enhance their competitiveness (Buciuni and Finotto, 2016). At the same time, other scholars have highlighted the need to closely control manufacturing processes – both organizationally and geographically – to increase customization opportunities, interaction with consumers and online communities (i.e. Flynn and Flynn Vencat, 2012). Studies on backshoring shed further light on the implications of an international location of manufacturing activities by considering the advantages of being close to the markets, managing coupled R&D/productive activities and exploiting positive country-of-origin effects (Fratocchi et al., 2014).

This scenario raises interesting challenges for the global organization of value chain activities depicted by the GVC framework. In fact, it emphasizes the many drivers influencing firms' choices concerning the localization of production in different countries and regions on the basis of competences and knowledge available. Lead firms may be attracted by the opportunity to rethink how they can organize their activities – i.e. the case of General Electric or Ford (Fratocchi et al., 2013) – with consequences on the entire global industry. Our perspective is to examine how firms in developed countries are approaching their strategies of international management of value chains within the GVC framework (Cattaneo et al., 2010), on the basis though of a series of studies on clusters. In fact, we are interested in exploring how leading cluster firms behave in this scenario, taking into account clusters' role as specialized systems where competitiveness has been traditionally based on a tight relationship between manufacturing and innovation. Indeed, literature on clusters still describes them as local manufacturing systems offering positive externalities in terms of innovation opportunities, quality control over production, and close connections with advanced customers (i.e. for Italian industrial districts) (Becattini et al., 2009). More recently, some researches have explored the transformation of clusters towards more open systems: lead firms invest in the international production process with the potential loss or weakening of relationships within local business-to-business networks (Zucchella, 2006; Chiarvesio et al., 2010). However, very few analyses have tried to understand the relative importance of manufacturing localized in clusters of developed countries in a globalized world.

From this perspective, the chapter aims at exploring the cluster firms' strategies concerning manufacturing location within the GVC framework, by considering the cluster's role as local manufacturing system. In fact, after several years of intense internationalization of production, little has been said on how leading cluster firms are now organizing their value chains at local and global levels and the implications for other actors, taking into account recent backshoring trends.

Manufacturing in global value chains and value generation: new trends

Studies on GVCs investigate the international structure of industries and, through the governance concept, they describe how firms (and countries) gain the value produced through fragmented international activities (Feenstra, 1998; Gereffi et al., 2005; Bair, 2009). In the GVC perspective, manufacturing activities are mainly located in developing countries and emerging economies, where (large) lead firms usually control their suppliers through captive – or modular – forms of governance. According to Mudambi (2007), the "smile" model considers manufacturing (and standardized services) at the lowest level of value creation, whereas R&D and design on the one hand, and marketing, brand management or specialized logistics on the other hand, are the most important value sources for an internationalized firm. R&D and marketing knowledge support this process of value creation. From a dynamic perspective, manufacturing and tangible-related activities are progressively located or developed in emerging economies; meanwhile, advanced countries (and new industries) are focusing on intangibles.

This model describes the progressive relocation of manufacturing activities that took place in the past decades from the North to the South of the world, as well as the opportunities for Western firms to control high value-added activities (Buckley, 2009). Countries such as the United States have experienced a strong decrease in manufacturing employment over time, as well as the rise of a service-based economy.

Schmitz and Knorringa (2000) suggest that small firms supplying large international buyers can benefit from this link through knowledge acquisition, which allows them to upgrade and increase their position in the GVC. Specifically, the upgrading concept describes the evolutionary process of manufacturers from assembler to Original Equipment Manufacturer (OEM), to Original Design Manufacturer (ODM) up to Original Brand Manufacturer (OBM). This highlights how, from low value-added manufacturing activities, a firm can gain more value in a path oriented to intangibles. In this "shift," manufacturing can become more and more marginal in an evolution that includes innovation and marketing functions. From this point of view, GVC recalls the "smile" approach, although considering the process mainly from the perspective of upgrading firms in developing countries (Elms and Low, 2013; Gereffi and Lee, 2014).

Despite the emphasis on the economic advantages of becoming a "post-industrial" economy, a clear and definitive picture of how manufacturing processes organized among firms and countries are far from being conclusive. The debate concerning the relevance of manufacturing activities is in fact not new (i.e. Cohen and Zysman, 1987; Merchant and Gaur, 2008). However, this issue has become more crucial due to the rise of a new technological landscape, new social trends and institutional transformations. Recently, in fact, several scholars have proposed a more nuanced framework to interpret the internationalization of production and the need to revalue manufacturing activities, in particular facing innovation. Pisano and Shih (2012) suggest considering the maturity of a manufacturing technology and the degree of modularity that characterizes a product's design. An international production can take place only when there is a high degree of modularity and high process maturity or pure process innovation. On the contrary, in other situations where there is a process-embedded innovation or a process-driven innovation, separating innovation (R&D or design) and manufacturing may reduce firms' ability (or the country's ability) to create new knowledge and to compete.

By studying firms' spatial location in relation to the advantages of agglomeration, Alcacer and Delgado (2013) highlight that geographically bounded intra-firm linkages (e.g. between R&D and manufacturing) are relevant in explaining firms' choices to co-locate activities. In their review on the debate concerning the evolutionary international trends of manufacturing organization and related empirical analysis, Buciuni and Finotto (2016) show the crucial role of co-location of production and development in low-tech industries: new knowledge and innovation activities are possible whenever industrial production occurs. From a different perspective, the rise of the maker movement and the increasing role of consumers as innovators (i.e. Anderson, 2012) open new scenarios where manufacturing activities are more distributed and connected with innovation.

From another viewpoint, marketing studies also consider the implications – for Western firms – of offshoring or recurring to global sourcing for their products. Firms offering high-end productions rely on high-skilled small producers or craftsmen to carry out their production, by locating where crucial manufacturing competences are available (Bettiol and Micelli, 2014). Proximity to consumers also offers the opportunity to be more reactive and interpret their needs for customization purposes. Moreover, a growing number of consumers explicitly consider the country-of-origin effect, by comparing country-of-design and country-of-production (Hamzaoui and Merunka, 2006) with impacts on their purchasing processes. Firms that want to exploit the positive country-of-origin image can choose to locate their manufacturing activities in their own countries, despite the potential disadvantages from the point of view of production costs. Consumers are also more interested in participating in production activities through the do-it-yourself (DIY) approach, where communities of consumers are involved in innovation, production, as well as marketing processes once limited to the firms' sphere (von Hippel, 2005).

Studies on backshoring (Fratocchi et al., 2014; Bailey and De Propris, 2014; Kinkel, 2014) scrutinize the location choice of manufacturing activities and emphasize a multifaceted scenario. According to this point of view, internationalized firms reorganize their manufacturing processes – either based on offshoring or global sourcing decisions – towards the firms' country (headquarter location) so as to exploit the advantages of co-location between R&D and production, to be close to their customers (better service, improved quality) or to gain from the country-of-origin effect. Moreover, said studies also consider the opportunity to increase efficiency in operations and to cope with increased costs of global supplying (e.g. Chinese labour costs). In fact, along with hidden organizational costs, a firm may have to manage international manufacturing processes not forecast at the beginning.

Among these emerging trends, recent GVC studies have also highlighted the rise of large (global) suppliers (e.g. Foxconn), capable of modifying the structure of GVCs and power distribution among GVC players (Gereffi and Lee, 2012). Due to their control over manufacturing activities, large suppliers are proposing interesting forms of competition and new models (i.e. platform leaders) that are reshaping the way through which production and consumption are taking place even in developing countries (Sturgeon and Kawakami, 2011).

Firms' strategies in clusters as local manufacturing systems

While studies on GVCs have considered the global organization of (manufacturing) activities, studies concerning clusters have focused their attention on the localized effects of manufacturing processes. The vast literature on clusters (Becattini et al., 2009; Lazzeretti et al., 2014) outlines the peculiarities of this model of economic development compared to large organizations: the extensive division of labour among firms localized in the same area (local sourcing), and the high number of small firms in a context where industry specialization increases specialized know-how. The spatial, social and cognitive proximity among firms (entrepreneurs, workers) support knowledge flows. Clusters are manufacturing systems where localized innovation occurs due to learning-by-doing processes characterizing the single firm as well as inter-firm linkages.

The cluster can be viewed as a cognitive system (Camuffo and Grandinetti, 2011), where localized knowledge is embedded in a specific institutional, economic and social setting that enables the production and diffusion of specialized knowledge (oriented to innovation and production). In this perspective, many studies show how multinational companies have been interested in investing in clusters to exploit the location advantages for knowledge acquisition – via manufacturing processes or research units (De Propris and Driffield, 2006); on the other hand, recent acquisitions of cluster brands by foreign companies are explained by their interest in exploiting local competences and knowledge (e.g. the acquisition of Italian Rossimoda located in the shoe cluster of Riviera del Brenta by the French group LVMH, OECD, 2014).

GVC studies have considered clusters in developing countries mainly for efficiency-seeking in manufacturing activities where innovation and in general value-added activities are controlled by the lead firm (overseas) (Bair and Gereffi, 2001; Pietrobelli and Rabellotti, 2007). Studies on clusters have proposed a different perspective that stresses the tight link between innovation and manufacturing in localized activities within clusters.

Moreover, recent studies on clusters have depicted a dynamic scenario concerning the cluster model (e.g. De Marchi and Grandinetti, 2014; Fornahl et al., 2015). Multiple forces are reshaping the cluster systems, which are characterized by increased internal and external variety. The rise of groups (as discussed by Giuliani and Rabellotti, Chapter 2 in this book) and the increased firm size modify inter-firm relationships at cluster level. Among the consequences of these processes, studies have noticed the transformation of the traditional cluster – where innovation was "in the air" and economies were external to the firms but internal to the cluster – in contexts where lead firms explicitly rely more both on internal competencies and international relationships to develop strategies that can be competitive regardless the conditions of the cluster as a whole.

In a few cases, cluster lead firms may be considered also as lead firms from a GVC perspective, such as Luxottica in the Italian eyewear district (Camuffo, 2003) or Geox in the sportsystem district (Camuffo et al., 2008). In most of the other cases, cluster lead firms are cluster mid-sized firms (Coltorti et al., 2013) that followed intense processes of product and process upgrading, by investing in design and/or brand competences and changing from OEM to ODM or OBM companies (Albino et al., 1999; Lazerson and Lorenzoni, 2008; Buciuni et al., 2013). However, usually lead firms in clusters do not outsource their manufacturing processes completely to local (or international) suppliers to become pure brand vendors, but often they maintain control over the production for competitive reasons.

On the one hand, internationalization processes put in place by cluster firms positively influence their performances; on the other hand, they affect the local division of labour among firms and the relationship between local and global (Chiarvesio et al., 2010, Chiarvesio et al., 2013). Cluster firms that internationalize manufacturing activities abroad modify their connections with local suppliers – rationalization vs. more intense supplying relationships (i.e. Grandinetti and Tabacco, 2015; Giansoldati and Pauluzzo, 2011) – with consequences also on the management of innovation. In fact, the rise of cluster lead firms – and the internationalization processes they put in place – affects the cohesion of the local system. Indeed, scholars (Furlan et al., 2007) discuss cluster suppliers' evolution owing to their relationships with internationalized lead firms, where some suppliers upgrade by improving their internal organizational and technological processes to become specialized suppliers. This process is consistent with learning processes of cluster small suppliers connected to GVC lead firms (Humphrey and Schmitz, 2002; Giuliani et al., 2005). However, upstream internationalization of leading firms may weaken the local sourcing structure, due to the effect of the substitution between local and international suppliers.

Many studies highlight the advantages of clusters' openness from a knowledge management viewpoint in terms of innovation opportunities. Camuffo and Grandinetti (2011), for example, stress the positive implications of internationalization processes for clusters, where cluster leading firms can play the role of gatekeepers between the local and the global. However, we should also consider that the depletion of the social and economic activity at local level, together with easy communication and interaction at a distance mediated by network technologies, can contribute in lowering the perceived relevance of localizing manufacturing activities within clusters.

In this scenario, the aim of our research is to explore the leading cluster firms' strategies of manufacturing location locally and globally, and more specifically to identify the role played by clusters – considered as local *manufacturing* systems – in such international location strategies. In particular, we are interested in considering whether the location of manufacturing activities by leading firms in clusters – and the forms of governance adopted between hierarchy and market – is still important for firms' competitiveness in the framework of GVCs and within the emerging phenomenon of backshoring. In other words, does (local) geography still matter? We would like to understand if there is a link between the cluster's choice of the location for manufacturing activities and the cluster firms' perceptions on local externalities and the advantages of agglomeration economies related to innovation and manufacturing flexibility. In particular, we will explore the role of local actors (leading firms, suppliers), their activities and their position in the value chain. Moreover, due to the recent hype on backshoring initiatives, we devoted specific attention in understanding the link between cluster firms' past internationalization strategies and backshoring initiatives at cluster level.

Location of cluster firms' manufacturing activities between local and global: an analysis of three Italian clusters

Methodology and analysis of clusters

For the aim of our research, a qualitative analysis was carried out based on comparative case studies (Eisenhardt, 1989). Firms specialized in low- and medium-tech industries (mechanics, fashion and furniture) were selected with reference to relevant clusters in the northeastern Italian regions (Veneto and Friuli Venezia Giulia). The latter are among the most important areas due to the presence of clusters with strong economic impacts on both the regions and the country itself. Moreover, compared to other geographical areas, Veneto and Friuli Venezia Giulia have been the most open toward internationalization (Chiarvesio et al.,

Table 9.1 Overview of the Italian clusters analysed

	Montebelluna Sport System	Furniture clusters (Livenza, Quartier del Piave, Manzano)	Belluno eyewear cluster
Products	Sport technical equipment for footwear: (i.e. hiking, backpacking, ski, motocross boots, inline and ice skating, football and tennis shoes) More recently: sportswear in general and every day shoes but with technical components (Geox, the main producer of every day shoes accounts for 70% of the district's turnover.	Middle end furniture: – Livenza and Q. Piave more specialized in furniture – Manzano more specialized in chairs, with an upgrading of some companies to furniture	High-end glasses (Frames, Sunglasses) Lenses Cases
# of firms*	525 firms (2014)	2,436 (2014)	313 firms (2014)
Export§	949 Ml Euro export (2015) +7.1% (2014/2015)	2,765 Ml Euro (2015) +5.5% (2014/2015)	2,753 Ml Euro +12.6% (2014/2015)
GVC key actors	Italy is leader in winter sports (70% of world production of ski boots – and of high-end niches in other sports)	China is the largest furniture exporter (38% of world export), followed by Germany, Italy, Poland and USA	Italy (leader in high-end eyewear production) China (80% of world total production in middle-low eyewear market)
Main markets	USA, Germany, France	United Kingdom, Germany, France, Russia, USA	US, France, Germany (frames), Spain (sunglasses) Europe counts 50% of total Italian export

Source: Authors, based on Movimprese (*) and Banca Intesa Sanpaolo (§).

2004). Table 9.1 provides an overview of the clusters considered, while Table 9.2 gives a GVC-wise description.

The research analysed firms of different size, but specialized in final goods. Moreover, the focus was on cluster lead firms' internationalization strategies. Within a cluster perspective, the role and the features of a lead firm are slightly different compared to those of a traditional GVC lead firm. More than being large players – either as large manufacturers or retailers – capable of setting standards and strong brands at global level, cluster lead firms emerge because of their specific technological competencies, innovation proactiveness, marketing strength, and international propensity. All the latter factors enable firms to identify new paths in clusters' evolution, capable of being a benchmark for other firms and, very often, of acting as gatekeepers between local and global contexts (Corò and Grandinetti, 1999). Sometimes said firms grow not by increasing their size as single firms, but through the acquisition of other firms, with the aim to enlarge their portfolio of products and/or brands; the business group can also remain informal when a single entrepreneur (or his/her family) and not a company acquires control over other firms (Cainelli et al., 2006).

We selected six case studies in three clusters: sportsystem (shoes and sportswear), furniture, and eyewear. The selected firms, although not necessarily large lead firms in a GVC

Table 9.2 Overview of the Italian sportsystem, furniture, eyewear clusters in the GVC

	Montebelluna Sport System	Furniture clusters	Belluno eyewear cluster
Types of firms	OBMs (some brands have a global presence and are leader in their niches) OEMs Small specialized suppliers	OBMs (some brands have a global presence and are leader in their niches) OEMs Small specialized suppliers	Top global brands (4 firms) with high number of brands in their portfolio OBMs, OEMs Small specialized suppliers
GVC Governance model	Producer-driven	Producer-driven mainly Some cases of buyer-driven relationships (e.g. Ikea)	Producer-driven
Distribution	Traditional specialized national and international retailers Large international retailers	Traditional specialized national and international retailers Large international retailers	Large national and international retail chains Independent optical shops Discount/department stores Non-store retailers (catalogues, TV channels, online shopping) Branded boutique chains
Upgrading strategies	Product Upgrading: Functional Upgrading: design; branding; retail (only for Geox)	Product upgrading Functional upgrading: – branding	Product upgrading Functional upgrading: – from production to distribution – branding
Supporting industries	Machinery productions, Chemical industry	Machinery productions	Machinery productions, Plastic industry; Chemical industry
Local institutions	Fondazione Museo dello Scarpone (Museum dedicated to the history of hiking and sky boots)	Catas (quality test and certification) Furniture cluster for Livenza and Manzano (enhancement of projects for the clusters)	Certottica (Italian Institute for the Certification of optical products) Museo dell'occhiale (Eyewear museum)

Source: Authors.

perspective, have high power in the value chain due to market-related factors and internal innovation capabilities. Moreover, they are able to design and control their value chain at the cluster level but also in an international setting. From this point of view, they are considered leading players within the district by other firms and local institutions.

First of all, in the sportwear cluster, the research focused on Aku and Diadora Sport. Aku is a traditional family business specialized in hiking and trekking boots, that can be defined an ODM. It followed several firms' evolution in the district, delocalizing its production in Romania (FDI), but without losing bonds with manufacturing at home. In particular, Aku kept a manufacturing plant in Montebelluna, specializing in assembly, quality control and product development. At the same time, Aku focused on product design, branding and communication. Eventually, the firm developed an interesting program (one of the first in the cluster) for improving product environmental sustainability. Diadora Sport produces sneaker and running shoes. In the past, especially in the 1970s and 1980s it was a worldwide leader in tennis shoes (the testimonial was the tennis champion Bjorn Borg) and one of the key players in other sports shoes. After that the firm declined and passed through several changes of ownership, until it was bought in 2009 from LIR, the holding company of the Polegato Family (the one behind Geox) and completely relaunched. This project was successfully executed and was based on a relaunch strategy focusing on three key factors: authenticity, craftsmanship and innovation that are part of the brand identity and heritage.

Second, in the furniture cluster, we interviewed Moroso, a company related to the chair district in the region of Friuli Venezia Giulia, and Arper, located in Veneto. Moroso is a medium, family-owned firm that produces high-quality design furniture (sofas, armchairs, accessories) for a high-end target, both consumers and businesses. The company's brand reputation is that of a design-setting company devoted to quality production, and it is considered a world leader in design furniture. Moroso exports 70% of its turnover, mainly in Europe and North America, but with an increasing interest in emerging markets; it has settled commercial subsidiaries in London, New York and Dubai and several showrooms or flagship stores in strategic towns. Arper, instead, is a medium-sized company specialized in high-quality design products (mainly) for the office (chairs, tables, armchairs, sofas). The market is typically business-to-business (B2B) and international, as 95% of its turnover is produced abroad (70% in Europe – above all Germany and Northern Europe); in the last few years, the company has opened 11 showrooms in cities relevant for design (from London to New York, Chicago, Stockholm). Arper has a well-known brand based on design (attested by the many awards received) and on its products' manufacturing quality, the result of a balanced mix of artisan competencies and robotics.

Finally, in the eyewear cluster, we interviewed two firms specialized in different products: cases and eyewear (frames and sunglasses). De Rigo Vision is a historical cluster eyewear manufacturer (OEM) founded in 1978 that upgraded to become an OBM in the last decade. Currently, De Rigo Vision has one manufacturing plant within the cluster, many brands in its portfolio (three proprietary brands – Police, Lozza- Lozza Sartoriale, and Sting – as well as 15 licensed brands in the middle-high market) and owns three retail chains leaders in their respective countries (General Optica in Spain, Mais Optica in Portugal, and Opmar Optik in Turkey, plus Boots Opticians in the UK which is also an international subsidiary of the company). Whereas, Giorgio Fedon & Figli is an OEM specialized in the production of cases with about a century-long history (founded in 1925). The company developed a complex upgrading process in order to become an ODM first and then an OBM: product upgrading, with investments in the quality of the product (cases) to produce high-quality cases for licensed global brands together with a more recent inclusion also of eyewear labelled with the Fedon brand in addition to cases; functional upgrading, by investing in design and marketing so as to develop its own brand and enhance its visibility on international markets, also through the development of its own retail stores internationally (mainly located in airports); chain upgrading, through product diversification including leather cases (i.e. for tablets) and other leather-based products (i.e. bags and related accessories), through the exploitation of productive synergies and internal competences.

Data were collected through face-to-face interviews carried out between October 2015 and March 2016 with entrepreneurs, CEOs, operational managers and sales managers. We completed and checked information through secondary sources (websites and company reports). Interviews focused on the firms' manufacturing location strategies between the cluster and the global scenario, the organization of the supply chain management and innovation management. Table 9.3 presents an overview of the selected case studies.

Table 9.3 Case studies overview

Company	Aku Italia	Diadora Sport	Arper	Moroso	Giorgio Fedon & Figli	De Rigo Vision
Turnover	21 Ml€	247 Ml€	50 Ml€	24 Ml€	54 Ml€	222 Ml€
Employees	50	176	90	130	240 (Italy)	890
Year of foundation*	mid 1980s (2009)	1948 (2009)	1989	1973	1925	1978 (1992) (2004)
Strategy	Medium-high quality trekking and outdoor footwear	Medium-high quality performance and lifestyle shoes & clothing	High end (total quality + design) furniture (B2B market)	Luxury sofas and seating	High-quality leather cases for glasses; Leather products; Eyewear	Medium-high quality glasses
Headquarter Location	Montebelluna (sportsystem cluster)	Caerano San Marco (sport system cluster)	Monastier di Treviso (furniture cluster)	Udine (furniture cluster)	Pieve d'Alpago (eyewear cluster)	Longarone (eyewear cluster)
Distribution strategy	One shop in Montebelluna Indirect distribution	Indirect distribution	11 showrooms in Europe and USA (NY, Chicago) Indirect distribution	Indirect distribution 3 commercial subsidiaries (London, New York, Dubai); showrooms Flagship stores in Milan, London, Amsterdam, NY	Four commercial branches (Paris, Hong Kong, Monaco, New York) 18 shops Indirect distribution	Three retail chains (Spain, Portugal, Turkey) Two subsidiaries (UK, Korea) Indirect distribution

* The first year reported is that of the foundation, while the year in parenthesis is that in which the company changed its legal status. Turnover and employment data refer to 2014

The Montebelluna cluster

The industrial district of Montebelluna is a shoemaking centre of worldwide importance, with extraordinary industrial integration: over 500 businesses and a turnover of around €1.9 billion, three-quarters of which realized on foreign markets. Montebelluna accounts for 25% of the world's production of skates, around half of the world's technical mountain boots, two thirds of after-ski boots, three-quarters of ski boots and almost all of the world's motorcycle boots.

Historically, the area was famous for the production of the traditional "gallozze," that is, heavy leather boots with a carved wooden sole, ideal for working the land in the mountain areas, especially for lumberjacks, a very popular profession in the area due to the presence of extensive wooded areas. In more recent years, the cluster started to produce leather-based ski and trekking boots with a rubber sole. A dramatic transformation occurred in the 1970s with the introduction of plastic for the production of ski boots. The original idea came from the outside, specifically from American Bob Lange (his brand still today is one of the most famous in the industry), who launched the idea of producing plastic ski boots in the 1960s. However, this invention took off in the market when local producers (i.e. Tecnica, Nordica and Dolomite, three leading boot producers, once independent and now part of the Tecnica Group) developed the idea with skill and experience, inventing a system to inject plastic into pre-assembled moulds. This led to a less-expensive, mass-produced, and lightweight ski boot that changed the sport and the industry forever. Eventually, the cluster's firms diversified their production in two main directions: 1) enlarging the range from ski boots, trekking boots and motorcycle boots, to dancing shoes, after-ski boots, ice skates and roller skates, tennis and football shoes etc.; and 2) extending the product portfolio with sportswear, ski technical equipment, t-shirts and other sports garments, in line with similar transitions of other footwear firms (e.g. Adidas, Nike).

In the 1990s a process of progressive delocalization of manufacturing activities began to unfold, especially in the more labour-intensive stages of production. The focus was on Timisoara, a Romanian town, with historical expertise in shoemaking. This process was so intensive that scholars and local experts refer to Timisoara as a twin cluster of Montebelluna, due to the fact that several local entrepreneurs went to Romania to open workshops in order to take advantage of less expensive labour costs (Crestanello and Tattara, 2011). Asia and China are also other relevant areas of delocalization, but are marginal compared to Timisoara. Delocalization led to a new division of labour: a different organization of activities between the two clusters on the one hand, and the development of new or higher capabilities (upgrading) on the other hand. This led to a specialization in product development, design, marketing and communication of the lead firms. It also produced a change in local subcontractors that are now focused on qualitative production such as prototypes, samples and first series of the products. The cluster is formed mainly by OBMs and several specific OEMs for soles ("suolettificio") and other very specific parts of the shoes. Some of the OBMs can be considered global brands, such as Nordica, Dolomite, Tecnica, Lotto, Geox, and Alpinestars. Some of these companies, such as Geox, can be comparable with the typical GVC lead firm. Others, instead, like Alpinestar, are niche players with very strong international brands in their specific segment (in this case technical boots and protections for motocross), due to product quality, innovation and constant interaction with lead users.

The clusters' specific skills and competences drew the attention of global multinationals in the sports industry that decided to tap into this knowledge pool via FDI in the cluster (as the case of Lange and Rossignol) or the acquisition of local companies (as the case of Amersports group, Nike and Salomon), highlighting the double dimension of clusters in GVCs, inserted both through home-grown multinationals and inward FDIs (as well depicted by Belussi et al., Chapter 5 in this book).

Between the 1990s and the 2000s another revolution occurred in the cluster with the diversification of every day shoes. Geox was the first mover, but with a differentiation strategy based on innovation: in fact, the company introduced an innovative technical component in traditional shoes (a breathable tissue patented in the aerospace industry and adapted for the shoe soles). This led to the creation of a new product category called "the shoe that breaths." This innovation opened up an important opportunity for growth, and now Geox accounts for 50% of the district's turnover, although not specialized in the sportswear.

The furniture clusters

The furniture cluster analysed is composed of three different historical industrial districts located across the regions of Veneto and Friuli Venezia Giulia: two specialized in different products for home furniture, and one focused on the production of chairs. In all, 2,500 firms that together constitute the biggest pole in Italy for the production of furniture, mainly in the middle and middle-high end of the market, with some companies in the high end (while, for example, the furniture cluster of Brianza is mainly focused on the very high-end target). Their export share on the total of Italian exports accounts for almost 40%, giving an important contribution to Italy's furniture industry, which is the third worldwide exporter, after China and Germany.

For a long time the district of Manzano was one of the most important areas for the production of chairs in Europe and even in the world. Then, a series of events (the increasing competition coming from low-cost markets, the delocalization of some local firms, the loss of price competition due to the adoption of the Euro as new currency and the economic crisis) put cluster firms in front of many difficulties. In order to face the new challenges, the most dynamic companies underwent a process of product and functional upgrading by investing in product distribution, communication and branding as well as product innovation (enlarging also the product portfolio to include tables and other products mainly for the living room). Similar paths were followed by the companies in the furniture cluster, where there was also a hierarchization process of relationships through the creation of company groups. In fact, most companies increased their size (and their market) by acquiring companies located in the same area and very often specialized in complementary products (so as to offer a complete product portfolio for home furnishing). In these clusters, groups are very often informal, as companies are controlled by the same entrepreneur, but remain autonomous from a legal viewpoint; in this case, grouping strategies are more driven by market purposes (enlargement of product portfolio, branding) than financial ones (Cainelli et al., 2006).

The furniture cluster is made of many OBMs, some with a very strong presence at international level, more visible in districts proposing general home furniture, compared to those focused on chairs. In the latter, in fact, companies are generally smaller, with few resources to be invested in marketing and communication. Some companies operate mainly for the consumer market, but most serve both consumers and B2B markets (the so called "contract market") in the chair district. There are also many small OBMs that work both in national and international markets, with a more selected network of customers. Besides, a number of OEMs and ODMs work for the contract market or for national and international distributors/buyers. Among the latter, in the area of Livenza, the two biggest ones are big suppliers of global brands such as Ikea, which has its second supplier market for furniture here after the Far East. Finally, as typical of industrial clusters, a huge number of small suppliers are specialized in specific phases of the production value chain (production of components or specific operations on behalf of other companies).

The Belluno eyewear cluster

The Belluno eyewear cluster is the most important cluster in Italy and worldwide specialized in the production of high-end glasses (frames, sunglasses, lenses, and cases). It is located in a mountainous region in the north of Italy (the region of Veneto) in the areas of Cadore, Agordo, Longarone, Belluno (provincial capital) and other municipalities. By exporting almost all of its domestic production, Italy has one-third of the global market share and ranks first in the manufacturing of high-end eyewear, while China is the absolute leader in the middle-low market.

The cluster has undergone a strong vertical hierarchization process over the years, with a decrease in the number of firms and the rise of important global lead firms. Luxottica is the largest global eyewear leader (OBM) specialized in design, production and distribution of luxury and sport eyewear and sunglasses, operating in more than 150 countries (12 manufacturing facilities, 18 distribution centres, 7,200 retail stores). Other internationally recognized OBMs located in the cluster are Safilo, De Rigo Vision, and Marcolin that manage large brand portfolios and control retail stores in multiple foreign markets. In addition, within the cluster, there are small-sized OBMs and OEMs producing for large buyers (licensing). As a reaction to the crisis and the market power of the biggest firms in the cluster, interesting strategies are emerging aimed at finding market niches (high-quality and customized products) or differentiation through services or innovation. There are also a large number of specialized suppliers providing selected activities along the value chain (i.e. galvanic and painting, whereas the components for obtaining final products refer to: screws, lenses, bridges, nose pads, hinges, rods, fronts and washers). However, the production process is composed of multiple activities that can be efficiently integrated through vertical integration (Design and Prototyping, MIM and Casting, Production of moulds, Tumbling, Sandblasting and Cleaning, Galvanic and Painting, Decoration, Engravings, Machining, Welding and Assembly).

Comparative analysis of company case studies

The research analysed how cluster firms tend to structure their organization of manufacturing activities between the cluster and the global scenario, as well as the forms of governance adopted. Moreover, the related innovation activities were also considered and in particular how cluster lead firms approach and manage new product development. Table 9.4 presents in detail the internationalization strategies of the six case studies analysed.

Concerning the internationalization of production, all case studies have located their production in the cluster. At the same time, however – except for Moroso – all of the firms have also invested in the development and management of international manufacturing activities.

The companies' different strategies can be analysed and compared considering three main aspects: 1) the governance of the value chain, where the choice is between hierarchical models or outsourcing – relational, modular or captive (in line with Gereffi et al., 2005); 2) the location of the production, both in the form of hierarchy or outsourcing; 3) the reasons why to maintain (backshore) the production in the cluster.

From the viewpoint of the governance of value chain (see Table 9.4 and Figures 9.1, 9.2, and 9.3), Arper and Giorgio Fedon & Figli have invested mainly in FDIs (to better control operations and quality output) with limited recourse to global sourcing. On the contrary,

Table 9.4 Internationalization strategies of the cluster firms analysed

Company	Aku Italia	Diadora Sport	Arper	Moroso	Giorgio Fedon & Figli	De Rigo Vision
Production location (hierarchy)	Italy (cluster) (re-shoring) Romania	Italy (cluster) (re-shoring)	Italy North Carolina	Italy (cluster)	Italy (cluster and other regions) (leather cases, accessories) Romania (bags) China (cases)	Italy (cluster) China Japan (some lines)
Supplier location	Italy (cluster) Romania	Italy (cluster) and rest of the World	Italy China Vietnam	Mainly Italy	Italy China	Italy (cluster) China Japan
Forms of governance (upstream)	Local sourcing: relational Global sourcing: modular and captive Hierarchy (FDI)	Local sourcing: relational Global sourcing: captive	Local sourcing: relational Global sourcing: relational Hierarchy (FDI)	Local sourcing: relational	Local sourcing: relational and captive Global sourcing: captive Hierarchy (FDI)	Local sourcing: market/captive Global sourcing: captive/market
Employees in operation dept.	30 (cluster) 300 (Romania)	46 (cluster)	60	n.a.	140 (cluster) 120 (Romania) 1000 (China)	600
Location of the design function	Global	Cluster	Global	Global	Cluster/Global	Global
Location of product development process	Cluster	Cluster	Cluster	Cluster	Cluster China	Cluster

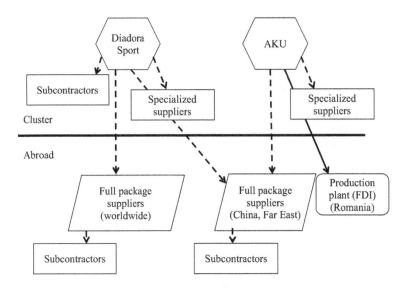

Figure 9.1 Governance of value chain in the case studies analysed: the Montebelluna cluster
Source: Authors.

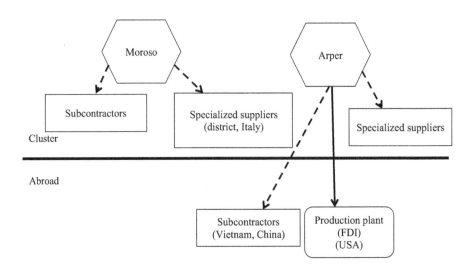

Figure 9.2 Governance of value chain in the case studies analysed: the furniture cluster
Source: Authors.

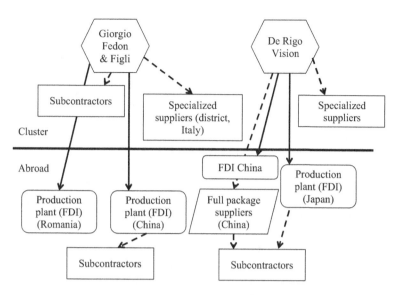

Figure 9.3 Governance of value chain in the case studies analysed: the Belluno eyewear cluster
Source: Authors.

De Rigo Vision has completely outsourced manufacturing activities at the global scale, while in-house production is carried out only at the cluster level and limited to selected brand products. Aku Italia adopts different forms of governance, recurring to FDIs as well as global sourcing (both captive and modular, in the same countries of the FDI location). Nevertheless, as regards employment related to manufacturing activities, it is possible to observe that production carried out in-house within the local manufacturing system counts a limited amount of human resources compared to foreign subsidiaries. In general, the scale of the international production is much higher than the production carried out at the cluster level (i.e. Giorgio Fedon & Figli produces 50 million cases each year in China, while in Italy the production is mostly for low volumes of luxury cases and handcrafted items).

When considering suppliers' location, firms evaluate suppliers' expertise and quality, but also production costs; in this way, they combine sourcing from the cluster and other Italian regions – mainly managed through relational forms of governance – with global sourcing from low-cost countries (within the European Union and also the Far East). Compared to the other case studies, Moroso has developed a strategy focused on Italy characterized by artisanship as a peculiarity of its manufacturing processes. Moroso stresses the Made in Italy origin of its products by emphasizing the hand-made side of production, which is possible through internal competences as well as small suppliers located close to the headquarters and with whom it is easy to interact. At the same time, all of the companies consider as strategic the fact of maintaining a presence at the local level, where suppliers can be managed mainly through a relational model of governance, fundamental for dealing with complex activities and innovation processes. In fact, local suppliers' competences should be considered in relation to the need of high-quality and/or complex and innovative products that require customization and interaction with customers.

The location within the cluster is the result of a historical path and a link with the firms' social fabric. Giorgio Fedon & Figli or De Rigo Vision maintain the production at the local level because of the embeddedness in the local context. Said companies are interested in preserving cluster employment due to the lead firm's social role in the cluster, but also in exploiting the local workforce's expertise. However, in order to justify the location of operational processes in a high-cost area such as Italy (and the region of Veneto), the mentioned firms have carried out an upgrading process of their productions focusing on high-end and luxury products. This is consistent with the request of selected global customers who ask for Made in Italy production. In the case of Aku Italia, the cluster firm has explicitly implemented backshoring processes to bring back to the cluster manufacturing activities previously carried out in other European countries (Romania). Diadora Sport production is mostly located in the Far East and Europe, but recently the company has decided to re-open an old factory in the cluster to produce high-quality sneakers. Reasons for this choice are related to the need of improving the control over the production in terms of quality performance linked to the exploitation of the Made in Italy effect. This is particularly true for Diadora Sport that did the history of many shoe products over the last decades. When the owners of another famous cluster company (Geox) purchased in 2009 the company that was in crisis, the new CEO decided to reintroduce the production of high-end products and limited editions (recently eco-shoes too) at the cluster level in order to reinforce and re-launch the Diadora historical brand. This was possible also by exploiting the machineries already available in the former operation department. Arper has invested to internationalize its manufacturing processes beyond its cluster location, but for other reasons. In particular, it has selected another important area for furniture production: the furniture cluster of High Point in North Carolina. This area is a major productive context for furniture production in the USA. The location of a subsidiary has allowed Arper to enter in the US market proposing customized products (contract), and to be close to main customers, becoming ever more effective in logistics. In the meantime, it has invested in increasing the cluster production's efficiency and quality by improving the degree of automation in the operational department, thanks to internal R&D-based knowledge applied to its machineries and plant processes.

It is important to note that the case studies innovate their products by recurring to global inputs for design, collaborating with international designers or studios. At the same time, however, product development is managed, generally speaking, within the cluster, through a dedicated internal department. Hence, the cluster is still the place where critical activities are located, which then require managing the interaction among design, innovation and operations (and suppliers) accordingly. It is worth noting however, that in the case of Giorgio Fedon & Figli, the firm has replicated its design department in China (within its Chinese subsidiary) in order to manage product development processes more efficiently and to be more consistent with international market requests.

Manufacturing (and geography) still matters

This chapter sheds light on clusters' manufacturing role in the present, and cluster firms' future manufacturing location strategies. Our research contributes to the theoretical debate concerning clusters' evolution and the relationship between GVC and localized production in clusters, within the context of developed countries. Our analyses confirm the transformation of the cluster model and, in particular, the internationalization processes occurring in the upstream activities of the manufacturing process. Cluster firms combine hierarchical control over internationalized manufacturing activities with different forms of governance of global suppliers. However, clusters are still considered an important place in which to locate manufacturing, but only selected ones and related to innovation and marketing purposes.

The case studies examined show the relevance for lead firms to be located in the cluster and maintain their manufacturing activities in order to exploit the expertise of local labour force and specialized local competences. In particular, the location of production activities within the cluster seems a strategy mainly related to different possible objectives: 1) the opportunity to enhance (or not to lose) the part of creativity and product innovation connected with the manufacturing process and the physical handling of the product; 2) the interest to strictly control the quality of the strategic components of the product; 3) the possibility to exploit local competencies with the aim to produce high-quality or even luxury products or limited editions that match quality and the Made in Italy; 4) the possibility to better react to customization requests.

Nevertheless, GVCs and local clusters are not in opposition, but are part of a more complex division of labour that is based on the optimization of specific competitive advantages: the search for *quality* in the case of clusters and the search for *quantity* (scale and low cost) in the case of global value chains. From the global perspective, the location of manufacturing in foreign markets – namely in Eastern Europe or the Far East – is part of the internationalization strategy of most of the firms considered, particularly relevant in case of large-scale production, where labour-intensive activities ask for location in manufacturing countries characterized by the large labour market (low-cost countries). From this point of view, cluster lead firms have followed the same strategies of large multinationals depicted in the GVC studies, by considering both FDI and global sourcing. In the latter case, captive or modular forms of governance seem to prevail, while the relational one characterizes the interaction with local suppliers. Moreover, some suppliers are chosen locally because of their competencies, but also because it is possible to have a rich and interactive relationship whenever innovation and quality issues are involved. At the same time, cluster-led firms that have created international manufacturing subsidiaries (FDI) are now reorganizing their foreign activities along two directions. On one hand, some of them (Aku Italia, Diadora) are taking back some productions or re-opening old factories; on the other hand, others (Arper and Giorgio Fedon) are investing in automation (i.e. advanced robots) in manufacturing processes – both internationally (i.e. China) and at the district level – to cope with the trend of increasing labour wages and to better control manufacturing and innovation within the firm. In all of the cases, a wide backshoring seems not to be among the options considered by the firms.

From the local perspective, cluster production is dedicated to a limited scale, where the cluster is perceived as "*a boutique*" (as defined by one of the interviewees), a specialized manufacturing system that is able to support high-quality (or luxury) productions, limited editions (where firms in some cases have self-limited their production scalability). Moreover, cluster location sustains firms' country-of-origin strategy and the opportunity to exploit artisanal competences for upgrading processes. Most important, firms are conscious that losing control over production means losing innovation opportunities, the ability to identify potential innovation trends, and remarkable knowledge concerning products and processes.

To sum up, it is possible to state that manufacturing still matters for cluster lead firms as a value chain activity to be controlled externally – through appropriate forms of governance – as well as executed internally. In this perspective, comparing Italian cluster lead firms and US OBMs, it is worthwhile to observe that most of the cluster firms' value chains are producer-driven. Moreover, production remains the core activity of the value chain, where the company has the best competencies, and it is important to support innovation activities, in addition to marketing ones. On the contrary, said firms are not always able to directly control retail (through hierarchical or captive forms of governance), with few exceptions (e.g. Luxottica).

Nevertheless, this strategic choice is made taking into consideration the global scope of manufacturing activities, beyond the cluster boundaries. Clusters can be seen as "sources of uniqueness", as these local manufacturing systems provide firms with the culture of the product (sticky knowledge – *à la* von Hippel (1994) – that is difficult to transfer). Manufacturing activities persists at the cluster level – both carried out by OBM, ODM and specialized suppliers – mainly related to high-quality production and with reference to selected upgrading processes (i.e. Diadora Sport's eco-shoes). There are also industry specificities, such as investments in automation (as mentioned, Arper developed its machineries internally) aimed at improving efficiency and reducing the need for outsourcing (locally or globally).

It is interesting to note that backshoring initiatives involve only two firms – Aku Italia and Diadora Sport – but do not imply an end to international production and the management of value chain activities at the global level, as described in the GVC literature concerning global brands such as Nike or GAP. On the contrary, backshoring is focused on the exploitation of the country-of-origin effect and the mix between production and innovation dynamics characterizing clusters (local know-how).

After a huge internationalization of production, needed to maintain companies' competitiveness (and sometimes survival), firms are approaching manufacturing in a different and more conscious way. As highlighted by the literature on backshoring, in some cases companies are not totally satisfied with past decisions, which sometimes are not reversible in the short term. However, they have learned the value of manufacturing and are considering it in a different way in order to cope with the new challenges coming from the market, often within an upgrading perspective. This suggests a different path compared to the "smile" model (Mudambi and Swift, 2011) and confirms the relevance of cluster location in terms of competences to support firms' competitiveness. Future research should work on two issues: on the one hand, understanding to what extent these processes, quite clear in the case of high and middle-high quality goods, can be extended also to other segments of the market; on the other hand, the maintenance and renovation of cluster manufacturing competences in the long run, also facing the transformation of the ongoing digital manufacturing revolution.

References

Albino, V., Garavelli, A.C., and Schiuma, G. (1999). Knowledge transfer and inter-firm relationships in industrial districts: The role of the leader firm. *Technovation*, 19: 53–63.

Alcacer, J., and Delgado, M. (2013). Spatial organization of firms and location choices through the value chain. *Working Paper Harvard Business School*, 25: 31.

Anderson, C. (2012). *Makers: The New Industrial Revolution*. New York: Crowd Business.

Bailey, D., and De Propris, L. (2014). Manufacturing reshoring and its limits: The UK automotive case. *Cambridge Journal of Regions, Economy and Society*, 7(3): 379–395.

Bair, J. (ed.). (2009). *Frontiers of Commodity Chain Research*. Berlin: Stanford University Press.

Bair, J., and Gereffi, G. (2001). Local clusters in global chains: The causes and consequences of export dynamism in Torreon's blue jeans industry. *World Development*, 29: 1885–1903.

Banca Intesa Sanpaolo. (2015). *Monitor dei distretti*. Direzione studi e ricerche.

Becattini, G., Bellandi, M., and De Propris, L. (eds.). (2009). *Handbook on Industrial Districts*. Cheltenham: Edward Elgar.

Bettiol, M., and Micelli, S. (2014). The hidden side of design: The relevance of artisanship. *Design Issues*, 30(1): 7–18.

Buciuni, G., Coro', G., and Micelli, S. (2013). Rethinking manufacturing in global value chains: An international comparative study in the furniture industry. *Industrial and Corporate Change*, 23(4): 967–996.

Buciuni, G., and Finotto, V. (2016). Innovation in global value chains: Co-location of production and development in Italian low-tech industries. *Regional Studies*, 50(12): 2010–2023.

Buckley, P.J. (2009). The impact of the global factory on economic development. *Journal of World Business*, 44: 131–143.

Cainelli, G., Iacobucci, D., and Morganti, E. (2006). Spatial agglomeration and business groups: New evidence from Italian industrial districts. *Regional Studies*, 40(5): 507–518.

Camuffo, A. (2003). Transforming industrial districts: Large firms and small business networks in the Italian eyewear industry. *Industry & Innovation*, 10(4): 377–401.

Camuffo, A., Furlan, A., Romano, P., and Vinelli, A. (2008). Breathing shoes and complementarities: Strategic innovation in a mature industry. *International Journal of Innovation Management*, 12(2): 139–160.

Camuffo, A., and Grandinetti, R. (2011). Entrepreneurship & Regional Development Italian industrial districts as cognitive systems: Are they still reproducible? *Entrepreneurship & Regional Development*, 23(9–10): 37–41.

Cattaneo, O., Gereffi, G., and Staritz, C. (2010). Global value chains in a postcrisis world: Resilience, consolidation, and shifting end markets. In O. Cattaneo, G. Gereffi and C. Staritz (eds.), *Global Value Chains in a Postcrisis World: A Development Perspective*. Washington, DC: The World Bank, pp. 3–20.

Chiarvesio, M., Di Maria, E., and Micelli, S. (2004). Strategie di internazionalizzazione dei distretti italiani: I principali risultati dell'osservatorio sulle imprese. In Aa.Vv. (eds.), *La governance dell'internazionalizzazione produttiva. L'osservatorio*. Roma: Quaderni Formez, p. 28.

Chiarvesio, M., Di Maria, E., and Micelli, S. (2010). Global value chains and open networks: The case of Italian industrial districts. *European Planning Studies*, 18: 333–350.

Chiarvesio, M., Di Maria, E., and Micelli, S. (2013). Sourcing from Northern and Southern countries: The global value chain approach applied to Italian SMEs. *Transition Studies Review*, 20(3): 389–404.

Cohen, S.C., and Zysman, J. (1987). Why manufacturing matters: The myth of the post-industrial economy. *California Management Review*, 29(3): 9–26.

Coltorti, F., Resciniti, R., Tunisini, A., and Varaldo, R. (2013). *Mid-sized Manufacturing Companies: The New Driver of Italian Competitiveness*. Italia: Springer-Verlag.

Corò, G., and Grandinetti, R. (1999). Evolutionary patterns of Italian industrial districts. *Human Systems Management*, 18(2): 117–129.

Crestanello, P., and Tattara, G. (2011). Industrial clusters and the governance of the global value chain: The Romania, Äì Veneto network in footwear and clothing. *Regional Studies*, 45(2): 187–203.

Dedrick, J., Kraemer, K.L., and Linden, G. (2009). Who profits from innovation in global value chains? A study of the iPod and notebook PCs. *Industrial and Corporate Change*, 19(1): 81–116.

De Marchi, V., and Grandinetti, R. (2014). Industrial districts and the collapse of the Marshallian model: Looking at the Italian experience. *Competition & Change*, 18(1): 70–87.

De Propris, L., and Driffield, N. (2006). The importance of clusters for spillovers from foreign direct investment and technology sourcing. *Cambridge Journal of Economics*, 30(2): 277–291.

Eisenhardt, K.M. (1989). Building theories from case studies research. *Academy of Management Review*, 14(4): 532–550.

Elms, D.K., and Low, P. (2013). *Global Value Chains in a Changing World*. Switzerland: WTO Publications.

Feenstra, R. (1998). Integration of trade and disintegration of production in the global economy. *The Journal of Economic Perspectives*, 12: 31–50.

Flynn, A., and Flynn Vencat, E. (2012). Custom Nation: Why Customization Is the Future of Business and How to Profit From It. Dallas: BenBella Books.

Fornahl, D., Hassink, R., and Menzel, M.P. (2015). Broadening our knowledge on cluster evolution. *European Planning Studies*, 23(10): 1921–1931.

Fratocchi, L., Barbieri, P.N., Di Mauro, C., Nassimbeni, G., and Vignoli, M. (2013). *Manufacturing Back-Reshoring – An Exploratory Approach for Hypotheses Development,*. XXIV Riunione Scientifica Annuale Associazione italiana di Ingegneria Gestionale, "Entrepreneurship, innovation and the engine of growth", Politecnico di Milano, Milano, 2013 October, 17-18. Available at SSRN: https://ssrn.com/abstract=2333106

Fratocchi, L., Di Mauro, C., Barbieri, P., Nassimbeni, G., and Zanoni, A. (2014). When manufacturing moves back: Concepts and questions. *Journal of Purchasing and Supply Management*, 20(1): 54–59.

Furlan, A., Grandinetti, R., and Camuffo, A. (2007). How do subcontractors evolve? *International Journal of Operations & Production Management*, 27(1): 69–89.

Gereffi, G., Humphrey, J., and Sturgeon, T. (2005). The governance of global value chains. *Review of International Political Economy*, 12(1): 78–104.

Gereffi, G., and Lee, J. (2012). Why the world suddenly cares about global supply chains. *Journal of Supply Chain Management*, 48(3): 24–32.

Gereffi, G., and Lee, J. (2014). Economic and social upgrading in global value chains and industrial clusters: Why governance matters. *Journal of Business Ethics*, 133(1): 25–38.

Giansoldati, M., and Pauluzzo, R. (2011). The international evolution of Italian and Chinese districts: What role for lead firms? *Transition Studies Review*, 18(2): 471–486.

Giuliani, E., Pietrobelli, C., and Rabellotti, R. (2005). Upgrading in global value chains: Lessons from Latin American clusters. *World Development*, 33: 549–573.

Grandinetti, R., and Tabacco, R. (2015). A return to spatial proximity: Combining global suppliers with local subcontractors. *International Journal of Globalisation and Small Business*, 7(2): 139–159.

Hamzaoui, L., and Merunka, D. (2006). The impact of country of design and country of manufacture on consumer perceptions of bi-national products' quality: An empirical model based on the concept of fit. *Journal of Consumer Marketing*, 23(3): 145–155.

Humphrey, J., and Schmitz, H. (2002). How does insertion in global value chains affect upgrading in industrial clusters? *Regional Studies*, 36: 1017–1027.

Kinkel, S. (2014). Future and impact of backshoring-some conclusions from 15 years of research on German practices. *Journal of Purchasing and Supply Management*, 20(1): 63–65.

Lazerson, M.H., and Lorenzoni, G. (2008). Transforming industrial districts: How leading firms are escaping the manufacturing cage. In S. Cropper, M. Ebers, C. Huxham and P.S. Ring (eds.), *The Oxford Handbook of Inter-Organizational Relations*. Oxford: Oxford University Press.

Lazzeretti, L., Sedita, S.R., and Caloffi, A. (2014). Founders and disseminators of cluster research. *Journal of Economic Geography*, 14(1): 21–43.

Merchant, H., and Gaur, A. (2008). Opening the Non-Manufacturing envelope: The next big enterprise for international business research. *Management International Review*, 48: 379–396.

Mudambi, R. (2007). Offshoring: Economic geography and the multinational firm. *Journal of International Business Studies*, 38: 206.

Mudambi, R., and Swift, T. (2011). Leveraging knowledge and competencies across space: The next frontier in international business. *Journal of International Management*, 17: 186–189.

OECD. (2014). *Italy: Key Issues and Policy*. OECD Studies on SMEs and Entrepreneurship. Paris: OECD Publishing.

Pietrobelli, C., and Rabellotti, R. (2007). *Upgrading to Compete: Global Value Chains, Clusters and SMEs in Latin America*. Cambridge, MA: Harvard University Press.

Pisano, G.P., and Shih, W.C. (2012). Does really America need manufacturing. *Harvard Business Review*, 90(3): 94–102.

Schmitz, H., and Knorringa, P. (2000). Learning from global buyers. *Journal of Development Studies*, 2: 177–205.

Sturgeon, T.J., and Kawakami, M. (2011). Global value chains in the electronics industry: Characteristics, crisis, and upgrading opportunities for firms from developing countries. *International Journal of Technological Learning, Innovation and Development*, 4: 120.

Von Hippel, E. (1994). Sticky information and the locus of problem solving: Implications for innovation. *Management Science*, 40(4): 429–429.

Von Hippel, E. (2005). *Democratizing Innovation*. Boston: MIT Press.

Zucchella, A. (2006). Local clusters dynamics: Trajectories of mature industrial districts between decline and multiple embeddedness. *Journal of International Economics*, 2(1): 21–44.

10 Networks of clusters within global value chains

The case of the European ceramic tile districts in Spain and Italy

Jose Luis Hervas-Oliver and Mario Davide Parrilli

Introduction

In recent years, clusters and Industrial Districts – IDs- around the world find themselves constrained by the growth and opening of global markets to an extent that has never been experienced before (Parrilli and Blazek, Chapter 4 in this book). If in the 1970s, 1980s and 1990s local and regional development was studied from an inward-led perspective focused on the internal drivers of economic development (Piore and Sabel, 1984; Becattini, 1990; Schmitz, 1995), over the past 20 years, the importance of the global context in which these clusters and IDs are competing has become more crucial than ever before. Scholars have understood this process early on and contextualized the development dynamics of such clusters and IDs within wider landscapes, frameworks, chains and networks (Gereffi and Korzeniewicz, 1994; Gereffi et al., 2005; Humphrey and Schmitz, 2002,2004; Guerrieri and Pietrobelli, 2004; Elola et al., 2013; Parrilli et al., 2013; Hervas-Oliver and Boix, 2013).

Within such contexts, the competitiveness of clusters and IDs is determined by a set of factors that include business assets such as human capital, investments, intangible assets and innovation capacities, as well as territorial assets such as institutional support, access to finance, joint actions, technological and market spillovers and social capital, among others (Bellandi, 2009; De Marchi et al., Chapter 1 in this book).

However, the competitiveness of business and clusters/IDs depends on their own resources as much as on the productive capacities of competitors. The latter can also upgrade their competitiveness and gain market shares. This situation makes this production and market context very fluid and open, and obliges businesses and policy-makers to take a dynamic approach to those local specificities, considering also other non-local aspects that can be of advantage for their local turf.

One of the most recent and relevant dynamics refers to the systemic innovation processes in which clusters/IDs have been involved. Currently, innovation is one of the most competitive assets for businesses and their clusters/IDs. For many years, SMEs have been able to work with a set of organizations and institutions based in their regions and that form the so-called 'regional innovation system' (RIS) (Cooke, 2001; Asheim and Gertler, 2005; Parrilli et al., 2010; Asheim et al., 2011). However, in the past 10 years the SME clusters led by large, often multinational, companies (e.g. hub-and-spoke clusters or satellite platforms, see Markusen, 1996, for a full review) have extended their reach in international markets, setting up production and even innovation plants abroad and in emerging economies (e.g. Vestas in China in the wind energy industry; Intel in Costa Rica in semiconductors). In addition, these companies have formed their own global innovation network (Ernst, 2009; Cooke, 2013; Parrilli et al., 2013), which to some extent jeopardizes the former collaboration with their own RISs (Elola et al., 2013; Parrilli and Blazek, Chapter 4 in this book).

All these aspects and their nuances are going to be analysed in this work based on the case of the tile industry in Castellon, Spain, and Sassuolo, Italy. This chapter examines the role of innovation and manufacturing of two intertwined clusters in the ceramic tile industry in Europe: Castellon (Spain) and Sassuolo (Italy). These clusters are undisputedly the world leaders in tile technology and innovation. Our research question is central to this volume: how do IDs link up with GVCs? Answering this question sheds light on two key issues that have received less attention by scholars: 1) which firms lead the process of ID connection to GVC, and 2) how innovation and manufacturing activities upgrade though such connection.

In particular, our analysis shows two interestingly new and complementary directions of the GVC in industrial districts: the role of home-grown multinationals connecting and coordinating clusters and GVCs, and the key importance of not offshoring manufacturing activities for the sake of innovation upgrading. On these key issues, our study dissects and concludes in the following way; on the one hand, the literature on GVC and specifically on local upgrading has been too biased toward the role of foreign and large MNEs connecting territories (see Gereffi's works), while we revise a case that shows that home-grown MNEs are also key (though usually neglected) actors. On the other hand, our analysis suggests that the well-known pattern of the *smiling curve of the value chain* (see Mudambi, 2008) does not fully account for IDs, as most of their value is based upon manufacturing activities embedded into local innovation systems. The latter argument provokes a reflection on the one-size-fits-all idea of offshoring activities from traditional social capital-rich IDs. The selected cases offer a glance at how clusters and IDs can fight these tendencies (that in other cases diverge in a sort of trade-off) thanks to the work of specific local firms, i.e. the home-grown multinationals (Sedita and Belussi, 2013; Hervas and Albors, 2008). These are a type of SME that has been embedded in IDs from the very beginning and that has been able to grow into a larger company that has progressively taken the lead in the production and innovation process, as well as in the coordination of the value chain that has globalized its operations over time.

Clusters/IDs and GVCs: issues of governance and upgrading

Recent evolution of GVCs

The globalization dynamics affecting clusters and IDs have taken place in different forms in distinct moments. Five forms of value chain integration (see Figure 10.1) have spread worldwide over the past few decades, a few of which are more operative in these days.

In the 1950s-1970s, value chains were hardly global (apart from the case of commodities). Most production (clusters) targeted national markets. Clusters and IDs were part of national value chains, particularly in Europe (ADEFI, 1985). In the late 1970s-1980s, value chains involving clusters became more typically GVCs, thus connected to global markets, both in traditional and more advanced industries. This is when districts and clusters focused on the EU market. Here, the global aspect was the market (Gereffi and Korzeniewicz, 1994; Boomgard et al., 1992). From the 1990s and till the 2010s to a different extent, large firms delocalized production abroad (e.g. Italian furniture industry delocalized to Eastern Europe, the US car industry to Mexico). However, the most important operations remain at home, e.g. headquarters, R&D, design and logistics (Sturgeon et al., 2008). Simultaneously, in the 2000s-2010s, new emerging countries' GVCs arise and produce for both their national market and global markets, e.g. Chinese and Indian MNCs (Sturgeon and Kawakami, 2010; De Marchi et al., Chapter 1 in this book).

From the 2000s till now, GVCs internationalized not only input acquisition and production, but also their most advanced activities (e.g. R&D, logistics etc.). This is the combination

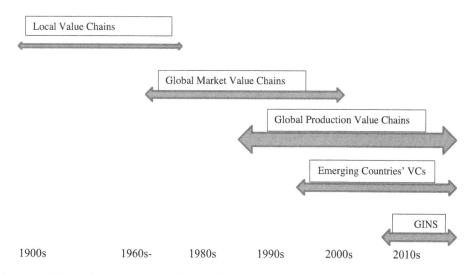

Figure 10.1 Historic transformation of value chains

Source: Author. The length of the arrows indicates the duration of these GVC forms, and the width suggests the volume of exchanges taking place in these formats.

of the GVC approach with the global innovation network (GIN) approach. The critical part of this new variant of the GVC concept is the focus on the most creative and value-added activity within the GVC 'smiling curve' stages: R&D and innovation. Lead companies in GVCs realized that they need to form the most advanced networks of global innovators as a means of capturing the frontier of knowledge in the core industry and related fields, and for this reason they are willing to neglect their previous association with their home-country innovation organizations, and to promote stronger associations with such leading global companies or organizations. In the end, the formation of GINs has been bolstered not just to control current markets, but also future markets and industry development (Parrilli et al., 2013; Chaminade and Bernard, 2012). It is a trend that any industry attains, e.g. automobile, aircraft and energy, among others.

This synthetic evolution implies that the position of clusters and IDs within GVCs has changed several times from quite a simplistic integration to a much more complex form in which not only market and production dynamics are involved, but also innovation dynamics. The final stage shows the complexity of interaction among different levels, i.e. market, production, innovation, institutions, regulations. This final stage opens up a number of challenges that clusters and IDs are currently facing and to which they have to find adequate competitive responses so as to be able to maintain their relevant and compact/cohesive position in GVCs.

Leadership, governance and upgrading in clusters and IDs

The GVC changes observed over time modify the 'relationships' among the different 'actors' that participate in GVCs (De Marchi et al., Chapter 1 in this book). The most typical current GVC variants (the latter three of Figure 10.1) exhibit governance patterns that have critical implications for the effective upgrading opportunities of such GVCs, and of the collective agents involved (i.e. clusters and IDs). As Humphrey and Schmitz (2002,2004) pointed out, the various types of GVC (i.e. modular, relational, captive, hierarchical and market-based, for a full review see Gereffi et al., 2005) operate to different extents within a number of clusters and IDs. The seminal work of Markusen (1996) indicated the existence of a wide range of local production systems (i.e. Marshallian industrial districts, hub-and-spoke clusters, satellite platforms, among others). These different types show a variety of governance systems and situations. Some of these clusters/IDs present a horizontal production and governance environment (e.g. Marshallian Industrial Districts – MIDs) based on a large set of SMEs that share a form of local collective leadership, whereas others involve vertical relations (e.g. Hub&Spoke clusters – H&S- and satellite platforms) with more defined individual leadership styles (i.e. usually led by Multinational Companies or MNCs). These and other structural characteristics related to the leadership style and governance system of these local systems influence their development prospects. For instance, in the case of MIDs, the firms expand their operations in a compact form. There are various leaders of local development, including firms and other organizations, in any of the value-adding activities (e.g. R&D, design or export). This is the case of IDs such as Sassuolo (Italy), Castellon (Spain), Stoke-on-Trent (UK) in the tile industry (Brioschi and Cainelli, 2002; Hervas-Oliver and Albors-Garrigos, 2014; Hervas-Oliver et al., 2011), but also in a wide number of traditional industrial districts (e.g. Prato in textiles, Italy (Dei Ottati,2014), among others).

In the case of H&S clusters, the large hubs (usually MNCs) take the lead and shift the GVC into a new stage. This is what happened with the car manufacturers moving operations to Mexico and Brazil; wind energy leaders (Vestas and Gamesa) to China and India; Intel to Costa Rica, among others (Humphrey, 2003; Elola et al., 2013; Lema et al., 2015; Parrilli and Sacchetti, 2008). This is likely to happen in either case, whether MNCs are embedded locally or not (i.e. Foreign Direct Investment in H&S clusters or satellite platforms).

The particular structure and governance of any specific cluster/ID leads to peculiar patterns of innovation and upgrading. The work of Humphrey and Schmitz (2002,2004) shows the relationship between these aspects in different types of clusters/IDs. Hierarchical clusters (e.g. H&S clusters and satellite platforms) tend to promote hierarchical or captive types of linkages controlled by the lead companies. These patterns lead to a few kinds of innovation and upgrading, particularly product and process innovation. In contrast, flatter/networked clusters (i.e. MIDs) tend to produce balanced governance styles, in which several local agents participate and contribute. These local systems are more inclined to promote relational and modular types of relations, which in addition to the former types of innovation, are more likely to generate functional and sometimes inter-sectoral/chain upgrading and innovations.

These different governance styles throughout different types of GVCs and clusters/IDs will lead to distinct forms of learning and upgrading (Pietrobelli and Rabellotti, 2011). In particular, hierarchical and captive linkages throughout GVCs are more likely to promote unilateral top-down decisions, such as direct training or technical assistance or even managerial supervision from the lead factories or the headquarters. Modular linkages would be spurred by raising standards and technical specifications as well as by trying to upgrade one's own standards in production, design and commercialization. Relational linkages of interdependence between lead companies and their suppliers would be promoted through face-to-face interactions in which the key aspects of a product or a process or even a function are discussed and developed. Finally, market relationships are more likely to promote observation, reverse engineering and other imitation and learning practices oriented to upgrading production and commercialization.

More recent work shows that learning and innovation take place increasingly on the basis of a stronger connection of some lead agents in clusters/IDs with global knowledge pipelines, otherwise known as global innovation networks (GINs) (Ernst, 2009; Cooke, 2013; Parrilli et al., 2013). Large companies and 'home-grown multinationals' are best positioned to connect to such global sources of advanced knowledge. In innovation activities, they tend to involve other smaller companies that are often their first- and second-tier suppliers; yet most second-, third- and fourth-tier suppliers are not in condition to follow them in either their innovation activities or their internationalization practices. This might lead to an internal fracture within clusters/IDs with a small group of firms that upgrade and internationalize their operations, whilst another larger group of SMEs remain cut off from GVCs and innovation activities (Elola et al., 2013; Blažek, 2016; Chapters 3 and 4 in this book). These dynamics can be observed for example in the wind energy cluster of the Basque country, Spain, where the lead companies (Iberdrola and Gamesa/Siemens) internationalized their operations and started to outsource the production of basic components (e.g. towers and nacelles) to large companies in the host countries (e.g. China, Brazil and the USA). This process had led to the incapacity of a number of Basque SME suppliers to follow their leaders in their internationalization process, in part for the lack of financial capacities to develop relevant FDIs in those new markets, and in part due to the generic nature of the components supplied (Elola et al., 2013). As a result, a process of fragmentation of the local cluster/ID takes place with the marginalization of a significant number of second-, third- and fourth-tier suppliers, thus the progressive weakening of the territorial development process (i.e. across the whole cluster/ID).

With these dynamics, the role of regional innovation systems becomes essential in order to ensure that all SMEs can get involved in innovation and upgrade and maintain their position in the GVC. This is a key to maintaining a higher consistence in the business profiles of local firms and a higher compactness of the cluster/ID itself (Elola et al., 2013; Parrilli and Blazek, Chapter 4 in this book). Simultaneously, the role of 'home-grown multinationals' matters a great deal as they may support the insertion of local/regional innovation systems in the GVCs. This is a more comprehensive way to understand the bottom-up cluster or territorial perspective. In fact, the cases that we discuss in this chapter represent a way out of the excess fragmentation of the GVC that is due to current internationalization processes. They show that, under certain conditions, the local/clustered SMEs maintain their operations within the GVC, whilst GINs and RISs work in synergy and benefit both lead firms and local SME suppliers.

In the next section, the analysis turns to the specific case of 'home-grown multinationals', which are shown to represent a critical feature of the most competitive IDs and clusters in recent years (De Marchi et al., Chapter 3 in this book). They may also represent a sort of new model or at least a key pattern of current successful local production systems.

The role of 'home-grown multinationals' as knowledge broker/catalyst

Following Belussi and Hervas-Oliver (2017), multinational enterprises or MNEs are taken for granted as foreign and large companies, disregarding those MNEs that are home-grown thanks to a cluster's vibrant local buzz. These have been named as *home-grown MNEs* (Sedita et al., 2013) or *indigenous MNEs* (Hervás-Oliver and Albors-Garrigós, 2008). These companies used to be small family-run firms that over time have been able to extend their operations overseas, yet maintaining a deep embeddedness in their home cluster. These firms foster competitiveness in their local milieus and co-ordinate local networks, connecting them to global value chains and orchestrating innovation in local agglomerations, acting as technology gatekeepers, as well as feeding small sub-contractors with new knowledge, technology and techniques to keep up with the latest changes. One special and outstanding feature of these firms is that they informally help to connect the cluster with other territories, while keeping strong and intense ties with their home territory, mainly based on social capital and family ties. This is mainly achieved through two complementary actions: 1) home-grown MNEs trade and invest with and into other clusters/territories, taking and bringing knowledge and information, and 2) their role as gatekeepers facilitating the entrance and interacting with foreign MNEs that tap into the local IDs.

In this respect, this type of home-grown MNC is in between the typical Marshallian Industrial Districts and Markusen's Hub-and-Spoke Cluster. The home-grown MNC is the leader of local development, which tends to shape up as a more vertical cluster than a typical ID; yet, it is strongly embedded in the local production system, thus striving for a consensus within it as a means to produce a sort of inclusive development, rather than a purely competitive space in which second-, third- and fourth-tier suppliers strive not to be squeezed out of the GVC and the market. The cluster opening process was mostly accomplished through the development of indigenous or 'home-grown MNEs' (previously SMEs) that connect to other territories and their reinforcing interaction with foreign MNEs. The insertion of the cluster/ID in GVCs also permitted the continuous renewal of the stock of competences: openness and connection to GVCs, leveraged by the entrance of new actors (MNEs), has positively transformed the cluster/ID into a complex industrial-based competitive hot spot, confirming previous studies in a diverse set of clusters/IDs that vindicated the benefits of and necessity for cluster openness and insertion in GVCs (e.g. Hervas-Oliver and Boix, 2013; Eisingerich et al., 2010; Sedita et al., 2013). In addition, and in line with Chiarvesio's et al. (2010) "open networks" in which IDs become a key node of global value chains (see also Amin and Thrift, 1992), these home-grown MNEs are also displaying sophisticated firm strategy benchmarks for other local firms. In general, those home-grown MNEs are the ones that best adapt to the global challenges and respond to them not only connecting to GVCs, but also developing in-house capabilities and strategies that help the ID to evolve and serve the purpose of the GVC.

Empirical analysis

Research setting in the tile industry: Castellon, Spain, and Sassuolo, Italy

First, a qualitative analysis has been undertaken of the Castellon ceramic tiles ID in Spain based on interviews carried out during 2013 and 2014. This industry is a very good research setting because it is mainly formed by a GVC with many local clusters (see Hervas-Oliver and Boix, 2013), constituting a formidable *testing bench* for examining the connection of IDs with GVCs. In total, 48 interviewed respondents included managers, ex-managers, policy-makers, technicians, engineers and representatives from trade associations, most of whom had a great deal of experience dealing with both Castellon and Sassuolo issues. Information for the case study was supplemented by secondary data drawn from archives. Research triangulation was achieved comparing the responses of interviewees with information collected through discussion with industry experts and policy-makers, as well as with the archival secondary data. The primary unit of analysis was the connection of the IDs to GVCs, with special emphasis on their respective innovation and manufacturing capabilities, inquiring also about the same phenomenon in Sassulo (Italy) IDs.

In Table 10.1 the main features of each ID are explained in detail. Following Hervás-Oliver and Albors-Garrigós (2007),[1] the Castellon (Valencia Region, Spain) ceramic tiles ID is a typical Marshallian ID, well-endowed with world-class public R&D organizations (Institute of Ceramic Technology, ITC), educational centres such as the Universitat Jaume I, and

Table 10.1 Overview of the Castellon and Sassuolo clusters in the GVC

Variables	Castellon (Spain, Valencia Region)	Sassuolo (Italy, Emilia-Romagna)
Product	Generally, red-clay ceramic tile as leading product in medium and medium-low markets; special emphasis on wall tile.	Generally, white-clay *porcelain* tile as leading product; premium targets, higher-end markets
Firms and employees	Around 180 tile firms in 2016; around 220 in 2006 15,500 employees in 2016, around 26,000 in 2006 Production of 460 million of square meters in 2016, around 600 in 2006 Traditionally SMEs firms	Around 140 tile firms in 2016; around 200 in 2006 19,000 employees in 2016, around 28,000 in 2006 Production of 410 million of square meters in 2016, around 570 in 2006 Traditionally SMEs but changing to more concentrated large groups of medium-size firms
Export intensity and markets	80% of exports in 2016 First European producer and second most export-led cluster in relative terms as % of production Main markets are Europe, Asia and USA (France, USA, UK or Israel, among the top). Around 50% to Europe, 24% Asia and 14% USA	85% of exports in 2016 Number one export-leading cluster in relative terms as % of production Main markets are Europe, Asia and USA
Local firms	Presence of leading home-grown MNEs very innovative in both product and process, undertaking all activities: manufacturing, innovation, marketing, R&D etc.	Presence of leading home-grown MNEs very innovative in both product and process, undertaking all activities: manufacturing, innovation, marketing, R&D etc.
Supporting industries	Very powerful chemical (ceramic tile decoration) companies, world-class leading industry multi-located in Asia, America, Europe and North Africa. Includes the presence of leading Sassuolo mechanical (kilns and production-oriented) firms.	Very powerful mechanical (ceramic tile production) companies, world-class leading industry multi-located in Asia, America, Europe and North Africa. Includes the presence of leading Castellon chemical (tile decoration) firms.
Local institutions	Very comprehensive array of local institutions: R&D centre (ITC), local university focused on engineering for ceramics (UJI), powerful trade associations (ASCER) etc. ITC is the leading ceramic R&D centre in the world.	Presence of important institutions, such as Assopiastrelle trade association, R&D centre (Ceramic Center of Bologna), the most powerful international trade fair (CERSAIE) etc.

(Continued)

Table 10.1 Overview (cont.d)

Variables	Castellon (Spain, Valencia Region)	Sassuolo (Italy, Emilia-Romagna)
Major recent transformations	Castellon always connected to Sassuolo, leading the latest digital transformation to inkjet tile decoration. Still focused on manufacturing and innovation, providing world-class knowledge on tile decoration to the rest of clusters worldwide. Venue for the most important patents in tile decoration.	Sassuolo well connected to Castellon through the presence of Castellon chemical firms. World-class and leading cluster for mechanical and engineering ceramic tile applications. Still focused on manufacturing and innovation, providing world-class knowledge on tile production and technology to the rest of clusters worldwide. Venue for the most important patents in tile production
Major activities/ capabilities	All of them: clay mining, refining and atomizing; tile manufacturing, including pressing, decoration (chemical) and burning in kilns; machinery and equipment provision and repair; especially relevant the production of frits and glazes (chemical components) for tile decoration. Design, marketing, logistics, all focused on tiles. Home-grown MNEs, mainly from the chemical tile activity, present in all clusters worldwide., such as Esmalglass, Torrecid, Ferro, Coloronda, Esmalfrit, Kerafrit, Fritta, Kerajet etc.[1]	All of them: clay mining, refining and atomizing; tile manufacturing, including pressing, decoration (chemical) and burning in kilns; especially relevant the production of machinery and equipment for tile production (including kilns, presses, and other equipment). Design, marketing, logistics, all focused on tiles. Home-grown MNEs, mainly from the machinery and equipment tile activity, present in all clusters worldwide, such as Sacmi, Barbieri-Tarozzi, System etc.

[1] www.anffecc.com/es/empresas

Source: Author's elaboration, based on Ascer and Assopiastrelle, and Hervas-Oliver and Albors-Garrigos (2007).

private institutions such as trade associations, all of which are focused on ceramic tiles. The Castellon cluster is a Marshallian ID that includes all the activities necessary for the ceramics value chain: clay processing, ceramic tile production, frit and glaze decoration based on high-tech chemistry and ceramic equipment production and services such as logistics, design and other related activities. It is significant to state that the industries in the cluster providing key knowledge and innovation are the frit and glaze (chemistry for tile surface decoration) and the ceramic equipment manufacturers (kilns, production lines, presses etc.), following a supplier-driven innovation pattern in the sense of Pavitt (1984). Along with Spain, Italy also has one of the largest ceramic tile industries in the world. Around 80% of Italy's ceramic tile production is concentrated in the Emilia – Romagna region, around Sassuolo (Russo, 2004). Both IDs (Castellon and Sassuolo) are mentioned in Porter's (1990) seminal contribution.[2]

An important characteristic and strength of the Italian district, deeply embedded in the Emilia-Romagna regional innovation system, is that it contains a strong ceramic tile equipment manufacturing sector. These machine manufacturing firms lead the ceramic tile equipment world and are present in Castellon through some subsidiaries. The Castellon frit and glaze industry is the most powerful auxiliary industry in the Castellon cluster and is the absolute world leader[3] in the frit and glaze activity for tiles, having extensive operations in other clusters worldwide, including Sassuolo. Both IDs form a network of clusters, channelling information back and forth through their multinational companies in their respective industries co-located in both IDs (Meyer-Stamer et al., 2004).

It is well documented that most of the innovations produced in the world's ceramic tiles industry have occurred through interactions between these two IDs, and the development of each can be explained in part by the other's support (Meyer-Stamer et al., 2004; Hervas-Oliver and Albors, 2009). Both clusters have been, and still are, the major source of tile innovation in the world of industrial ceramics, feeding the other important clusters such as the Brazilians (Santa Gertrudes and Criciuma), China (Foshan) and Turkey, among others.[4] A crucial part of the "innovation engine", and the true strength of the Castellon cluster, is its *systemic behaviour*, exemplified by the inter-organizational interaction of the ITC (Tech Institute of Ceramics), within the Jaume I Universitat, the frit and glaze subsector and the ceramic tile producers. This mechanism of innovation dissemination is very difficult to replicate elsewhere (Meyer-Stamer et al., 2004). Similarly, in Sassuolo the innovation system is exceptional but rather centred around ceramic equipment manufacturers (Russo, 2004, p. 5), conforming also a systemic innovation around ceramic tile producers and tile equipment manufacturers.

This virtuous circle of innovation, driven by the strong collaboration and knowledge exchange between the ceramic tile producers and the tile equipment manufacturers is well described in Russo (2004), featuring the key strength that the interrelationships form, as sources of agglomeration externalities and as a key factor to access to them, describing how different industries (technology and knowledge suppliers of ceramic equipment and tile producers) interact and exchange knowledge at the local level in Sassuolo:

> This virtuous circle of interrelations among the actors of the Sassuolo district – enabling the innovation process to be maintained – emerged not only as the result of the purely cooperative game, but also from the interplay of competitive relations: both of these are important in interpreting the dynamics of the district. Cooperation occurs each time the ceramic firms find in the machine producers the answer to a particular technical problem, the solution for obtaining a special effect, the right (even formal) partnership in order to perfect a new technology.
>
> (Russo, 2004, p. 5)

For the sake of clarity and contextualization, we briefly remark on the objective and main results. The research question guiding this study consists of understanding how IDs link up with GVCs. This means getting to know what firms lead the process of connecting IDs to GVCs, and how innovation and manufacturing activities upgrade in this connection. Our findings unfold two main points. First, home-grown MNEs trade and invest with and inside other clusters/territories, while acting as gatekeepers that promote and complement the localization of foreign MNEs in the ID and their effort to tap into local knowledge and production capabilities. Second, manufacturing activities are not usually offshored from these traditional IDs, as such activities are closely linked to innovation, thus representing the best way to keep the IDs (and their firms) vital and connected to GVCs.

Global innovation networks: inter-cluster connection

Ceramic tile production and tile decoration GVC

Sassuolo has been, since the 1960s, the major European force for tile manufacturing, displaying a strong mechanical and engineering base from the Emilia-Romagna regional innovation system that fuelled and boosted the tile industry (Porter, 1990).

Since the 1970s, the second pole of tile manufacturing in Europe was Castellon. Castellon possessed, at that time, a poorer mechanical and equipment technology for tile manufacturing, being totally dependent on Sassuolo expertise. Following Hervas-Oliver et al., (Chapter 10 in this book), leading equipment firms from the Sassuolo ID (System, Sacmi, Barbieri-Tarozzi, among many others) have been operating in Castellon since the 1970s. These multinational companies transferred mechanical knowledge about tile manufacturing, nurturing Castellon from knowledge generated in the Sassuolo ID. Since the 1980s, all those firms gained a foothold in Castellon establishing their own commercial subsidiaries in order to deal with those host markets, offering installation, repair and maintenance, although tile equipment manufacturing was kept in Sassuolo. All these small multinationals were very different from the traditional foreign multinationals mainly depicted in the GVC approach, being heavily embedded in their home locations but also developing strong ties and relational strategies with local Castellon firms. They were the first and foremost important "global pipelines" or links between Castellon and Sassuolo, building up a knowledge highway. All R&D activities from Sassuolo firms remained in Sassuolo, whilst production was never transferred to Castellon, but sales and post-sales activities were.

Simultaneously, since the early 1980s, a technological revolution around glazing and frits decoration tile activities, originated in Castellon (porous single-fired decoration for wall tiles[5]) boosted the decoration capabilities of Castellon and upgraded Castellon tile decoration activities, creating a specific subsector of Castellon firms specialized in frits and glaze, that is, the decoration process of tile production. The knowledge about decoration in Castellon flourished and the Sassuolo firms were also bringing back home not only market information and mechanical knowledge from the day-to-day operations but also knowledge about decoration. By the late 1980s and early 1990s the process reversed: this time Castellon chemical (frit and glaze) firms were the ones setting a foothold in Sassuolo, transferring Castellon decoration knowledge. All R&D activities from Castellon firms remained in Castellon and frits manufacturing was never transferred to Sassuolo, but sales, technical assistance and marketing were, in a similar way to Sassuolo equipment manufacturing firms. This phenomenon constituted the second "global pipeline" or link between Castellon and Sassuolo, reinforcing the existent knowledge circuit or a network of clusters in which tile equipment manufacturing, based on mechanical knowledge, was stronger in Sassuolo, while tile decoration, based on industrial chemistry, was concentrated in Castellon. Since the 1990s, the two Marshallian IDs established a fruitful informal bottom-up inter-cluster connection, constituting a 'cluster of clusters' where the innovation systems of both were intertwined, connected and mutually reinforced, being responsible for the main knowledge and patents for the entire world tile industry. This process, accumulated over decades, constitutes the most important inter-cluster knowledge transfer ever observed in the world tile industry. As a result, the current development observed in the tile industry in emerging giants (e.g. Brazil or China, among others), is occurring thanks to the knowledge transfer and the synergies developed from this European network of clusters. This knowledge exchange, led by their respective indigenous or home-grown multinationals (tile equipment firms from Sassuolo investing and locating in Castellon, and tile decoration firms from Castellon locating in Sassuolo), was accompanied by a reciprocal move of expats, executives, technicians and other personnel who were permanently travelling from one place to another, developing personal ties in both territories. This newly-established GVC around tile production, decoration and commercialization expanded both clusters and reinforced their respective local buzz, in addition to feeding other world ceramic tile production centres (e.g. Turkey, Brazil, Foshan in China etc.) with advanced knowledge, expertise and patents (see Hervas-Oliver et al., 2017; Hervas-Oliver and Boix, 2013; Hervas-Oliver and Albors, 2008; Meyer-Stamer et al., 2004; Russo, 2004) since the early 2000s.

The ranking of world industry production[6] (2015 figures) are as follows: China (5.7 billion square meters, sqm), Brazil (871 million sq. m), India (750 million sq. m), Iran (500 sq. m), Spain (440 sq. m) and Italy (390 sq. m), but with Italy leading exports (85% of its turnover) and achieving the top average price (>15$) per sq. m, showing the type of segments they addressed. Spain is the second exporter (80% of its turnover) and China third (20% of its turnover). In 2000, Spain and Italy dominated all rankings. The interesting point is that Spain and Italy combine manufacturing with the world's best innovation and engineering industry. Currently, Spain and Italy with their respective IDs constitute the leading innovation hubs, while preserving the core of the manufacturing process. See Figures 10.2 and 10.3 about production and employment,[7] respectively, evolution in both IDs during the period 1976–2015.

Decoration technology was organized in both clusters by leading Castellon firms, while leading Sassuolo tile equipment manufacturers did the same in both territories. The main

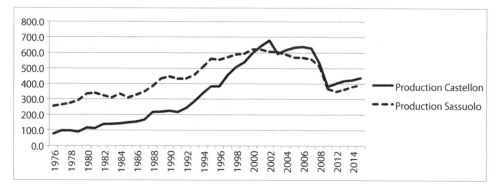

Figure 10.2 Production evolution in Castellon and Sassuolo IDs

Note: Production reported in million square meters.

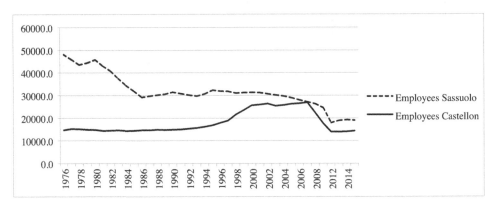

Figure 10.3 Employment evolution in Castellon and Sassuolo IDs

Castellon firms connected to Sassuolo's are: Torrecid, Ferro and Esmalglass, only Ferro being a major foreign MNE (trading in the New York stock exchange). The principal Sassuolo firms in Castellon are Sacmi, System and Barbieri-Tarozzi. In the beginning, these Italian firms disseminated knowledge in the district through their trade/exports, and later on by gaining a foothold with sales offices in Castellon (FDI). Sassuolo firms only manufacture equipment in Italy. Castellon firms followed a similar pattern, and started by locating in Sassuolo. Furthermore, the Castellon chemical firms' knowledge transfer includes the inter-cluster exchange of engineers as a means to move tacit knowledge on decoration. Castellon chemical firms also manufacture some low-value compounds in some locations overseas (mainly commodities) as well as some parts of product development (tailored to each territory's specificity, e.g. the type of clay and the consequent kiln temperature) but concentrate R&D and high value-added activities in Castellon. One important difference between the two districts is that the Castellon chemical firms provide more services, and the internationalization process differs slightly from that pursued by those Italian machinery partners. In both cases, the home-grown multinationals account for a diverse average size, with the leading group (Torrecid 500 employees, Ferro, 600, Esmalglass, 300) and the smaller group (Coloronda, Kerafrit etc.) with around 60–80 employees[8] (See Table 10.1).

Thus, each territory specialized fully on one side of the production process, accessing the best first-hand knowledge about the other side from the other cluster. Simultaneously, all this technology was exported to the rest of the world. By the 1990s, Castellon and Sassuolo were the top exporters in terms of world export share, constituting around 90% of the total exports. Since 2000, China also entered in the statistics, taking the first position in terms of tile exports, but importing frits (decoration) and equipment from Castellon and Sassuolo, respectively. A really interesting fact of this network of clusters not previously addressed in the GVC literature is that the inter-clusters connection is led by the leading Sassuolo and Castellon *home-grown* (see more at Belussi and Hervas-Oliver, 2017) which are established in all tile production centres worldwide, including the Chinese clusters around Foshan. In fact, Castellon and Sassuolo have pursued excellent product and process upgrading by moving to more sophisticated high-quality products and high-technology processes. In terms of governance, in both IDs relational networks are observed, with stable groups sustained by an informal and formal process of cooperation. In no small part, the special embeddedness of the home-grown multinationals has facilitated the absence of strictly vertically hierarchical relations, despite the existence of large industrial groups in Sassuolo.

The reason for those upgrading strategies is based on the absence of offshoring manufacturing, the latter being kept in both clusters, triggering innovation. This has fuelled and facilitated a mutually reinforcing manufacturing and innovation interrelationship within and throughout both IDs. This has also promoted the existence of all the relevant activities in both IDs, with innovation and manufacturing activities standing out.

These leading firms in both clusters, named also as home-grown MNEs, were mainly spin-offs from local firms. They were SMEs that soon excelled and grew through their own strategies (different to those adopted by other local firms). Among these, they were leading groups of small SMEs and proactively influencing the local system; they were the first to reach global markets, pioneering marketing and design activities, incorporating R&D activities and, in general, undertaking the riskiest changes, and providing the best skilled labour to the local system (see more at Chapter 10 in this book).

In terms of upgrading, in both territories firms have kept all activities, including manufacturing and innovation, not offshoring key activities and using all available actors from territories (R&D centres, training centres etc.), developing sophisticated marketing and innovation activities. In each territory, the auxiliary industries (decoration and equipment) that fuel both IDs with technology have developed the most cutting-edge technologies. The latter, despite being also exported worldwide, are first proved and tested at home, giving the local Castellon and Sassuolo firms a clear advantage.

Connecting the Castellon tile industry to the UK printing industry: chain upgrading

Since 2000 a new disruption has occurred in Castellon in relation to tile decoration (see more at Hervas-Oliver and Albors-Garrigos, 2014). A new firm from Castellon designed a new system of decoration, substituting the mechanical decoration system and turning decoration from mechanical to digital (known as Kerajet), using the same technology of inkjet printers. Those entrepreneurs at Kerajet dreamed of a digitalized process to decorate the tiles as was the case in other industries, e.g. graphic design. The necessary knowledge was available neither in Castellon nor in Sassuolo. It was absent in the entire tile GVC. This limitation was based on the poor development of the digital technology (developed by the printing industry in the USA around Silicon Valley and the UK around Cambridge) in Spain or Italy, never before applied in the ceramic tile industry.

Kerajet was searching for knowledge outside the network of IDs and throughout many industries. The new Castellon firm Kerajet connected externally with the firm Xaar, located in the Cambridge inkjet printing cluster. In 1998 they developed a first prototype based on inkjet printing, their main aim being to digitalize the decoration process of ceramic tiles. The new technology involved a dramatic change in the knowledge base, moving from a *mechanical* type of decoration (using pressure on the surface, the Rotocolor) to digital printing decoration.

Even though the new inkjet application (i.e. software, print heads and equipment) was developed, the new issue became the frits, which were not optimized. Traditional chemical frits did not work. In Castellon the innovation system worked very well and the three leading frits incumbents from Castellon (Ferro, Esmalglass and Torrecid) started a race in order to secure the best "inks" (digital version of frits and glaze) for the new inkjet decoration technology. In 2005 the new inks and the inkjet technology became fully established and operational in Castellon. The new inkjet technology provided significant productivity improvements. A comparison between the new (inkjet printing) and the old technology (Rotocolor) showed new important benefits or advantages, which could be classified in relation to process, product, management and design aspects. Sassuolo was left behind, as they were too reluctant to abandon the mechanical processes of the decoration activity, even though they still dominated the tile equipment industry. The problem was the cognitive inertia process by which many clusters failed to adopt new innovations (see more at Hervas-Oliver, 2016), and Sassuolo was too embedded in the mechanical system, which was the core in the Emilia-Romagna region (RIS). In synthesis, the adoption of new knowledge located outside the thematic and technology boundary of the two IDs was crucial to understanding the process of 'creative destruction' that occurred in Castellon and opened the former GVC to knowledge inputs (i.e. inkjet printing) produced in the UK, and then transferred to Castellon first, and to Italy later.

Nowadays, the Castellon cluster encompasses new capabilities based in inkjet printing, optics, electronics and digitalizing for the ceramic tile decoration process, while the formerly dominant mechanical decoration paradigm has gradually been abandoned. By 2013, the process of creative-destruction had almost been completed. The Cambridge printing cluster in the UK is connected, mostly through the companies Xaar and Xennia, to the Castellon cluster, as Silicon Valley is through the EFI Company. In this way, they are continuously channelling/sourcing new knowledge related to software and print heads for digital printing. The Castellon cluster is still linked to Sassuolo in relation with the best mechanical production equipment (production lines, kilns etc.) and also transfers knowledge about frits and glaze for tile decoration (especially as regards the new inks and inkjet technology) to the Italian cluster (through the number of co-located companies) and, more indirectly, to other production sites worldwide.

Discussion of results

The innovation in Castellon turned the world industry upside down, upgrading the existing ceramic tile GVC and thus creating a new digital decoration process fully controlled by IT systems. Moreover, the network of IDs, formed by Castellon and Sassuolo, opened up and connected to a new knowledge domain: inkjet printing, connecting also to Cambridge (UK) to source printing technology, and kept on exporting their tile technology worldwide. This change enriched the production of ceramic tiles, incorporating new phases and agents on a global scale. This chain upgrading and the rejuvenation of the GVC is depicted with the following three main facts:

- Both IDs remained open and mutually connected, combining from the beginning their local buzz and innovation activities with external linkages. The reason for this connection was the special embeddedness of their respective home-grown multinationals. In fact, the foreign multinationals in each ID are those home-grown in the partner ID.
- Both IDs kept manufacturing as well as innovation activities as core engines of their firms' strategies; most of the offshoring carried out has been done in terms of seeking markets, whilst keeping the full range of activities at the headquarters.
- Thanks to their local embeddedness, the home-grown MNEs have maintained and even strengthened their relationships with the relevant RISs and their innovation-focused institutions (e.g. ITC in Castellon, and Centre of Ceramics in Bologna, among others). As a result, the local SMEs have continued to benefit from fresh and relevant knowledge that helps them maintain a competitive position in the ceramics GVC. In general, both IDs present all the necessary activities that boost competitiveness,

displaying also synergies amongst the constituent elements (R&D centres, training facilities, related subsectors, strong associations etc.).

Overall, our analysis has shown two new complementary tendencies throughout GVCs and industrial districts: 1) the role of home-grown multinationals connecting IDs and coordinating the GVC, and 2) the key importance of connecting manufacturing and innovation within the local production systems. Upgrading and rejuvenating IDs also require firms' strategies based upon chain upgrading, connecting and diversifying into new value chains.

Conclusions

This chapter has examined the role of the connectedness between innovation and manufacturing activities of two intertwined ceramic tile IDs in Europe: Castellon (Spain) and Sassuolo (Italy). These clusters/IDs are undisputedly the world leaders in tile technology and innovation. Taking a GVC perspective, our results shed light on a very key question on GVCs: how IDs link up with GVCs. Our findings suggest 1) the key importance of both home-grown MNEs linking up IDs and connecting to GVCs and, 2) the necessary and positive relationship between manufacturing and innovation activities in traditional IDs, to the extent that manufacturing is not the type of activity that can be offshored, contradicting the smiling curve of the value chain issue (see Mudambi, 2008): manufacturing activities are closely linked to innovation and both are the only way to keep the IDs vital and connected to those GVCs.

Addressing home-grown MNEs, we learned about their process of connecting to GVCs and transferring knowledge from cluster to cluster. First, home-grown MNEs used to be special SMEs that chose different, innovative and more risky strategies, then becoming leading firms acting as gatekeepers. Second, home-grown MNEs trade and invest with and into other clusters/territories, while acting as gatekeepers that promote and complement the entry and interaction with foreign MNEs that tap into the local ID resources. Our novelty consists of identifying a new critical player, more involved in the development of the local ID and pro-active in promoting a competitive connection to GVCs, thus complementing the role of large foreign MNEs.

In addition, the selected cases show that the local embeddedness of the home-grown MNEs creates the conditions for the whole cluster/ID to adopt and develop innovations and, as a result, to upgrade in a way that keeps them cohesive and compact. The dynamic role of the RIS helps avoid the formation of separate GINs that would prevent second-, third- and fourth-tier suppliers to continue their innovation and upgrading processes, thus maintaining their competitive position in GVCs. Overall, this case differs substantially from those literatures that only stress the presence and dominant role of large foreign MNEs.

Acknowledgements

We are financially thankful to ECO2015:63645-R Open Innovation in Clusters, (MINECO and FEDER).

Notes

1 The cluster provides around 16,000 direct jobs (in 2014) and there are around 200 firms in related industries, see www.ascer.es (industry statistics)

2 The agglomeration indices for the Castellon and Sassuolo ceramic tiles industries are reported to be around 4.5 (450%) in both cases (See Boix, 2009 and ISTAT, 2006).
3 In 2014, 26 Castellon frit firms exported around 66% of their total production valued at 1.2 billion Euros, and employed around 3,400 workers. Five of them account for 75% of those exports, the leading group. See www.anffecc.es (www.anffecc.com/es/cifras-del-sector)
4 See more at Hervas-Oliver and Boix, 2013
5 This was an improvement from Sassuolo (Marazzi firm) 'monocottura' for floor tiles.
6 www.ceramicindustry.com/articles/94429-world-tile-production-increases-64 (accessed January 2nd, 2017)
7 ASCER and Indagine Stadistica Nazionale, Assopiastrelle, own elaboration
8 For instance, Torrecid, with 500 workers in its Castellon headquarters, has production and sales representative offices in 25 countries, including China, Indonesia, Italy, Brazil and USA. Despite moving part of the manufacturing to those countries (China, Brazil or USA, for instance), the R&D activities are concentrated in the Castellon facilities and the most high-tech activities are also carried out there. Nevertheless, there are activities carried out in bulk that are better carried out in the host market of consumption in order to save logistics costs. Torrecid, Esmalglass and Ferro are the worldwide leaders in frits and glazes, representing around 75% of world exports in the ceramic tile industry (see more in Hervas-Oliver and Boix, 2013).

References

ADEFI. (1985). *L'analyse de filieres*. Paris: Economica.

Amin, A., and Thrift, N. (1992). Neo-Marshallian nodes in global networks. *International Journal of Urban and Regional Research*,16(4): 571–587.

Asheim, B., Boschma, R., and Cooke, P. (2011). Constructing regional advantage: Platform policies based on related varieties and differentiated knowledge bases. *Regional Studies*, 45: 1–12.

Asheim, B.T., and Gertler, M.S. (2005). The geography of innovation: Regional innovation systems. In J. Fagerberg, D.C. Mowery and R.R. Nelson (eds.), *The Oxford Handbook of Innovation*. Oxford: Oxford University Press.

Becattini, G. (1990). The district as a socioeconomic notion. In F. Pyke, G. Becattini and W. Sengenberger (eds.), *Industrial Districts and Local Economic Cooperation*. Geneva: ILO.

Bellandi, M. (2009). External economies, specific public goods and policies. In G. Becattini, M. Bellandi and L. De Propris (eds.), *Handbook of Industrial Districts*. Cheltenham: Edward Elgar, pp. 712–725.

Belussi, F. and Hervas-Oliver, J.L. (2017). Understanding cluster evolution: Beyond life cycles. In F. Belussi and J.L. Hervas-Oliver (eds.), *Unfolding Cluster Evolution*. New York: Routledge.

Blažek, J. (2016). Towards a typology of repositioning strategies of GVC/GPN suppliers: The case of functional upgrading and downgrading. *Journal of Economic Geography*, 16(4): 849–869.

Boomgard, J., Davies, S., Haggblade, S., and Mead, D. (1992). A subsector approach to small enterprise promotion and research. *World Development*, 20: 199–212.

Brioschi, F., Brioschi, M.S., and Cainelli, G. (2002). From the industrial district to the district group: Insight into the evolution of capitalism in Italy. *Regional Studies*, 36: 1037–1052.

Chaminade, C., and Bernard, H. (2012). *Global Innovation Networks: A Taxonomy*. Circle Working Papers, 2011/04, Lund.

Chiarvesio, M., Di Maria, E., and Micelli, S. (2010). Global value chains and open networks: The case of Italian industrial districts. *European Planning Studies*,18(3): 333–350.

Cooke, P. (2001). Regional innovation systems, clusters and the knowledge economy. *Industrial and Corporate Change*, 10(4): 945–974.

Cooke, P. (2013). Asian dynamics: From global production networks to global innovation networks in ICTs. *European Planning Studies*, 21(7): 1081–1094.

Dei Ottati, G. (2014). A transnational fast-fashion industrial district: The Chinese businesses in Prato. *Cambridge Journal of Economics*, 38(5): 1247–1274.

Eisingerich, A., Bell, S.J., and Tracey, P. (2010). How can clusters sustain performance? The role of network strength, network openness, and environmental uncertainty. *Research Policy*, 39: 239–253.

Elola, A., Parrilli, M.D., and Rabellotti, R. (2013). The resilience of clusters in the context of increasing globalization: The Basque wind energy value chain. *European Planning Studies*, 21(7): 989–1006.

Ernst, D. (2009). *A New Geography of Knowledge in the Electronics Industry? Asia's Role in Global Innovation Networks*, Policy Studies 54. Honolulu: East-West Centre.

Gereffi, G., Humphrey, J., and Sturgeon, T. (2005). The governance of global value chains. *Review of International Political Economy*, 12(1): 78–104.

Gereffi, G., and Korzeniewicz, M. (1994). *Commodity Chains and Global Capitalism*. Westport, CT: Greenwood Press.

Guerrieri, P., and Pietrobelli, C. (2004). Industrial districts' evolution and technological regimes: Italy and Taiwan. *Technovation*, 24(11): 899–914.

Hervas-Oliver, J.L. (2016). What about disruptions in clusters? Retaking a missing debate. In M.D. Parrilli, R.D. Fitjar and A. Rodriguez-Pose (eds.), *Innovation Drivers and Regional Innovation Strategies*. New York: Routledge, pp. 105–122.

Hervás-Oliver, J.L., and Albors-Garrigós, J. (2007). Do clusters capabilities matter? An empirical application of the resource-based view in clusters. *Entrepreneurship and Regional Development*, 19(2): 113–136.

Hervás-Oliver, J.L., and Albors-Garrigós, J. (2008). Local knowledge domains and the role of MNE affiliates in bridging and complementing a cluster's knowledge. *Entrepreneurship and Regional Development*, 20(6): 581–598.

Hervas-Oliver, J.L., and Albors-Garrigos, J. (2009). The role of the firm's internal and relational capabilities in clusters: When distance and embeddedness are not enough to explain innovation. *Journal of Economic Geography*, 9(2): 263–283.

Hervas-Oliver, J.L., and Albors-Garrigos, J. (2014). Are technology gatekeepers renewing clusters? Understanding gatekeepers and their dynamics across cluster life cycles. Entrepreneurship and Regional Development, 26: 5–6.

Hervas-Oliver, J.L., and Boix-Domenech, R. (2013). The economic geography of the meso-global spaces: Integrating multinationals and clusters at the local–global level. *European Planning Studies*, 21(7): 1064–1080.

Hervas-Oliver, J.L., Jackson, I., and Tomlinson, P.R. (2011). 'May the ovens never grow cold': Regional resilience and industrial policy in the North Staffordshire ceramics industrial district–with lessons from Sassoulo and Castellon. *Policy Studies*, 32(4): 377–395.

Hervas-Oliver, J.L., Lleo, M., and Cervello, R. (2017). The dynamics of cluster entrepreneurship: Knowledge legacy from parents or agglomeration effects? The case of the Castellon ceramic tile district. *Research Policy*.

Humphrey, J. (2003). Globalization and supply chain networks: The auto industry in Brazil and India. *Global Networks*, 3(2): 21–41.

Humphrey, J., and Schmitz, H. (2002). How does insertion in global value chains affect upgrading in industrial clusters? *Regional Studies*, 36: 1017–1027.

Humphrey, J., and Schmitz, H. (2004). Chain governance and upgrading. In H. Schmitz (ed.), *Local Enterprises in the Global Economy: Governance and Upgrading*. Chelthenham: Elgar, pp. 349–381.

Lema, R., Quadros, R., and Schmitz, H. (2015). Reorganizing global value chains and innovation capabilities in Brazil and India. *Research Policy*, 44: 1375–1386.

Markusen, A. (1996). Sticky places in slippery space: A typology of industrial districts. *Economic Geography*, 72(3): 293–313.

Meyer-Stamer, J., Maggi, C., and Siebel, S. (2004). Upgrading in the Tile Industry of Italy, Spain and Brazil: Insights from cluster and value chain analysis. In H. Schmitz (ed.), *Local Enterprises in the Global Economy: Issues of Governance and Upgrading*. Cheltenham: Elgar, pp. 174–199.

Mudambi, R. (2008). Location, control and innovation in knowledge-intensive industries. *Journal of Economic Geography*, 8(5): 699–725.

Parrilli, M.D., Aranguren, M.J., and Larrea, M. (2010). The role of interactive learning to close the 'Innovation Gap' in SME-based local economies. *European Planning Studies*, 18: 351–370.

Parrilli, M.D., Nadvi, K., and Yeung, H.W. (2013). Local and regional development in global VCs, PNs and INs: A comparative review and challenges for future research. *European Planning Studies*, 21: 1–21.

Parrilli, M.D., and Sacchetti, S. (2008). Linking learning and governance in clusters and networks. *Entrepreneurship and Regional Development*, 20: 387–408.

Pavitt, K. (1984). Sectoral patterns of technical change: Towards a taxonomy and a theory. *Research Policy*, 13(6): 343–373.

Pietrobelli, C., and Rabellotti, R. (2011). Global value chains meet innovation systems: Are there learning opportunities for developing countries. *World Development*, 39(7): 1–9.

Piore, M., and Sabel, C. (1984). *The Second Industrial Divide*. New York: Basic Books.

Porter, M. (1990). *The Competitive Advantage of Nations*. New York: The Free Press.

Russo, M. (2004). *The Ceramic Industrial District Facing the Challenge From China*. Dipartimento di Scienze Sociali, Cognitive e Quantitative. Università degli Studi di Modena e Reggio Emilia.

Schmitz, H. (1995). Collective efficiency: Growth path for small-scale industry. *Journal of Development Studies*, 31(4): 529–566.

Sedita, S., Caloffi, A., and Belussi, F. (2013). *Heterogeneity of MNEs Entry Modes in Industrial Clusters: An Evolutionary Approach based on the Cluster Life Cycle Mode*. DRUID 2013 Barcelona.

Sturgeon, T., and Kawakami, M. (2010). *Global Value Chains in the Electronic Industry: Was the Crisis a Window of Opportunity for Developing Countries*. Policy Research Working Papers, 5417, The World Bank.

Sturgeon, T., van Biesebrock, J., and Gereffi, G. (2008). Value chains, networks and clusters: Reframing the global automotive industry. *Journal of Economic Geography*, 8: 297–321.

Tomlinson, P.R. (2012), Industry institutions, social capital and firm participation in industrial development. *Industrial and Corporate Change*, 21(1): 1–29.

11 The role of manufacturing within industrial districts

Proposing and testing an innovative methodology

Ruggero Golini and Albachiara Boffelli

Introduction

The division of labour across specialized co-localized firms is one of the key elements of an industrial district (ID). Under the pressure of globalization and, more specifically, the nesting process of IDs within global value chains (GVCs), such division of labour – with special regard to manufacturing activities – has followed a non-linear evolution and led to greater firm-level heterogeneity within IDs, as increasingly observed by researchers (e.g. Rabellotti et al., 2009; Chiarvesio et al., 2010). To grasp this evolutionary process, this chapter proposes an original methodology to map and analyse production activities and their heterogeneity among firms within an ID. Consequently, we elaborate on the role of manufacturing in industrial districts. However, whereas in Chapter 9 Bettiol et al. analyse the role played by IDs in manufacturing location strategies, we investigate the choices of firms within a district in terms of activities performed and how these affect their competitive position in the global value chain, within the *general aim of understanding the role of manufacturing in supporting the participation of the ID firms in GVCs.*

We present the application and results of this analysis as part of a major survey-based research project conducted by the University of Bergamo across 145 manufacturing firms in the textile and clothing ID of the province of Bergamo (Northern Italy, Lombardy region). This ID has been heavily subjected to that process of fragmentation and globalization which has significantly driven the evolution of firms in other industrial districts (Rabellotti et al., 2009; Chiarvesio et al., 2010; De Marchi and Grandinetti, 2014; Buciuni and Pisano, 2015). Hence, the project aimed to analyse the distribution of manufacturing activities performed by firms in the ID across the different production stages (from spinning to final product manufacturing).

To elaborate, we employed the GVC framework at the ID level to understand which production activities are more common across firms, the extent and forms of vertical integration, and the variety and uniqueness of the activities performed. The starting point is that firms in this region do not exist in isolation, but each one forms part of a local and global supply chain (Belso-Martínez, 2008; Rabellotti et al., 2009; Chiarvesio et al., 2010; De Marchi and Grandinetti, 2014). Moreover, each firm is driven to find an optimal position within its supply chain, which extends outside the ID, and to maintain its role within the ID at the same time. This effort becomes more complicated with each passing day due to globalization, which has caused a great deal of fragmentation and dispersion of production and non-production activities and led to a very intricate global network of supply chain partners (Gereffi, 2005; Gereffi and Fernandez-Stark, 2016). To analyse such a complex context, we employ the GVC framework to understand the nature and content of the linkages between production stages (De Marchi et al., 2013). We rely on the input-output structure of the GVC, which requires the identification of the value chain stages in order to reveal the flow of tangible and intangible goods and services (Gereffi and Fernandez-Stark, 2016).

In conclusion, in this chapter, we propose a methodology aimed at the following: 1) creating a value chain map of the production activities performed at the ID level; 2) analyzing the position of the different firms within this map; and 3) analyzing firm-level heterogeneity, namely, the extent to which firms are involved in different production activities in terms of uniqueness and variety. This contribution is original as we provide a replicable methodology and quantitative indicators for the analysis of IDs through the lens of the GVC framework. It follows that this work attempts to contribute to the GVC literature by presenting a case of extensive activity-level mapping applied to an ID, employing a methodology that could be replicated in future studies and for different IDs.

The Bergamo textile and clothing district

This section will provide an overview of the textile and clothing district in Bergamo, to which the methodology proposed in this chapter has been applied. However, as we will explain later, the same approach could be used to analyse different IDs or industries. The decision to focus on a single industry is in line with the GVC literature, which is often industry-specific; therefore, we could rely on existing works and better control the variables and the context considered. Moreover, the textile and clothing industry has attracted a great deal of interest from GVC scholars (e.g. Appelbaum and Gereffi, 1994; Gereffi, 1994; Gereffi, 1997; Gereffi, 1999; Bair and Gereffi, 2003; Gereffi and Memedovic, 2003; Abecassis-Moedas, 2006; Frederick and Cassil, 2009), because it is one of the world's largest industries and is relevant to almost every country in the world. One additional element that makes this industry so appealing for our research purposes is the turmoil faced in recent decades in terms of the fragmentation and global dispersion of production activities (e.g. Gereffi, 1999).

The two major disruptions in the textile and clothing industry were the removal of quotas[1] in (2005), which not only increased global competition but also resulted in a global supplier base for the large retailers (Taplin, 2006), and the financial crisis that started in 2008, which hit the textile and clothing industry as a whole and resulted in the textile industry experiencing a more significant decline as a provider of intermediate products (Curran and Zignago, 2010). The direct effects have been the decline in the number of companies and the downsizing of surviving firms, leading to a loss of jobs in the industry. Despite these difficulties, some firms were able to react, and a significant number are still active and profitable (Euratex, 2014). As a result of this trend, China and India became the top two countries in the exports of textile and apparel products. In 2013, China was the world's largest exporter of both textile and apparel products with a global share of 32.6% and 40.1%, respectively, followed by India with shares amounting to 6.3% for textiles and 3.8% for apparels. The third-highest exporter, and the largest within the developed countries, was Italy with shares of 4.1% and 5.3% in the textile and apparel markets, respectively (Sistema Moda Italia, 2016). However, Italy lost 40% of its share in the last 10 years, but it is now recovering through restructuring processes.

In the textile and apparel industry, the province of Bergamo comprised 1,294 registered companies in 2014 (marking a decrease by 1.82% from 2013) and 12,106 employees in 2013 (also having decreased by 12.95% from 2012). The value of exports was €870 million in 2014, indicating an increase of 2.64% from 2013 (Osservatorio Nazionale Distretti

Table 11.1 Overview of the Bergamo cluster in the GVC

	Bergamo Textile and Clothing District	
	Valcavallina Oglio	*Valseriana*
Products	• Clothing products • Dyeing preparation for fur • Furniture and accessories	• Textiles
ID Position in the GVC	Firms are engaged in production activities (e.g., spinning, weaving, finishing, dyeing, printing, tailoring). Some firms also perform pre-production (e.g., R&D, product design) and post-production activities (e.g., branding and marketing).	
GVC key actors	The textile and clothing GVC is characterized by large Original Brand Manufacturers (e.g. Zara, H&M, GAP), some of them purchase intermediate and finished products from the districts, by relying on quick and flexible suppliers.	
ID Export propensity	€870 million (2014)	
ID # of firms/ employees	1,294 firms in 2014, decreased by 1.82% from 2013 12,106 employees in 2013, decreased by 12.95% from 2012.	
ID Local firms	Strong presence of craftsmen (usually stage suppliers or specialized suppliers)	• Small and very small businesses are stage suppliers • Medium-sized companies are specialized suppliers or Original Equipment Manufacturers (OEMs) • A small group of leading firms (usually home-grown) control the innovation dynamic
ID Supporting industries	Machinery production; Chemicals; Logistics; Packaging	
ID Local institutions	Confindustria Bergamo (Textile and Clothing Firms Association)	
ID Major recent transformations	The districts underwent a major restructuring process in recent years. In terms of *products,* the companies moved toward high-quality products (while the medium-quality ones had been outsourced to Eastern European countries). The *population of companies* faced a decline over the last decade, but some of the bigger companies started an integration process driven by the need for greater control of all the manufacturing stages, and these companies eventually became leading companies for the districts.	

Italiani, 2014). Further, two districts were formally recognized in the province: the Bergamasca Valcavallina Oglio and the Valseriana (Osservatorio Nazionale Distretti Italiani, 2014). The characteristics of the districts are summarized in Table 11.1.

The specialization of the Bergamasca Valcavallina Oglio district is split across two sectors: the tailoring of clothing products and dyeing preparation for fur, and manufacture of furniture and accessories, the latter not considered in this study. The Valseriana district specializes in textile activities. Most of the companies here are involved in cotton-yarn weaving and tailoring of textile products, except for apparel items, and the manufacturing of moquettes and carpets.

Despite the high number of active firms, both districts have faced significant reductions in the number of firms in the last 15 years. This resulted in a concentration process, with few companies (e.g. Cotonificio Albini, Martinelli Ginetto, Carvico) growing by vertical integration and acquisition of smaller suppliers. Such firms are now the backbone of the local district, supporting smaller local suppliers, promoting innovation and engaging with international customers. These *local dynamic actors* are usually Original Brand Manufacturers (OBMs) that rely on a network of specialized suppliers or Original Equipment Manufacturers (OEMs). However, a plethora of small companies has specialized in niches where they have an internationally recognized brand (e.g. Santini, Radici Pietro Industries and Brand), which still provides a fundamental contribution to innovation and brings to the district some sort of resilience to the aforementioned global shifts. Hence, the district followed a hierarchization trajectory, similar to what described by De Marchi et al. in Chapter 3 in this book, but did so with many smaller firms that proved adaptable to the changing context (De Marchi and Grandinetti, 2014).

As the two districts are very closely located, they are considered to be within the same ID of Bergamo, and we analysed them jointly. The research aimed to survey the production activities performed by firms and their connections within and outside the district by using information that is not available from secondary sources, such as economic databases based on NACE[2] codes, which do not take into account the fragmentation of activities or the linkages among firms within the district.

Methodology

This chapter describes the methodological steps followed in our analysis, which can theoretically be applied to map any ID. The steps we followed are described below.

Identification of the value chain stages

The first step aims to define the input-output structure of the GVC within the ID. Several sources can be used, such as the literature, industry reports and preliminary interviews with companies and associations. In our case, we relied on the previous GVC studies in the same industry (Gereffi, 1999; Bair and Gereffi, 2003; Gereffi and Memedovic, 2003; Gereffi and Frederick, 2010; Gereffi and Fernandez-Stark, 2016) and on national industry reports (Sistema Moda Italia, 2016). Additional sources of information were obtained from preliminary interviews with industry experts or with vertical integrated firms belonging to the district.

As shown in Figure 11.1, the textile and clothing value chain comprises three phases:

1   The *raw materials phase* involves the fibre growing/production stage, where the raw materials are grown (in case of natural fibres) or produced (in case of manmade fibres) for textile manufacturing.
2   The *manufacturing phase* involves seven stages: the raw materials pass through the spinning, spinning supplementary activities, weaving preparation activities, weaving and final product manufacturing (namely, the tailoring activities) stages. The finishing stage, which comprises all the activities to ennoble the yarn/fabric, and the printing/dyeing stage can be performed before or after each one of the previously mentioned manufacturing stages; this is why these two stages are represented in parallel to the other stages.
3   The *distribution phase* comprises the retail stage, where the final products are brought to the end consumers.

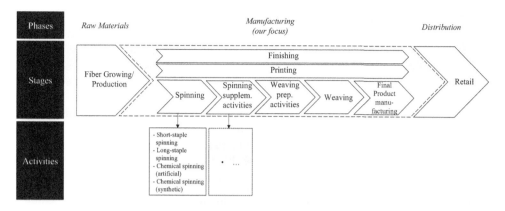

Figure 11.1 Phases, stages and activities in textile and clothing value chain

Note: Activities are reported only for spinning as an example.

Identification of the production activities in each stage

Among the three phases previously described, we decided to focus on the manufacturing activities. In fact, fibre growth and production are not performed in the district, as well as retailing, since the large majority of final products are sold to other companies. Within the manufacturing phase, we identified the *production activities* involved in each of the seven stages described previously.

A preliminary list of activities was defined based on information obtained from technical sources (Fondazione ACIMIT, 2003; Grana, 2005). The list was refined following several interviews with industry experts, leading firms (Gereffi and Fernandez-Stark, 2016) and the most dynamic actors in the district (Rabellotti et al., 2009), since some activities were obsolete and some others were not applicable to the district. At the end of the process, 111 different production activities were identified at different stages of the value chain:

- 4 spinning activities (e.g. cotton fibre spinning and wool fibre spinning);
- 7 spinning supplementary activities (e.g. spooling and twisting);
- three weaving preparation activities (e.g. warping and sizing);
- 10 weaving activities (e.g. weaving with jacquard looms and weaving of non-woven fabrics);
- 31 printing/dyeing activities (e.g. bleaching and digital printing);
- 49 finishing activities (e.g. finishing with softener and antibacterial treatment); and
- seven final product manufacturing activities (e.g. cutting and sewing).

For brevity sake, we do not list all the activities; however, the logic we followed is to consider each activity to be different from the other when it employs a different technology, auxiliary materials or equipment.

Survey design

The next step was to design a survey to gather data on which of the previously identified production activities are performed by the firms in the district. Moreover, we requested some general information about the company that could be used as control variables. The survey we administered had the following structure:

1   General information about the company: characteristics of the company, products offered, final markets and pre- and post-production activities performed;
2   Production activities performed: both stage-level and activity-level, as described in the previous steps of the methodology;
3   Upgrading: the main investments in strategic initiatives related to product, process, functional, chain and environmental and social upgrading;
4   GVC participation indicators: extent of purchases and sales inside and outside the district and the home country (in our case, Italy).

Definition of the population of companies in the district

We derived the initial list of companies from AIDA (a Bureau Van Dijk database, which includes data about limited liability companies) selecting the firms on the basis of the geographic area (Bergamo, in the case of this study) and the industry[3] (textile and cloth-ing). We excluded the codes related to the manufacture of furniture, since it belongs to a different GVC even though it may involve the use of textile products. On the other hand, we included companies classified as distributors as they also perform production activi-ties in many cases. Finally, we conducted some interviews with experts and local industry associations to validate the list of companies and identify the leading companies and their main local suppliers, to ensure that the most prominent firms in the area were included in the sample.

Later, we restricted the number of companies to be contacted based on the availabil-ity of economic data in the database and a contact reference (i.e. telephone number and e-mail). We then eliminated companies belonging to holdings (the parent company was asked to fill the survey for the entire group), small companies (those with less than ten employees) involved only in the distribution phase, and companies that, after a check, resulted as not actually operating in the textile industry. This last activity was completed after having directly contacted the company by e-mail or telephone. In the end, from an initial database of almost 700 companies, we arrived at an available population of 443 companies.

Data collection

To reach out to the companies, we asked the local association of textile companies to distribute the survey across its associates (118 companies). With the remaining firms, we established preliminary telephonic contact in order to ensure an adequate response rate and the quality of the responses. In fact, by contacting the firms by telephone, we obtained the direct e-mail address of the most appropriate persons who could fill the questionnaire (in general, a manager with an overall view of the company or the produc-tion or the operations manager). Next, we sent them an e-mail containing a description of the project and instructions on filling the survey. As a reward for completing the survey, we promised the participating companies a customized report. The overall process took place between January and February 2016. In the end, we obtained a response rate of 32.7% with 145 companies completing the questionnaire from the total available popula-tion of 443 companies.

Development of the indicators

After having obtained the data on the production stages and activities performed by the companies, we defined the indicators needed to describe the district characteristics. In particular, we looked for indicators that could provide information about firm-level heterogeneity internal to the ID, which is one of the key concerns in the literature on IDs (Molina-Morales and Martínez-Fernández, 2009; Rabellotti et al., 2009; De Marchi and Grandinetti, 2014). The indicators were developed both at the stage-level (e.g. spinning) and the activity-level (e.g. the four production activities within spinning). Therefore, in this work, we use some general indicators that could be potentially applicable to every district and every industry.

Below are the details of the indicators we employed:

- Stage-level indicators (with reference to the stages of the value chain in Figure 11.1):

   1) Number of companies in each production stage;
   2) Vertical integration: the number of production stages performed by a company.

- Activity-level indicators (with reference to the activities in each stage as in Figure 11.1):

   1) Variety: the number of activities performed by a company in each stage;
   2) Uniqueness: the degree to which the activities performed by the company are exclusive or performed by a limited number of other companies.

Results

Following the methodology discussed in the previous paragraphs, we now illustrate the results of its application to the textile and clothing district in Bergamo. Given our focus on manufacturing activities, we excluded from the analysis pure retailers, wholesalers or producers of accessories (e.g. buttons, zippers). Thus, the results relate to only 79 companies, from the sample of 145 respondents, engaged in manufacturing activities. Comparing the population of firms (443), the collected sample (145), and the manufacturing firms considered (79) in terms of turnover and number of employees, both the sample and the group of manufacturing companies considered have fewer micro-sized companies (those with less than 10 employees) and are slightly overrepresented in terms of medium-sized companies. This is due to the difficulty in reaching key respondents in micro-sized companies or their lack of interest/time in participating in a survey. Nevertheless, micro-companies are well represented in our sample, accounting for 27% compared to the 44% in the overall population. Moreover, for the purpose of this study, larger companies can be more interesting as they have been recognized as the key actors in IDs (Rabellotti et al., 2009). Table 11.2 summarizes the distribution in terms of turnover and number of employees in the manufacturing companies, as considered in the data analysis.

Other interesting descriptive statistics of the sample relate to the location of sales and purchases. Particularly, we have found a strong connection with the district (on average, 31% of purchases and 30% of sales are exchanged with other firms in the district) and, generally, with the home country of the respondents. On average, 69% of the inputs used by the companies come from Italy and 71% of the output is sold in Italy, including within-district exchanges. For the remainder, 13% of inputs are purchased from European suppliers and 18% from suppliers outside the continent. On the other side, 18% of the production is exported to other European countries and 11% outside Europe.

Table 11.2 Turnover and number of employees of the manufacturing companies

Turnover (million €)			Employees		
Range	# of companies	Share	Range	# of companies	Share
0–2	37	47%	1–10	21	27%
2–10	25	32%	10–50	39	49%
10–50	15	19%	50–250	17	22%

Source: Data elaboration from AIDA, a Bureau Van Dijk database. Turnover in € million

In addition, a more detailed analysis at the stage-level has been performed in order to understand the connections with the GVC (Figure 11.2). In terms of purchases, the linkages with global suppliers (i.e. outside EU) are in the upstream stages (spinning or weaving preparation) or in finishing, the latter result being explained by the fact that the chemical products for the finishing activities are usually bought from large multinational companies. In the downstream phases (weaving and final product manufacturing) and printing prevails the linkage with local and domestic suppliers. In terms of sales, the stages with the major global connections are the spinning supplementary activities and finishing, which are the stages mostly performed by OEMs in contract manufacturing.

Stage-level analysis

The first analysis focuses on the stages of the value chain to verify whether all the stages are covered within the district and the concentration (i.e. number of companies) in each stage (Figure 11.3). Moreover, the evaluation of the vertical integration and how the companies spread along the value chain provides some preliminary insights on the heterogeneity of firms within the district.

In our sample, we found a greater presence of firms while moving downstream in the value chain. In other words, the spinning, spinning supplementary activities and weaving preparation activities are scarcely represented (accounting for eight, 13 and 14 companies, respectively). On the other end of the spectrum, weaving and final product manufacturing are the most well-represented stages (with more than 20 and 50 companies, respectively). With regard to the major transformations that the district faced in recent years (see Table 11.1), this result can be explained by the fact that the activities abandoned over time in the district are mainly the upstream ones. Further, cross-stage activities (finishing, printing and dyeing) are highly frequent across the sample (more than 20 companies perform such activities). We identified two reasons for this. First, being cross-stage activities, there are higher chances that they are performed in combination with other activities. Second, these activities enable product differentiation, thus providing a significant value-added.

Vertical integration, on the other hand, refers to the number of stages performed by a company. We acknowledge that the majority of companies are active in only one stage of the value chain (55.6%). Regarding the other cases, 20.2% of the companies perform two stages; 12.6% three stages; the remaining 11%, four or more stages. Only one company is integrated along the whole value chain. This proves the presence of few broadly integrated companies, which gained a leading role over the years (see the positive correlation between

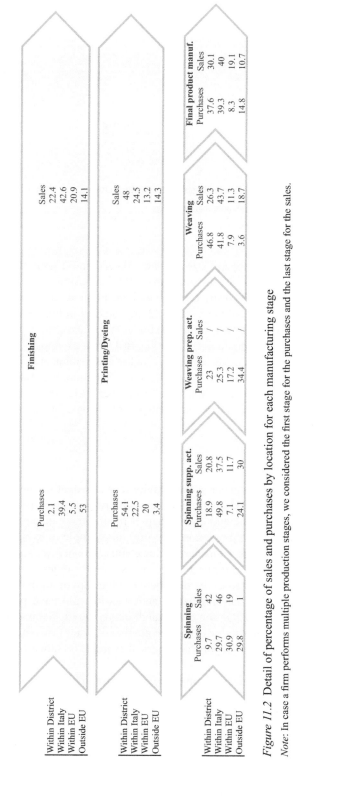

Figure 11.2 Detail of percentage of sales and purchases by location for each manufacturing stage

Note: In case a firm performs multiple production stages, we considered the first stage for the purchases and the last stage for the sales.

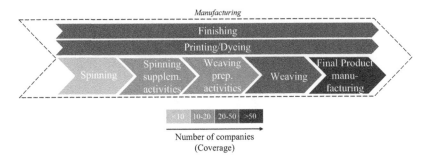

Figure 11.3 Coverage of value chain stages by the manufacturing companies in the sample

Note: One company can be active in more than one stage.

vertical integration and company size presented later), and a great fragmentation among the other firms belonging to the district. Table 11.2 demonstrates the presence of different integration models within the district. In line with the previous analyses, the majority of the companies are involved in only one stage: 32 are engaged in final product manufacturing, four in printing/dyeing, and two in the remaining stages except for the weaving preparation activities. It is interesting to note, however, that when a company increases its level of vertical integration, it tends to differentiate from the other companies in the district in terms of the stages. Consequently, it is very uncommon to find more than two to three companies with the same integration model (Table 11.3). Moreover, there are cases in which companies skip some intermediate stages, generating integration models that are not continuous along the value chain.

Activity-level analysis

The second analysis goes deeper at the activity level, evaluating the variety of activities performed by a company and their uniqueness with respect to the other companies in the sample. The appendix at the end of the chapter reports the mathematical expressions of the indicators, whereas in this section, we offer an example to explain how to calculate the value of these indicators. Consider a value chain with only two stages. A company can perform a subset of activities for each stage, and so can the other firms in the sample. The *variety* indicator is calculated as the ratio between the sum of all the activities performed by the company and the total number of activities it could have performed within the stages in which it is active. On the other hand, *uniqueness* is the maximum ratio of 1 (if the company performs that activity) and the number of other firms in the sample performing such activity.[4] Table 11.4 reports a numerical example on how to calculate variety and uniqueness.

Figure 11.4 displays the distribution of the companies in terms of variety and uniqueness. It can be noted that very few companies demonstrate both high variety and uniqueness, while the majority of the firms fall in the lower left area, which corresponds to low scores for both indicators. Moreover, a group of companies displays very high uniqueness. This indicates a clear firm-level heterogeneity in production activities within the sample.

Table 11.3 Integration models of the sample

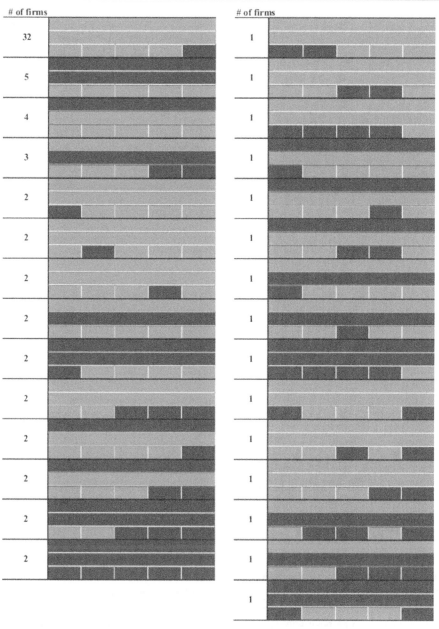

Table 11.4 An example on how to calculate variety and uniqueness in a two-stages value chain

Production stage	Stage 1					Stage 2		
	Act. 1	*Act. 2*	*Act. 3*	*Act. 4*	*Act. 5*	*Act. 1*	*Act. 2*	*Act. 3*
Does the company perform the activity?	Yes	No	No	Yes	Yes	No	Yes	Yes
Stage variety			3/5				2/3	
Total variety					5/8			
Number of other firms in the sample performing the activity	4	10	6	8	2	1	10	3
Activity Uniqueness	1/4	–	–	1/8	1/2	–	1/10	1/3
Total Uniqueness					Max(1/4,1/8,1/2,1/10,1/3)=1/2			

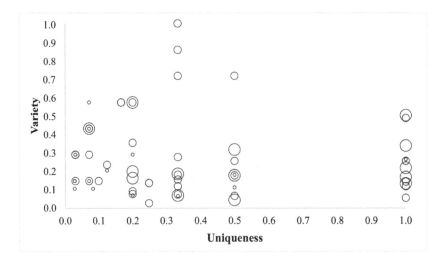

Figure 11.4 Companies distribution in terms of variety and uniqueness

Note: The dimension of the marker reflects the company size: small for micro companies, medium for small companies and big for medium and large companies.

Linking the ID and the GVC level of analysis

We also performed additional analyses, obtained through simple correlations among the different indicators and testing for differences between groups of firms with different characteristics. Examining the correlation among the previously analysed indicators (vertical integration, variety, and uniqueness) and the company size (measured in terms of the number of employees), we found uniqueness to be positively correlated with both vertical integration and company size, meaning that the bigger the company, the more vertically integrated it is and the more unique are the activities it performs within the district (see Table 11.5). Future developments of this study should investigate if a company's growth was driven by it being characterized by high uniqueness or whether only larger firms could invest in expanding their uniqueness.

Interestingly, we did not find evidence of correlation between the activity-level indicators and sales and purchases by location. In other words, companies that are highly unique or those that perform a broad variety of activities are not more internationalized than the

Table 11.5 Correlations among the indicators and the company size

	Company size	Vertical Integration	Variety	Uniqueness
Company size	1.00			
Vertical Integration	0.52*	1.00		
Variety	0.15	−0.19	1.00	
Uniqueness	0.36*	0.55*	−0.09	1.00

Table 11.6 Kruskal-Wallis test results and mean of the sub-samples of finished products producers and not

Variable		Mean (Not producer of a finished product)	Mean (Producer of a finished product)	Kruskal-Wallis test significance level
Vertical integration		2.1	1.7	0.121
Variety		0.2	0.4	0.000**
Uniqueness		0.5	0.2	0.005**
Purchases	District	48%	41%	0.486
	Italy	67%	71%	0.701
	EU	15%	10%	0.755
	Extra EU	18%	19%	0.839
Sales	District	42%	43%	0.850
	Italy	73%	67%	0.405
	EU	19%	17%	0.844
	Extra EU	8%	16%	0.181
# of companies		44	35	

others. Finally, we split the sample between firms involved in the production of a finished product (35 firms) and those that were not (44 firms). We tested for differences on the following variables: vertical integration, variety, uniqueness, distribution of purchases (within the district, within Italy, within Europe and outside Europe) and distribution of sales (within the district, within Italy, within Europe and outside Europe). The last two variables (i.e. distribution of purchases and sales) are measures of backward and forward participation in a GVC, respectively (WTO, 2014; WTO, 2015). As the variables are not normally distributed, we used non-parametric tests (Kruskal-Wallis).

The analysis highlights that being involved in the production of a finished product influences a firm's variety and uniqueness. Generally, a company that focuses on the production of finished products has higher variety but less unique activities. However, there are no differences in the percentage of purchases and sales in the different locations: the companies are in any case closely linked to the local territory (40% to 50% of purchases and sales are within the district). The results suggest that other factors, besides variety and uniqueness, should be examined in order to explain how well integrated a company is in its GVC.

Discussion

To complement the results of the survey, we interviewed two firms that are among the largest and most successful in the district and have significant participation in GVCs. Via the definitions provided in Chapter 3 by De Marchi et al., we could define these two firms as *local dynamic actors* because of their abilities to innovate, build strong brands and contribute to district growth. Due to our focus on production activities, we used these cases to better understand to what extent their manufacturing strategy – i.e. choices in terms of variety, uniqueness and vertical integration and relationships with local suppliers – contributes to their competitiveness in the GVC.

Company A

Company A was established in 1965 as an artisan factory producing clothes for other companies. After a while, the founder's deep passion for sports, particularly cycling, led them to specialize in clothing for cyclists. One of the distinctive characteristics of the company is their decision to design and manufacture products exclusively in Italy, which also led to the need to develop long-term relationships with local suppliers based on trust and reputation. In 2014, the company recorded €13 million in turnover and an employee count of sixty-three, classifying them as a medium-sized enterprise. Currently, the company manufactures more than 3,000 items every day and exports 70% of its production. The firm is directly involved in research and development (R&D); in fact, it has a team of dedicated designers that develops a new collection yearly and tailors their products to the customers' requests. The speed and efficiency of the new product development process, which also involves the overall supply chain, is one of the competitive advantages of the company. Over the years, the firm has been able to develop a strong and recognizable brand through consistent investments in marketing and branding activities, such as through partnerships with athletes participating in world championships.

Critical success factors are features that allow a firm to succeed in a specific market segment (Brun et al., 2008), and hence, they are strictly related to the firm's competitive strategy. Company A follows a niche strategy focused on product quality, innovation and flexibility.

With respect to the stage-level analysis, Company A is involved in the printing/dyeing and the final product manufacturing stages. Thus, its level of vertical integration is equal to 2. Considering the activity-level analysis, Company A is involved in the following activities:

- Printing/dyeing stage: transfer printing and digital printing;
- Final product manufacturing stage: cutting, sewing, removal of defects and thermal fastening.

Its level of variety of the production activities is 0.16 and its uniqueness is 0.2.[5] As per Figure 11.4, Company A belongs to the group with low variety and uniqueness in terms of its manufacturing activities. In particular, Company A is not a pure original design manufacturer, but in line with its critical success factors, it keeps some basic manufacturing activities in-house to control quality (e.g. removal of defects) and add high-value customizations (e.g. printing). All the other activities, and especially those with higher uniqueness, are outsourced mainly at local suppliers' (65.8% of the total inputs come from the district). This network of local suppliers supported Company A in the creation of competitive advantage in terms of market responsiveness and development of technical innovations. It appears that this company compensated its scarce variety and uniqueness (well below the district mean) by establishing strong relationships with local partners, to find support for its innovative endeavours and differentiate its own products. In this manner, and thanks to its renowned brand, the company can reach a global market, with 70% of its products being exported all over the world. This company participates in the GVC leveraging uniqueness of local suppliers to conquer global markets, that, according to Caniato et al. (2013), reflects a *Baron* configuration (namely, local purchases, local production and global sales).

Company B

Company B is a well-known family-firm in Valseriana. The family became active in the textile sector in 1891; however, the company was established in 1947, when the first woollen blanket production line was opened. Thereafter, the production was extended by adding cotton and linen as raw materials. The firm has initially focused on the high-end home-textiles market; however, over time it has entered other markets, such as casual wear and furnishings. Company B also began a vertical integration process that allowed it to take control over a large part of the value chain. In 2014, Company B recorded a turnover of €75 million and employed 420 workers.

R&D activities are particularly important for this company, both in terms of products and processes. The firm renews its fabrics every year to meet new customer needs, which are gathered by participating in the most important industry fairs and via collaborations with national and international customers. Today, Company B has built strong and recognizable brands in every market niche it targets.

Company B needs to fulfil many critical success factors simultaneously: product quality, craftsmanship and exclusivity, Made in Italy, flexibility, innovativeness and technical characteristics, and, to a lesser extent, sustainability. This reflects the plurality of markets it addresses and the orientation towards high-end niches, which are also highly demanding. Regarding the stage-level analysis, Company B is highly integrated, with involvement in all the value chain stages, except final product manufacturing. Thus, its level of vertical integration is equal to 6.

Per the activity-level analysis, Company B has a variety equal to 0.5 and a uniqueness equal to 1.0.[6] Consequently, both high variety and uniqueness characterize Company B; in fact, thanks to its broad vertical integration, the firm controls a wide range of manufacturing stages with varying degrees of uniqueness of the activities performed (from low to very high). Differently from Company A, Company B decided to insource uniqueness rather than looking for it at suppliers. As a consequence, connections with local suppliers are less important and Company B exploits the advantages of global sourcing to find the best supply markets (85% of its raw materials and intermediate products are imported from outside Italy). The only exception regards local suppliers of textile machineries, which are involved in R&D projects to develop cutting-edge production technologies. In conclusion, Company B extended its supply chain globally, but kept production local. This configuration allows the firm to add value through its unique and integrated manufacturing processes and serve customers by means of fast and flexible manufacturing cycles.

Although both companies A and B are recognized as leading firms within the district, they have very different features. Company A has low vertical integration, variety and uniqueness, while much higher values of these indicators are registered for Company B. From a strategic perspective, both firms focus on market niches: Company A addresses a single market, while Company B addresses multiple markets, which is reflected by the greater number of production activities and critical success factors that characterize it. Interestingly, Company A has strategic ties with suppliers within the district and takes the final product to global markets, acting as a *gatekeeper* (Morrison, 2008). Conversely, Company B is a global player that has invested in its own manufacturing capabilities and keeps limited ties with other firms in the district. Still, some positive spillovers are generated from the presence of Company B in the district, such as temporary business opportunities and involvement in R&D projects.

Conclusions

In this chapter, we presented a methodology and its application to the textile and clothing ID in the province of Bergamo to map which production activities in the value chain are performed and how companies in the same ID differentiate themselves. To the best of our knowledge, this study represents the first attempt to extensively map the value chain stages and the elementary production activities performed by the companies in an ID. In particular, we propose two new indicators: *variety* (i.e. related to a number of different production activities performed by a company) and *uniqueness* (i.e. related to the extent to which the activities performed are rare in the sample). These indicators, together with vertical integration and the distribution of the different integration models can provide insights on the heterogeneity of firms in an ID in greater detail. Hence, the results contribute to the debate on the heterogeneity of IDs by proving that the Marshallian concept of the ID is undergoing a change.

The application of the methodology on the Bergamo textile and clothing ID shows that companies tend to concentrate in the final stages of the value chain and on supporting activities. Moreover, a significant number of companies are focused on one or few stages in the value chain, which is in line with the literature (i.e. increasing fragmentation of specialization in the global value chains). However, almost half of the sample comprises companies that are vertically integrated, often in a discontinuous way, and this opens new possibilities for research as vertical integration has usually been considered for stages that immediately precede or follow the current one. The fact that many different integration models have been found highlights one major difference with other studies conducted, for instance, in developing countries where a large portion of the firms' population is concentrated in the same production stage (Gereffi and Frederick, 2010). In addition, the analysis of vertical integration allows the identification of the larger firms within the district, which are often autonomously engaged in the GVCs. This is the case of Company B, which followed a process of vertical integration that included the acquisition of smaller companies to control the entire supply chain. However, as in the case of Company A, leading firms at the ID level can also be those that source locally and act as gatekeepers, with lower levels of vertical integration (Morrison, 2008). In both cases, such *local dynamic actors* find in the ID a source of competitive advantage and, in turn, they foster innovation and establish a connection between the ID and the GVCs.

Such competitive advantage generated in the ID is tightly related to the concepts of variety and uniqueness proposed in our study. The results of our mapping methodology show how the ID includes a broad range of firms with different specialization in terms of production stages and activities performed. Such diversity creates the possibility to configure and reconfigure firms in *temporary local value chains*, which are self-orchestrated or orchestrated by local lead firms to reach global markets. In these chains, each firm contributes thanks to the uniqueness and/or variety of its processes and, as a whole, the ID is able to adapt to changing conditions of the global markets thanks to the heterogeneity of its actors. Such heterogeneity in the production activities is also reflected in the heterogeneity of knowledge possessed and shared by the firms. This makes the ID a very fertile environment for innovation and explains why global buyers engage with firms in the ID at all stages, as the high percentage of sales outside the country at each stage of the value chain demonstrates.

In this complex picture, it is still possible to observe some general trends: for instance, variety and uniqueness alone are not related to a higher or lower participation in a GVC in terms of purchases and sales outside the country – which, from the case studies, seem to be rather related to the presence of R&D and branding activities within the firm. As a consequence, future developments of this work can concentrate on the impact of R&D and branding activities, which is an additional source of firm-level heterogeneity.

In conclusion, the analysis presented in this paper contributes both to the literature on GVC and ID and moves a step forward in reconciling the global-local issue by presenting an objective and quantitative methodology and, therefore, paving the way for a more structured interaction between the two fields. Our conviction is that such methodology is generalizable to different districts, once the basic activities characterizing the value chain have been identified. Moreover, this mapping effort can be of help for companies in the ID to know their role and contribution in the GVC. In our case, companies from the textile and clothing ID of Bergamo are currently using our data to strengthen their connections and evaluate joint investments on the production activities which can be of mutual interest.

One primary limitation is that the focus is only on production activities and we left out pre- and post- production stages of the value chain. However, our methodology can be easily extended to include such activities. Another limitation of this study is its focus on a single ID. For future developments of this work, a comparison with other IDs mapped using the same methodology would be highly beneficial. In particular, two kinds of strategic comparisons are foreseeable for multiple IDs: on the one hand, the comparison of IDs in the same industry and country and, on the other hand, the comparison of different product IDs in the same region. Moreover, given the scattered situation in terms of vertical integration, variety and uniqueness, more case studies should be developed to establish causal relationships between the different variables. Finally, a dynamic analysis of how companies have evolved over time, for instance, by replicating the study after five years, could also prove important in highlighting how firms in IDs evolve over time.

Acknowledgements

The project was done in collaboration with Confindustria Bergamo (Gruppo Tessili e Moda) and was funded by the Pro Universitate Bergomensi association.

Appendix

The mathematical expressions of the two activity-level indicators are as follows:

$i \in I$, I set of companies;
$j \in J$, J set of stages;
$k \in K[1, n_j]$, K set of activities with $n_j =$ maximum number of activities in stage j

$$\text{Variety}_i = \frac{\sum_j \sum_k x_{ijk} * j_{ij}}{\sum_j j_{ij} * n_j}$$

$$\text{Uniqueness}_i = \max[\text{Uniqueness}_{ijk}]$$

$$\text{Uniqueness}_{ijk} = \frac{x_{ijk}}{\sum_i x_{ijk}}$$

With $x_{ijk} = \begin{cases} 1 & \text{if company } i \text{ perform activity } k \text{ in stage } j \\ 0 & \text{otherwise} \end{cases}$ and

$$j_{ij} = \begin{cases} 1 & \text{if company } i \text{ is in stage } j \\ 0 & \text{otherwise} \end{cases}$$

Notes

1 The Multi-Fiber Arrangement (MFA) and the following Agreement on Textile and Clothing (ATC) restricted exports to the major consuming markets by imposing limits (i.e. quotas) on the volume of imported apparel and textile items. The system was designed to protect the domestic industries of the United Stated and the European Union by limiting imports from highly competitive suppliers such as China.

2 NACE (Nomenclature statistique des Activités économiques dans la Communauté Européenne) is the statistical classification of economic activities in the European Communities. NACE is a four-digit classification providing the framework for collecting and presenting a large range of statistical data according to economic activity in the fields of economics and statistics (e.g. production, employment and national accounts) and in other statistical domains developed within the European statistical system (ESS). NACE Rev. 2, a revised classification, was adopted at the end of (2006), and it began implementation in 2007. (http://ec.europa.eu/eurostat/statistics-explained/index. php/Glossary:Statistical_classification_of_economic_activities_in_the_European_Community_ (NACE)).

3 NACE codes used in this research: 13 and 14 (with all the subsets); 46.16, 46.41, 46.42; 47.51, 47.53, 47.71, 47.82.

4 We used the maximum to calculate uniqueness for sharper results; however, similar results were obtained using the average (the correlation between maximum and average uniqueness equals 0.820, sig. 0.000).

5 Company A performs two out of 31 activities in the first stage and four out of seven activities in the second stage, thus the variety score for Company A can be calculated as $6/38 = 0.16$. In order to evaluate its uniqueness, it is necessary to count, for each activity in which the company is involved, the number of other firms in the sample that perform the same activity. For example, there are other six companies involved in digital printing, so the uniqueness of this activity can be calculated as $1/6 = 0.167$. Accordingly, Company A's uniqueness score is 0.2.

6 Company B is involved in 52 different activities of the 104 it could perform; namely, the total number of activities of the 6 stages in which it is involved. Therefore, the variety score for Company B is 0.5. This firm is the only one in the sample performing the following activities: chintzing (treating fabric with waxes and resins to give a shiny appearance and a pleasant texture), crease-care treatment, anti-slip treatment and easy-wash treatment. Thus, Company B's uniqueness score is equal to 1.0.

References

Abecassis-Moedas, C. (2006). Integrating design and retail in the clothing value chain: An empirical study of the organisation of design. *International Journal of Operatios & Production Management*, 26(4): 412–428.

Appelbaum, R., and Gereffi, G. (1994). Power and profits in the apparel commodity chain. In E. Bonacich, L. Cheng, N. Chinchilla, N. Hamilton, and P. Ong (eds.), *Global Production: The Apparel Industry in the Pacific Rim*. Philadelphia, PA: Temple University Press, pp. 42–62.

Bair, J., and Gereffi, G. (2003). Upgrading, uneven development, and jobs in the North American apparel industry. *Global Networks*, 3(2): 143–169.

Belso-Martínez, J.A. (2008). Differences in survival strategies among footwear industrial districts: The role of international outsourcing. *European Planning Studies*, 16(9): 1229–1248.

Brun, A., Caniato, F., Caridi, M., Castelli, C., Miragliotta, G., Ronchi, S., Sianesi, A., and Spina, G. (2008). Logistics and supply chain management in luxury fashion retail: Empirical investigation of Italian firms. *International Journal of Production Economics*, 114(2): 554–570.

Buciuni, G., and Pisano, G.P. (2015). Can Marshall's clusters survive globalization? *Harvard Business School Working Paper*.

Caniato, F., Golini, R., and Kalchschmidt, M. (2013). The effect of global supply chain configuration on the relationship between supply chain improvement programs and performance. *International Journal of Production Economics*, 143(2): 285–293.

Chiarvesio, M., Di Maria, E., and Micelli, S. (2010). Global value chains and open networks: The case of Italian industrial districts. *European Planning Studies*, 18(3): 333–350.

Curran, L., and Zignago, S. (2010). The financial crisis: Impact on key clothing markets and suppliers. *Journal of Fashion Marketing and Management: An International Journal*, 14(4): 530–545.

De Marchi, V., Di Maria, E., and Micelli, S. (2013). Environmental strategies, upgrading and competitive advantage in global value chains. *Business Strategy and the Environment*, 22: 62–72.

De Marchi, V., and Grandinetti, R. (2014). Industrial districts and the collapse of the Marshallian model: Looking at the Italian experience. *Competition & Change*, 18(1): 70–87.

Euratex. (2014). *Taking Action for the Future of the European Textile and Clothing Industry*. Available at: http://euratex.eu/fileadmin/user_upload/images/do_not_miss/Euratex_brochure_2015.pdf

Fondazione ACIMIT. (2003). *Quaderni di tecnologia tessile*. ACIMIT Servizi (eds.)

Frederick, S., and Cassil, N. (2009). Industry clusters and global value chains: Analytical frameworks to study the new world of textiles. *The Journal of the Textile Institute*, 100(8): 668–681.

Gereffi, G. (1994). The organization of buyer-driven global commodity chains: How US retailers shape overseas production networks. In G. Gereffi, and M. Korzeniewicz (eds.), *Commodity Chains and Global Capitalism*. Westport, CT: Praeger, pp. 95–122.

Gereffi, G. (1997). Global shifts, regional response: Can North America meet the full-package challenge? *Bobbin*, 39(3): 16–31.

Gereffi, G. (1999). International trade and industrial upgrading in the apparel commodity chain. *Journal of International Economics*, 48(1): 37–70.

Gereffi, G. (2005). The global economy: Organization, governance and development. In N.J. Smelser and R. Swedberg (eds.), *The Handbook of Economic Sociology*. Princeton: Princeton University Press, pp. 160–182.

Gereffi, G., and Fernandez-Stark, K. (2016). *Global Value Chain Analysis: A Primer*. Durham, North Carolina: Center on Globalization, Governance & Competitiveness (CGGC).

Gereffi, G., and Frederick, S. (2010). The Global Apparel Value Chain, Trade and the Crisis: Challenges and Opportunities for Developing Countries. World Bank Policy Research Working Paper Series.

Gereffi, G., Humphrey, J., Kaplinsky, R., and Sturgeon, T. (2001). Introduction: Globalization, value chains and development. *IDS Bulletin*, 32(3): 1–8.

Gereffi, G., Humphrey, J., and Sturgeon, T. (2005). The governance of global value chains. *Review of International Political Economy*, 12: 78–104.

Gereffi, G., and Memedovic, O. (2003). *The Global Apparel Value Chain: What Prospects for Upgrading by Developing Country*. Vienna, Austria: United Nations Industrial Development Organization (UNIDO).

Grana, C. (2005). Tecnologia e merceologia tessile per la formazione degli operatori del settore tessile-abbigliamento. Bergamo, Italy: Editrice San Marco.

Molina-Morales, F.X., and Martínez-Fernández, M.T. (2009). Does homogeneity exist within industrial districts? A social capital-based approach. *Papers in Regional Science*, 88(1): 209–229.

Morrison, A. (2008). Gatekeepers of knowledge within industrial districts: Who they are, how they interact. *Regional studies*, 42(6): 817–835.

Osservatorio Nazionale Distretti Italiani. (2014). *Osservatorio Nazionale Distretti Italiani*. Available at: www.osservatoriodistretti.org/node/218/distretto-bergamasca-valcavallina-oglio

Rabellotti, R., Carabelli, A., and Hirsch, G. (2009). Italian industrial districts on the move: Where are they going? *European Planning Studies*, 17(1): 19–41.

Sistema Moda Italia. (2016). *Rapporto di settore 2015/2016. L'industria tessile-moda in Italia. Il quadro generale*. Available at: www.sistemamodaitalia.com/it/area-associati/centro-studi/item/9894-l-industria-tessile-moda-in-italia-rapporto-2015-2016

Taplin, I.M. (2006). Restructuring and reconfiguration: The EU textile and clothing industry adapts to change. *European Business Review*, 18(3): 172–186.

WTO. (2014). *World Trade Report 2014*. Available at: www.wto.org/english/res_e/booksp_e/world_trade_report14_e.pdf

WTO. (2015). *International Trade Statistics 2015*. Available at: www.wto.org/english/res_e/statis_e/its2015_e/its2015_e.pdf

12 New frontiers for competitiveness and innovation in clusters and value-chains research

Valentina De Marchi, Eleonora Di Maria and Gary Gereffi

Starting from different premises, both studies on industrial districts (IDs) or clusters and on global value chains (GVCs) have witnessed a profound transformation over the last decade in *how* value chain activities are structured at the local and global levels and *where* those activities are performed. In addition, studies have discussed *who* are the actors involved in such dynamics and the implications in terms of *what* activities are controlled by firms in the pre-production, production and post-production scheme over time (*when*). In this concluding chapter, we present the key contributions emerging from the chapters in this book, focusing on four key cross-cutting themes: 1) the co-evolution of IDs driven by insertion in GVCs; 2) the diverse actors driving such heterogeneous outcomes; 3) the role of manufacturing and upgrading in IDs in the new global scenario; and 4) the future of globalization.

The co-evolution of clusters and global value chains

The increasing heterogeneity between and within IDs

Based on fresh analyses from clusters in the countries where this type of industrial organization formed the backbone for development starting in the 1980s, this book provides evidence that contemporary clusters are quite heterogeneous. Reviewing the recent literature on Italian industrial districts, in Chapter 3 De Marchi et al. suggest that the major dimensions of ID differences include: 1) the degree of concentration of cluster resources within few firms; 2) the rate of decline in the population of cluster firms; and 3) the ability of the ID to produce local added value in order to remain competitive. Together these phenomena drive three different trajectories: *decline*, *hierarchization* and *resilience*. Industrial districts that resemble the hierarchization and resilience trajectories are still performing well in final markets and can retain a large portion of value-added in the ID. In the hierarchization case, such capacity is concentrated in only a few companies, whereas in the resilience trajectory, growth is driven and value is spread among a larger range of actors, often small and medium-sized enterprises (SMEs).

Giuliani and Rabellotti (Chapter 2) take a different perspective in analyzing the heterogeneity across IDs, focusing on the value chain activities performed and the value added at the district level. In their model, *locally rooted GVC-led IDs* as well as *outward-oriented GVC-led IDs* are outperforming *low-road IDs* because they are able to engage in pre- and/or post-production activities along the smile curve, entailing the possibility to capture higher value-added activities.

Drawing on the examples of well-studied districts such as Riviera del Brenta footwear, Montebelluna sportsystems, and Belluno eyewear, both chapters clearly suggest that Italian

IDs are nowadays quite distinct from the traditional model that made Italy a benchmark for local development until the 2000s. Two key insights are emerging from their analyses. First *within-ID* heterogeneity has increased. The Italian ID landscape is no longer homogeneous: some IDs are better able to cope with global challenges than others, which has important policy implications. Second, within-ID heterogeneity is related to *between-ID* heterogeneity: the "cluster effect" has been substituted by the increased ability of local companies to take advantage of ID characteristics to cope with global markets. This is reinforced by a higher prevalence of large firms within IDs, which is even more dramatic if one considers the business group phenomena described in Chapter 2.[1]

Drivers in the co-evolution of IDs and GVCs

Globalization has played a crucial role in the deep transformations of the cluster model. Clusters that proved to be resilient in the new scenario are better able to cope with and adapt to the needs of global markets. Adopting a term increasingly used in GVC studies (Lee and Gereffi, 2013; Sturgeon and Lee, 2005), we propose that a key contribution emerging from our book is the co-evolution of IDs and GVCs – i.e. the competences and specialization of firms based in local districts co-evolve with the needs and features of their global buyers and production partners, who are playing a more prominent role in most clusters. In other words, phenomena related to both IDs and GVCs have jointly shaped the emergence of the three evolutionary trajectories, reinforcing each other.

Entrepreneurship and entrepreneurial dynamics are among the main drivers of cluster evolution, referring both to the birth of new companies and to the ability of existing firms to discover and exploit international business opportunities (Oviatt and McDougall, 2005). The traditional Marshallian cluster model, which earned Italy global renown for its diversified and vibrant local development, featured the rise of new firms, particularly through spin-off processes. Studies presented in this book suggest that clusters facing difficulties in coping with international competition have witnessed a decrease in their rate of new-firm formations and actual reductions of active firms (as in the Vicenza gold jewellery case presented in Chapter 3 in this book). In other cases, entrepreneurship is still a key driver of local development, such as the case of Prato where the cluster proved particularly attractive for Chinese entrepreneurs to open up new businesses by exploiting socio-communitarian dynamics linked to foreign communities (Chapter 8 in this book). The presence of dynamic local companies, some of which became lead firms that succeeded in leveraging local knowledge while managing global supply chains, is another factor in explaining ID trajectories, which we will delve into below.

Gereffi (2014) sees several major elements shaping the current phase of the global economy: 1) the increasing role of emerging economies as economic and political powers; 2) the geographic consolidation and value chain concentration in the global supply base; and 3) a shift in GVC end markets (growing consumption in emerging economies and increasing attention to corporate responsibility, supply chain transparency, customization and flexibility in developed countries). These global drivers shape the evolution of industrial districts analysed in this book. Veneto IDs (investigated in Chapters 2, 3 and 9 in this book) are particularly illuminating in this regard. The consolidation in the gold jewellery value chain and the disappearing middle segment in the EU and US markets have been identified as key transformations of the industry, to which the Vicenza ID firms have not been able to cope (De Marchi et al., 2014). Similarly, the push by consolidated global buyers to preside over the distribution phase in the luxury footwear industry co-evolved with the abandonment by Riviera del Brenta ID firms of post-production activities to focus on production and pre-production activities within their local hub. In the Belluno eyewear cluster, similar global trends co-evolved with the increasing relevance of local original brand manufacturers (OBMs), which developed into global lead firms for that industry.

In the evolution of clusters, there is a *tension between place-based variables*, on the one hand, and *global drivers*, on the other. The studies in this book reinforce the insight that geography matters, in the sense that localization of activities within ID boundaries offers the opportunity to grasp local know-how and exploit economic and social relationships for innovation purposes. At the same time, the internationalization of local firms (home-grown multinational enterprises or MNEs) as well as the entrance of foreign MNEs transforms clusters both internally and externally by creating different evolutionary paths among them. The study by Belussi et al. (Chapter 5 in this book) suggests that the impact of the entrance of foreign MNEs at the cluster level depends on the cluster life cycle, i.e. whether MNEs were among the key actors that gave rise to the cluster or they entered during the maturity phase.

Thus, transformation at the cluster level may signal an evolution that occurs also at the global level and the two processes are mutually reinforcing. To sum up, we should view the trajectories of both clusters and GVCs as interdependent, which results in their co-evolution.

Investigating the evolution of IDs in GVCs

The co-evolution of local clusters and global chains calls for an increasing effort by scholars to link both perspectives in the analysis of development dynamics. Indeed, all chapters suggest the need to analyse local and global forces in an integrated way, and Chapter 3 explicitly suggests the joint impact of ID-related and GVC-related elements as determinants of ID resilience.

As noted in Chapter 1 by the editors, the GVC and ID perspectives are complementary and not contradictory. In the former approach, GVCs can be conceived as nested structures in which clusters are agglomerations of firms whose specialization in manufacturing activities was amplified by the global sourcing strategies of lead firms and first-tier suppliers (Sturgeon et al., 2008). In the ID perspective, the connection with external firms and the relevance of 'downstream' internationalization has been a constituent feature of clusters. However, the co-evolution of both levels in the current scenario requires improving our capacity to interpret how industries are globally structured, allowing for novel empirical approaches.

The study by Golini and Boffelli (Chapter 11 in this book) is a clear case in point, as it provides an original methodology to capture the intertwined relationships between clusters and GVCs with respect to divisions of labour and value production. Cluster studies have usually approached internal divisions of labour in terms of supplier-client relationships, looking at the implications for innovation and development spin-offs. GVC studies focus on value chain mapping to identify the main activities needed to make a product and how value is created and captured by firms, according to the range of activities performed (pre-production, production and post-production). Golini and Boffelli apply the methodology of value chain mapping at the local level to analyse the evolutionary processes of clusters and their internal and cross-cluster heterogeneity. Based on a survey of firms in the textile and clothing cluster in Bergamo (Italy), they define the stages of the value chain and the activities within each stage that are carried out at the local level, and assess how many actors perform these activities. This methodology, based on detailed firm-level data, captures the variety of activities performed by each firm and their level of uniqueness, as well as the global connections of such activities.

Another methodological contribution is found in Chapter 7 by Molina-Morales and colleagues, which evaluates the role of internal and external connections in support of ID development analyzing the network of the firm. Finally, it is worth mentioning the attempt by De Marchi et al. (Chapter 3 in this book) to suggest a parsimonious set of variables, which can be easily adopted in other empirical contexts, to classify the evolutionary trajectories of IDs and measure their heterogeneity.

The diversity of key actors

The heterogeneity within and among clusters centres around the evolution of the firms based within clusters and their strategies to cope with globalization. Indeed, the chapters of this book suggest that it is not possible to understand ID evolution without focusing on the main actors highlighted in both the ID and GVC literatures. However, ID studies have tended to ignore the role of global buyers or MNE producers, while GVC studies often overlooked the specificities and strategies of local firms. A cross-cutting theme emerging from this book is the diversity of local and global actors that are determining the evolution of IDs.

Home-grown vs. foreign global lead firms

A first set of relevant actors to understand cluster evolution are global lead firms (GLFs), defined by GVC studies as buyers or producers that exert power in the chain to shape the development of their industry, and how, where, when and by whom value is added and captured (Gereffi, 1994; Gibbon et al., 2008). Many GVC studies have focused on learning possibilities and upgrading trajectories for developing country clusters or regions by participating in GVCs with GLFs (Gereffi, 1999; Navas-Alemán, 2011; Pietrobelli and Rabellotti, 2011; Staritz et al., 2011). Studies on IDs based in developed countries, including contributions in this book, have stressed the other direction of learning: clusters offer crucial knowledge to GLFs so that cluster firms in GVCs can be knowledge-providers rather than just knowledge-seekers. In most districts, lead firms – both foreign and home-grown – play a key role in ID evolution (in Chapters 2 and 3 in this book, their presence is a major determinant of cluster resiliency).

A wide literature (spanning both the GVC and ID traditions) describes clusters as preferred destinations for foreign MNEs. Analyzing the entrance of foreign MNEs in different clusters in Italy, Romania and China using a cluster-life cycle approach, Belussi et al. suggest in Chapter 5 that there is not a singular impact of such firms on cluster trajectories. When the cluster is built around pioneering MNEs whose goal is to discover and exploit local resources, the MNEs' intention is to create "place-anchored" value chains, with direct connections between MNE subsidiaries and headquarters. Under these circumstances, knowledge spillovers are quite limited and local SMEs are usually excluded. By contrast, in the maturity phase when the local engines of innovation and growth are slowing down, MNEs are interested in rejuvenating cluster competences and we see different results (i.e. hierarchization, functional downgrading, etc.). Hence clusters are heterogeneous because of the different exposure to and goals of foreign MNEs.

In the early ID literature, local firms were viewed as largely homogeneous. In some cases, specific firms were considered crucial in influencing the origin and development of IDs, often a solo firm or pioneer company (Belussi, 2015; Lazerson and Lorenzoni, 1999). Cluster firms have become more differentiated, as medium and large firms have started to internationalize, which affects the structure of cluster networks. Following Pisano and Shih (2009,

2012), Barzotto and colleagues argue that by maintaining activities at the cluster level, such home-grown MNEs not only benefit from but also nurture the local industrial commons (labour pool, supply networks etc.). These firms thus choose to anchor their actions in the cluster. Because of their simultaneous role as *local* and *multinational* companies, they transfer to the cluster knowledge acquired globally, while also investing and maintaining local assets through global market opportunities. The cases of ceramic production in Sassuolo (Italy) and Castellon (Spain) developed in Chapter 10 suggest two-way flows of foreign investments across the two IDs, with the large Italian MNEs specialized in the production of ceramic equipment making investments in the Castellon cluster, and vice versa, generating deep knowledge flows across the two IDs.

More recently, the growth of *within-district* heterogeneity has received more attention. The IDs described in this book are characterized not only by GLFs, but also by the presence of local firms that have been called *cluster lead firms* (CLFs) (or as suggested in Chapter 3, *local dynamic actors*). Smaller in size than GLFs, CLFs are usually specialized in niche markets where they are recognized for specialized technical knowledge and advanced production, design or branding capabilities (see Chapter 6 in this book). Cluster lead firms shape the evolutionary processes of the cluster by modifying the set of activities carried out at the local level (Camuffo, 2003). Even if they do not exert power the way GLFs do, CLFs occupy a distinctive position beyond their district boundaries (e.g. driving the innovation frontier of the industry and being internationalized upstream and downstream – see e.g. Chapters 3 and 8 in this book).

Cluster lead firms can also become global lead firms. Perhaps the clearest (and maybe exceptional) example is Italian MNE Luxottica (see Chapters 3 and 9 in this book) in the eyewear cluster of Belluno (Italy), which recently merged with French group Essilor to create the largest eyewear group in the world with more than 50 billion Euro and 140,000 employees worldwide (Reuters, 2017). From a GVC perspective, CLFs can become global players if they have an impact on the governance of the GVC and shape the evolution of the industry beyond their impact at the cluster level. In general terms, home-grown MNEs (Chapter 5 in this book) are companies born in the district that still take part in the activities there; they have developed specific strategies to combine global and local sourcing as well as to approach foreign markets, gaining a leadership position in their global industries. In Chapter 6 Barzotto et al. suggest that home-grown MNEs developed by exploiting the industrial commons characterizing clusters.

In conclusion, home-grown and foreign MNEs are important players in our co-evolutionary model: they connect the local (cluster) and the global (GVC) levels and they can both impact the evolutionary trends of clusters and GVC.

Cluster actors beyond global lead firms

Large multinationals are not the only actors that shape the evolutionary paths of clusters. Chapters 5, 6 and 9 in this book suggest that internationalization is a peculiar characteristic of CLFs since they are able to structure appropriate strategies that impact on their local supply base and knowledge repositories. Internationalization may refer to downstream or upstream activities and include pre-production, production or post-production processes. However, not all cluster firms that become internationalized can be considered lead firms. Cluster lead firms developed a distinctive bundle of capabilities that may include manufacturing-related capabilities, pre-production (i.e. design) and/or post-production activities (brand, retail) that support their roles within and outside the district (see Chapters 9 and 3).

In many cases, CLFs are medium or large-sized firms, even though size is not the only proxy to identify them (unlike in GVC studies where GLFs tend to be quite large). In Italian clusters, where firms often grow through mergers, acquisitions and the creation of business groups (Cainelli et al., 2006), it is also important to explore changes in ownership. Local companies can become members of global groups via inward foreign direct investment (FDI) at the cluster level, or they can extend their organizational (and cluster) boundaries through outward FDI. This issue, like the distinction between home-grown and foreign MNEs, is a central contribution of this book.

From a knowledge-management point of view, CLFs can play the role of gatekeepers transferring external knowledge to the cluster and their local suppliers, thereby facilitating upgrading processes. In their analysis of the Spanish clusters of ceramic tiles and toys in Chapter 7, Molina-Morales et al. suggest that cluster firms may play different brokerage roles and that networks accessing technical or market knowledge do not necessarily overlap. As far as complex technical knowledge is concerned, the global connections of cluster actors (brokers) is key and such firms – oriented externally, beyond cluster boundaries – are the main contributors to the system. Interestingly, they report that only brokerage positions providing access to diverse repositories of knowledge provide valuable systemic contributions, which highlights the importance of within-ID heterogeneity.

Entrepreneurship is also relevant. The study of Prato by Guercini (Chapter 8 in this book) is particularly revealing. Through immigration from China, the Italian Prato cluster has witnessed a deep internal transformation with the rise of numerous Chinese firms specializing in textile activities. Through upgrading processes, those firms have been able to acquire more knowledge and extend their activities (product and process upgrading), and control more value. Most importantly, Chinese companies have acted as mediators between the cluster level (Prato) and the global level (China), impacting the role of native Italian firms in the cluster.

Hence, clusters are heterogeneous both internally (due to different communities of entrepreneurs and firms) and externally (due to different degrees of immigration at the local level). This offers an additional layer to the relationship between clusters and GVCs by taking into account international mobility and the role of foreigners in establishing globally oriented business activities.

In their analysis of the evolutionary trajectories of clusters, De Marchi et al. (Chapter 3) recommend the adoption of a broader framework to include so-called Local Dynamic Actors (LDAs), beyond just CLFs. They propose a classification of the local actors supporting ID resiliency that includes: 1) original equipment or original design manufacturers (OEMs or ODMs), with advanced production capabilities; 2) original brand manufacturers (OBMs) with advanced post-production capabilities; 3) highly specialized suppliers with distinctive manufacturing or service capabilities; and 4) local institutions, which support cluster development by providing technical and market knowledge. Evidence on the roles of LDAs spans the ID literature and incorporates theoretical concepts employed in GVC studies (e.g. Gereffi, 1999), thereby providing a bridge across the two literatures and enriching our comprehension of cluster evolution and the heterogeneity of local actors. (In Chapter 3, the authors suggest that global and local actors jointly sustain the ID resilient trajectory, while their absence is associated with the decline of IDs.)

The role of manufacturing and upgrading

In the GVC perspective, clusters have been identified as agglomerations of firms whose specialization in manufacturing activities has coincided with the global sourcing strategies of lead firms (Sturgeon et al., 2008). With reference to the smile curve (Gereffi and Fernandez-Stark, 2016; Mudambi, 2008), GVC scholars have stressed a clear division of labour between advanced countries and emerging economies, where manufacturing activities are considered low value-added activities as compared to innovation/R&D, marketing, retail management, and logistics. In this context, analyzing clusters specialized in low-tech industries in developing countries, early GVC contributions suggested that cluster upgrading trajectories were associated with moving away from assembly manufacturing to perform pre-production or post-production activities, thanks to the knowledge absorbed from the global buyers (Gereffi, 1999; Bair and Gereffi, 2001; Humphrey and Schmitz, 2002; Schmitz and Knorringa, 2000).

Analyzing highly competent clusters located in advanced economies, this book contests this perspective in several respects. First, it is shown that the "linear" upgrading scheme suggested in traditional GVC contributions – from assembly to higher value-added activities – is just one of the possible upgrading trajectories, as suggested in recent GVC studies (Cattaneo et al., 2010; Gereffi, 2015; Low and Pasadilla, 2016). For cluster firms to be competitive in the global context, they must focus on a meaningful bundle of capabilities. Different capabilities might reflect both the starting position of each of the IDs (i.e., local history, culture and institutions matter), as well as understanding the shifting context of global structures and players. In this sense, the smile approach is just one possible representation of the relative importance of different value chain activities.

In Chapter 4, Parrilli and Blažek suggest that upgrading can be interpreted as a manifold process where the variety of activities distributed among suppliers is intertwined with the streamlining of the lead firms' supply base. Consistent with the rise of global suppliers mentioned in other GVC studies (e.g. Azmeh and Nadvi, 2014; Gereffi, 2014), these two authors highlight specific implications at the cluster level: in some cases, cluster second-tier suppliers are developing new functions voluntarily transferred from first-tier suppliers; in other cases, the process of mergers and acquisitions allows cluster suppliers to cope with efficiency requests of GLFs.

Second, contributions in this book challenge the view of manufacturing as a low value-added activity for firms based in developed countries, a discussion that recently has become a hot topic in the current global political and economic agenda. Recent discussions about backshoring and re-shoring scrutinize the consolidated position of advanced and emerging countries in the "smile" curve (Gray et al., 2013; Fratocchi et al., 2014), notwithstanding the challenges to relocate manufacturing activities in domestic economies (Bailey and De Propris, 2014). The new scenario suggests the need for a more fine-grained analysis of the linkages between pre-production, production and post-production activities in terms of actors, geography and value generated. It requires a conceptualization of the role of manufacturing in advanced economies, which takes into account both the sources of competitiveness of local contexts as well as its connection with innovation capabilities (Berger, 2013; Buciuni and Finotto, 2016; Cano-Kollmann et al., 2016).

The value of manufacturing and its link with innovation

To understand cluster and GVC co-evolution, the relationship between manufacturing and geography is important. A first issue involves understanding how labour and value are distributed within IDs. As shown by Golini and Boffelli (Chapter 11), one important contribution of GVC studies to the evolution of clusters is to map which activities (and stages of activities) are located at the cluster or global levels. This is particularly relevant from an evolutionary perspective, since one can explore upgrading trajectories and also the profiles of LDAs and their impact on the evolution of the cluster itself.

A second and related issue concerns those activities that should remain at the local level within the ID to support its growth or resilience. Giuliani and Rabellotti (Chapter 2) suggest that not all production activities are equally relevant for the competitiveness of ID firms in each of the three possible development trajectories they identify (low-road, locally rooted GVC-led, and outward-oriented GVC-led IDs). From a geographic point of view, there is a dynamic process between local and global manufacturing. On the one hand, clusters are the receivers of the location choices of foreign-MNE lead firms; on the other hand, cluster firms also dynamically change their own – and collectively the entire cluster's – value chain. This dynamic process can be better understood by adopting the GVC lens, which identifies the specific activities and governance structures that link IDs and GVCs within an industry.

A third issue concerns the relevance of manufacturing competences to nurture the ID's innovation capability. As suggested by Buciuni and Finotto (2016), the proximity between R&D and production activities is an important spur for innovation; cutting such links because of offshoring may affect the firms' (and cluster's) ability to innovate. Similarly, Berger (2013) shows the importance of control over manufacturing for innovation and how knowledge transfer (or loss) relates to the physical and organizational separation between R&D and manufacturing. The disadvantages refer not only to single firms, but also to entire territories (i.e. regions) where the possibilities for firms to benefit from the industrial commons will be reduced (Pisano and Shih, 2012).

Contributions in Part III of this book provide fresh evidence from diverse empirical settings in support of this idea. Hervas-Oliver and Parrilli (Chapter 10) suggest that the control of key manufacturing activities (and knowledge) by ceramic tile producers in Castellon (Spain) is what allowed them to understand the innovation possibilities linked with the ink-jet applications developed for other industries in the UK. This introduced a break-through innovation with the potential to completely transform ceramic production worldwide. It is exactly this strong connection that has generated difficulties in the case of the Prato cluster for the adjoining communities of Chinese immigrants and native firms, the former extending the control over manufacturing activities to the detriment of the latter (Chapter 8).

When investing in specialized manufacturing activities to generate high value-added products, clusters can build a sustainable role in the global economy. The discussion about manufacturing in GVCs is crucial not only for emerging economies and developing countries, but even more so for advanced economies. Countries explored in this book, such as Italy or Spain – which over the years accumulated important competences and manufacturing know-how in manufacturing products and processes – could leverage such assets to support their competitiveness at the global level, especially considering their primacy vis-à-vis countries such as the USA or UK, where many manufacturing skills have been lost due to decades of offshoring (Bailey and Propris, 2014). Developing place-anchored strategies (as suggested in Chapters 5 and 6) can be a fruitful solution to maintain critical knowledge at the local level through the control of manufacturing activities.

Of course, this should not be considered an impediment for local firms to internationalize. Cluster lead firms can structure their internationalization to maintain part of their production within the firms, and at the local level to combine the *genius loci* with the advantages of scale at the global level (Chapter 9). The six case studies presented by Bettiol et al. in Chapter 9 seek to capture – from an inside-out perspective – how cluster firms in GVCs can structure their own manufacturing activities in terms of employment within the cluster boundaries. A recent study by Barzotto et al. (2016) provided a different measure to describe the implications at the local level of foreign MNEs, showing how those firms can contribute to the (re)generation of host country labour markets and investments in high-skilled workers, with greater effectiveness than national firms. The implication on the skills available at the cluster (or regional) level within the GVC scheme is an important and up-to-date research domain that could be further explored.

Manufacturing, services and new technologies

An important trend that will impact how manufacturing activities produce value in the global scenario is the importance of *services*, especially manufacturing-related services, including pre-manufacturing, manufacturing, post- manufacture, back office or post-sales services (Low and Pasadilla, 2016). Low value-added or labour-intensive services (e.g. call centres) are increasingly outsourced and offshored (Fernandez-Stark et al., 2011).

The cluster cases scrutinized in this book provide fresh evidence to explore the role and the strategies of manufacturing-related services located in IDs, and in particular those focused on innovation, such as design or R&D, which have been called *Knowledge-Intensive Business Services* or KIBS (Di Maria et al., 2012; Miles, 2005). In Chapter 3, De Marchi et al. include them within the LDAs that might support the development of resilient ID trajectories. Indeed, having developed a strong know-how about the manufacturing process (technology, product, materials etc.), they nurture the cluster competitiveness of manufacturing firms through knowledge transfer and knowledge sharing (Camuffo and Grandinetti, 2011; Grandinetti, 2011). With internationalization, they become important knowledge gatekeepers between the local and the global contexts (e.g. Claudio Franco Design&Develop, reported in Chapter 3).

The increasing relevance of service activities is not confined just to service firms. Due to new technologies, the border between goods and services is blurring, and the process of servitization of products is a notable trend (Roy et al., 2009). Classifying and measuring manufacturing activities and their international organization becomes difficult. For instance, Nike as a brand vendor in GVC terms is not a manufacturing company but a service company since it carries out only service activities – by focusing on R&D, marketing and retailing. At the same time, Decathlon (and the French group Oxylane) is not only one of the world's largest sporting goods retailers, but it is also involved in managing manufacturing activities directly. Such examples show that classification of goods and services (NACE classification) should be updated to take into account the evolutionary trends of manufacturing firms. Macro analysis can be misleading. In this sense, the application of the GVC mapping approach, such as proposed in Chapter 11, could contribute to the theoretical discussion about the relationship between manufacturing and services by showing exactly which activities are insourced or not by firms and hence depicting the real nature of firms (beyond an ex-ante classification).

Another research frontier is the implications for GVCs and clusters of new technological developments that go under the label of "Industry 4.0". Emerging digital technologies such as 3D printing are enabling a new paradigm, known as Industry 4.0 (Rüßmann et al., 2015), characterized by customization and distributed-manufacturing processes. This will impact the organization of value-chain activities, both in terms of the geographic location of activities and the role of national labour markets (Rehnberg and Ponte, 2017). The adoption of additive manufacturing may modify location choice of manufacturing activities to exploit the advantages of customer proximity. Indeed, digitalization of manufacturing production via 3D printing firms can increase product customization and create scale-free production processes. New market opportunities arise for SMEs, with a potential decrease in the market power of large MNEs. This will impact the future of GVCs shaped by GLFs, with important implications for a value-chain governance perspective. Based on new consumer interfaces and "big data" enabled by technological solutions such as the smart grid (i.e. Internet of Things), firms can enrich their innovation potential.

From this point of view, the control of retail becomes a crucial asset. Rehnberg and Ponte (2017) suggest that 3D printing technologies may lead to two opposing scenarios: 1) such technologies will become *complementary* to others, hence increasing efficiency within mass-oriented manufacturing production; and 2) the *substitution* of traditional manufacturing with 3D printing technologies. In the second scenario, the distance between extraction, process and consumption decreases, modifying the smile curve. Value-chain activities will be closer to end-users, often reducing the need for low-skill, labour-intensive functions in the processing (manufacturing) stage. (For an early analysis of the Internet's impact on consumer choice and governance structures in GVCs, see Gereffi, 2001.)

Cluster firms may be ready to adopt such technologies, particularly in advanced countries, since they are accustomed to organization of manufacturing and innovation activities based on collaboration and have developed the competencies to translate a client's requests into products. This book has not explored these issues widely. However, the cluster model can indeed embrace new technologies at the manufacturing level – even disruptive ones (as in the case of inkjet applications in the Castellon ceramic tiles cluster described in Chapter 10) – through adoption and adaptation to the local context. This can be done via GLFs entering into the cluster as well as through LDAs, in particular cluster lead firms. This is also supported by strong local (diffused) competencies on how to manage manufacturing processes and collaborative innovation. As the evidence is very recent, future research should further explore whether clusters can sustain the renovation and upgrading of local competencies to cope with such technological trends in an industrial commons framework (Barzotto et al., Chapter 6 in this book; Pisano and Shih, 2009).

The future of globalization

The interplay between the local and global elements that support cluster development, and the recent challenges to the role of manufacturing, spur a discussion about the future of globalization, especially considering the recent evidence of stagnation in world trade starting at the end of 2016.[2] It is too early to depict whether we are going towards the conclusion of the globalization era, but certainly globalization dynamics will be different from what we have observed in the last 20–25 years.

In its Outlook 2017, the Credit Suisse Research Group (2017) examines the end of globalization as we know it and describes a potentially new scenario that stresses the rise of a multipolar world. Trade and manufacturing activities become more regional. The power of GLFs decreases while regional champions emerge. In this scenario, clusters – particularly those located in advanced countries – might increase their relevance within regional value chains, led by cluster lead firms and home-grown GLFs.

The recent focus on the economic relevance of manufacturing activities – both through direct and indirect impacts – heightens our attention on the places where such activities are carried out. The chapters in this book emphasize the utility of the cluster model within local manufacturing systems, where manufacturing and innovation reinforce each other within a set of favourable local conditions. This is true for both advanced and developing countries.

The growth of South-South trade over the last decade (UNCTAD, 2015) is a signal of a transformation in the well-established North-South interactions shaped by GLFs in the

GVC perspective (Lee, 2016). The technological and political scenario is opening new trajectories characterized by the decreased relevance of being global and the rise of regional value chains (Gereffi, 2014; Ferrantino and Taglioni, 2014). In addition to "multipolar" governance within GVCs (Ponte and Sturgeon, 2013), we are likely to see multiple geographical centres – namely, North America, Europe, and East Asia (Credit Suisse, 2017).

Based on the competencies among suppliers and lead firms in different countries, GVC studies have identified regional divisions of labour within industries (Sturgeon et al., 2008; Gereffi and Frederick, 2010), which leads to a production hierarchy where manufacturers may have an impact at the regional level. In the coming years, this may strengthen the competencies embedded in specific territories and become an important asset for economic development and for sustaining competitiveness at the global level. The experiences of local clusters and the transformations in advanced countries described in this book provide powerful examples of the strengths and limitations of local production and innovation systems. The co-evolution of clusters and GVCs analysed here could be an ideal observatory to explore the complexity of globalization in the next decade.

Notes

1 Business groups are groups of firms with the same ownership but which are legally independent; they are more likely to be widespread in district than in non-district areas.
2 Data available at: www.cpb.nl/

References

Azmeh, S., and Nadvi, K. (2014). Asian firms and the restructuring of global value chains. *International Business Review*, 23(4): 708–717.

Bailey, D., and Propris, L. De. (2014). Manufacturing reshoring and its limits: The UK automotive case. *Cambridge Journal of Regions*, 7(3): 379–395.

Bair, J., and Gereffi, G. (2001). Local clusters in global chains: The causes and consequences of export dynamism in Torreon's blue jeans industry. *World Development*, 29(11): 1885–1903.

Barzotto, M., Corò, G., Mariotti, I., and Mutinelli, M. (2016). The Impact of Inward FDI on Host Country Labour Markets. A Counterfactual Analysis on Italian Manufacturing Companies. C-MET Working Papers No. 1612.

Belussi, F. (2015). The international resilience of Italian industrial districts/clusters (ID/C) between knowledge – Re-shoring and manufacturing off (near) -shoring. *Journal of Regional Research*, 32(8): 89–113.

Berger, S. (2013). *Making in America: From Innovation to Market*. Cambridge, MA: The MIT Press.

Buciuni, G., and Finotto, V. (2016). Innovation in global value chains: Co-location of production and development in Italian low-tech industries. *Regional Studies*, 50(12): 2010–2023.

Cainelli, G., Iacobucci, D., and Morganti, E. (2006). Spatial agglomeration and business groups: New evidence from Italian industrial districts. *Regional Studies*, 40(5): 507–518.

Camuffo, A. (2003). Transforming industrial districts: Large firms and small business networks in the Italian eyewear industry. *Industry and Innovation*, 10(4): 377–401.

Camuffo, A., and Grandinetti, R. (2011). Italian industrial districts as cognitive systems: Are they still reproducible? *Entrepreneurship and Regional Development*, 23(9–10): 815–852.

Cano-Kollmann, M., Cantwell, J., and Hannigan, T. (2016). Knowledge connectivity: An agenda for innovation research in international business. *Journal of International Business Studies*, 47(3): 255–262.

Cattaneo, O., Gereffi, G., and Staritz, C. (eds.). (2010). *Global Value Chains in a Postcrisis World: A Development Perspective*. Washington, DC: The World Bank.

Credit Suisse Research Group. (2017). *Getting Over Globalization*. Available at: http://publications.credit-suisse.com/tasks/render/file/index.cfm?fileid=BCD82CF0-CF9D-A6CB-BF7ED9C29DD02CB1

De Marchi, V., Lee, J., and Gereffi, G. (2014). Globalization, recession and the internationalization of industrial districts: Experiences from the Italian gold jewellery industry. *European Planning Studies*, 22(4): 866–884.

Di Maria, E., Bettiol, M., De Marchi, V., and Grandinetti, R. (2012). Developing and managing distant markets: The case of KIBS. *Economia Politica*, 29(3): 361–380.

Fernandez-Stark, K., Bamber, P., and Gereffi, G. (2011). The offshore services value chain: Upgrading trajectories in developing countries. *International Journal of Technological Learning, Innovation and Development*, 4(1/2/3): 206.

Ferrantino, M., and Taglioni, D. (2014). Global value chains in the current trade slowdown. *Economic Premise*, The World Bank, 137: 1–6.

Fratocchi, L., Di Mauro, C., Barbieri, P., Nassimbeni, G., and Zanoni, A. (2014). When manufacturing moves back: Concepts and questions. *Journal of Purchasing and Supply Management*, 20(1): 54–59.

Gereffi, G. (1994). The organization of buyer-driven global commodity chains: How US retailers shape overseas production networks. In G. Gereffi and M. Korzeniewicz (eds.), *Commodity Chains and Global Capitalism*. Westport: Praeger, pp. 95–122.

Gereffi, G. (1999). International trade and industrial upgrading in the apparel commodity chain. *Journal of International Economics*, 48(1): 37–70.

Gereffi, G. (2001). Shifting governance structures in global commodity chains, with special reference to the Internet. *American Behavioral Scientist*, 44(10): 1616–1637.

Gereffi, G. (2014). Global value chains in a post-Washington consensus world. *Review of International Political Economy*, 21(1): 9–37.

Gereffi, G. (2015). *Global Value Chains, Development and Emerging Economies*. UNIDO/UNU-MERIT Working Paper Series n. 047, November 27. Available at: www.merit.unu.edu/publications/working-papers/abstract/?id=5885.

Gereffi, G., and Fernandez-Stark, K. (2016). *Global Value Chain Analysis: A Primer*. Durham. Available at: www.cggc.duke.edu/pdfs/Duke_CGGC_Global_Value_Chain_GVC_Analysis_Primer_2nd_Ed_2016.pdf

Gereffi, G., and Frederick, S. (2010). The global apparel value chain, trade and the crisis: Challenges and opportunities for developing countries. In O. Cattaneo, G. Gereffi and C. Staritz (eds.), *Global Value Chains in a Postcrisis*. Washington, DC: World Bank Publications.

Gibbon, P., Bair, J., and Ponte, S. (2008). Governing global value chains: An introduction. *Economy and Society*, 37(3): 315–338.

Grandinetti, R. (2011). Local/global cognitive interfaces within industrial districts: An Italian case study. *The Learning Organization*, 18(4): 301–312.

Gray, J.V., Skowronski, K., Esenduran, G., and Johnny Rungtusanatham, M. (2013). The reshoring phenomenon: What supply chain academics ought to know and should do. *Journal of Supply Chain Management*, 49(2): 27–33.

Humphrey, J., and Schmitz, H. (2002). How does insertion in global value chains affect upgrading in industrial clusters? *Regional Studies*, 36(9): 1017–1027.

Lazerson, M.H., and Lorenzoni, G. (1999). The firms that feed industrial districts: A return to the Italian source. *Industrial and Corporate Change*, 8(2): 235–266.

Lee, J. (2016). Global value chains and the changing pattern of North-South trade: Apparel, electronics and automotive sectors in 2005–2014. *Journal of International Trade and Commerce*, 12(6): 1–21.

Lee, J., and Gereffi, G. (2013). The Co-Evolution of Concentration in Mobile Phone Global Value Chains and Its Impact on Social Upgrading in Developing Countries. Capturing the Gains Working Paper No. 2013/25.

Low, P., and Pasadilla, G. (2016). *Services in Global Value Chains: Manufacturing-Related Services*. Singapore: World Scientific Publishing.

Miles, I. (2005). Knowledge intensive business services: Prospects and policies. *Foresight*, 7(6): 39–63.

Mudambi, R. (2008). Location, control and innovation in knowledge-intensive industries. *Journal of Economic Geography*, 8(5): 699–725.

Navas-Alemán, L. (2011). The impact of operating in multiple value chains for upgrading: The case of the Brazilian furniture and footwear industries. *World Development*, 39(8): 1386–1397.

Oviatt, B., and McDougall, P. (2005). Defining international entrepreneurship and modeling the speed of internationalization. *Entrepreneurship Theory and Practice*, 29(5): 537–554.

Pietrobelli, C., and Rabellotti, R. (2011). Global value chains meet innovation systems: Are there learning opportunities for developing countries? *World Development*, 39(7): 1261–1269.

Pisano, G., and Shih, W. (2009). Restoring American competitiveness. *Harvard Business Review*, 87(7–8): 114–125.

Pisano, G., and Shih, W. (2012). *Producing Prosperity: Why America Needs a Manufacturing Renaissance*. Boston: Harvard Business School Press.

Ponte, S., and Sturgeon, T. (2013). Explaining governance in global value chains: A modular theory-building effort. *Review of International Political Economy*, 21(1): 195–223.

Rehnberg, M. and Ponte, S. (2017), From smiling to smirking? 3D printing, upgrading and the restructuring of global value chains. *Global Networks*. doi:10.1111/glob.12166

Reuters. (2017). *Luxottica and Essilor in 46 Billion Euro Merger to Create Eyewear Giant*. 16/01/2017. Available at: www.reuters.com/article/us-essilor-m-a-luxottica-group-idUSKBN14Z110

Roy, R., Shehab, E., Tiwari, A., and Baines, T. (2009). The servitization of manufacturing: A review of literature and reflection on future challenges. *Journal of Manufacturing Technology Management*, 20(5): 547–567.

Rüßmann, M., Lorenz, M., Gerbert, P., and Waldner, M. (2015). *Industry 4.0: The Future of Productivity and Growth in Manufacturing Industries*. Boston Consulting. Available at: www.inovasyon.org/pdf/bcg.perspectives_Industry.4.0_2015.pdf

Schmitz, H., and Knorringa, P. (2000). Learning from global buyers. *Journal of Development Studies*, 37(2): 177–205.

Sturgeon, T., and Lee, J.-R. (2005). Industry co-evolution: A comparison of Taiwan and North American electronics contract manufacturers. In V. Berger and R.K. Berger (eds.), *Global Taiwan: Building Competitive Strengths*. Armonk, NY: M.E. Sharpe, pp. 35–75.

Sturgeon, T., Van Biesebroeck, J., and Gereffi, G. (2008). Value chains, networks and clusters: Reframing the global automotive industry. *Journal of Economic Geography*, 8(3): 297–321.

UNCTAD. (2015). *Global Value Chains and South-South Trade*. Available at: http://unctad.org/en/PublicationsLibrary/gdsecidc2015d1_en.pdf

Index

Page numbers in italics indicate tables.

advanced countries 9, 11, 33, 96, 109, 156, 219, 222–3
AIDA Bureau Van Dijk dataset 36
Aku Italia *163*, *167*, 169, 170–2
Alpinestar 40, 81, 164
Amighini, A. 26, 41
Arcad 84
Armani 10, 38–9, 41, 84
Arzignano leather district 35
Arper 162, *163*, 166, *167–8*, 170–2
Asolo Gold 38
Audi 62
Apple 13n6, 82

backshoring 2, 155–7, 159, 170–2, 219
Balenciaga 84
Banatim 84
Barzotto, M. 11, 217, 220–1
BBK Electronics 82
Becattini, G. 1–2, 21, 30n3, 52
Belluno eyewear district 27–8, 35–6, *37*, 38–9, *43*, 46, 47n6, *160–1*, 166, *169*, 213, 215, 217
Belussi, F. 11, 27, 87n1, 179, 186, 215
Bergamo textile and clothing district 194–6
Better Silver 38, *45*
Bettiol, M. 12, 193, 220
Biella cluster 24
"black swan" phenomenon 137
Boffelli, A. 12, 215, 219
brokerage 11, 114–28, 218
Buciuni, G. 84, 157, 220
Bulgari 38
Burberry 55
buyer-driven commodity chains 4–5, 10, 55, 134

Cainelli, G. 23
Caloffi, A. 11
Calvino, F. 29
Calzaturificio Magli 85
Calzaturificio Renè Caovilla 84
Calzaturificio SCARPA 40–1

Castellani, D. 99
Castellon 12, *58*, *77*, 176, 178, 180–90
Castellon frit and glaze industry 183
ceramic tile clusters 11–12, 24, 114, *120*, 121–2, *123*, 126, 175–89, 218, 222
Cesare Paciotti 85
Chanel 26
Chiarvesio, M. 12, 180
Chimento 38
China 5–6, 37, 39, 79, 82, 136, 142, 144, 175, 178, 218
Chrysos 38
Cielo Venezia 38
Citroen 62
CLF *see* cluster lead firms
cluster lead firms (CLF) 72, 158–60, 166, 171, 217–18, 220, 222
Codara, L. 39
co-evolution 9–10, 19–68, 213–16, 219, 223
collaboration 3, 47, 51, 59, 96, 105, 107–9, 117, 142, 146, 175, 183, 207, 222
competitiveness 1, 3, 33–4, 94, 97, 155, 159, 172, 213–23
Confindustria 22
Consorzio Maestri Calzaturieri 42
cooperation 1, 127, 137, 183, 186
Corò, G. 11, 100
Credit Suisse Research Group 222

Delgado, M. 157
Delta Electronics 82
De Marchi, V. 10, 26, 28, 51, 95, 196, 205–6, 213, 216, 218, 221
De Rigo Vision 39, 162–3, *166–7*, 169, *169*
development 1–2, 26–9, 51–2, 102, 105, 107, 157–8, 161–2, 206, 213
Diadora Sport 40, 161–2, *163*, *167–8*, 170–2
Di Giacinto, V. 22
Di Maria, E. 51, 95, 196
Dior 26, 84
district effect 22, 25, 30n4

diversity 12–13, 22–8, 40, 110, 114, 117–18, 126, 208, 216–18
Dolomite 81, 164
Dolpi 39
Dongguan electronics cluster 71–2, 79, *79*, 80, 82–3, 86
drivers 9, 34, 36, 51–2, 65, *76*, 115, 155, 175, 214–15

electronics 71, *79,* 82–3, 86, *120,* 188
emerging cluster 73
emerging countries 2, 11–12, 22, 59, 62, 81, 96, 137, 147, 176, 219
entrepreneurship 3, 11, 34, 85–6, 133–4, 137–8, 140, 142, 144, 146–8, 214, 218
evolution 33–47, 51–2, 57, 71–3, *74*, 87, 127–8, 137–8, 140, 142, 144–7, 156, 159, 161, 170, 176–7, *185–6*, 193, 213, 216–20
eyewear 27–8, 35–6, *37*, 38–9, *43*, 46, 47n6, *160–1*, 166, *169*, 213, 215, 217

fashion industry 72, *80*, 82, 84, 108, 134, 136–8, *139*, 140, *141*, 142, *143*, *145*, 147
Fedon 39, 47n6, 162, *163*, 166, *167*, 169–71
Feldman, M. P. 30n4, 87n1, 106–7
Felman, M.P. 30n4, 87n1, 106–7
Fernandez, R. M. 116–17, 123
Fiat 62
Filk 38
Filty 84–5
Finotto, V. 157, 220
footwear cluster 26–7, 36–7, *37*, 41–2, *43–5*, 46–7, 72, 79, *79–80*, 83–4, 86–7, 158, 213, 215
Ford 62, 155
foreign global lead firms 216–17
foreignness, liability of 133, 135, 144, *145*, 147
Foxconn 82
fragmentation 53–4, 64–5, 94, 96, 100, 117, 179, 193–6, 202, 208
furniture 27, 57, *58–9*, 59–60, *77*, 100, 102, *103*, 109, *160–1*, 162, *163*, 165–6, *168*, 170, 176, 195, *195*, 198
furniture district clusters 27, 57, *58–9*, 59, 60, *77*, 100, 102, *103*, 109, *160–1*, 162, *163*, 165–6, *168*, 170, 176, 195, *195*, 198

Galunic 116
General Electric 10, 155
Geox 40, 43, 45, 47n6, 81, 85, 158, 160, *161*, 162, 164–5, 170
Gereffi, G. 10, 26, 28, 51, 95, 196, 205–6, 213, 216, 218, 221
Gigabyte Electronics 82
GINs *see* global innovation networks
Giovannetti, G. 24
Giuliani, E. 7, 9, 115, 118, 126, 158, 213, 220

global drivers 214–15
global factors 34, 53, 115, 214, 220
global innovation networks (GINs) 10, 51, 60–4, 175, 177, 179, 184–9
globalization 4, 9, 21–2, 33–4, 38, 42, 47n1, 47n5, 51, 57, 95, 98, 119, 121, 136, 144–5, 147, 176, 193, 213–14, 216, 222–3
Golini, R. 12, 215, 219
Google 62
Gould, R. V. 116–17, 123
governance 5, 8–11, 52, 54, 86, *141,* 156, 159, 166, 217, 220, 222–3
Grandinetti, R. 10, 205–6, 213, 216, 218, 221
growth 1, 6, 21, 29, 33, 35, 40, 42, 73, 81, 87, 94–9, 106, 109, 121, 137, 142, 147, 165, 175, 197, 204, 213, 216, 220
Guban 84–5
Gucci 84
Guercini, S. 11, 218
GVC Corporation 82

Hardin, G. 96
Hargadon, A. B. 116
Head 81
Hennessy, L.V.M. 26
Herrigel, G. 55
Hervas-Oliver, J. L. 12, 179–80, 184, 220
heterogeneity 4, 9, 11, 36, 42, 86, 95, 115, 193–4, 199–200, 202, 208–9, 213–18
high road development 51, 60–1, 63
home-grown global lead firms 12, 40, 42, *43*, 44, *44–5*, 216–17, 222
home-grown multinational enterprises *77*, 87, 102, 165, 176, 179, *181–2*, 184–9, 195, 215, 218; knowledge broker/catalyst 179–80
Honda 62
Humphrey, J. 52, 159, 178
Hyundai 62

IKEA 27, 55, 165
immigrant 134, 137, 140, 141, 142–3, 143, 220
industrial commons 3, 9, 11, 94–102, 105–6, 109–11, 217, 220, 222
innovation 2–4, 8–12, 22, 27, 35, 39, 40, 51, 54, 57, 60–5, 79, *80*, 82, 86, 96–7, 99, 101, 104, 107, 114–26, 135, 155–62, 165, 170–2, 175–89, *195*, 206, 208, 215–23
institutions 1–3, *8*, 10, 36–8, 41, *43*, *44*, 45–7, *58*, 72, 75, *78*, *80*, 85, 96–7, 104–10, 114, 117, *120*, 122, *143*, *146*, 161, 175, 177, 181, 183, 188, *195*, 218
International Labour Organization 1
Iris by Gibò 84
ISI-Thomson Reuters Web of Science database 87n4
ISTAT 36

Italy 2, 7, 9, 11, 21–30, 33–39, 47, 51, 52, 59, 60, 63, 79, 82, 85–7, 100–9, *120*, 121, 134, 137, 143, *160*, *163*, 165–70, 175–8, 180, *181*, *182*, 183, 185–90, 193–4, 198, *205*, 206–7, 214–20
Iuzzolino G. 22

jewellery *45*

Kerajet 187
Kering Group 41, 72, 84
Kering-Gucci 84
Knorringa, P. 156
knowledge-intensive business services 45, 48n16, 221
knowledge sharing 3, 114, 117, 221
Kramer, M. R. 98–9

Lamos by Prada 84
Lange, B. 164
LDAs *see* local dynamic actors
lead firms 4–13, 24, 27, 33–4, 39, *43*, 44–6, 55, 59–62, 72, *80*, 95, 99, 102, 155–60, 164, 166, 171, 179, 208, 214–23
Lee, J. 26, 28
liability of foreignness 133, 135, 144, *145*, 147
liability of outsidership 133, 135–6, 144–6, *145*, 147–8
local dynamic actors (LDAs) 44, *44*, 45, *45*, 46–7, 196, 217–18, 220, 222
local liabilities 11, 133–48
locally rooted global value chains 9, 25–8, 213, 220
local production systems 1, 52, 60, 94–111, 178–9, 189
Lorenzo Muraro 38
Lotto 47n6, 81, 164
Louis Vuitton Moët Hennessy (LVMH) 26, 41, *45*, 72, 84, 158
low-road industrial districts 9, 25–8, 213, 220
Luxottica 23, 27–8, 39, 47n6, 158, 166, 171, 217
LVMH 26, 41, *45*, 72, 84, 158

Manufacture de Souliers Louis Vuitton 84; *see also* LVMH
manufacturing 1–3, 5, 9, 11–13, 21–2, 24–8, 33–4, 37, 39–42, 44–5, 72, 81–2, 85, 87, 94–102, 109–10, *120*, 136–8, 142, *143*, 147, 155–72, 176, 180, *181–2*, 183–4, 193–210, 215, 217–22
map 12, 123, 193–4, 196, 208, 219
Marchon 39
Marco Bicego 38
Marcolin 39, 47n6, 166
Mares 81
Markusen, A. 3, 71, 178, 180

Marshall, A. 2–3, 30n1
Marshallian model 3, 7, 21, 29, 42, 47n1, 47n3, 52–3, 83–4, 122, 178, 180, 183, 208, 214
Martin, R. 28–9
Martinez-Cháfer, L. 11
McCann, P. 79
Menon, C. 22
Micelli, S. 12
MNEs *see* multinational enterprises
Molinda-Morales, F. X. 11, 216, 218
Monique 84
Montebelluna SportSystem cluster 27, 35–6, *37*, 39–41, *43*, *45*, 46, 72, 79, *79–80*, 81–2, 86–7, 109, *160*, 161, *161*, 164–5, *168*, 213
Morato, E. 39
Moroso 162, *163*, 166, *167–8*, 169
Morrison, A. 95, 115
Mudambi, R. 73, 79, 156
multinational enterprises (MNEs) 1, 27, 71–87, 135, 179, 215

National Labour Committee 83
Native 138, *138*, 142–4
network 1–5, 10–13, 27, 39, 44–5, 51–7, 61, 64, 71, 73, *75*, *77*, 86–7, 94–9, 105–11, 114–19, 121–23, 126–28, 135, 145–48, 165, 173, 175, 177, 179, 183–90, 193, 196, 206, 216, 218
Nike 10, 40, 72, 81, 87, 87n2, 164, 172, 221
Nintaus Digital 82
Nordica 81, 164
Nordic School of Industrial Marketing 136
Novation Tech 40, *45*, 81

OBMs 37–41, 45–6, 48n8, 164–6, 171, 196, 218
OECD *see* Organization for Economic Cooperation and Development
Open Automotive Alliance 62
Organization for Economic Cooperation and Development (OECD) 1, 6, 29
original brand manufacturers 218
Ostrom, E. 97
outsidership 133, 135–6, 144–6, *145*, 147–8
outward-oriented global value chains 9, 25, 27–8, 213, 220
Özatağn, G. 55

Panasonic 62
Parrilli, M. D. 10, 12, 219–20
Pieri, F. 99
Piore, M. J. 1–2, 52
Pisano, G. P. 84, 96, 98, 157, 216–17
Plank, L. 55
policy 2, 9, 12, 21, 28–9, 36, 39, 42, 47, 51, 61, 63, *74*, *75*, 84, 95, 101, 110, 175, 180
Politecnico Calzaturiero 84, 87n3
Pomini, F. 29

Ponte, S. 222
Porter, M. E. 1, 52, 98–9, 122, 183
Prada 39, 41, *45*, 84
Prato 11, 24, 134, 137–48
producer-driven commodity chains 4–5, 10, 134, 171
Puma 84
Pyke, F. 30n3

Qisheng Electronics 82

Rabellotti, R. 9, 21, 26, 30n3, 41, 57, 115, 213, 220
Ray-Ban 39
R&D 3, 5, 27, 33, 40, 45, 51, *58*, 60–1, 63, *75*, *76*, *78*, 94, 96, 98, 102, 108, *120*, *141*, 155–7, 170, 176–89, *195*, 206–9, 219–21
regional innovation systems (RISs) 10, 51, 54, 61–4, 83, 175, 179, 183–4, 188
Rehnberg, M. 222
resilience trajectory 35–6, 42, 44, 46, 213
RISs *see* regional innovation systems
Riviera del Brenta footwear cluster 26–7, 36, *37*, 41–2, *43*, *45*, 46–7, 72, 79, *79–80*, 83–4, 86–7, 158, 213, 215
Rodan 116
Rossignol 81, 164
Rossimoda 26, 81, 84, 158, 164
Roster-Recall methodology 122
Rueda-Cantuche, J. M. 100
Russo, M. 183

Sabel, C. 1–2, 52
Salomon 81, 164
Santangelo, G. D. 73
Scatena, A. 29
Schmitz, H. 52, 60, 156, 178
Sedita, S. R. 11, 87n1
Sengenberger, W. 30n3
service 5, 11–13, 22, 38, 40, 60, *75–6*, 86, 94, 96–7, 155–7, 183, 186, 194, 221–2
Shih, W. 96, 98, 157, 216–17
size 4, 10, 22, 26–7, 34–40, *43*, 46, 62, *74*, *79*, 81, 84–7, *103*, 114, 122–26, 133, 145, 158, 160, 162, 165, 176, 186, *195*, 199, 202, 204, 218, 222
small-and-medium-sized enterprises (SMEs) 1–4, 8–9, 13n1, 21, 29, 35, 38, 41–2, 54, 57, 62–4, 72, 81, 175, 178–80, 187–9, 213, 216, 221
SMEs *see* small-and-medium-sized enterprises
SNA *see* Social Network Analysis

Social Network Analysis (SNA) 123
Spain 9, 12, 21, 52, 100–1, *120*, 121, 126, 162, 175–89, 220
sportsystem 35, 39–41, *43*, *45*, 46, 72, 79, *79*, 81–2, *103*, 109, 158, 160, *161*, *163*
Staritz, C. 55
Stonefly 47n6, 81
Sturgeon, T. J. 7, 29
Sunley, P. 28–9
Sutton, R. I. 116
Swarovski 38

Tecnica 47n6, 81, 164
Tecsun 82
textile and clothing 12, 22–4, 28, 40, 47, 48n10, 52, 60, *80*, 100, 102, *103*, 136–8, *138*, 140, *140*, *143*, 147–8, 178, 194–6, *197*, 198–9, 208–9, 215
Tiffany 38
Torrecid 186–7, 190n8
toy valley cluster 119–21, *120*, *123*, *125*, 126
trajectories 33–47, 52, 60, 213–16, 218–21, 223
Tyrolia 81

UK 12, *61*, 63, 99, *160*, 162, *163*, 178, *181*, 187–8, 220
United Nations conference on Trade and Development 1
upgrading 2, 5–12, 26–7, 38, 41–2, 52, 54–5, 57, *58–9*, 60–4, 109, 111, 145, 156, 158, *160–1*, 162, 164–5, 176–80, 213, 216, 218–22
USA 1, 6, 21, 37, 39, 41, 57, 83, 108, 156, *160*, *163*, *168*, 170, 179, *181*, 187, 220

value chain stages 194, 196–7, *202*, 207–8
Veneto 10–11, 23, 27, 34, 36–42, 59, 81, 83, 85, 87, 99–102, 109, 159, 162, 165–6, 170, 214
Versace 38–9
Vicenza 26, 36, *37,* 37–8, 42, *43,* 46, *103,* 214
Vieri 38
Volpe, M. 11
Voltan 83
von Hippel, E. 172

World Bank 1, 6

Yin, R. K. 36, 101
Yves Saint Laurent 26, 38, 84

Zaheer, S. 135
Zylan 82

For Product Safety Concerns and Information please contact our EU
representative GPSR@taylorandfrancis.com Taylor & Francis Verlag GmbH,
Kaufingerstraße 24, 80331 München, Germany

Printed and bound by CPI Group (UK) Ltd, Croydon, CR0 4YY

01/05/2025

01858405-0002